RESTITUTIONARY RIGHTS TO SHARE IN DAMAGES

Rights and obligations can arise *inter alia* in tort or in unjust enrichment. This book deals with the phenomenon whereby a stranger to litigation is entitled to participate in the fruits of that litigation. Two prominent examples of this phenomenon are the carer, who is entitled to share in the fund of damages recovered by a victim of tort, and the indemnity insurer, which is entitled to participate in the fruits of the insured's claim against the wrongdoer. Degeling demonstrates that both are rights raised to reverse unjust enrichment.

Careful examination of these two categories reveals the existence of a novel policy motivated unjust factor called the policy against accumulation. Degeling argues that this is an unjust factor of broad application, applying to configurations other than that of the carer and the indemnity insurer.

The conceptual relevance of this work is that it assists in solving certain three-party cases which lie at the border between tort and unjust enrichment. In solving the stranger's entitlement to share in the damages recovered, the policy motivated unjust factor called the policy against accumulation is identified. This book will interest restitution lawyers and tort lawyers, academic and practitioner, as well as academic institutions and court libraries.

SIMONE DEGELING is Senior Lecturer in the Faculty of Law, The University of New South Wales, Australia. At the time of writing, she was City Solicitors' Educational Trust Lecturer in the Law of Restitution at the University of Nottingham. She teaches, researches and publishes in the law of unjust enrichment. Dr Degeling has practised as a commercial lawyer and is admitted as a Solicitor of the Supreme Court of New South Wales.

RESTITUTIONARY RIGHTS
TO SHARE IN DAMAGES

Carers' Claims

SIMONE DEGELING

CAMBRIDGE
UNIVERSITY PRESS

CAMBRIDGE UNIVERSITY PRESS
Cambridge, New York, Melbourne, Madrid, Cape Town, Singapore, São Paulo

Cambridge University Press
The Edinburgh Building, Cambridge CB2 8RU, UK

Published in the United States of America by Cambridge University Press, New York

www.cambridge.org
Information on this title: www.cambridge.org/9780521800655

First published 2003
This digitally printed version 2007

A catalogue record for this publication is available from the British Library

ISBN 978-0-521-80065-5 hardback
ISBN 978-0-521-03696-2 paperback

CONTENTS

Preface   vii

Table of cases   viii

List of key works   xxii

1   Introduction   1

PART I

2   Three leading carer cases   13

3   Claims based on contractual and non-contractual promises to pay   29

4   The carer's claim in unjust enrichment   47

5   The carer's claim in tort   111

PART II

6   Direct claims: the problem remains unsolved   149

7   Insurance subrogation analogy   159

8   The policy against accumulation   191

PART III

9   The proprietary claim   233

10   Conclusion   271

Bibliography   276

Index   284

PREFACE

My doctoral research, which forms the basis of this book, was submitted to the University of Oxford in 1998, and was funded by the Commonwealth Scholarship Commission and St Peter's College Oxford. Some of the chapters are updated versions of those written for my thesis. Other chapters, particularly chapters 8 and 9, are the result of work done since.

My greatest debt of gratitude is to my thesis supervisor Peter Birks. As his student I had the benefit of his patience, wisdom and generosity. He is a great scholar and teacher and I am privileged to have been his student. I am also indebted to my thesis examiners, Gareth Jones and Lionel Smith, for their thoughtful and helpful comments on my work. In this respect, I am particularly grateful to Lionel Smith, who has continued to provide advice and inspiration. Mention must also be made of Ewan McKendrick, who has always been a source of support and encouragement.

In completing this project, I was also assisted by various people who were kind enough to give me their views, or engage in conversation about my work. Listed alphabetically they include: John Armour, Robert Chambers, Simon Gardner, Charles Mitchell, George Panagopoulos, Francis Rose and Robert Stevens. I am also grateful for the assistance given by the School of Law, University of Nottingham. I would not have been able to complete the manuscript without sabbatical leave, and the moral support given by colleagues, particularly at the end, was much appreciated.

Finally, I wish to acknowledge the support and encouragement given by my parents, without whom this book would not have been written.

The publisher has used its best endeavour to ensure that the URLs for external websites referred to in the book are correct and active at the time of going to press. However, the publisher has no responsibility for the websites and can make no guarantee that a site will remain live or that the content is or will remain appropriate.

Simone Degeling
Sydney, August 2002

TABLE OF CASES

123 East Fifty-Fifth Street Inc *v.* United States (1946) 157 F Rep
  (2d) 68   265
A *v.* National Blood Authority [2001] 3 All ER 289   67, 242
AG for Hong Kong *v.* Reid [1994] 1 AC 324   252, 259
Air Jamaica Ltd *v.* Charlton [1999] 1 WLR 1399   239
Alcock *v.* Chief Constable of South Yorkshire Police [1992] 1
  AC 310   125, 130, 131
Alexander Enterprises *v.* Dobbin (1987) 63 Nfld & PEIR 1   67
Allied Maples Group Ltd *v.* Simmons & Simmons [1995] 4 All
  ER 907   145
Altmann *v.* Dunning [1995] 2 VR 1   93, 96, 243
Ambrose *v.* Kerrison (1851) 10 CB 776   90, 168
Amoco (UK) Exploration Co *v.* Imperial Chemical Industries plc
  unreported 30 July 1999   102
Angelopoulos *v.* Sabatino (1995) 65 SASR 1   56
Anns *v.* Merton London Borough Council [1978] AC 278   116, 141, 142
Arab Bank plc *v.* John D Wood Ltd [2000] 1 WLR 857   186, 203
Arnold *v.* Teno (1978) 83 DLR (3d) 609   21, 52, 57, 93, 106
Astopolos Konstantine Ventouris *v.* Trevor Rex Mountain (The Italia
  Express No 2) [1992] 2 Lloyd's Rep 281   204
Attorney General for Ontario et al *v.* Crump (1976) 74 DLR
  (3d) 345   125
Attorney General *v.* Blake [1998] Ch 439 (CA) [2001] AC 268
  (HL)   45, 46
Austin *v.* Zurich General Accident and Liability Insurance Co Ltd
  [1944] 2 All ER 243   164
B, re [2000] NSWSC 44   25, 26, 85, 199, 243
Baker *v.* TE Hopkins & Son Ltd [1959] 1 WLR 966   125, 128

Bank of America *v.* Arnell [1999] Lloyd's Rep Banking 399   249

Banque Financière de la Cité *v.* Parc (Battersea) Ltd [1999] 1
    AC 221   48, 173, 178, 180, 181

Barclays Bank Ltd *v.* Quistclose Investments [1970] AC 567   247

Barclays Bank Ltd *v.* WJ Simms Son and Cooke (Southern) Ltd
    [1980] QB 677   194

Barnett *v.* Chelsea and Kensington Hospital Management Committee
    [1969] 1 QB 428   145

Baron Napier and Ettrick *v.* RF Kershaw [1993] 1 Lloyd's
    Rep 10   174

Baron Napier and Ettrick *v.* RF Kershaw unreported Saville J
    14 May 1992   174

Beasley *v.* Marshall (1996) 10 SASR 544   25, 85

Beasley *v.* Marshall (No 4) (1986) 42 SASR 407   51, 199, 243

Benstead *v.* Murphy (1994) 23 Alta LR (3d) 251   48, 93, 94, 98, 113

Berkeley Applegate (Investment Consultants) Ltd, in re [1989]
    Ch 32   90, 168

Beswick *v.* Beswick [1968] AC 58   266

Bissky *v.* Trottier (1984) 54 BCLR 288   245

Blaaupot *v.* Da Costa (1758) 1 Eden 130   173

Blundell *v.* Musgrave (1956) 96 CLR 73   37, 40, 151, 152, 153, 154

Bordin *v.* St Mary's NHS Trust unreported Queen's Bench Division
    26 January 2000   238, 245

Bourhill *v.* Young [1943] AC 92   125

Bow Valley Husky (Bermuda) Ltd *v.* St John Shipbuilding Ltd (1997)
    153 DLR (4th) 385   143

BP Exploration Co (Libya) *v.* Hunt (No 2) [1979]
    1 WLR 783   54, 227

Bradburn *v.* The Great Western Railway Company (1874) LR 10
    Ex 1   170

Bradstock Trustee Services Ltd *v.* Nabarro Nathanson (A Firm)
    [1995] 1 WLR 1405   266

Brandon *v.* Osborne Garrett and Company Limited [1924]
    1 KB 548   125, 133

British Transport Commission *v.* Gourley [1956] AC 185   15, 195

Britliffe *v.* Britliffe (1990) Aust Torts Rep ¶81–060   60, 94

Brown et al *v.* University of Alberta Hospital et al (1997) 145 DLR
    (4th) 63   51, 52, 93, 245

Brownton Ltd *v.* Edwards Moore Inbucon Ltd [1985] 3
    All ER 499   268
Burdis *v.* Livesey [2001] 1 WLR 1751   238
Burford *v.* Allen (1992) Aust Torts Rep ¶81–184   93
Burnicle *v.* Cutelli [1982] 2 NSWLR 26   48
Burns Philp & Co Ltd *v.* Gillespie Brothers Pty Ltd (1947) 74
    CLR 148   90
C, re (Adult: Refusal of Medical Treatment) [1994] 1 All
    ER 819   50, 51
Caledonia North Sea Ltd *v.* Norton (No 2) Ltd (in liquidation) [2002]
    1 All ER (Comm) 321   186, 203, 204
Caltex Oil (Australia) Pty Ltd *v.* The Dredge 'Willemstad' (1976) 135
    CLR 529   111, 138, 139
Canadian National Railway Co *v.* Norsk Pacific Steamship Co (1992)
    91 DLR (4th) 289   141, 142, 143, 144
Candlewood Navigation Corporation Ltd *v.* Mitsui OSK Lines Ltd
    [1986] AC 1   115
Canwest Geophysical Ltd et al *v.* Brown et al [1972]
    3 WWR 23   163
Caparo Industries plc *v.* Dickman [1990] 2
    AC 605   116, 118, 126, 129
Car & Universal Finance *v.* Caldwell [1965] 1 QB 525   246
Carr-Glynn *v.* Frearsons [1999] Ch 326   120
Cassell *v.* Hammersmith and Fulham Health Authority [1992] 1
    PIQR Q1   236
Castellain *v.* Preston (1883) 11 QBD 380   186, 187, 203, 204, 206
Cavanaugh *v.* MacQuarrie (1979) 62 APR 687   60
Central Insurance Co Ltd *v.* Seacalf Shipping Corporation
    (The Alios) [1983] 2 Lloyd's LR 25   170
Chadwick *v.* British Railways Board [1967] 1 WLR 912   125, 128
Chase Manhattan Bank NA *v.* Israel-British Bank (London) Ltd
    [1981] Ch 105   249, 265
China Pacific SA *v.* Food Corporation of India [1982]
    AC 939   90
Chubbs *v.* O'Brien (1980) 28 Nfld & PEIR 314   37
Clark *v.* Kramer [1986] WAR 54   93, 96
Clark *v.* Warrington (1958) 26 WWR 673   21, 150
Cleadon Trust Limited, in re [1939] 1 Ch 286   163

Coderre *v.* Ethier (1978) 85 DLR (3d) 621   4, 22, 48, 57, 61, 71,
  80, 81, 82, 99, 176, 212, 214, 244
Cole *v.* Lawrence (2001) 33 MVR 159   69
Commissioner of State Revenue (Victoria) *v.* Royal Insurance Ltd
  (1994) 182 CLR 51   72, 200, 201, 202, 265
Crane *v.* Worwood (1992) 65 BCLR (2d) 16   52, 60, 68, 81, 94,
  98, 245
Craven-Ellis *v.* Cannons Ltd [1936] 2 KB 403   59
Crossley *v.* Rawlinson [1982] 1 WLR 369   125
Cunningham *v.* Harrison [1973] QB 942   17, 18, 21, 30, 31, 34,
  38, 40, 41, 42, 43, 44, 67, 81, 82, 83, 84, 86, 135, 151, 155, 200, 243,
  245, 247
Curator of Estates *v.* Fernandez [1976] 16 ALR 445   62, 245
Cutler *v.* United Dairies (London) Limited [1933] 2 KB 297   125
D'Amato *v.* Badger [1996] 8 WWR 390   142, 143
D'Ambrosio *v.* DeSouza Lima [1983] 60 ACTR 18   60, 93, 96, 110
Daly *v.* General Steam Navigation Co Ltd [1980]
  3 All ER 696   94
Darrell *v.* Tibbitts (1880) 5 QBD 560   186, 203
David Securities Pty Ltd *v.* Commonwealth Bank of Australia (1992)
  175 CLR 353   194
Dextra Bank & Trust Company Limited *v.* Bank of Jamaica [2002] 1
  All ER (Comm) 193   101, 102, 103, 104
Dimond *v.* Lovell [2000] 1QB 216 (CA); [2002] 1
  AC 384 (HL)   9, 223, 224, 225, 269
DJR, re and the Mental Health Act 1958 [1983] 1
  NSWLR 557   25, 26, 85, 199, 236, 243
Donnelly *v.* Joyce [1974] 1 QB 454   16, 17, 21, 34, 38, 43, 52, 66,
  68, 80, 84, 86, 93, 94, 96, 106, 140, 197, 198, 244
Donoghue *v.* Stevenson [1932] AC 562   116, 127
Donovan *v.* Stirling (1986) 183 APR 104   37
Dorset Yacht Co Ltd *v.* Home Office [1970] AC 1004   116
Dziver *v.* Smith (1983) 146 DLR (3d) 314   32, 37, 38, 49, 56, 59, 74
Eagle Star Insurance Co Ltd *v.* Provincial Insurance plc [1993] 1 All
  ER 1   204
Einarson *v.* Keith [1961] 36 WWR 215   30, 36, 64
England *v.* Guardian Insurance Ltd [2000] Lloyd's Rep IR 404
  186, 203, 205, 236

ES and the Mental Health Act, re 1958 [1984]
    3 NSWLR 341   25, 85, 199, 243
Esanda Finance Ltd *v.* Peat Marwick Hungerfords (Reg) (1995–1997)
    188 CLR 241   137
Esso Petroleum Co Ltd *v.* Hall Russell & Co Ltd [1989]
    AC 643   1, 163, 176, 220, 266, 268
Esso Petroleum Company Limited *v.* Niad Limited Unreported
    22 November 2001   45
Esterhuizen *v.* Allied Dunbar Assurance plc [1998]
    2 FLR 668   120
Exall *v.* Partridge (1799) 8 TR 308   59, 60, 98, 194
F (Mental Patient: Sterilisation), in re [1990] 2 AC 1   90, 91, 93,
    94, 97
Fairhurst *v.* St-Helens and Knowsley Health Authority [1995]
    4 PIQR Q1   57, 236
Falcke *v.* Scottish Imperial Insurance Company (1886)
    34 Ch D 234   89, 163
Feng *v.* Graham (1988) 25 BCLR (2d) 116; (1988)
    44 CCLT 52   47, 72, 86, 94, 98, 199, 200, 245
Firme C-Trade SA *v.* Newcastle P&I Association [1991]
    2 AC 1   204
Fitzgerald *v.* Ford [1996] 5 PIQR 73   93, 96
Foodlands Association Ltd *v.* Mosscrop [1985] WAR 215   137
Foskett *v.* McKeown [1998] Ch 265 (CA); [2001]
    1 AC 102 (HL)   258, 259, 264
Frost *v.* Chief Constable of South Yorkshire Police [1998] QB 254,
    [1999] 2 AC 455   125, 126, 128, 130, 131, 133
Gage *v.* King [1961] 1 QB 188   48
Garland *v.* Clifford (1996) 67 SASR 47   52, 60, 69, 93
Gaydon *v.* Public Transport Commission [1976]
    2 NSWLR 44   37, 151, 153
GDM and the Protected Estates Act 1983 (NSW), in the Matter of
    (1992) Aust Torts Rep ¶81–190   25, 26, 85, 86, 198, 199, 244
Gerow *v.* Reid (1989) 225 APR 34   94, 245
Gertsch *v.* Atsas [1999] NSWSC 898   102, 103, 105
Gibeault *v.* Schultz (1978) 11 AR 584   32, 37, 41, 49, 56, 59, 62,
    63, 74, 243
Giles *v.* Thompson [1994] 1 AC 142   267, 268

Gillick *v.* West Norfolk and Wisbech Area Health Authority [1986] 1
    AC 112   52
Godin *v.* London Assurance Company (1758) 1 Burr 489   204
Goldcorp Exchange Ltd, re [1995] 1 AC 74   247
Goldfinch *v.* Scannell [1993] 2 PIQR Q143   93, 96
Goode *v.* Thompson and Anor (2001) Aust Torts Reports
    ¶81–617   25, 52, 69, 85, 199, 244
Goodwill *v.* British Pregnancy Advisory Service [1996] 2 All
    ER 161   121
Gorham *v.* British Telecommunications Plc [2000]
    1 WLR 2129   120
Gow *v.* Motor Vehicle Insurance Trust [1967]
    WAR 55   51, 64, 93, 243
GRE Insurance Ltd *v.* Q.B.E. Insurance Ltd [1985] VR 83   164
Great Northern Railway *v.* Swaffield (1874) LR 9 Ex 132   90, 168
Greatorex *v.* Greatorex [2000] 1 WLR 1970   125
Greenaway *v.* CPR Co et al [1925] 1 DLR 992   97
Griffiths *v.* Kerkemeyer (1977) 139 CLR 161   1, 23, 26, 36, 49, 54,
    58, 85, 93, 140, 149, 195, 199, 245
Grincelis *v.* House (2000) 201 CLR 321   3, 24, 48, 51, 69, 85, 93,
    149, 159, 160, 195, 199, 230, 234, 235
Grover *v.* Lowther (1982) 52 NSR (2d) 22   20, 81, 93, 94, 245
Grovewood Holdings plc *v.* James Capel & Co Ltd [1995]
    2 WLR 70   269
Guinness Mahon & Co Ltd *v.* Kensington and Chelsea Royal London
    Borough Council [1998] 2 All ER 272   76
Ha *v.* New South Wales (1997) 189 CLR 465   202, 226
Haggar *v.* de Placido [1972] 2 All ER 1029   30, 36, 41, 135, 243
Haig *v.* Bamford [1977] 1 SCR 466   141
Hall *v.* Miller (1989) 41 BCLR (2d) 46   48, 61, 98, 99, 245
Hamilton *v.* Hayes [1962] 38 WWR 506   37
Harrison *v.* British Railways Board [1981] 3 All ER 679   125, 128
Hasson *v.* Hamel (1977) 78 DLR (3d) 573   75, 77, 80, 244
Haynes *v.* Harwood [1935] 1 KB 146   125, 133
Hedley Byrne & Co Ltd *v.* Heller & Partners Ltd [1964]
    AC 465   112, 115, 116, 117, 118, 120, 121, 122, 123, 124, 137, 141
Henderson *v.* Merrett Syndicates Ltd [1995] 2 AC 147   118, 119
Hendrie *v.* Rusli (2000) 32 MVR 240   69

Hercules Managements Ltd *v.* Ernst & Young (1997) 146 DLR
    (4th) 577   143
Hill (Trading as RF Hill & Associates) *v.* Van Erp (1995–1997) 188
    CLR 159   126, 128, 134, 138
Hobbs *v.* Marlowe [1978] AC 16   170
Hogan *v.* Gill (1992) Aust Torts Rep ¶81–182   57
Horsfall *v.* Haywards [1999] 1 FLR 1182   120
Hotson *v.* East Berkshire Health Authority [1987]
    2 All ER 909   145
Housecroft *v.* Burnett [1986] 1 All ER 332   34, 68, 123, 135, 151, 245
Howe *v.* Campbell (1974) 7 NBR (2d) 144   21, 150
Hunt *v.* Severs [1993] QB 815 (CA); [1994] 2 AC 350 (HL)   1, 2,
    13, 14, 16, 17, 18, 19, 22, 25, 27, 34, 36, 47, 48, 54, 62, 63, 66, 67,
    83, 84, 86, 93, 94, 97, 111, 135, 136, 149, 151, 154, 156, 159, 171,
    176, 195, 196, 210, 211, 212, 214, 215, 233, 234, 235, 240, 241, 245,
    254, 255, 269, 274
Hunter *v.* British Coal Corporation [1999] QB 141   125
Hyett *v.* Great Western Railway Company [1948] 1 KB 345   125
Island Records Ltd *v.* Tring International plc [1996]
    1 WLR 1256   136
Jaensch *v.* Coffey (1984) 155 CLR 549   125
Jaggard *v.* Sawyer [1995] 1 WLR 269   45
James Hardie & Co *v.* Newton (1997) 42 NSWLR 729   58, 64, 69
Jameson *v.* Central Electricity Generating Board [1999]
    3 WLR 141   206, 207
Jeffrey *v.* Commodore Cabaret Ltd (1995) 128 DLR
    (4th) 535   125
Jenkins *v.* Tucker (1788) 1 Hy Bl 90   90, 168
John Edwards and Co *v.* Motor Insurance Co Ltd [1922]
    2 KB 249   164
Johns *v.* Prunell [1960] VR 208   77, 151, 153
Johnson *v.* Shelest (1988) 22 BCLR (2d) 230   32, 41, 48, 49, 56,
    59, 75, 93, 94, 243
Jolley *v.* London Borough of Sutton [1998] 1 Lloyd's Law Rep 433,
    [1998] 1 WLR 1546 (CA) and [2000] 1 WLR 1082 (HL)   240, 242
Jones *v.* Moylan [No 2] (2000) 23 WAR 65   25, 26, 85, 199, 244
Joy *v.* Newell unreported Queen's Bench Division 27 February
    1998   67, 242

Kamloops (City) *v.* Nielsen (1984) 10 DLR (4th) 641   141

Kars *v.* Kars [1995] Aust Torts Reports ¶81–369 (QLD CA), (1996)
    187 CLR 354 (HCA)   1, 3, 22, 23, 24, 25, 34, 47, 48, 68, 85, 93,
    137, 149, 151, 156, 159, 160, 190, 195, 199, 208, 209, 233, 234,
    245

Kiddell *v.* Kulczycki [1977] 3 WWR 216   111, 113

King *v.* Victoria Insurance Company Limited [1896] AC 250
    163, 164, 165, 166, 186, 266

Kirby *v.* British Columbia (Attorney General) British Columbia
    Supreme Court 15 July 1997   245

Kirkham *v.* Boughey [1958] 2 QB 338   111, 113

Kite *v.* Malycha (1998) SASR 321   69

Kleinwort Benson *v.* Birmingham City Council [1997]
    QB 380   72

Kleinwort Benson Ltd *v.* Lincoln City Council [1998]
    3 WLR 1095   194

Kleinwort Benson Ltd *v.* South Tyneside Metropolitan Borough
    Council [1994] 4 All ER 972   72

Kobs *v.* Merchants Hotel (1990) 62 Man R (2d) 210 approved (1991)
    70 Man R (2d) 178   59, 94, 244

Kovac *v.* Kovac [1982] 1 NSWLR 655   51

L Shaddock & Associates Ltd *v.* Parramatta City Council [No 1]
    (1981) 150 CLR 225   137

Lady Hood of Avalon *v.* Mackinnon [1909] 1 Ch 476   78

Lang *v.* Ballash (1989) 72 Alta LR (2d) 306   21, 111, 150

Lankenau *v.* Dutton (1989) 56 DLR (4th) 364   93, 94, 245

Lapensée *v.* Ottawa Day Nursery (1986) 35 CCLT 129   21, 52, 93,
    106, 150

Leduc *v.* British Canadian Insurance Co [1924] 1 DLR 196   164

Lee *v.* Taunton and Somerset NHS Trust [2001] 1 FLR 419   122, 123

Lefebvre *v.* Kitteringham (1985) 39 Sask R 308   93, 96

Legal and General Assurance Society Ltd *v.* Drake Insurance Ltd
    [1992] QB 887   204

Levesque *v.* Grondin (1974) 7 NBR (2d) 98   62, 63

Liffen *v.* Watson [1940] 1 KB 556   59

Lipkin Gorman *v.* Karpnale [1991] 2 AC 548   101, 103, 104

London, Chatham and Dover Railway Company *v.* South Eastern
    Railways [1893] AC 429   44

Lonrho Exports Ltd *v.* Export Credits Guarantee Department [1996]
    4 All ER 673   179, 181, 182, 218
Lonrho plc *v.* Fayed [1992] 1 WLR 1   247
Lord Napier and Ettrick *v.* Hunter [1993] AC 713   1, 173, 174,
    175, 176, 179, 180, 187, 205, 206, 217, 218, 220, 236, 257, 259, 260,
    261, 263, 266, 274
Louth *v.* Diprose (1992) 175 CLR 621   78
Lunnon *v.* Reagh (1978) 25 NSR (2d) 196   52, 93, 106, 235, 245
Lusignan (Litigation Guardian of) *v.* Concordia Hospital [1997] 6
    WWR 185, supplementary reasons at [1999]
    1 WWR 733   51, 93, 245
Macclesfield Corporation *v.* Great Central Railway [1911]
    2 KB 528   163
Macdonald (Guardian ad litem of) *v.* Neufield (1993) 85 BCLR (2d)
    129   21, 150
Mackinlay *v.* MacEachern (1983) 123 APR 175   245
Mahesan s/o Thambiah *v.* Malaysia Government Officers'
    Co-Operative Housing Society Ltd [1979] AC 374   136
Malat *v.* Bjornson (No 2) [1979] 4 WWR 673   21, 94
Marc Rich & Co AG *v.* Bishop Rock Marine Co Ltd [1996]
    1 AC 211   115, 116, 126, 132
Marin *v.* Varta (1983) 218 Sask R 173   48, 93
Marinko & Anor *v.* Masri (2000) Aust Torts Rep ¶81–581   26, 85
Marsland *v.* Andjelic [No 2] (1993) 32 NSWLR 649   243
Martel Building Ltd *v.* Canada (2000) 193 DLR (4th) 1   143, 144
Martorana *v.* Lee (1994) 17 Alta LR (3d) 409   37, 77
Matheson *v.* Bartlett (1993) 335 APR 373   245
McFarlane *v.* EE Caledonia Ltd [1994] 2 All ER 1   125, 128, 129
McFarlane *v.* Tayside Health Board [2000] 2 AC 59   119, 120, 121, 125
McGregor *v.* Rowley [1928] SASR 67   32, 77
McLeod *v.* Palardy (1980) 4 Man R (2d) 218   48, 51, 93, 106, 245
McLoughlin *v.* O'Brien [1983] 1 AC 410   125, 131
Michols *v.* McWilliams (1980) AR 102   37, 77
Miller, Gibb & Co Ltd, re [1957] 2 All ER 266   186, 203
Millett *v.* McDonald's Restaurants of Canada Limited (1984) 29 Man
    R (2d) 83   21, 94, 241
Mills *v.* British Rail Engineering Limited [1992]
    PIQR Q130   111

Ministry of Defence *v.* Ashman [1993] 2 EGLR 102   53

Mitchell *v.* U-Haul Co of Canada Ltd (1986) 73 AR 91   57, 94, 245

Mollgaard *v.* ARCIC [1999] 3 NZLR 735   88

Morris *v.* Ford Motor Co Ltd [1973] 1 QB 792   179

Morrison Steamship Co Ltd *v.* Greystoke Castle (Cargo Owners) [1947] AC 265   115

Moule *v.* Garrett (1872) LR 7 Exch 101   194

Mulcahy *v.* Ministry of Defence [1996] 2 All ER 758   116

Murphy *v.* Brentwood District Council [1991] 1 AC 398   116, 126

Mutual Life & Citizens' Assurance Co Ltd *v.* Evatt (1968) 122 CLR 556   137

N, re (2001) 33 MVR 237   25, 26, 85, 199, 244

Nahhas *v.* Pier House (Cheyne Walk) Management Ltd (1984) 270 EG 328   163, 166, 167, 168

Nash *v.* Inman [1908] 2 KB 1   107

National Bank of New Zealand *v.* Waitaki International Processing Ltd [2000] 2 NZLR 1   102

National Westminster Bank plc *v.* Somer International (UK) Ltd [2002] 1 All ER 198   102

Neste Oy *v.* Lloyd's Bank [1983] 2 Lloyd's Rep 658   247, 249

Newby *v.* Reid (1763) 1 Wm Bl 416   204

Newell *v.* Hawthornthwaite (1988) 26 BCLR (2d) 105   241

Nicholls *v.* Jack [1963] Qd R 1   37, 151, 153

North British and Mercantile Insurance Company *v.* London, Liverpool and Globe Insurance Company (1876) 5 Ch D 569   204

O'Keefe *v.* Schluter (1979) Qd R 224   48

Oasis Merchandising Services Ltd, in re [1998] Ch 170   267

Ogwo *v.* Taylor [1988] 1 AC 431   125

Oliver (Guardian ad Litem of) *v.* Ellison unreported British Columbia Court of Appeal 18 May 2001   245

Orakpo *v.* Manson Investments Ltd [1978] AC 95   163, 180, 189

Ostapowich *v.* Benoit (1982) 14 Sask R 233   1, 21, 47, 150

Owen *v.* Tate [1976] 1 QB 402   60, 98, 163, 164, 168, 194

Page *v.* Smith [1995] 2 All ER 736   125, 130, 131

Parkinson *v.* St James NHS Trust [2001] 3 WLR 376   122

Parry *v.* North West Surrey Area Health Authority unreported Queen's Bench Division 29 November 1999   67, 242

Peel (Regional Municipality) v. Canada (1993) 98 DLR
    (4th) 140   53
Perre v. Apand (1999) 198 CLR 180   138, 139
Peter v. Beblow [1993] 3 WWR 337   263
Pettkus v. Becker (1980) 117 DLR (3d) 257   72
Phillip Collins Ltd v. Davis [2000] 3 All ER 806   102, 103
Phillips v. L & SW Ry (1879) 5 CPD 280   113
Pickering v. Deakin [1985] 1 WWR 289   235, 245
Poirier v. Dyer & Dyer (1989) 91 NSR (2d) 119   1
Polly Peck (No 2), re [1998] 3 All ER 813   238
Prager v. Blatspiel, Stamp and Heacock Ltd [1924]
    1 KB 566   90
Price v. Gebert (1952–53) 7 WWR 426   21, 150
Proctor & Gamble Philippine Manufacturing Corporation v. Peter
    Cremer GmbH (The Manilla) [1988] 3 All ER 843   53
R v. Bournewood Community and Mental Health N.H.S. Trust ex
    parte L [1998] 3 All ER 289   91
Rand v. East Dorset Health Authority [2000] Lloyd's Rep
    Med 181   122
Randal v. Cockran (1748) 1 Ves Sen 98   173
Rathwell v. Rathwell (1978) 83 DLR (3d) 289   72
Rawson v. Kasman (1956) 3 DLR (2d) 376   4, 20, 22, 27, 48, 57,
    71, 80, 99, 212, 214, 244
RBC Dominion Securities Inc v. Dawson (1994) 111 DLR
    (4th) 230   102, 103, 105
Redden v. Hector (1980) 42 NSR (2d) 96   32, 41, 49, 56, 59, 74,
    241, 243
Rhodes, in re (1890) 44 Ch D 94   90, 108
Richardson v. Schultz (1980) 25 SASR 1   51, 93
Riordon v. Palmer (1989) 226 APR 326   21, 111, 150
Roach v. Yates [1938] 1 KB 256   51, 52, 66, 93, 94, 97, 106, 244
Roberts v. Bailey (1975) 10 NBR (2d) 212   21, 111, 150
Roberts v. Johnstone [1988] 3 WLR 1247   51, 93, 94, 106
Rogers v. Price (1829) 3 Y&J 28   168
Rosecrance v. Rosecrance (1996) Aust Torts Rep ¶81–374   68
Roxborough v. Rothmans of Pall Mall Australia Limited [2001] HCA
    68, 185 ALR 335   9, 10, 201, 202, 203, 223, 225, 226, 227, 228,
    230, 273

Ruch *v.* I & H Transfer Limited (1969) 1 NBR (2d) 379   71

San Sebastian *v.* The Minister (1986) 162 CLR 341   137

Sauve *v.* Provost (1990) 66 DLR (4th) 338   32, 37, 38, 49, 56, 59, 74, 75

Scaramanga *v.* Stamp (1880) 5 CPD 295   132, 133

Scarff *v.* Wilson (1986) 39 CCLT 20   266

Schebsman, re [1944] Ch 83   81, 93, 96, 245

Schneider *v.* Eisovitch [1960] 2 QB 430   27, 51, 62, 63, 64, 80, 93, 107, 110, 244

Scottish Equitable *v.* Derby [2001] 3 All ER 818   102, 103

Shaw et al *v.* Roemer et al (1981) 46 NSR (2d) 629 affirmed (1981) 134 DLR 590 (3d)   63, 94

Simpson *v.* Portsmouth & South East Hampshire Health Authority unreported Queen's Bench Division 16 July 1997   240, 242

Sinclair *v.* Brougham [1914] AC 398   106

Smith *v.* Eric Bush [1990] 1 AC 831   118, 119

Society of Lloyd's *v.* Robinson [1999] 1 WLR 756   174

Soulos *v.* Korkontzilas (1997) 146 DLR (4th) 214   238

South Australia Asset Management Corp *v.* York Montague Ltd [1996] 3 All ER 365   128

South Tyneside Metropolitan BC *v.* Svenska International [1995] 1 All ER 545   102, 103

Spring *v.* Guardian Assurance plc [1995] 2 AC 296   117, 118, 119

Stacey *v.* National Leisure Catering Ltd [2001] EWCA Civ 355   242

Stevens et al *v.* Kachman (1978) 10 AR 192   21, 111, 150

Stewart et al *v.* Mayer (1990) 243 APR 298   21, 111, 150

Stovin *v.* Wise [1996] 3 All ER 801   129

Sullivan *v.* Gordon (1999) 47 NSWLR 319   49, 69

Surrey County Council *v.* Brodero Homes Ltd [1993] 1 WLR 1361   45

Sutherland Shire Council *v.* Heyman (1984–1985) 157 CLR 424   126

T (Adult: Refusal of Treatment), in re [1992] 3 WLR 782   50, 51, 53, 96, 108

Tang Man Sit *v.* Capacious Investments Ltd [1996] AC 514   136

Taylor *v.* Bristol Omnibus Co [1975] 1 WLR 1054   97, 235, 245, 255, 256

Tepko Pty Ltd *v.* Water Board [2001] 178 ALR 634   137
TH Knitwear (Wholesale) Ltd, in re [1988] 1 Ch 275   189
The Winson [1982] AC 939   98
The 'Zuhal K' and 'Selin' [1987] 1 Lloyd's Rep 151   60, 98, 168, 194
Thomas et al *v.* City of Winnipeg (1937) 45 Man R 422   21, 150
Thomas *v.* Eyles (1998) 28 MVR 240   27, 80
Thomson *v.* MacLean (1983) 57 NSR (2d) 436; (1983) 120 APR 436
    20, 80, 87, 93, 245
Thornton *v.* Board of School Trustees of School District No 57
    (Prince George) (1976) 73 DLR (3d) 35 (BCCA) (1978) 83 DLR
    (3d) 480 (SCC)   1, 3, 19, 20, 21, 22, 34, 48, 52, 67, 93, 172,
    173, 175, 195, 240, 241, 245
Tito *v.* Waddell (No 2) [1977] Ch 106   45
Tomlinson *v.* Bentall (1826) 5 B & C 738   90, 168
Trendtex Trading Corporation *v.* Credit Suisse [1980] 1QB 269 (CA);
    [1982] AC 679 (HL)   267
Treonne Wholesale Meats *v.* Shaheen (1988) 12 NSWLR
    522   110
Turnbull *v.* Hsieh (1990) 108 NBR (2d) 33, (1990) 269
    APR 33   4, 22, 70, 93, 94, 96, 212, 214, 244, 245
Twinsectra Limited *v.* Yardley [2002] 2 AC 164   239, 247
Urbanski *v.* Patel (1978) 84 DLR (3d) 650   21
Valois *v.* Long (1984) 146 APR 191 varied on other grounds (1986)
    167 APR 434   94, 244
Van Gervan *v.* Fenton (1992) 175 CLR 327   36, 68, 140, 149, 156, 243
Vandepitte *v.* Preferred Accident Insurance Corp of New York [1933]
    AC 70   266
Veivers *v.* Connolly (1994) Aust Torts Rep ¶81–309   111, 137,
    139, 140, 141
Veldhuizen and Stevens *v.* Blokzyl [1977] 1 WWR 526   21, 32, 62, 63
Vernon *v.* Bosley (No 1) [1997] 1 All ER 577   125, 131
Videan *v.* British Transport Commission [1963] 2
    QB 650   125, 128, 133
W *v.* Essex County Council [2000] 2 WLR 601   125, 130
W *v.* Q (1992) 1 Tas R 301   25, 85, 244
Wadsworth *v.* Lydall [1981] 1 WLR 598   44
Wattson *v.* Port of London Authority [1969] 1 Lloyd's
    Rep 95   244

Weinman *v.* Boten (1991) 104 FLR 146   60, 94

Westdeutsche Landesbank Girozentrale *v.* Islington London Borough
    Council [1994] 4 All ER 890, [1994] 1 WLR 938 (CA), [1996] AC
    669 (HL)   76, 106, 238, 248, 249, 250, 265

Wheatley *v.* Cunningham [1992] 1 PIQR Q100   71

White *v.* Jones [1995] 2 AC 207   117, 118, 120, 121, 123, 124, 135

Williams *v.* Natural Life Health Foods Ltd [1998] 1 WLR 830
    116, 119, 121

Williams *v.* Wentworth (1842) 5 Beav 325   108

Wills *v.* Cook and Others unreported Chancery Division 2 April
    1979, (11 July 1979) Law Society's Gazette 706   266

Wilson *v.* McLeay (1961) 106 CLR 523   51, 62, 93, 107, 244

Winnipeg Condominium Corp No 36 *v.* Bird Construction Co
    (1995) 121 DLR (4th) 193   143

Wipfli *v.* Britten (1984) 13 DLR (4th) 169   123

Woodrup *v.* Nicol [1993] 2 PIQR Q104   71

Woolwich Building Society *v.* IRC (No 2) [1993] AC 70   76

Wrotham Park Estate Co Ltd *v.* Parkside Homes Ltd [1974] 1
    WLR 798   45

Yepremian et al *v.* Scarborough General Hospital et al (1980) 110
    DLR (3d) 513   51, 60, 93, 94, 106, 241

Yorkshire Insurance Co Ltd *v.* Nisbet Shipping Co Ltd [1962]
    2 QB 330   176

KEY WORKS

Birks   Birks, P., *An Introduction to the Law of Restitu-*
                             tion (revised edn., Oxford, 1998)

Birks and Mitchell   Birks, P. and Mitchell, C. "Unjust Enrichment",
                             in P. Birks (ed.), *English Private Law, Volume*
                             II (Oxford, 2000), chapter 15

Burrows   Burrows, A., *The Law of Restitution* (London,
                             1993)

Burrows and McKendrick   Burrows, A. and McKendrick, E., *Cases and*
                             Materials on the Law of Restitution (Oxford,
                             1997)

Chambers   Chambers, R., *Resulting Trusts* (Oxford, 1997)

Clerk and Lindsell   Dugdale, A. (et al.) (eds.), *Clerk and Lindsell*
                             on Torts (Eighteenth edn., London, 2000)

Elias   Elias, G., *Explaining Constructive Trusts* (Ox-
                             ford, 1990)

Goff and Jones   Goff, R. and Jones, G., *The Law of Restitution*
                             (5th edn., London, 1998)

Maddaugh and McCamus   Maddaugh, P. and McCamus, J., *The Law of*
                             Restitution (Aurora, 1990)

Mason and Carter   Mason, K. and Carter, J., *Restitution Law in*
                             Australia (Sydney, 1995)

Mitchell   Mitchell, C., *The Law of Subrogation* (Oxford,
                             1994)

Smith   Smith, L., *The Law of Tracing* (Oxford, 1997)

Tettenborn   Tettenborn, A., *Law of Restitution in England*
                             and Ireland (2nd edn., London, 1996)

Trindade and Cane   Trindade, F. and Cane, P., *The Law of Torts in*
                             Australia (2nd edn., Oxford, 1993)

Virgo   Virgo, G., *The Principles of the Law of Restitu-*
                             tion (Oxford, 1999)

1

Introduction

This book is about particular three-party cases occurring at the boundary between tort and unjust enrichment. The conceptual problem to be addressed is to explain why a stranger to litigation should ever be entitled to participate in the fruits of that litigation. The paradigm example of such cases is the victim of a tortious injury and her carer. An incapacitated victim of tort may receive help from her friends and family who intervene in order to ameliorate the effects of the tortfeasor's negligence. They may give assistance in the form of services provided to the victim or payment of her debts. The victim is entitled to sue the wrongdoer in respect of the value of this assistance.[1] However, in general the carer has no right to sue the wrongdoer,[2] and it is widely assumed that she cannot compel the victim to do so on her behalf. In some cases, the victim will recover damages subject to the carer's entitlement to share in the fund. In these cases, the carer is a stranger to the victim's suit, but is nonetheless entitled to participate in the victim's judgment. The carer's entitlement to share in the fund has never been explained. In addition, the fact that in some cases the carer's right is proprietary adds to the confusion.

The same pattern is evident in the rights available to an indemnity insurer. The insurer indemnifies the insured for loss. The proper claimant in any suit against the wrongdoer is the insured.[3] The insured will hold any damages recovered subject to an equitable lien in favour of the insurer.[4] The insurer is thus a stranger to the insured's suit, but is nonetheless entitled to participate in the insured's judgment.

---

[1] *Hunt* v. *Severs* [1994] 2 AC 350; *Griffiths* v. *Kerkemeyer* (1977) 139 CLR 161; *Kars* v. *Kars* (1996) 187 CLR 354; *Thornton* v. *Board of School Trustees of School District No 57 (Prince George) et al* (1978) 83 DLR (3d) 480.

[2] There are exceptional cases in which the carer has sued the wrongdoer directly: *Ostapowich* v. *Benoit* (1982) 14 Sask R 233; *Poirier* v. *Dyer & Dyer* (1989) 91 NSR (2d) 119.

[3] *Esso Petroleum Co Ltd* v. *Hall Russell and Co Ltd* [1989] AC 643.

[4] *Lord Napier and Ettrick* v. *Hunter* [1993] 1 AC 713.

The problem stated: victims and carers

The examples set out above reveal the core conceptual problem addressed by this book. That is to explain why a stranger to litigation should ever be entitled to participate in the fruits of that litigation. Litigation is conducted by a claimant against a defendant. One remedy which might be sought by the claimant is an award of damages. A third party, a stranger to the litigation, is not entitled in the ordinary course to the benefit of these damages. However, there are categories of case in which a different pattern emerges. In these examples, the court departs from the general position and awards damages to the claimant on terms which recognise the interest of the stranger. This book explains why such an entitlement arises. In addition, it is necessary to explain why, if ever, the stranger's right to participate is expressed via a proprietary mechanism, rather than a mere personal entitlement. Finally, the book exposes a hidden anomaly. Given that the carer's position is recognised via an entitlement to share in the fruits of the victim's claim, it is surely incongruous that the carer has no means of forcing the victim to realise this entitlement via a suit against the wrongdoer. Each of these three core questions is outlined below.

The right to participate in the fund

An incapacitated victim requires the assistance of others. This assistance may be provided by the carer who is a friend or relative of the victim. The carer may nurse the victim, assist with the day-to-day management of the victim's life and affairs or provide household help. In other cases, the carer intervenes by paying those of the victim's debts associated with her negligently inflicted injury. The carer's intervention is of great benefit to the victim but often comes at a substantial financial and personal cost to the carer. In these circumstances, the question arises as to what remedies are available to carers. *Hunt* v. *Severs*[5] confirms that in England, the proper claimant in any action against the tortfeasor is the victim, and denies the carer her own claim.[6] Their Lordships also held that in general, although not on the special facts of that case, the victim will recover damages calculated by reference to the carer's services and hold them in trust for the carer.[7]

---

[5] *Hunt* v. *Severs* [1994] 2 AC 350. The leading speech was delivered by Lord Bridge with whom the rest of the House agreed.
[6] *Ibid.*, 358.   [7] N. 5 above at 363.

Other appellate courts have also given decisions on this factual pattern. The Supreme Court of Canada in *Thornton* v. *Board of School Trustees of School District No 57 (Prince George)*[8] held that the carer has no direct claim,[9] but that the victim may claim the value of such assistance from the wrongdoer. Consistently with the result proposed by the House of Lords, this part of the victim's damages award was to be held in trust for the carer. The High Court of Australia has adopted a divergent position. *Kars* v. *Kars* confirms that the victim may '...as part of his or her damages (without joining that person [the carer] as a party to the action), recover damages in respect of the cost to a family member of fulfilling the natural obligations to attend to the injuries and disabilities caused to the plaintiff by the tort.'[10] However, unlike the position in Canada and England, the carer in Australia is denied any right of access to the fund.[11] This has led to anomalous results. This book ultimately rejects the logic of the Australian cases and proposes that, leaving aside the form of access, the carer should be entitled to share in the fund of damages recovered by the victim. Such reform would remove the injustice produced by the current position which is vividly described by Callinan J:[12]

> Experience recalls to mind the incredulous expressions of delight of plaintiffs, and of disbelieving dismay of defendants, on being told that damages for gratuitous care and services at common law are available, and that there is no legal obligation in this country for them to be paid to the gratuitous carer and provider of services.

The right to force litigation against the wrongdoer

A related mystery is that the carer has no apparent means of ensuring that the victim exercises her claim against the wrongdoer. At least in England and Canada, where the carer is indirectly recognised via an entitlement to share in the proceeds of the victim's claim, it is curious that the carer is left without any means of forcing suit against the wrongdoer. Rather, the law appears

---

[8] *Thornton* v. *Board of School Trustees of School District No 57 (Prince George)* (1976) 73 DLR (3d) 35 (British Columbia Court of Appeal) upheld in the Supreme Court of Canada at (1978) 83 DLR (3d) 480.

[9] *Thornton* v. *Board of School Trustees of School District No 57 (Prince George)* (1976) 73 DLR (3d) 35 at 55 PER TAGGART JA.

[10] *Kars* v. *Kars* (1996) 187 CLR 354 at 368 PER TOOHEY, MCHUGH, GUMMOW AND KIRBY JJ.

[11] *Ibid.*, 380.   [12] *Grincelis* v. *House* (2000) 201 CLR 321 at 339 PER CALLINAN J.

to endorse the peculiar model whereby the carer's position is recognised, because she is entitled to share in the victim's damages. However, in reality the carer is not protected, because the carer has no means to ensure that these damages actually are recovered.

The nature of the right to participate

The dominant position is that a carer in England and Canada is entitled to participate in the victim's damages via the mechanism of a trust. However, there are also examples in which the carer's entitlement is only ever personal.[13] The carer's trust has come under scrutiny and the UK Law Commission has recommended its statutory abolition.[14] It is therefore a relevant question to determine how, if ever, the carer's entitlement will be proprietary.

Solutions and structure of this book

The primary configuration under examination is the legal relationship between the victim of a tort, her carer and the wrongdoer. However, in investigating this relationship, this book utilises a powerful conceptual tool, which is to observe that the phenomenon under investigation in the victim and carer cases is also manifest in the case of the indemnity insurer and insured. It will be shown that a structural analogy may be drawn between an indemnity insurer and the carer of a victim of tort. The insurer and the carer both intervene to assuage the loss experienced by the claimant. The carer does so by providing necessary services to the victim. The insurer does so by paying money for loss pursuant to its contractual obligations under the policy of indemnity insurance. The insurer intervenes under the constraint of legal liability founded on an antecedent contract. The constraint upon the carer arises from compassion and moral obligation.

In drawing this analogy, it is apparent that the questions arising from the victim and carer configuration also require explanation in the case of the indemnity insurer and insured. Where possible, the book therefore places

---

[13] *Coderre* v. *Ethier* (1978) 85 DLR (3d) 621 at 632 PER LERNER J; *Turnbull* v. *Hsieh* (1990) 269 APR 33 at 42 PER HOYT JA who delivered the judgment of the court; *Rawson* v. *Kasman* (1956) 3 DLR (2d) 376 at 381 PER SCHROEDER JA with whom Hogg and MacKay JJA agreed.

[14] UK Law Commission, *Damages for Personal Injury: Medical, Nursing and Other Expenses; Collateral Benefits* (Law Com No 262, 1999), para. 3.62.

in parallel each of these paradigm cases, and attempts to make sense of both as constituent parts of a larger pattern. It will be argued that the rights of the carer to share in the victim's damages mirror those of the insurer to claw back the value of any indemnity provided to the insured. Similarly, it will be argued that although not visible on the present state of the law, those rules which allow the insurer to compel the insured to bring litigation against the wrongdoer should be reflected in a right for the carer to force the victim to sue. The proprietary nature of the insurer's and the carer's entitlement will also be addressed.

An important caveat must be given about the approach that has been taken in drawing this analogy. Reference is made to other contextual categories of law, such as the law of negligence, the law of trusts and the law of unjust enrichment. The position is complicated further by the fact that the evidence for this study, the victim and carer cases, have been drawn from England, Australia and Canada. The point must be made that it is not the purpose of this book to conduct a detailed analysis of the relevant rules in each jurisdiction. Rather, the focus is on a higher level of principle, dealing with what seem to be the common structural tendencies. To this extent, the analysis attempts to draw out the underlying pattern of the victim and carer cases. A more elaborate analysis would not only require a much larger piece of work, but might also be hindered by the myopic focus of greater detail. We will now briefly return to the three core questions posed in this book and outline the arguments to be presented.

The right to participate in the fund

The carer's entitlement is given to reverse the unjust enrichment of the victim which would otherwise remain. The insurer's entitlement is likewise given to reverse unjust enrichment. The difficulty in revealing the juridical basis of these rights to share is twofold. The first is that there are apparently many grounds upon which we might justify the right to share in the fund. For example, the carer's right may on some facts be given in response to a contract, and has erroneously been attributed to the law of tort.[15] The second is that there appears to be no relevant unjust factor. Unjust enrichment is a likely explanation for the carer's right to share. However, the utility of this analysis is hampered by the fact that the existing unjust

---

[15] R. Williams, 'Preventing Unjust Enrichment' [2000] *Restitution Law Review* 492 at 510.

factors fail adequately to account for the carer's entitlements. The solution suggested by this book is that the law of unjust enrichment discloses a novel policy motivated unjust factor called the policy against accumulation. This unjust factor convincingly accounts for both the insurer's and also the carer's right to participate.

In order to advance these arguments, some ground clearing is therefore essential. Part I (chapters 1–5) commences with a short exposition of the leading victim and carer cases in England, Australia and Canada in order to provide a basis for analysis in the remainder of the book (chapter 2). The discussion then explores the possibility that the carer might hold a right to sue for her own loss directly. Such a right might exist against either the victim or the tortfeasor. Against the victim, the carer may allege an obligation in either contract or unjust enrichment. These possible claims are the concern of chapters 3 and 4, which will show that, superficially at least, an obligation may bind the victim to pay the carer. However, as will be explored more fully in part II, these claims are of themselves incapable of explaining the carer's right to share in the fund. Chapter 5 will briefly survey the possible claim by the carer against the victim in tort. While some cases adopt this route, there is very little scope for this type of claim.

Part II (chapters 6–8) concentrates on the argument that in order to understand the carer's right to share in the fund, it is helpful to look at the position of the indemnity insurer. Chapter 6 documents the fact that, even if the carer does hold any one of the direct rights of claim identified in part I, none provides an adequate explanation for the carer's right to share in the victim's damages. The analysis then returns to the observation that the relevant rules regulating the carer and the indemnity insurer may be closely related. Chapter 7 draws a detailed analogy between the position of the carer and the indemnity insurer, drawing on the groundbreaking work of Mitchell, and adopting the nomenclature described in his model of subrogation.[16] This analogy reveals the similar position of the carer and the indemnity insurer. One consequence of this similarity is that our understanding of the rules which regulate the position of one may be used to inform our understanding of the rules regulating the position of the other.

Chapter 8 contains a more sophisticated unjust enrichment analysis. As has been said, chapter 4 demonstrates that the victim is enriched at the

---

[16] Mitchell, pp. 4–8.

expense of the carer. However, chapter 4 cannot convincingly advance an unjust enrichment explanation for the carer's entitlement, because the existing unjust factors do not sit well with the victim and carer cases. Chapter 8 successfully completes the unjust enrichment analysis. It demonstrates the existence of a novel policy motivated unjust factor called the policy against accumulation. The policy against accumulation applies whenever a claimant (RH) receives a benefit, or has the right to recover damages, from another party such as the wrongdoer (PL) and receives, or has the right to receive in respect of the same debt or damage from a third party (S). The policy against accumulation dictates that RH may not accumulate in respect of the same debt or damage. To the extent that RH has accumulated, she must return value. In the configurations investigated in this book, RH returns value to the carer and the indemnity insurer (S) in order to reverse her enrichment which would otherwise remain. Chapter 8 therefore applies the policy against accumulation to explain the right of both the carer, and also the insurer, to participate in the fund of damages recovered. There are broader ramifications flowing from the identification of this unjust factor. Chapter 8 identifies other factual configurations which appear to invite the application of the policy against accumulation. One of the great merits of a detailed analysis of the victim and carer relationship is to disclose the existence of this novel unjust factor.

The right to force litigation against the wrongdoer

The analogy in chapter 7 does not only assist in explaining the stranger's right to participate in the fruits of the litigation. If correct, it shows how the anomaly by which the carer is not able fully to protect her position is removed. The rights of the insurer form a template for the law's future development. Chapter 7 argues that the carer should enjoy a right similar to the indemnity insurer's ability to compel litigation against the wrongdoer. Following the work of Mitchell, it is easy to see how these rights to force litigation work to reverse unjust enrichment.

The nature of the right to participate

Part III (chapter 9) explains why in some cases the carer's right to share in the victim's damages is proprietary, and in others is merely personal. It will be argued that on the current structure of the law of unjust enrichment, it is very difficult to explain why the carer is a beneficiary of a trust. The task is not impossible. Although controversial, it will be suggested that the policy against accumulation itself triggers the proprietary nature of the carer's entitlement. The key to understanding the proprietary claim is that the carer's intervention increases the victim's patrimony. The valuation of the victim's claim is in part a direct function of the assistance provided by the carer. This assistance creates new value in the hands of the victim, by increasing the worth of the victim's chose in action against the wrongdoer. Arguably, it is this contribution which justifies a proprietary response to unjust enrichment.

The insurer's equitable lien has likewise been difficult to reconcile with accepted principles. Chapter 9 ventures an explanation of the proprietary quality of the insurer's entitlement which is likewise linked to policy against accumulation. However, it is conceded that this analysis is not wholly convincing. Rather, the insurer's entitlement, while understood as resting on the reversal of the insured's unjust enrichment by accumulation, should be understood only as triggering a personal claim. Chapter 10 is a brief conclusion.

Conclusion

The task of this book is to explain how and why the carer, a stranger to the victim's litigation, is entitled to share in the fruits of that litigation. In addition, it attempts to shed some light on the issue of why in some cases this right is proprietary and in others it is not. In answering these questions, we observe that the indemnity insurer and the carer are in an equivalent position. The crucial similarity between them is that each intervenes to make good or indemnify the loss of another, yet has no claim of her own against the wrongdoer who caused that loss. An argument may be made that there are two methods which the law gives to protect the position of a person who intervenes in circumstances such as these.

The first is that the stranger is entitled to share in the fruits of the claimant's litigation. This right is given to reverse the unjust enrichment which would otherwise remain. The unjust factor supporting the entitlement is the policy against accumulation. As outlined in chapter 8, the law discloses a novel policy motivated unjust factor called the policy against accumulation. This applies whenever the claimant (RH) receives a benefit, or has the right to recover damages, from another party such as the wrongdoer

(PL) and receives, or has the right to receive, in respect of the same debt or damage from a third party (S). The policy against accumulation dictates that RH may not accumulate in respect of the same debt or damage. To the extent that RH has accumulated, she must return value. The configurations investigated in this book are of the indemnity insurer and insured and the carer and victim. RH returns value to the carer and the indemnity insurer (S) in order to reverse her enrichment which would otherwise remain.

It is immediately obvious that these examples concern the ability of a claimant to sue a wrongdoer in respect of loss already made good by the intervention of the carer and the insurer. However, the operation of the policy against accumulation is not confined to these categories. Chapter 8 discusses additional configurations which appear to invite the application of the policy. One of these is typified by *Dimond* v. *Lovell*,[17] and is similar to the victim and carer cases in that it involves a claimant who has received a loss ameliorating benefit. The other is *Roxborough* v. *Rothmans of Pall Mall Australia Limited*,[18] which concerns accumulation by a claimant who is entitled to recover from the revenue money paid on account of an unconstitutional tax. Difficulty was caused by the fact that the claimant had passed the burden of the tax onto a third party. Recognition of the policy against accumulation allows us better to solve these configurations. The role of the policy against accumulation as an unjust factor is not limited to explaining the rights of the carer and the indemnity insurer to share in the fund. Rather, it is an unjust factor of wider application.

The second method of protection given to an intervener, most obviously present in the case of the indemnity insurer, is to allow the intervener to force the claimant to sue the wrongdoer. This book argues that a carer occupies an equivalent position, and should likewise be given the right to force litigation against the wrongdoer. The novel right suggested for the carer, the right to compel suit by the victim against the wrongdoer, is simply the corollary of the carer's existing right to share in the fund. The award of subrogation, literally the right to be substituted as claimant, is an equitable remedy and is thus discretionary. The parallel right for the carer should be exercised only if it is just and equitable to do so.

---

[17] *Dimond* v. *Lovell* [2002] 1 AC 384.
[18] *Roxborough* v. *Rothmans of Pall Mall Australia Limited* [2001] HCA 68, 185 ALR 335. *Roxborough* was reported as this book went to press. References in the remaining footnotes are to neutral citation.

On the facts of the core configurations in this book, there are two rights available: the right to share in the fund, irrespective of the nature of that right, and the right to compel suit against the wrongdoer. These rights work in tandem to protect the position of the intervener. However, it is not necessarily the case that these rights will co-exist. For example, let us take the facts of a case such as *Roxborough*, in which the claimant paid to the revenue tax pursuant to a liability which turned out to be unconstitutional. The claimant had already passed the cost of the tax onto tobacco consumers. Chapter 8 shows that the claimant is thereby unjustly enriched by accumulating in respect of the same debt or damage. The claimant is obligated to return value to these consumers on the basis of the policy against accumulation. It is the author's own view that the additional right available to the intervener, the right to force litigation, may also be available to these consumers. This argument is not fully explored in this book and is no doubt controversial. However, irrespective of the right to force litigation, it remains the case that the right to recover value from the claimant is available.

PART I

2

Three leading carer cases

Courts fail coherently to explain why the carer, a stranger to the victim's suit against the wrongdoer, is entitled to share in the fruits of the victim's claim. The limited purpose of this chapter is briefly to document judicial opinion in Australia, England and common law Canada as revealed by the leading cases in each jurisdiction. This introduction to the leading cases provides a basis for the discussion which follows in the remaining chapters of this book.

The factual pattern under examination is the negligently injured victim suing the wrongdoer in order to obtain damages in tort. The victim may be cared for prior to trial by friends and family. In addition, there may be evidence that the intervention of friends and family will continue after the date of judgment to meet the victim's future care needs. The victim generally is entitled to recover an amount by way of damages which is referable to the assistance provided by the carer.[1] However, there is no uniform approach to two important questions: (1) whether the carer is entitled to share in the proceeds of the litigation; and (2) whether or not this right is proprietary. In England and Canada, the carer is entitled to participate in the fruits of the victim's claim. In Australia, the carer is denied access to the fund of damages. Each of these jurisdictions will be considered in turn. The discussion will describe the method by which the courts account for the value of the carer's intervention, and whether the carer is entitled to share in the victim's damages.

England

The position in England is recorded in the decision of the House of Lords in *Hunt* v. *Severs*.[2] The victim Miss Hunt was a pillion passenger on a

---

[1] There are statutory modifications to this rule which are not discussed in this book. These statutes are referred to for the sake of completeness only in nn. 20 and 33 below.

[2] *Hunt* v. *Severs* [1994] 2 AC 350. Discussed in S. Degeling, 'Carers' Claims: Unjust Enrichment and Tort' [2000] *Restitution Law Review* 172; L. Hoyano, 'The Dutiful Tortfeasor in the House of

motorcycle driven by her fiancé Mr Severs. Unfortunately, they crashed and Miss Hunt was gravely injured. As a result, Miss Hunt was made a paraplegic, requiring constant and intensive care. Miss Hunt and Mr Severs subsequently married and her tortfeasor husband provided much of her care.

Mr Severs admitted liability in negligence and Miss Hunt commenced proceedings against him, or more accurately, against his insurer. At trial, Miss Hunt recovered special damages calculated by reference to her husband's travelling expenses while visiting her in hospital and a sum representing the value of his past services when caring for her at home. An amount was also awarded for Miss Hunt's future loss, including a sum estimated to be the value of her husband's future care.

The tortfeasor Mr Severs appealed against the damages award, ultimately taking his challenge to the House of Lords.[3] He sought, *inter alia*, to reduce the damages to be paid to Miss Hunt. Against his own interests, and that of the victim, his appeal was successful and the value of damages awarded to Miss Hunt was reduced.[4] For reasons which are explained immediately below, that part of the victim's claim referable to the carer's assistance was denied. It would normally have been upheld. As will be explained, the special fact influencing the House was the dual identity of Mr Severs as both carer and tortfeasor.

Three issues arose for review in the House of Lords:[5] (1) the award in relation to the tortfeasor's travelling expenses; (2) the award in relation to the past and future care of the victim by the tortfeasor; and (3) the multiplier to be used in calculations. For the purpose of this discussion,

---

Lords' (1995) 3 *Tort Law Review* 63; H. Luntz, 'Voluntary Services Provided by the Defendant: A Postscript' (1994) 2 *Torts Law Journal* 184; P. Matthews and M. Lunney, 'A Tortfeasor's Lot is not a Happy One?' (1995) *Modern Law Review* 395; A. Reed, 'A Commentary on *Hunt* v. *Severs*' (1995) 15 *Oxford Journal of Legal Studies* 133.

[3] *Hunt* v. *Severs* [1994] 2 AC 350. The matter went first to the Court of Appeal where Sir Thomas Bingham MR, who delivered the judgment of the court, dismissed his appeal holding that the trial '... judge reached the right conclusion ...'. *Hunt* v. *Severs* [1993] QB 815 at 831 PER SIR THOMAS BINGHAM MR.

[4] In bringing this appeal, Mr Severs was no doubt motivated by his insurer. This case illustrates the impact that the presence of an insurer may have. As a result of his agreement with his own liability insurer, Mr Severs was forced to co-operate in an appeal which was against his own interests. As a matter of practical reality, the damages which had been recovered by his wife would have been paid by his insurer. This fund would have indirectly assisted him in caring for his wife.

[5] *Hunt* v. *Severs* [1994] 2 AC 350. Lord Bridge delivered the only judgment of any length and the other members of the House agreed with him.

only the first two grounds of appeal are relevant. The key fact around which argument proceeded was that it was the tortfeasor himself, rather than another member of the victim's family not involved in the wrongdoing, who was the carer. The tortfeasor had already incurred expenses in visiting the victim in hospital, and later contributed his labour in caring for her at home. Mr Severs argued that no claim could lie for the value of services voluntarily rendered to the victim by a defendant tortfeasor. Expressing the interest of his insurer, he questioned whether he should in effect be asked to pay twice by also paying damages which were not adjusted to reflect the value of his prior contributions.

This argument was rejected by their Lordships. Rather, their decision was founded on the view that the carer's intervention does not discharge the tortfeasor's obligation to compensate the victim. This result is obtained irrespective of the identity of the carer. The tortfeasor was thus unable to discharge his own liability by himself providing services to the victim. His obligation to pay damages remained undiminished. It was therefore not open to Mr Severs to argue that he had already met his obligations to Miss Hunt in kind. Given that the services provided by the carer did not curtail the victim's right to sue, it was necessary for the House to account for the value of the carer's intervention, and consider whether the carer was entitled to participate in the fund of damages recovered.

Accounting for the carer's intervention

The purpose of an award of damages in negligence is to compensate the claimant for loss. The court seeks to put the claimant in the position he would have been had the tort not been committed.[6] Within this framework it might be argued that, leaving aside the underlying non-pecuniary loss associated with his injuries[7] and any other losses unaffected by the carer's intervention, the victim has suffered no loss in relation to the carer's assistance. Rather than allowing the tortfeasor's liability to be reduced, the House identified two methods of accounting for the carer's intervention which are discussed below: (1) the 'needs of the victim' approach; and (2) the

---

[6] *British Transport Commission* v. *Gourley* [1956] AC 185.

[7] The accepted heads of damage for non-pecuniary loss are: pain and suffering, loss of amenities and loss of expectation of life. There are many expositions of these rules. For example: Trindade and Cane, pp. 495–9; Clerk and Lindsell, pp. 1583–8.

'compensate the carer' approach. *Hunt* v. *Severs* tells us that in England the latter is the correct approach.[8]

Needs of the victim

This approach, ultimately rejected in *Hunt* v. *Severs*,[9] attempts to adhere strictly to the traditional and seemingly elementary rule which directs the court to award damages in order to compensate the victim for loss. The assistance provided by the carer is regarded as a loss to the victim, rather than as a matter affecting the position of the carer. This is done by contemplating the provision of necessary assistance as indicative of the needs of the victim which have been created by the wrongdoer, and for which compensation can be awarded.

The leading example is *Donnelly* v. *Joyce*[10] in which the victim Christopher Donnelly was negligently injured in a road accident. He was treated as an in-patient in hospital for the months immediately following the accident but was then released to be cared for at home. His mother gave up her job in order to care for him during this period and as a result was not paid by her employer. Donnelly, suing by his father and next friend, claimed damages from the wrongdoer including an amount referable to his mother's lost wages for a six-month period.[11] The amount of £147.16 was awarded by the trial judge and upheld in the Court of Appeal.[12]

The Court of Appeal reasoned that this amount was recoverable by the victim because, notwithstanding that the wages forgone were those of his mother, the relevant loss was the victim's need for the services which had been provided by her. Having been satisfied that the victim's need for these services was generated by the wrongdoer's negligence, the mother's lost wages were used as a method of quantifying the victim's loss, represented by his need for the care which she had provided:[13]

> The plaintiff's loss, to take this present case, is not the expenditure of money to buy the special boots or to pay for the nursing attention. His loss is the existence of the need for those special boots or for those nursing services, the value of which for purposes of damages – for the purpose of the ascertainment

---

[8] N. 5 above at 363 PER LORD BRIDGE.

[9] N. 5 above at 361 and 363 PER LORD BRIDGE.   [10] *Donnelly* v. *Joyce* [1974] QB 454.

[11] The period claimed was two years but the trial judge awarded damages only for six months.

[12] N. 10 above at 464 PER MEGAW LJ who read the judgment of the court.

[13] N. 10 above at 462 PER MEGAW LJ.

of the amount of his loss – is the proper and reasonable cost of supplying those needs. That, in our judgment, is the key to the problem. So far as the defendant is concerned, the loss is not someone else's loss. It is the plaintiff's loss.

The approach of the court in *Donnelly* v. *Joyce* is not without difficulty. If it is accepted that the victim's loss lies in his need for care, it would be more natural to put a value on that need without reference to the carer's own loss. There is obviously some artificiality in using the actual loss to the carer as the measure of the victim's needs.

Compensate the carer

The alternative approach is that which was endorsed by the House in *Hunt* v. *Severs*. The practical reality is that when the victim is injured and receives nursing and other assistance, the impact of the tortfeasor's negligence flows not only to the victim, but will also be felt by those who provide that assistance. This model assumes that the carer has no right to sue the tortfeasor directly, and awards to the victim an amount which is explicitly associated with the impact of the negligence on the carer.[14] The central purpose of an award in respect of the voluntary care received by the claimant victim is thus to compensate the voluntary carer:[15]

> But it is nevertheless important to recognise that the underlying rationale of the English law, as all the cases before *Donnelly* v. *Joyce* [1974] QB 454 demonstrate, is to enable the voluntary carer to receive proper recompense for his or her services... By concentrating on the plaintiff's need and the plaintiff's loss as the basis of an award in respect of voluntary care received by the plaintiff, the reasoning in *Donnelly* v. *Joyce* diverts attention from the award's central objective of compensating the voluntary carer.

If there is any artificiality in the 'needs of the victim' approach, as we have suggested there is, there is an obvious illogicity in this one. Helpful as the result may be, it can only be regarded as very curious to deny the carer any claim of his own and then nonetheless so explicitly to allow him to share in the fruits of the victim's suit against the tortfeasor.

---

[14] N. 5 above at 358 PER LORD BRIDGE. The carer's possible direct claim in tort is dealt with in chapter 5.

[15] N. 5 above at 363 PER LORD BRIDGE. This approach is also referable to the earlier Court of Appeal decision in *Cunningham* v. *Harrison* [1973] QB 942.

Carer's participation in the fund

Having decided in *Hunt* v. *Severs* that the purpose of an award was to compensate the carer, it was necessary to determine how in the normal case to transmit these damages to the carer. Their Lordships noted that in Scotland, the Administration of Justice Act 1982 confers a statutory obligation on the victim to account to the carer for any damages recovered.[16] In order to achieve a similar result in England the House confirmed that '... in England the injured plaintiff who recovers damages under this head should hold them on trust for the voluntary carer.'[17] It was difficult to apply this trust analysis on the unique facts of *Hunt* v. *Severs* in which the carer and the tortfeasor were the same person. Their Lordships' solution was to create a regime which distinguished between the case when the carer is not the tortfeasor and the carer is also the tortfeasor.

Carer not the tortfeasor

When the carer and the tortfeasor are different people, the tortfeasor pays damages to the victim reflecting the carer's contribution. The victim holds these damages in trust for the carer.

Carer also the tortfeasor

When the carer and the tortfeasor are the same person, *Hunt* v. *Severs* shows us that the result is different. The difference lies in the use of a trust to allow the carer access to these damages. The House noted that it would be pointless to require the tortfeasor to pay damages to the victim as these would then be immediately carried back by the trust to the tortfeasor in his capacity as carer:[18]

> Once this [referring to the award's central objective of compensating the voluntary carer] is recognised it becomes evident that there can be no ground

---

[16] The legislation states: 'The relative shall have no direct right of action in delict against the responsible person in respect of the services or expenses referred to in this section [being necessary services rendered as a consequence of the injuries in question], but the injured person shall be under an obligation to account to the relative for any damages recovered from the responsible person under this section.' Administration of Justice Act 1982 s. 8(2).

[17] N. 5 above at 363 PER LORD BRIDGE. As is explored in chapter 9, this was a view which had earlier been expressed by Lord Denning MR in *Cunningham* v. *Harrison* [1973] QB 942 at 952. Orr LJ at 955 and Lawton LJ at 958 agreed with his view.

[18] N. 5 above at 363 PER LORD BRIDGE.

in public policy or otherwise for requiring the tortfeasor to pay to the plaintiff, in respect of services which he himself has rendered, a sum of money which the plaintiff must then repay to him.

In order to remove this anomaly, the House reduced the quantum of the victim's damages by the value of the carer's contribution. Accordingly, the victim's award was reduced by the value attributed to the tortfeasor's travelling expenses incurred in visiting the victim in hospital, and the cost of his past and estimated future care of the victim.[19] This reduction was only to avoid the bizarre configuration which would have resulted had the trust been imposed. The liability of the tortfeasor to pay damages remained undischarged by his contribution as carer. The House could have ordered the tortfeasor to pay damages to his wife and then required her to hold these damages in trust for him in his capacity as carer. The result would have been conceptually the same.

Canada

The Supreme Court of Canada in *Thornton* v. *Board of School Trustees of School District No 57 (Prince George)*[20] allowed the victim to recover the value of the carer's assistance and ordered that these damages would be held in trust for the carer. Gary Thornton was rendered paraplegic in an

---

[19] N. 5 above at 366 PER LORD BRIDGE. The Law Commission has recommended that there should be legislation reversing this aspect of *Hunt* v. *Severs*. According to the recommendations, the defendant's liability to pay damages to the claimant for nursing or other care should be unaffected by any liability of the claimant, on receipt of damages, to pay them or a proportion of them, to the defendant in his capacity as carer. UK Law Commission, *Damages for Personal Injury: Medical, Nursing and Other Expenses; Collateral Benefits* (Law Com No 262, 1999), para. 3.76.

[20] *Thornton* v. *Board of School Trustees of School District No 57 (Prince George)* (1978) 83 DLR (3d) 480. The effect of this case has been modified by statute in Ontario. The Family Law Act 1990 (Ontario) s. 61 gives relatives the statutory right to recover reasonable travel and other expenses and a reasonable allowance for services rendered where these arise from injury to any person with a claim for damages for personal injury. In those provinces which allow consortium and service actions, a husband may sue the tortfeasor directly to recover any expenses paid on behalf of his injured wife: This claim is no longer available in British Columbia, Manitoba, Saskatchewan and New Brunswick. Alberta has extended it to include a claim by either spouse for the loss of the society and comfort of the other: Domestic Relations Act 1980 (Alberta) s. 43(1). The legislative regime in Canada is discussed in K. Cooper-Stephenson, *Personal Injury Damages in Canada* (2nd edn., Scarborough, 1996), pp. 195–200; UK Law Commission, *Damages For Personal Injury: Medical, Nursing and Other Expenses* (Consultation Paper No 144, 1996), pp. 116–19.

accident which occurred during his school gymnastics class. The trial judge found that this accident had occurred as a result of the negligence of the instructor and the school board. Gary was cared for at home for a time by his mother and stepfather, Mr and Mrs Tanner, who claimed damages for the value of services that they had rendered to Gary. In determining his claim, the court both accounted for the carer's intervention and allowed the carer to participate in the fund.[21]

Accounting for the carer's intervention

The victim Gary Thornton successfully sued the wrongdoer in respect of the care provided by his mother.[22] In allowing his claim, Taggart JA stated:[23]

> I ... am of the opinion that while Mr and Mrs Tanner have no claim against the appellants the respondent Gary Thornton may claim as an item of special expense an appropriate amount to compensate those who have rendered services to him of a nursing character. That result should obtain irrespective of whether there exists between the respondent Gary Thornton and those rendering the services a contract pursuant to which he agrees to reimburse them ... [and later on the same page, referring to the sum of $7,500 awarded on this basis] That amount should be paid to Gary Thornton but held by him on trust to be paid over to Mrs Tanner.

---

[21] The British Columbia Court of Appeal awarded to Gary damages on trust for his mother on account of her nursing services. *Thornton v. Board of School Trustees of School District No 57 (Prince George)* (1976) 73 DLR (3d) 35 at 55 PER TAGGART JA with whom the other members of the British Columbia Court of Appeal agreed. The case subsequently went on appeal to the Supreme Court of Canada where the court was concerned with the capitalised cost of annual care required by the victim over his life expectancy. Dickson J (who delivered the judgment of the Supreme Court of Canada) upheld the decision of the British Columbia Court of Appeal. *Thornton v. Board of School Trustees of School District No 57 (Prince George)* (1978) 83 DLR (3d) 480 at 491 PER DICKSON J.

[22] The original claim was by Mr and Mrs Tanner in respect of their own loss in caring for Gary. The British Columbia Court of Appeal held that Mr and Mrs Tanner had no claim against the wrongdoer but that Gary did and allowed an amendment to the pleadings so that it was Gary who claimed in respect of their care. Gary was already a claimant in the action, claiming damages in negligence in respect of his loss. This result is confirmed by other decisions in which the carer has brought an action and an award was ultimately made to the victim on the basis that it is the victim who is the correct claimant: *Rawson v. Kasman* (1956) 3 DLR (2d) 376; *Grover v. Lowther* (1982) 52 NSR (2d) 22; *Thomson v. MacLean* (1983) 120 APR 436.

[23] *Thornton v. Board of School Trustees of School District No 57 (Prince George)* (1976) 73 DLR (3d) 35 at 55 PER TAGGART JA with whom the other members of the British Columbia Court of Appeal agreed.

Thornton appears to adopt the compensate the carer approach.[24] However, there is evidence that the needs of the claimant method has also found sympathy with Canadian judges.[25] It must also be admitted that there are some Canadian decisions which do allow the carer a direct right of action against the tortfeasor.[26] In some of these cases, the carer's claim is on the basis of compensation for what appears to be, but is not articulated as, breach of a tortious duty.[27] In others, the carer claims against the tortfeasor for restitution on the basis of the tortfeasor's unjust enrichment at the expense of the carer.[28]

When the carer is allowed his own claim against the tortfeasor, judgment is given in favour of the party ultimately interested in any damages, the carer. The issue with which this book is concerned does not then arise. We will come back to these cases in chapter 5. So far as they suggest that the carer may have a cause of action against the wrongdoer, they may in part explain why the carer obtains access to the fruits of litigation obtained by the victim. There are also a small minority of cases in which one carer sues the tortfeasor in respect of his own contribution as well as that of another carer and in which the second carer obtains access to the damages obtained by the first.[29] Despite these qualifications, the decision in *Thornton* is instructive to the extent that it represents an authoritative statement of the Canadian position.

---

[24] Although Taggart JA refers to the judgments of both Lord Denning MR in *Cunningham* v. *Harrison* and Megaw LJ in *Donnelly* v. *Joyce*, professing to agree with both statements of principle without distinguishing between the fact that *Cunningham* uses the 'compensate the carer' analysis while *Donnelly* is authority for the 'needs of the claimant' approach. *Ibid.*, 54–55.

[25] *Malat* v. *Bjornson (No 2)* [1979] 4 WWR 673; *Millett* v. *McDonald's Restaurants of Canada Limited* (1984) 29 Man R (2d) 83; *Urbanski* v. *Patel* (1978) 84 DLR (3d) 650.

[26] *Stevens et al* v. *Kachman* (1978) 10 AR 192; *Lapensée et al* v. *Ottawa Day Nursery Inc. et al* (1986) 25 CCLT 129; *Howe* v. *Campbell* (1974) 7 NBR (2d) 144; *Roberts* v. *Bailey* (1975) 10 NBR (2d) 212; *Clark* v. *Warrington* (1958) 26 WWR 673 (the carer's claim failed); *Price* v. *Gebert* (1952–53) 7 WWR 426 (the carer's claim failed); *Thomas et al* v. *City of Winnipeg* (1937) 45 Man R 422 (the carer's claim failed); *Riordon* v. *Palmer* (1989) 226 APR 326; *Stewart et al* v. *Mayer* (1990) 243 APR 298; *Lang* v. *Ballash* (1989) 72 Alta LR (2d) 306; *Macdonald (Guardian ad litem of)* v. *Neufield* (1993) 85 BCLR (2d) 129; *Ostapowich* v. *Benoit* (1982) 14 Sask R 233.

[27] *Stevens et al* v. *Kachman* (1978) 10 AR 192; *Lapensée et al* v. *Ottawa Day Nursery Inc. et al* (1986) 25 CCLT 129; *Howe* v. *Campbell* (1974) 7 NBR (2d) 144; *Roberts* v. *Bailey* (1975) 10 NBR (2d) 212; *Clark* v. *Warrington* (1958) 26 WWR 673 (the carer's claim failed); *Price* v. *Gebert* (1952–53) 7 WWR 426 (the carer's claim failed); *Thomas et al* v. *City of Winnipeg* (1937) 45 Man R 422 (the carer's claim failed); *Riordon* v. *Palmer* (1989) 226 APR 326; *Stewart et al* v. *Mayer* (1990) 243 APR 298; *Lang* v. *Ballash* (1989) 72 Alta LR (2d) 306; *Macdonald (Guardian ad litem of)* v. *Neufield* (1993) 85 BCLR (2d) 129.

[28] *Ostapowich* v. *Benoit* (1982) 14 Sask R 233.

[29] *Arnold* v. *Teno* (1978) 83 DLR (3d) 609; *Veldhuizen and Stevens* v. *Blokzyl* [1977] 1 WWR 526.

Carer's participation in the fund

The victim in *Thornton* held the relevant portion of his damages award in trust for his carers. This trust is a frequent but not invariable device employed by the courts in this type of case.[30] For example, in other cases a direction to pay is imposed.[31] For the purpose of this discussion this remedial diversity is not important. The point is that, irrespective of the form of the carer's access, there are authorities pursuant to which the carer is entitled to share in the fund.

Australia

In Australia the relevant case is the decision of the High Court of Australia in *Kars* v. *Kars*.[32] The facts were similar to those in *Hunt* v. *Severs* as in both cases the carer and the tortfeasor were the same person. However, despite this similarity, the High Court declined to follow the decision of the House. Instead the carer's right to share in the victim's damages was denied. As a result, the tortfeasor's damages liability was not reduced and the fund of damages available to the victim remained undiminished. At the risk of weakening the position of carers generally, the High Court thus broke the logic which had deprived Miss Hunt of part of her damages. As the carer had no legal entitlement to the victim's damages, it could not be said that what he paid as tortfeasor he would immediately receive back as carer. The fund of damages was not reduced.

The facts of *Kars* v. *Kars* are as follows. In September 1991 a motor vehicle accident occurred which was attributable to the negligence of Mr Kars. Mrs Kars, a passenger in the vehicle, was injured. This injury resulted in a 35 per cent permanent disability to her back. As a result of this back injury, Mrs Kars required a great deal of assistance with day-to-day life and was unable to do full-time, or even most part-time, work. At trial, the evidence indicated that Mrs Kars' neighbours had provided six hours of care per week and that her husband had provided an additional seventeen and a half hours of care per week. Mrs Kars sued her tortfeasor husband for damages

---

[30] L. Hoyano, 'The Dutiful Tortfeasor in the House of Lords' (1995) 3 *Tort Law Review* 63 at 73.

[31] *Rawson* v. *Kasman* (1956) 3 DLR (2d) 376; *Coderre* v. *Ethier* (1978) 85 DLR (3d) 621; *Turnbull* v. *Hsieh* (1990) 108 NBR (2d) 33.

[32] *Kars* v. *Kars* (1996) 187 CLR 354. Discussed in S. Degeling, '*Kars* v. *Kars* – Balancing the Interests of Victims and Carers' (1997) 71 *Australian Law Journal* 882; S. Degeling, 'Carers and Victims: The Law's Dilemma' (1997) 11 *Trust Law International* 30; H. Luntz, 'Damages for Voluntary Services Provided by the Tortfeasor' (1997) 113 *Law Quarterly Review* 201.

on account of her injuries. Her claim included an amount pursuant to the head of damages recognised by the High Court of Australia in *Griffiths* v. *Kerkemeyer*[33] which was formulated by the majority in *Kars* v. *Kars* as follows:[34]

> ... the principle that a plaintiff who brings an action in tort may, as part of his or her damages (without joining that person as a party to the action), recover damages in respect to the cost to a family member of fulfilling the natural obligations to attend to the injuries and disabilities caused to the plaintiff by the tort.

The Queensland Court of Appeal had ordered Mr Kars to pay damages including an amount calculated by reference to the cost of his future care of his wife.[35] Mr Kars, no doubt motivated by his insurer, took his case to the High Court of Australia, arguing that he should not pay damages with respect to the estimated future care that he would provide to his wife.[36] His appeal failed. The majority held that the tortfeasor was obligated to pay the full amount in damages, not an amount discounted by the value of the future care to be provided by him. Mr Kars' dual identity as carer

---

[33] *Griffiths* v. *Kerkemeyer* (1977) 139 CLR 161. The following statutes abolish or limit this right of claim: in Tasmania the Common Law (Miscellaneous Actions) Act 1986 (Tas) s. 5 abolishes the right to claim for gratuitous care in all actions accruing on or after 1 January 1987. However, payments under Tasmania's no fault traffic accidents scheme is permitted by s. 27A of the Motor Accidents (Liabilities and Compensation) Act 1973 (Tas) in relation to accidents occurring on or after 28 June 1991. In Victoria the Transport Accidents Act 1986 (Vic) ss. 93(10)(c) and 174 places a ceiling on car accident claims before 1987 and removes the right in relation to post-1987 claims. The Accident Compensation Act 1985 (Vic) s. 35A abolishes the right to claim for assistance arising out of work-related injury occurring on or after 1 December 1992. In New South Wales the right to claim in relation to actions arising out of motor vehicle accidents and claims against employers arising out of industrial accidents is subject to statutory limits. Motor Vehicles (Third Party Insurance Act) 1942 (NSW) s. 35C; Motor Accidents Act 1988 (NSW) s. 72 and s. 72A; Motor Accident Compensation Act 1999 (NSW) ss. 127, 128 and 129; Workers Compensation Act 1987 (NSW) ss. 151K and 151KA. In South Australia, the Wrongs Act 1936 (SA) s. 35a(1)(g), (h) and 35a(2) imposes a statutory minimum in relation to motor accidents occurring on or after 8 February 1987. In Western Australia a statutory limit is imposed in relation to injury arising out of industrial accidents on or after 1 July 1993 and traffic accidents in respect of which a claim accrues on or after 1 July 1993. Workers' Compensation & Rehabilitation Act 1981 (WA) ss. 93A and 93F; Motor Vehicle (Third Party Insurance) Act 1943 (WA) s. 3D. These are briefly discussed in UK Law Commission, *Damages for Personal Injury: Medical, Nursing and Other Expenses* (Consultation Paper No 144, 1996), pp. 107–8.

[34] *Kars* v. *Kars* (1996) 187 CLR 354 at 368 PER TOOHEY, MCHUGH, GUMMOW AND KIRBY JJ.

[35] *Kars* v. *Kars* [1995] Aust Torts Rep. ¶81–369 at 62,817 PER MCPHERSON JA. Davies JA agreed with this outcome although for differing reasons. Sheperdson JA dissented.

[36] The parties agreed that the value of Mr Kars' pre-trial care was $1,500. Neither this amount nor Mr Kars' entitlement to claim it was challenged. Only the amount in relation to the future care of Mrs Kars remained in dispute.

and tortfeasor did not reduce the value of his victim wife's claim. In their decision, the Justices of the High Court of Australia accounted for the value of the carer's intervention and denied the carer access to the fund of damages recovered.

Accounting for the carer's intervention

The approach which is taken by the High Court of Australia, contrary to the position adopted by the House in *Hunt* v. *Severs*, is that which seeks to make good the needs of the claimant. This method permits the victim to claim an amount by way of damages, in relation to the voluntary care provided by a friend or relative, on the basis that this care indicates a need of the victim which has been caused by the wrongdoer's negligence. Compensation is payable by the tortfeasor in order to meet this need. Thus Mr Kars was required to pay compensation to his wife on account of her future care needs, notwithstanding that it was anticipated that he would continue to meet those needs in kind.

Carer's participation in the fund

The court in *Kars* v. *Kars* rejected the trust proposed by *Hunt* v. *Severs*. In the course of argument Mr Kars had relied on the decision of the House, suggesting that his damages liability should be reduced by the value of the care to be provided by him in the future. The High Court of Australia rejected this submission, and declined to adopt their Lordships' rule that ordinarily the victim will hold the relevant portion of any damages awarded in trust for the carer, remarking that such a trust would be 'peculiar'.[37] Contrary to the position adopted in England and Canada, the carer in Australia is not entitled to participate in the victim's judgment:[38]

> Whereas in England a trust obligation to recompense the provider of services has been accepted as the law [citing *Hunt* v. *Severs*], such an obligation has been rejected by this country. While it may be conceded that, realistically, the fund for voluntary care provided in the plaintiff's verdict will often inure indirectly to the benefit of the tortfeasor, this is, in our legal theory, entirely a matter for the plaintiff to whom the damages are paid for the plaintiff's needs.

---

[37] N. 34 above at 371 PER TOOHEY, MCHUGH, GUMMOW AND KIRBY JJ.

[38] N. 34 above at 380 PER TOOHEY, MCHUGH, GUMMOW AND KIRBY JJ. This result has been confirmed by the High Court's decision in *Grincelis* v. *House* (2000) 201 CLR 321.

Thus, there is no necessity that the damages should be paid for the services provided to the tortfeasor, still less in the proportions which, for convenience, are used to calculate the sum that is provided to meet the plaintiff's needs.

The motivation of the court in *Kars* v. *Kars* in denying the carer access to the fund was in part to remove the aberrant result produced by *Hunt* v. *Severs*. This result is that when the carer and the tortfeasor are the same person, the fund of damages available to the victim is reduced. However, it is not at all clear that the High Court of Australia was right, on this occasion at least, to dissent from the analysis offered by the House of Lords. In rejecting the trust, the High Court fundamentally misunderstood the basis of the decision in *Hunt* v. *Severs*. Mr Severs' damages liability was reduced only to prevent the anomaly which would otherwise have arisen if he had been required to pay damages to Miss Severs which would have been immediately carried back to him by the trust. In the case where the carer and the tortfeasor are not the same person, this anomaly does not arise and, according to the regime proposed by *Hunt* v. *Severs*, the fund of damages available to the carer remains undiminished. However, the effect of the decision in *Kars* v. *Kars* is to deny all carers, even those not involved in the wrongdoing, the right to share in the damages obtained by the victim. As will be explored in chapter 8, this creates the risk that the victim will retain both the value of any assistance provided by the carer and also the damages paid by the tortfeasor on account of this assistance. It will be argued in chapter 8 that the victim is thereby unjustly enriched at the expense of the carer on the basis of the policy against accumulation.

Despite the High Court of Australia's commitment to the rule denying the carer access to the fund, brief mention must be made of a line of cases in which the carer is paid. These cases concern victims of tort who are so incapacitated by their injuries that the court appoints a trustee or protective commissioner to administer the fund on their behalf. In such cases, an application is sometimes made by the carer for payment on account of services rendered to the victim.[39] An example is *Re N*.[40] As a result of the

---

[39] For example: *Re B* [2000] NSWSC 44; *Beasley* v. *Marshall (No 4)* (1986) 42 SASR 407; *Re DJR and the Mental Health Act* [1983] 1 NSWLR 557; *Re ES and the Mental Health Act 1958* [1984] 3 NSWLR 341; *In the matter of GDM and the Protected Estates Act 1983 (NSW)* (1992) Aust Torts Rep ¶81–190; *Goode* v. *Thompson & Anor* (2001) Aust Torts Rep ¶81–617; *Jones* v. *Moylan [No 2]* (2000) 23 WAR 65; *Re N* (2001) 33 MVR 237; *W* v. *Q* (1992) 1 Tas R 301.
[40] *Re N* (2001) 33 MVR 237.

tortfeasor's negligence, N received compensatory damages and was also declared an incapable person. Her damages award included an amount for past gratuitous care provided by her husband. Her husband applied to the court for payment of an amount on account of this care. His claim succeeded:[41]

> ... although *Griffiths* v. *Kirkemeyer* (1977) 15 ALR 387 damages are damages which belong to the injured person and are not subject to any trust, the court on its protective side may permit the payment out of that person's estate of an appropriate amount for past care.

On the facts of *Re N* this payment was authorised pursuant to the scheme contained in the Protected Estates Act 1983 (NSW). However, there is authority suggesting that even in the absence of specific statutory entitlement, the court has jurisdiction to order such payments under its inherent jurisdiction.[42] The point is to realise that, although affirming the rule that the carer has no entitlement to share in the fund, such cases in result allow the carer access. We will return to these cases in chapter 8. At this point, all that must be observed is that despite adherence by the Australian courts to the rule denying the carer's access, there are some aberrations.

Structural paradoxes

The larger conceptual problem addressed by this book is to explain why a stranger to litigation is entitled in certain circumstances to participate in the fruits of that litigation. As the cases set out above demonstrate, there are two core positions. In the first, reflecting the position in England and in many Canadian cases, the carer is entitled to share in the fruits of the victim's suit. In the second, shown by the Australian position, the carer is not. In investigating this problem, three other peculiar features of these cases are revealed.

The first is that, in those cases which recognise the carer's right to participate, this right is visible only once the victim has successfully sued the tortfeasor. Superficially at least, the carer's right to share seems to be contingent

---

[41] *Ibid.*, 237–238 PER YOUNG J.

[42] *Marinko & Anor* v. *Masri* (2000) Aust Torts Rep ¶81–581 at 64, 204 PER HANDLEY JA; *Re B* [2000] NSWSC 44; *Re DJR and the Mental Health Act* [1983] 1 NSWLR 557 at 564–565 PER POWELL J; *In the matter of GDM and the Protected Estates Act 1983 (NSW)* (1992) Aust Torts Rep ¶81–190 at 61,686 PER POWELL J; *Jones* v. *Moylan* [*No 2*] (2000) 23 WAR 65 at 83 PER MCKECHNIE J.

in nature. There appears to be no case in which the carer's access to a portion of the victim's judgment is explicitly justified on the basis of a pre-existing obligation binding the victim to pay the carer. Rather, the carer's right to be paid out of the fund becomes visible only when the victim has successfully sued the wrongdoer.

The second is that the carer apparently is not able to compel the victim to sue the wrongdoer. Given that, in cases such as *Hunt* v. *Severs*, the purpose of the award of damages to the victim is in part to compensate the carer, it is surely surprising that the carer has no method of enforcing this indirect right to compensation. In those cases which recognise the carer's entitlement, the carer's right to participate is not matched by a correlative right allowing the carer to force the victim to sue the wrongdoer. In the absence of such a right to compel litigation, particularly in a system which denies the carer a direct claim, the carer is left to the vagaries of the victim in deciding whether or not to seek an award whose purpose is in part to compensate the carer. As the law now stands, the carer depends on the victim for redress.

The third is that, notwithstanding the undoubted utility of the carer's intervention, it does not discharge the tortfeasor's obligations to the victim. That the law adopts this rule is in part a function of various policy considerations which are not the subject of our inquiry.[43] Of relevance, however, is the consequence of this rule. Its application in a system which allows the victim to claim for the value of the carer's assistance means that it is possible that the victim will accumulate in respect of her loss. As at the date of judgment, the victim may hold both the value of the services provided by the carer and also the damages recovered pursuant to a suit against the tortfeasor.

Conclusion

In Australia, England and Canada the victim is permitted to sue the tortfeasor for an amount calculated by reference to the value of the carer's intervention. This unanimity of approach is not reflected in the rules relating

---

[43] For example: (1) because the wrongdoer should not benefit from the carer's intervention as cited in *Rawson* v. *Kasman* (1956) 3 DLR (2d) 376 at 378 PER SCHROEDER JA with whom the other members of the court agreed on this issue. As stated by Priestley JA '... where a favour is done to a disabled person, whether by a relative or a stranger, where the favour consists of the gratuitous provision (that is, a gift) of funds, services, or goods, then the plaintiff should reap the benefit rather than the tortfeasor defendant' *Thomas* v. *Eyles* (1998) 28 MVR 240 at 257 PER PRIESTLEY JA; (2) because the care is reasonably necessary and caused by the wrongdoer's negligence, as cited in *Schneider* v. *Eisovitch* [1960] 2 QB 430 at 440 PER PAULL J.

to whether or not the carer is entitled to participate in the fund of damages recovered by the victim. In England, and some Canadian cases, the victim is in general obliged to share the damages with the carer. In Australia, however, the contrary position has been adopted and the carer is denied access to the fund. Three core questions are addressed by this book. The first is to explain why a stranger to litigation, such as the carer, is entitled in some cases to participate in the fruits of the victim's suit against the wrongdoer. The second is to ask whether the carer holds the ability to compel the victim to sue the wrongdoer. Finally, we must explain why in some cases the right to participate in the fund of damages recovered is proprietary. In answering these questions, it will also be necessary to accommodate the structural paradoxes which have been outlined above.

3

Claims based on contractual and non-contractual promises to pay

There are cases in which the victim has promised to pay the carer. In some instances this promise is contained in a contract for care entered into between the victim and carer. In others, there is a promise which the courts have not treated as being enforceable as a matter of contract. In both categories there are examples in which the carer is entitled to share in the victim's damages. Such cases raise the question: is there any correlation between those cases in which the victim has promised to pay the carer, and those in which the carer is entitled to share in the fruits of the victim's claim?

This chapter determines whether the promise of remuneration is relevant to the carer's right to share. The evidence is that it is not. It is necessary to distinguish between the mere existence of a promise to pay the carer and breach of that promise. As this chapter will show, the victim's promise is not, of itself, capable of supporting the imposition of a mechanism by which the carer shares in the fund. On the other hand, breach of that promise may well be. The structure of this discussion will be as follows: the first section maps out the cases in which there is a promise to pay and the second section identifies the conceptual relevance of this promise. Irrespective of whether or not the promise to pay is contained in a contract, the existence of a promise is used by the court in a variety of ways. In some examples, the victim's promise to the carer is used to support the victim's claim against the wrongdoer for damages in tort. In others, the victim's promise appears to be neutral to the claim against the wrongdoer. Of interest is the relevance of the promise to the carer's entitlement to participate in the victim's damages.

The cases

This section maps out the pattern of the cases containing a promise by the victim to pay the carer. There is a division between those promises which are apparently contained in a contract between the victim and the carer and those which are not. Each will be described in turn.

Contract

In rare cases the victim and the carer may enter into a formal contract, pursuant to which the victim agrees to pay the carer for any services or other assistance which is given.[1] An example is *Cunningham* v. *Harrison*,[2] in which the victim Ronald Cunningham entered into a contract for care with his wife. Mr Cunningham had been rendered tetraplegic in a motor vehicle accident. As a result, he required twenty-four-hour nursing care. This care was provided by his wife. Although physically impaired, his mental capabilities remained unaffected by the accident. The victim's legal advisers seem to have thought, erroneously as it turns out, that it would be prudent for him to enter into a contract with his wife. They took the view that a contract would allow Mr Cunningham to claim the value of his wife's nursing services from the wrongdoer. Accordingly, on 11 June 1972 a written contract was entered into by Mr and Mrs Cunningham. He agreed to pay to her £2,000 per annum in respect of her nursing services. Mr and Mrs Cunningham were thus parties to an apparently binding and enforceable contract. The Court of Appeal certainly gave no indication that they did not regard it as such.[3] Mrs Cunningham fulfilled her contractual obligations to her husband up until three days before trial when sadly she committed suicide.[4]

---

[1] *Cunningham* v. *Harrison* [1973] 1 QB 942; *Haggar* v. *de Placido* [1972] 2 All ER 1029. *Einarson* v. *Keith* [1961] 36 WWR 215 may also be an example of a case in which the victim and carer entered into a contract. Although there was no written agreement, the judge found that in return for her services, the carer received $65 a month, room and board.

[2] *Cunningham* v. *Harrison* [1973] 1 QB 942.

[3] There is a question whether, for example, such a contract might be defective on the ground of unconscionability. This discussion will not examine whether the law would have enforced such a contract. We assume, as did the Court of Appeal in *Cunningham*, that such a contract does not suffer from any deficiency. However, it must be admitted that on certain facts, a different conclusion might be reached. For example, in *Haggar* v. *de Placido* [1972] 2 All ER 1029 at 1033 May J held that a contract for care which was dated 1 December 1970 did not actually bind the victim until December 1971 on the basis that May J did '... not think that he [the victim] knew what was going on until December 1971.'

[4] Her contractual obligations commenced on 11 July 1972, although she had been caring for her husband at home since his release from hospital in August 1971. She died on 24 November 1972 and the trial was due to begin on 27 November 1972.

Mr Cunningham sued the tortfeasor for compensatory damages, including an amount on account of his future care. Given that his wife had died, Mr Cunningham's award was calculated by reference to the cost of obtaining nursing and housekeeping assistance from a commercial provider. The trial judge awarded £33,250, an amount which was reduced by the Court of Appeal.[5] Although not strictly required by the facts, Lord Denning MR also dealt with what the position would have been had Mrs Cunningham not died. He held that the victim's right to claim damages was not contingent on whether the victim was legally liable to pay for this care, and decided that had Mr Cunningham recovered damages on account of any future assistance to be provided by his wife, he would have held this money in trust for her:[6]

> It seems to me that when a husband is grievously injured – and is entitled to damages – then it is only right and just that, if his wife renders services to him, instead of a nurse, he should recover compensation for the value of the services that his wife has rendered. It should not be necessary to draw up a legal agreement for them. On recovering such an amount, the husband should hold it on trust for her and pay it over to her. She cannot herself sue the wrongdoer (see *Best* v. *Samuel Fox & Co. Ltd.* [1952] AC 716); but she has rendered services necessitated by the wrongdoing and should be compensated for it.

The report of the case does not reveal whether any damages were claimed by Mr Cunningham in respect of his wife's past care. Prior to her death, she had performed her contractual obligations for the period 11 July 1972 until 23 November 1972. In addition, it is clear that her care had actually commenced earlier in time, when Mr Cunningham was discharged from hospital. We do not know whether Mr Cunningham had paid his wife prior to her death or even whether his contractual obligation to do so had yet arisen. The trial judge awarded the amount of £1,266 as special damages for the period up to the date of trial. This amount was not challenged on appeal and we cannot tell whether any component related to Mrs Cunningham's past care of her victim husband.

If damages were awarded in relation to Mrs Cunningham's past contribution, it is difficult to see how these could have escaped the trust proposed

---

[5] N. 2 above at 954 PER LORD DENNING MR. Orr LJ at 954 and Lawton LJ at 957 also reduced this amount.

[6] N. 2 above at 952 PER LORD DENNING MR. Orr LJ at 955 and Lawton LJ at 958 agreed with the views expressed by Lord Denning.

by Lord Denning MR. Assuming, as suggested by Lord Denning MR, that the contract was not relevant to the victim's right to claim for his wife's services, then the value of her care from the date of his discharge from hospital should have been impressed with a trust. Even if the amount of damages was limited to the contractual amount, the same problem arises. Assuming that Mr Cunningham had not yet paid his wife, and that his obligation to do so had arisen, it is not clear why Mr Cunningham's contractual obligation to pay for past care does not seem to have survived for the benefit of his wife's estate. Although the information is not apparent from the report of the case, one solution might be that he had already paid his wife.

Non-contractual promises

In other cases the arrangements between the carer and victim are less formal. There is an agreement between the victim and carer concerning the terms on which the carer will assist the victim. However, this agreement is treated as not having the status of contract, because the court is either unwilling or unable to discover a binding contract.[7] One example is *Dziver* v. *Smith*,[8] in which the victim had received extraordinary nursing and domestic services from her son and his wife, and also from her sister. We may infer from the report of the case that the victim promised to pay her carers, although the court did not accord these promises the status of contract. The victim sued the tortfeasor for damages including an amount calculated by reference to the care given by her family. Weatherston JA stated:[9]

---

[7] *Dziver* v. *Smith* (1983) 146 DLR (3d) 314; *Gibeault* v. *Schultz* (1978) 11 AR 584; *Redden* v. *Hector* (1980) 42 NSR (2d) 96; *Sauve* v. *Provost* (1990) 66 DLR (4th) 338; *Veldhuizen and Stevens* v. *Blokzyl* [1977] 1 WWR 526 (although the claim in this case was brought by the carer directly). In *McGregor* v. *Rowley* the victim stated: '... I have not paid Mrs Ward [carer], but I intend to pay her. Her husband is just a working man. I do not know what I will give her for her services ...' and 'I have not arranged to pay her, but I must pay her; she spent such a lot on me.' In result it was decided that there was insufficient evidence to determine whether an obligation to pay had been created, *McGregor* v. *Rowley* [1928] SASR 67 at 71 PER ANGAS PARSONS J. Another example might be *Johnson* v. *Shelest* (1988) 22 BCLR 230 in which the victim promised to pay the carers out of any damages recovered in her suit against the wrongdoer. The arrangement between the parties was not described by the court as a contract, reference being made merely to her promise to pay. It should be noted, however, that the court awarded damages on the basis of the victim's need for assistance rather than relying on the promise to pay.

[8] *Dziver* v. *Smith* (1983) 146 DLR (3d) 314.

[9] *Ibid.*, 316 PER WEATHERSTON JA who delivered the judgment of the Ontario Court of Appeal.

I do not think that this Act [Family Law Reform Act 1980 (Ontario)] prevents the assertion of a claim for damages to enable her to carry out promises to pay reasonable sums to her son and daughter-in-law and to her sister for domestic or nursing services rendered pursuant thereto. In the present case the plaintiff's promises may not have been legally enforceable, but they were at least moral obligations on her part.

The cases cited in this section are included merely to complete our survey. A more determined court might find a contract even from such informal dealings, and would probably be undeterred by obstacles such as the apparent absence of such requirements as the intention to create legal relations. The point here is simply to illustrate that in some cases the victim's promise to pay is not treated as being binding in contract. However, as will be shown below on pp. 42–4, the relevance for this analysis of the carer's promise to pay is not altered by its apparent informality.

Conceptual relevance of the victim's promise to pay

The purpose of this section is to assess the conceptual significance of the victim's promise to pay. In some cases, the court uses the existence of the victim's promise to support the victim's claim against the wrongdoer for damages in tort. However, it seems that the carer's promise is not used to justify the carer's access to the victim's damages. As between carer and victim, this discussion will reveal that there are no cases in which the mere existence of the victim's promise to pay the carer has been used by the court to justify the carer's participation in the victim's damages. While there are cases in which the victim has promised to pay the carer, and in which the carer is permitted to share in the victim's damages, it seems that there is no correlation between the mere presence of the promise in the factual matrix and the carer's right to the victim's damages. The discussion will deal with the use of the carer's promise to: (1) support the victim's claim against the wrongdoer; and (2) justify the carer's access to the victim's damages.

Supporting the victim's claim against the wrongdoer

Many cases treat the victim's obligation to pay the carer as supporting the victim's claim against the tortfeasor. However, it is as well to say at the start that the better and now prevailing view is that the measure of the victim's recovery against the wrongdoer is not necessarily linked to any such obligation. If the victim is obligated to pay the carer, the measure of this obligation may have some impact on the value of the victim's claim. However, it is no longer essential that such an obligation exists. Fully to understand the relationship between the carer and victim it is, nevertheless, still necessary to briefly document the other view. The following section will first set out the current position pursuant to which the victim's claim is not contingent on an obligation to pay the carer. The contrary view will then be considered.

Current position – no obligation to pay is required

In order for the victim to recover damages from the wrongdoer on account of the carer's contribution, it is not necessary that the victim has agreed to pay the carer. This statement remains true irrespective of whether the approach of the court is, ostensibly at least, to look to the needs of the victim[10] or the position of the carer[11] when quantifying the victim's claim. The position is stated by O'Connor LJ in *Housecroft v. Burnett*:[12]

> For the reasons given by Megaw LJ in *Donnelly's* case, I am very anxious that there should be no resurrection of the practice of plaintiffs making contractual arrangements with relatives to pay for what are in fact gratuitous services rendered out of love. Now that it is established that an award can be made in the absence of such an agreement, I would regard such an agreement made for the purposes of trying to increase the award as a sham.

Courts have however not always analysed the cases in this way, and there are cases in which the victim's promise to pay the carer was necessary for the victim's claim against the tortfeasor. It is to these cases that we now turn.

---

10 *Donnelly* v. *Joyce* [1974] QB 454; *Kars* v. *Kars* (1996) 187 CLR 354.
11 *Cunningham* v. *Harrison* [1973] QB 942; *Hunt* v. *Severs* [1994] 2 AC 350.
12 *Housecroft* v. *Burnett* [1986] 1 All ER 332 at 343 PER O'CONNOR LJ with whom the other members of the Court of Appeal agreed. This position is consistent with the following statements of principle, although the reason for the victim's recovery in each of these cases is not always the same. The point is, however, that recovery was not predicated on an obligation to pay the carer: *Kars* v. *Kars* (1996) 187 CLR 354 at 372 and 380–381 PER TOOHEY, MCHUGH, GUMMOW AND KIRBY JJ; *Hunt* v. *Severs* [1994] 2 AC 350 at 363 PER LORD BRIDGE; *Thornton* v. *Board of School Trustees of School District No 57 (Prince George)* (1976) 73 DLR (3d) 35 at 55 PER TAGGART JA with whom the other members of the British Columbia Court of Appeal agreed. Affirmed *Thornton* v. *Board of School Trustees of School District No 57 (Prince George)* (1978) 83 DLR (3d) 480 at 491 PER DICKSON J who delivered the judgment of the Supreme Court of Canada.

Past position – an obligation to pay is required

The underlying reason for the now repudiated doctrine that a contractual or other obligation to pay the carer was relevant to the measure of the victim's recovery was the law's insistence on dividing the victim's damages claim into one which concerned pecuniary or financial losses on the one hand and non-pecuniary losses on the other. In general terms[13] we may say that the '... function of the pecuniary heads of damage is to ensure that the claimant recovers, subject to the rules of remoteness and mitigation, full compensation for the loss that he has suffered.'[14] 'Loss' under this head of damage refers to the financial loss suffered by the victim. The view was that, in an action by the victim against the wrongdoer, it was impossible to take account of the care provided by or expenses incurred by a third party, save so far as they could be represented as an element of the victim's own financial loss. A contractual, or in some circumstances non-contractual, obligation on the victim to pay the carer was one way of doing this. The carer's obligation to pay bridged the gap between the victim's cause of action and the carer's loss, because the loss thereby became the victim's rather than the carer's.[15]

This strict approach has not prevailed, and other ways of bringing the carer's contribution into a calculation of the victim's loss have been found. This book is not specifically concerned with explaining why the law has softened its treatment of assistance provided by the carer, nor does the analysis attempt to rationalise this exception with the position that what is to be compensated is the victim's loss.[16] It is enough to note that, in those

---

[13] Specialist references on the law of damages include: H. McGregor, *McGregor on Damages* (16th edn., London, 1997); H. Luntz, *Assessment of Damages for Personal Injury and Death* (3rd edn., Sydney, 1990); and K. Cooper-Stephenson, *Personal Injury Damages in Canada* (2nd edn., Scarborough, 1996).

[14] H. McGregor, *McGregor on Damages* (16th edn., London, 1997), p. 1017.

[15] UK Law Commission, *Damages for Personal Injury: Medical, Nursing and Other Expenses* (Consultation Paper No 144, 1996), p. 13.

[16] There are clearly policy imperatives, such as the need to ensure that the tortfeasor does not benefit from the contribution of the carer, which are relevant. Trindade and Cane, p. 495 state: 'Although from one point of view the *Donnelly* v. *Joyce* principle is a generous extension of the compensatory principle, from another point of view, since the plaintiff has suffered no financial loss and is under no obligation to reimburse the benefactor, the major justification for this head of damages, as for the previous one, must be to ensure that the costs generated by the defendant's activity are borne by it. This is one aspect of the concern with efficient loss allocation which is interested not only in spreading losses but also in reducing accidents and not encouraging activities by relieving them of their true social costs.'

cases such as *Griffiths* v. *Kerkemeyer*, which apply the needs of the victim rule, the carer's intervention is regarded as demonstrating the negligently created need of the victim for care and assistance, and is therefore regarded as a loss for which compensation may be awarded.[17] The extent to which the courts have been prepared to be flexible is demonstrated by those cases which look not to the victim's need but to the position of the carer. Even in cases such as *Hunt* v. *Severs*, in which the House went out of its way to say that the purpose of the award is to enable the voluntary carer to receive proper recompense,[18] the amount awarded was recoverable as part of the victim's claim.

Contracts   *Haggar* v. *de Placido*[19] is a case which typifies the discredited line of reasoning. The victim was injured in a road accident which left him tetraplegic and in need of day-to-day nursing care and assistance with his life and affairs. He was cared for at home by his mother and brother, with whom he had entered into separate written contracts. Pursuant to these agreements, the victim agreed to pay an amount per week to each of his mother and brother for the nursing and other assistance which was to be provided to him. May J allowed the victim to recover an amount from the tortfeasor which reflected his past and future contractual liability to pay his carers. In May J's view, the victim's entitlement to claim damages was contingent on his obligation to pay his carers:[20]

> In my opinion, the principle which has to be applied to this first type of case is that a plaintiff is only entitled to recover the amount of expenditure incurred or loss sustained by a third party first, if he, the plaintiff, is under a legal liability to this third party in respect of that expenditure or loss; and, secondly, if it was reasonable for that expenditure to have been incurred or that loss to have been sustained.

There are other cases in which a similar rule has been applied. These are often cases in which the victim's claim against the wrongdoer has failed on

---

[17] *Griffiths* v. *Kerkemeyer* (1977) 139 CLR 161. Note that the super-added requirement of Gibbs J, that in order to support an award of damages the fulfilment of the claimant's need must be likely to be productive of financial loss, has now been overruled. *Van Gervan* v. *Fenton* (1992) 175 CLR 327 at 333 PER MASON CJ, TOOHEY and MCHUGH JJ with whom Brennan J at 340–341 and Gaudron J at 347 agreed. Deane and Dawson JJ did not deal with this issue.

[18] *Hunt* v. *Severs* [1994] 2 AC 350 at 363 PER LORD BRIDGE.

[19] *Haggar* v. *de Placido* [1972] 2 All ER 1029.

[20] *Ibid.*, 1032 PER MAY J. Another example may be *Einarson* v. *Keith* [1961] 36 WWR 215 at 216 and 218 PER FERGUSON J.

the ground that there was no obligation binding the victim to pay the carer. Courts have noted that if such an obligation had been present on the facts of the case, then the victim would have succeeded against the wrongdoer.[21]

Non-contractual promises   The same pattern is evident in those cases in which, although a formal contract between the parties was apparently not entered into, the victim has nonetheless promised to pay the carer.[22] In some of these cases there has been judicial concern that the non-contractual nature of the victim's promise to pay might allow the tortfeasor to escape paying a corresponding amount by way of damages. One technique which has found favour is to elevate these promises to the apparently superior level of moral obligations binding the victim to pay the carer. This moral obligation is then used to justify the victim's recovery from the tortfeasor of a corresponding amount by way of damages.

An example is *Sauve* v. *Provost*[23] in which the victim agreed to pay the carer $5 per hour if the victim recovered any damages for her injuries. The trial judge characterised this obligation as '...merely a moral and not a legal obligation'.[24] He noted that it was possible for the victim to suffer a pecuniary loss, and therefore, a loss capable of compensation, even though

---

[21] *Chubbs* v. *O'Brien* (1980) 28 Nfld & PEIR 314 at 320 PER GOODRIDGE J; *Donovan* v. *Stirling* (1986) 183 APR 104 at 105–106 PER TURNBULL J; *Hamilton* v. *Hayes* [1962] 38 WWR 506 at 508 PER LORD J. The minority judges in *Blundell* v. *Musgrave* held that a contractual obligation was a sufficient but not a necessary basis for the claim against the wrongdoer. *Blundell* v. *Musgrave* (1956) 96 CLR 73 at 79–80 PER DIXON CJ and 92 PER FULLAGER J. These dissenting judgments are not inconsistent with the decision of the majority and have been applied in later cases such as *Gaydon* v. *Public Transport Commission* [1976] 2 NSWLR 44 at 55 PER GLASS JA and 52 PER HUTLEY JA and *Nicholls* v. *Jack* [1963] Qd R 1 at 10–11 PER GIBBS J with whom the rest of the court agreed. The following cases may also be examples of cases in which the victim was denied recovery because there was no positive obligation to pay the carer. However, it is also possible that these victims were denied recovery because the carers in these cases intended that the victim should receive a gift of the care and that at all events, no payment was due to them: *Martorana* v. *Lee* (1994) 17 Alta LR (3d) 409 at 448 PER LOMAS J; *Michols* v. *McWilliams* (1980) AR 102 at 128 PER KRYCZKA J.

[22] *Dziver* v. *Smith* (1983) 146 DLR (3d) 314 at 316 PER WEATHERSTON JA who delivered the judgment of the Ontario Court of Appeal; *Gibeault* v. *Schultz* (1978) 11 AR 584 at 587–588 PER DECORE DCJ (although it is not clear whether the victim's claim was contingent on the promise to pay or was independent of the promise being based on the court's recognition that the victim was in need of care); *Sauve* v. *Provost* (1990) 66 DLR (4th) 338 at 345–346 PER GRANGER J. In *Blundell* v. *Musgrave* (1956) 96 CLR 73 at 79 Dixon CJ contemplates that if a victim has an unconditional social or moral obligation to pay the carer then he may recover. Fullager J at 92 links recovery to '... practical certainty, or at least a high degree of probability, that the payment [to the carer] will have to be made.'

[23] *Sauve* v. *Provost* (1990) 66 DLR (4th) 338.   [24] *Ibid.*, 345 PER GRANGER J.

there was no legal obligation on the victim to pay. The trial judge then confirmed that the victim's moral obligation to pay the carer was capable of supporting a claim for damages:[25]

> I find that the plaintiff is under an obligation to repay Carol Boulianne [the carer] for the domestic services rendered, as she agreed that Carol Boulianne would be paid if she recovered moneys from the defendant for her injuries. The fact that the obligation to repay was contingent does not make it unreasonable in the circumstances of the case that payment should be made. In my opinion, therefore, Carol Boulianne is entitled to be paid $3,250 for her services and Mrs Sauve [the victim] is entitled to recover these expenses from the defendants.

Supporting the carer's access to the victim's damages

The cases in which the victim has promised to pay the carer do not contain any examples in which the court has awarded damages to the victim on terms which impose, as at the date of judgment, a mechanism allowing the carer's right to share in the fruits of litigation. However, there are rare examples of cases in which the court has contemplated this possibility, and sets out the circumstances in which the carer will be granted access. This discussion is not concerned with the form that the carer's access takes, whether, for example, the carer is a beneficiary of a trust of the damages or is entitled to the benefit of a direction to pay. That question is reserved for chapter 9. All that this chapter is concerned to establish is whether there is any correlation between the victim's promise to pay, and the possibility that the carer will share in the victim's damages. Two leading cases in which such a possibility is raised are *Donnelly* v. *Joyce*[26] and *Cunningham* v. *Harrison*.[27] Each will be discussed in turn.

Donnelly v. Joyce

Donnelly v. *Joyce* concerned a claim by the infant victim Christopher Donnelly for compensatory damages for injuries sustained in a road

---

[25] N. 23 above at 345–346 PER GRANGER J. Another example is *Dziver* v. *Smith* (1983) 146 DLR (3d) 314 at 316 PER WEATHERSTON JA who delivered the judgment of the Ontario Court of Appeal.

[26] *Donnelly* v. *Joyce* [1974] 1 QB 454. The judgment of the Court of Appeal was delivered by Megaw LJ.

[27] N. 2 above.

accident. After his release from hospital, his mother Mrs Donnelly gave up her job in order to care for her son. He succeeded in his suit and was awarded, *inter alia*, damages calculated by reference to the value of his mother's forgone wages for the period in which he was in her care. The case is generally associated with the rule that the victim's right to claim damages from the wrongdoer is in part a function of the needs of the victim created by the tortfeasor's negligence. In this model, that part of the victim's claim which is calculated by reference to the value of the carer's services arises independently of any contract obligating the victim to pay the carer.

On the facts of the case there was no promise to pay. However, the court set out what would have been the position had there been such a promise. Given that the promise is irrelevant to the existence of the victim's claim against the tortfeasor, this leaves open the logical possibility that the promise to pay might generate the carer's right to participate in the fund. Megaw LJ made the point that even though it was not relevant for the victim's claim against the tortfeasor, the promise to pay might still be effective to create an obligation on the victim to pay the carer:[28]

> Hence it does not matter, so far as the defendant's liability to the plaintiff is concerned, whether the needs have been supplied by the plaintiff out of his own pocket or by a charitable contribution to him from some other person whom we shall call the 'provider' [the carer]; it does not matter, for that purpose, whether the plaintiff has a legal liability, absolute or conditional, to repay the provider what he has received, because of the general law or because of some private agreement between himself and the provider; it does not matter whether he has a moral obligation, however ascertained or defined, so to do. The question of legal liability to reimburse the provider may be very relevant to the question of the legal right of the provider to recover from the plaintiff. That may depend on the nature of the liability imposed by the general law or the particular agreement. But it is not a matter which affects the right of the plaintiff against the wrongdoer.

Subject to a proper construction of its terms, a contract obligates the victim to pay a portion of his damages to the carer. However, the importance of the above passage is that Megaw LJ does not contemplate that such a payment obligation will automatically justify the imposition of a mechanism, as at the date of judgment, pursuant to which the carer obtains access to the victim's damages. It might erroneously be thought that, in

[28] N. 26 above at 462, PER MEGAW LJ.

imposing a mechanism in these cases, the court is simply facilitating the performance by the carer of his contractual obligations. However, this chapter shows that the mere existence of the victim's promise to pay is neutral to the question of whether the court allows the carer to participate in the fund.[29] Something more is required to explain the carer's participation. The discussion on pp. 42–4 argues that it is not until the carer has breached his obligation to pay that a mechanism granting the carer access to the fund is triggered.

Cunningham v. *Harrison*

The facts of *Cunningham* v. *Harrison* were given at the start of this chapter. Mr Cunningham was a tetraplegic requiring on-going care and assistance. He had entered into a contract for care with his wife, pursuant to which he agreed to pay her £2,000 per annum in return for her nursing and domestic services. Mrs Cunningham performed her contract for a few months before committing suicide. Mr Cunningham sued the tortfeasor for damages including an amount for his future care. We do not know whether Mr Cunningham claimed an amount on account of the past care given by his wife.

For reasons which are not relevant to this discussion, the Court of Appeal reduced the victim's award on account of future care.[30] In addition, Lord Denning MR discussed what would have been the position had Mrs Cunningham not died and had she continued to care for her husband. He held that the victim's right to claim did not depend on the existence of a legal agreement between victim and carer. He also suggested that, had the carer not committed suicide before trial, she would have been the beneficiary of a trust of that portion of her husband's damages which correlated to the value of any necessary services provided by her.[31]

---

[29] An even stronger position is that taken in *Blundell* v. *Musgrave* (1956) 96 CLR 73 at 94 PER FULLAGER J. In his view the victim's recovery is predicated on the existence of an obligation to pay the carer which as a matter of practical certainty the court is satisfied will be complied with. Fullager J specifically refused the argument that the carer will be entitled to share in the victim's judgment: 'In an action for damages for personal injuries the court is concerned only with the interests of the plaintiff. It is in no way concerned with the interests of his creditors – still less with the interests of someone who may be thought to have a moral claim on him.'

[30] N. 2 above at 953 PER LORD DENNING MR. Orr LJ at 954 and Lawton LJ at 957 also reduced this amount.

[31] N. 2 above at 952 PER LORD DENNING MR. Orr LJ at 955 agreed with Lord Denning's views about the contract as did Lawton LJ at 958.

Part of the difficulty with this case is that we cannot be sure whether Mr Cunningham recovered damages on account of his wife's past care. If he did, it is difficult to see how these damages could have escaped the trust proposed by Lord Denning MR, the benefit of which could have inured for Mrs Cunningham's estate. Leaving aside these perplexing questions, this case still proves difficult to explain. Superficially at least, it seems to provide evidence of a case in which the carer's promise to pay his wife might be related to the existence, in the form of a trust, of a mechanism pursuant to which the carer obtained access to the victim's damages.

We will return to this case in more detail in chapter 9 when explaining the form that the carer's access to the victim's damages might take. In particular, what must be explained is why in some cases this access is proprietary and in others it is not. The task for this chapter is merely to explain the relevance, if any, of the victim's promise to pay to the right of the carer to share in the victim's fund. As will be discussed on pp. 42–4, it is possible that the contract did have a role to play in the court's conclusion that the carer would have been entitled to a portion of the victim's damages. However, Lord Denning MR's view that the carer would have been entitled to share in the victim's damages does not appear to have been a product merely of the existence of a contract for care. At this point all that must be noticed is that it was not the existence of the contract, of itself, which produced this result. There must have been another factor operative in the factual matrix.

Silence about the carer's entitlement

Leaving aside the above two cases, in many cases in which the victim has promised to pay the carer, the court is silent about whether the carer has any right to participate in the victim's damages.[32] One way of explaining these cases would be to regard them as neutral to the possibility of the carer's access to the victim's damages. It must also be admitted that the contents of a judicial opinion on any given set of facts will be in part a product of the arguments put to the court by counsel in the case. It would therefore be unwise to place undue emphasis on this phenomenon of silence, particularly

---

[32] *Gibeault* v. *Schultz* (1978) 11 AR 584 at 588 PER DECORE DCJ. In this case the court's silence is made even more apparent because in quantifying the value of the victim's claim against the wrongdoer, Decore DCJ specifically notes that the carer '... is claiming from the plaintiff [victim] $7,124.53 for her services including the cost of traveling back and forth ...' yet is silent on the question of mechanism. See also: *Redden* v. *Hector* (1980) 42 NSR (2d) 96; *Johnson* v. *Shelest* (1988) 22 BCLR (2d) 230; *Haggar* v. *de Placido* [1972] 2 All ER 1029.

when we cannot be sure whether the carer requested access to the fund. Even after having taken these considerations into account, however, it is still possible to advance one reason for judicial silence on the question of the carer's entitlement. This argument will be outlined below.

No breach of the promise to pay

It is possible to rationalise the evidence which has been presented in this chapter in the following way. It must be recognised that it is not necessary for the victim's claim against the wrongdoer that the victim has promised to pay the carer. However, this does not mean that such a promise to pay is inert. Rather, it is capable of producing a very powerful remedial reaction, albeit one that has not been obviously present in the cases in this study. That is to say, although the mere existence of the victim's promise to pay is not relevant to the carer's access to the fund, breach of that promise may well be.

Leaving to one side for the moment the position of the carer in *Cunningham* v. *Harrison*, there appears to be no case in this study in which the victim has been, at the date of judgment, in breach of a payment obligation to the carer. As we have seen, the victim and carer may in fact agree that the carer will intervene in return for payment when the victim is put in funds by the award of damages in his suit against the wrongdoer. There are of course many variations as to the contents of such an arrangement, because such matters fall to be decided by the parties. The important point which must be noticed is that, insofar as it is possible to tell, the victims in these cases were not, at the point when damages were recovered, in breach of an obligation to pay the carer. It is difficult to be certain about this conclusion because the cases in this study are primarily concerned with the victim's claim in tort against the wrongdoer. As has been said, the current position is that promises to pay the carer are not relevant to the victim's right to claim. We cannot therefore be completely confident that the reports of these cases would disclose any failure by the victim to pay the carer. However, to the extent that the evidence allows, it seems that, as at the date of judgment, there is no case in which the victim was in breach of an obligation to pay the carer.

In this situation it is hardly surprising that the court remains silent about whether or not the carer is entitled to share in the fund of damages. At the date of judgment, there is no breach of duty by the victim capable of triggering judicial intervention. As suggested by Megaw LJ in *Donnelly* v. *Joyce*, all that can be said about this situation is to identify the truism that a contract for payment will, other things being equal, create an obligation binding the victim to pay the carer.[33] Without a breach of this obligation, it is very difficult to see how the existence of a promise to pay, whether regarded as contractually binding or not, could have any relevance to the imposition of a mechanism granting the carer access to the victim's damages. The simple point is that the promise itself provides a sufficient basis for the carer to sue.[34] Hence, unless that promise has been repudiated, there is no need for any other mechanism to ensure the carer's access to the victim's damages.

Cunningham v. *Harrison* is also explicable in a manner which is consistent with the above solution. In that case the carer died before trial. It is not clear why Lord Denning MR reached the hypothetical conclusion that a trust of the damages would have been imposed if the carer had not killed herself. One inference which may be drawn on the facts is that the court may have held a suspicion that Mr Cunningham was not a man who could be trusted to keep his word. There are oblique references in the judgments of the members of the Court of Appeal to Mr Cunningham's unfavourable disposition. Lord Denning MR described him as a '... very autocratic and talkative man who would not fit well with others in a home for the disabled.'[35] Similarly, Lawton LJ noted the trial judge's observation that he had a '... personality which might not be congenial to many.'[36] Doubtless also the court was influenced by the plight of Mrs Cunningham, who felt compelled to take her own life before trial.

To the extent that the court may have been operating on the unarticulated assumption that Mr Cunningham was not likely to honour his payment obligation to his wife, the court may have been acting to protect the position of Mrs Cunningham. These suspicions may have convinced the court that Mr Cunningham would have repudiated his obligation to pay his wife, thus placing him, hypothetically at least, in breach of his contract. It might be argued that the carer's access to the fund was thus contemplated only as a response to the risk that Mr Cunningham would fail to pay his wife. The

---

[33] N. 26 above at 462–463 PER MEGAW LJ.

[34] This claim might be in subtractive unjust enrichment relying on failure of basis as the ground of claim or, more controversially, in restitution for wrongs. Of course, if the promise has the status of contract, a claim in contract might be brought.

[35] N. 2 above at 952 PER LORD DENNING MR.   [36] N. 2 above at 956 PER LAWTON LJ.

separate inquiry why a trust, rather than a personal mechanism such as a direction to pay, should be imposed will be addressed later. However, if these were the reasons in this case, then *Cunningham* v. *Harrison* does illustrate one set of facts which strongly justifies such a trust. For example, by awarding damages in trust, except as against a bona fide purchaser, the court ensured that the carer could, if necessary, trace her payment into the hands of any other recipient of the funds.

Claims founded on the breach

The existence of the victim's promise to pay will be relevant only if it is not honoured. The failure to pay will be a breach of duty and thus an event to which the law responds. The carer may hold a claim against the victim either in contract, in restitution for wrongs[37] or for restitution of unjust enrichment on the ground of failure of basis. The possible claim in unjust enrichment is considered in chapter 4, but a brief outline of the other claims is helpful here.

Contract

Assuming the contract is regarded by the court as enforceable, any breach would give rise to a claim for the carer pursuant to the relevant principles of the law of contract. Let us assume that the carer has done all that is required of him by the contract, but that the victim refuses to pay. If the time stipulated for payment has arisen, the victim is in breach of contract. The carer is entitled to an award for the agreed sum or contract price.[38] The carer may also choose to terminate the contract and sue for damages in respect of any additional loss caused by the victim's failure to pay.[39] Research has revealed no case in which the carer has pursued a contractual claim against the victim.

---

[37] Sometimes restitution or disgorgement is given in response to a wrong. P. Birks, 'Equity in the Modern World: An Exercise in Taxonomy' (1996) 26 *University of Western Australia Law Review* 1; P. Birks, 'The Law of Restitution at the End of an Epoch' (1999) 28 *University of Western Australia Law Review* 13; P. Birks, 'Equity, Conscience and Unjust Enrichment' (1999) 23 *Melbourne University Law Review* 1; P. Birks, 'Rights, Wrongs and Remedies' (2000) *Oxford Journal of Legal Studies* 1; L. Smith, 'The Province of the Law of Restitution' (1992) 71 *Canadian Bar Review* 672; 'Breach of Confidence – Constructive Trusts – Punitive Damages – Disgorgement of the Profits of Wrongdoing: *Ontex Resources Ltd* v. *Metalore Resources Ltd*' (1994) 73 *Canadian Bar Review* 259.

[38] *London, Chatham and Dover Railway Company* v. *South Eastern Railways* [1893] AC 429.

[39] *Wadsworth* v. *Lydall* [1981] 1 WLR 598.

Restitution for wrongs

The victim's failure to pay will also constitute a wrong for which a disgorgement or gain stripping remedy, rather than a compensatory remedy, may be sought. After earlier judicial uncertainty[40] and much academic activity[41] the House of Lords in *Attorney General* v. *Blake*[42] recognised that in exceptional cases an account of profits could be given to deprive the wrongdoer of the profits of his breach of contract. Lord Nicholls held:[43]

> ... there seems to be no reason, *in principle*, why the court must in all circumstances rule out an account of profits as a remedy for breach of contract... When, exceptionally, a just response to a breach of contract so requires, the court should be able to grant the discretionary remedy of requiring the defendant to account to the plaintiff for the benefits he has received from his breach of contract... the plaintiff's interest in performance may make it just and equitable that the defendant should retain no benefit from his breach of contract.

The remedy of account of profits is thus to be awarded only in exceptional cases when compensatory damages are inadequate. The general indicia of such a case is said to be when '... the plaintiff had a legitimate interest in preventing the profit making activity, and, hence, in depriving [the defendant] of his profit.'[44] As Fox points out, this remedy is strongly deterrent in effect, and operates to remove any financial incentive for the defendant to walk

---

[40] *Surrey County Council* v. *Brodero Homes Ltd* [1993] 1 WLR 1361; *Tito* v. *Waddell (No 2)* [1977] Ch 106; *Wrotham Park Estate Co Ltd* v. *Parkside Homes Ltd* [1974] 1 WLR 798; *Jaggard* v. *Sawyer* [1995] 1 WLR 269; *Attorney General* v. *Blake* [1998] Ch 439 (CA).

[41] P. Birks, 'Restitutionary Damages for Breach of Contract: Snepp and the Fusion of Law and Equity' [1987] *Lloyd's Maritime and Commercial Law Quarterly* 421; D. Friedmann, 'Restitution of Profits Gained by Party in Breach of Contract' (1988) 104 *Law Quarterly Review* 383; I. Jackman, 'Restitution for Wrongs' (1989) 48 *Cambridge Law Journal* 302; G. Jones, 'The Recovery of Benefits Gained From Breach of Contract' (1983) 99 *Law Quarterly Review* 442; L. Smith, 'Disgorgement of the Profits of Breach of Contract: Property, Contract and Efficient Breach' (1994) 24 *Canadian Business Law Journal* 121.

[42] *Attorney General* v. *Blake* [2001] AC 268; *Esso Petroleum Company Limited* v. *Niad Limited* Unreported 22 November 2001, Sir Andrew Morritt VC. J. Edelman, 'Restitutionary Damages and Disgorgement Damages for Breach of Contract' [2000] *Restitution Law Review* 129; J. Edelman, 'Profits and Breach of Contract' [2001] *Lloyd's Maritime and Commercial Law Quarterly* 9; D. Fox, 'Restitutionary Damages to Deter Breaches of Contract' (2001) *Cambridge Law Journal* 33.

[43] *Attorney General* v. *Blake* [2001] AC 268 at 284–285 PER LORD NICHOLLS who gave the leading speech.

[44] *Ibid.*, 285 PER LORD NICHOLLS.

away from his bargain. The theoretical question is whether such a claim is available to the carer.

Let us return to the example given above in which the victim reneges on his bargain and refuses to pay the carer. In determining the applicability of *Attorney General* v. *Blake*, it is necessary to ask the threshold question whether compensatory damages would be an adequate remedy for the carer? The simple answer is yes – compensatory damages would protect the carer's interest in performance. The performance contracted for by the carer is payment by the victim. There is a market value for the carer's services and it is easy to quantify his loss. It is possible to put the carer in the same position, via an award of compensatory damages, as if the contract had been performed. An account of profits does not seem a likely remedy.

Conclusion

The purpose of this chapter has been to reveal whether the existence of a promise given by the victim to pay the carer has any necessary conceptual relevance to the court's recognition that the carer is entitled to share in the victim's damages. Recent cases have made clear that the victim's promise to pay is no longer relevant to the question of whether or not the victim may claim from the wrongdoer the value of the carer's services. Similarly, such a promise is not, of itself, capable of supporting the imposition of a mechanism pursuant to which the carer participates in the victim's damages.

The existence of a promise to pay will be relevant only if it is not kept. There will be a breach of duty constituting an event to which the law responds. The carer may have a claim against the victim in contract. Although a theoretical possibility, it seems that a claim for an account of any profits made through the wrong of breach of contract will be of little assistance to the carer. The carer may also hold a claim against the victim for restitution of unjust enrichment on the ground of failure of basis. The victim's possible unjust enrichment liability to the carer is explored in the next chapter.

4

The carer's claim in unjust enrichment

This chapter determines whether the cases support a claim for the carer against the victim in unjust enrichment. The victim and carer cases contain little judicial discussion of the carer's possible unjust enrichment claim against the victim.[1] This chapter is therefore limited by the fact that it does not reflect any explicit judicial consideration of the carer's claim. Nonetheless, as the following analysis demonstrates, there is much to be said in support of the carer's unjust enrichment claim.[2] This chapter therefore determines the extent to which such a claim is sustainable by the carer against the victim.

[1] A rare example of a case which refers to unjust enrichment in this context is *Feng* v. *Graham* (1988) 44 CCLT 52 at 64 PER WALLACE JA who delivered the judgment of the court. *Hunt* v. *Severs* [1994] 2 AC 350 at 354–355 notes in the summary of counsel's submissions the possible unjust enrichment claim for the carer. Unfortunately, this line of argument was not referred to in the speeches of the House. *Ostapowich* v. *Benoit* (1982) 14 Sask R 233 also considers the carer's claim in unjust enrichment. However, the carer Ostapowich claimed against the tortfeasor, not the victim. This book does not pursue the possible unjust enrichment claim which may be brought by the carer against the tortfeasor. There has been little judicial discussion of this possibility (*Ostapowich* is a rare example). In addition, there is a fundamental structural barrier. It is widely accepted that the carer's intervention does not discharge the tortfeasor's liability to the victim. This premise does not align with the possibility that the tortfeasor is unjustly enriched at the expense of the carer. *Hunt* v. *Severs* [1994] 2 AC 350 at 363 PER LORD BRIDGE; *Kars* v. *Kars* (1996) 187 CLR 354 at 379–381 PER TOOHEY, MCHUGH, GUMMOW AND KIRBY JJ.

[2] This analysis deliberately adopts 'unjust enrichment claim' rather than 'restitutionary claim' in recognition of the view that, while restitution is the response given to reverse a subtractive unjust enrichment, this is not true for all restitutionary claims. Sometimes restitution or disgorgement is given in response to a wrong. P. Birks, 'Equity in the Modern World: An Exercise in Taxonomy' (1996) 26 *University of Western Australia Law Review* 1; P. Birks, 'Definition and Division: A Meditation on *Institutes* 3.13' in P. Birks (ed.), *The Classification of Obligations* (Oxford, 1997), pp. 20–1; P. Birks, 'The Law of Restitution at the End of an Epoch' (1999) 28 *University of Western Australia Law Review* 13; P. Birks, 'Equity, Conscience and Unjust Enrichment' (1999) 23 *Melbourne University Law Review* 1; P. Birks, 'Rights, Wrongs and Remedies' (2000) *Oxford Journal of Legal Studies* 1; L. Smith, 'The Province of the Law of Restitution' (1992) 71 *Canadian Bar Review* 672; 'Breach of Confidence – Constructive Trusts – Punitive Damages – Disgorgement of the Profits of Wrongdoing: *Ontex Resources Ltd* v. *Metalore Resources Ltd*' (1994) 73 *Canadian Bar Review* 259.

In order to demonstrate the victim's unjust enrichment at the expense of the carer, the following elements must be satisfied:[3] first, the victim must be enriched by the receipt of a benefit; secondly, this benefit must be received by the victim at the expense of the carer; thirdly, the carer must show that it would be unjust for the victim to retain the benefit. This last requirement is merely a way of saying that there must be an unjust factor present in the factual matrix which affects the quality of the victim's enrichment.[4] Finally, the victim must have no defence to the carer's claim. Each of these elements will be addressed below.

The victim is enriched

The victim receives services from the carer. These services may be nursing or domestic care.[5] There are also rare examples in which the services of the carer have been crop harvesting or other farm work.[6] In other cases, the carer pays the expenses incurred by the victim which result from the accident, for example medical and hospital bills[7] or meets the victim's non-payment obligations to third parties.[8] Despite the routine difficulties of establishing

---

[3] These elements are widely accepted. Birks, p. 21; Goff and Jones, p. 15; Burrows, p. 7; Mason and Carter, p. 38; Virgo, p. 49. *Banque Financière de la Cité* v. *Parc (Battersea) Ltd* [1999] 1 AC 221 at 227 PER LORD STEYN.

[4] Birks chapter IV.

[5] For example: *Grincelis* v. *House* (2000) 201 CLR 321; *Hunt* v. *Severs* [1994] 2 AC 350; *Kars* v. *Kars* (1996) 187 CLR 354; *Thornton* v. *Board of School Trustees of School District No 57 (Prince George) et al* (1978) 83 DLR (3d) 480.

[6] *Johnson* v. *Shelest* (1988) 22 BCLR (2d) 230; *Marin* v. *Varta* (1983) 28 Sask R 173; *O'Keefe* v. *Schluter* (1979) Qd R 224.

[7] *Coderre* v. *Ethier* (1978) 85 DLR (3d) 621; *Rawson* v. *Kasman* (1956) 3 DLR (2d) 376; *Gage* v. *King* [1961] 1 QB 188 might also be included here. However, Diplock LJ held at p. 194 that the carer was obliged to pay the victim's medical expenses. The expenses were recoverable in the carer's direct claim against the tortfeasor. Leaving to one side a consideration of the carer's direct claim, this case is an example of the difficulty inherent in deciding whether the debt is that of the victim or carer. It is only when the carer has discharged the victim's debt that any issue of the victim's enrichment arises.

[8] *Hall* v. *Miller* (1989) 41 BCLR (2d) 46. A difficult issue arises when the victim, carer and third party are all members of the same family. The carer may step in and, in lieu of the victim, perform services for the benefit of the third party. In order to be certain that the victim has been enriched by the carer's performance, it is necessary to demonstrate that the carer did not intervene pursuant to his own obligation to provide services. Examples of cases in which the victim, but not the carer, owed an obligation to provide services to a third party and in which the victim recovered damages include: *McLeod* v. *Palardy* (1980) 4 Man R (2d) 218; *Benstead* v. *Murphy* (1994) 23 Alta LR (3d) 251. However, the situation is far from resolved. *Burnicle* v. *Cutelli* [1982] 2 NSWLR 26 is a case in which the victim's claim for the value of services rendered

enrichment when what is received is not money, but benefits in kind, these benefits probably all satisfy at least one of the tests of enrichment which have been proposed. The third category of possible enrichment relates to the expenses incurred by the carer in assisting the victim. This will be dealt with separately.

Except for incontrovertible enrichment, the outcome of the tests of enrichment which are discussed below to an extent depends on the degree of incapacity suffered by the victim. Put simply, it is necessary to know the extent to which the victim is able meaningfully to communicate with the carer. Only then can the various tests of enrichment be applied. The analysis therefore commences with a survey of the cases in order to document the factual patterns of victim incapacity which are present.

Identification of factual patterns

The starting point is to ask whether the victim and carer have agreed the basis upon which the carer will assist. Of those cases in which there is no contract between the victim and the carer, there are cases in which there is nonetheless an agreed basis for the carer's intervention. In particular, the victim and carer may agree that the carer will be paid.[9] By far the majority of cases, however, are those in which there is no evidence of any agreement between the victim and the carer.

In analysing these cases the essential fact which must be known is whether the victim is able meaningfully to communicate with the carer. This will be assessed by examining: (1) the cognitive abilities of the victim, in essence asking whether the victim is capable of consenting to the carer's intervention; and (2) whether the victim is physically able to communicate with the carer.

Capacity to consent to the carer's intervention

The common law presumes that an adult has full legal capacity unless it is shown that he or she does not. The Law Commission notes: '[a] legal

by the carer to third parties failed. *Burnicle* was not applied in the subsequent case of *Sullivan* v. *Gordon* (1999) 47 NSWLR 319 at 331–332 PER BEAZLEY JA. Citing *Griffiths* v. *Kerkemeyer*, the New South Wales Court of Appeal allowed a claim in respect of the carer's services in looking after the victim's child.

[9] *Sauve* v. *Provost* (1990) 66 DLR (4th) 338; *Dziver* v. *Smith* (1983) 146 DLR (3d) 314; *Gibeault* v. *Schultz* (1978) 11 AR 584; *Redden* v. *Hector* (1980) 42 NSR (2d) 96; *Johnson* v. *Shelest* (1988) 22 BCLR (2d) 230.

incapacity arises whenever the law provides that a particular person is incapable of taking a particular decision, undertaking a particular juristic act, or engaging in a particular activity.'[10] A different test of capacity is adopted depending on the nature of the decision in question.[11] At present, the law offers no coherent test of capacity applicable to the victim's possible restitutionary liability in relation to the carer.[12] In the absence of a specific test of capacity, this book is guided by that applied to determine the capacity of a person to consent to medical treatment. An adult is regarded as competent to consent to medical treatment if he understands the nature, purpose and effects of the proposed treatment.[13] This is said to involve a division of the patient's decision making process into three stages:[14]

> ...first, comprehending and retaining treatment information, second, believing it and, third, weighing it in the balance to arrive at a choice.

In applying this test, account must be taken of the factors which may be operating on the mind of the patient or victim in question. A helpful authority is *In re T. (Adult: Refusal of Treatment)*[15] which concerned an application brought by T's father for a declaration that it would not be unlawful for the hospital to administer a blood transfusion to T without her consent. T had, on the ground of her apparent religious beliefs as a Jehovah's Witness, at

---

[10] UK Law Commission, *Mentally Incapacitated Adults and Decision-Making: An Overview* (Consultation Paper 119, 1991), p. 19.

[11] The tests of legal incapacity surveyed by the Law Commission included those relating to the Mental Health Act 1983, contracts, wills, medical treatment, marriage and divorce, sexual intercourse, jury service, voting in elections and giving evidence in court. *Ibid.*, pp. 24–42

[12] Birks, p. 432. The Law Commission has concluded a review of the law relating to mentally incapacitated adults and decision making, including those decisions relating to the care given by friends and family. As a result of this review, the following test of legal capacity has been proposed: '... a person is without capacity if at the material time he or she is: (1) unable by reason of mental disability to make a decision on the matter in question, or (2) unable to communicate a decision on that matter because he or she is unconscious or for any other reason.' 'Mental disability' is broadly defined to include 'any disability or disorder of the mind or brain, whether permanent or temporary, which results in an impairment or disturbance of mental functioning'. UK Law Commission, *Mental Incapacity. Item 9 of the Fourth Programme of Law Reform: Mentally Incapacitated Adults* (Law Com 231, 1995), p. 37.

[13] *Re C (Adult: Refusal of Medical Treatment)* [1994] 1 All ER 819 at 824 PER THORPE J.

[14] *Ibid.* This approach is very similar to that advocated by the Law Commission. The Commission has suggested that the ability of a disabled adult to understand, retain and use information, including with respect to the reasonably foreseeable consequences of deciding one way or another or failing to make the decision, should be taken account of. UK Law Commission, *Mental Incapacity. Item 9 of the Fourth Programme of Law Reform: Mentally Incapacitated Adults* (Law Com No 231, 1995), pp. 38–9.

[15] *In re T (Adult: Refusal of Treatment)* [1992] 3 WLR 782.

the last minute rejected a blood transfusion. At the time of the application she was sedated and on a ventilator. Although the facts of that case were rather extreme,[16] the observations of Lord Donaldson of Lymington MR are nonetheless helpful in identifying the factors which may be operating on the mind of the victim. Lord Donaldson stated:[17]

> An adult patient may be deprived of his capacity to decide either by long term mental incapacity or retarded development or by temporary factors such as unconsciousness, confusion or the effects of fatigue, shock, pain or drugs.

Turning to those cases in this study it is clear that those victims who are unconscious[18] are unable to consent. In those cases where the victim is suffering a mental disorder[19] or mental disability,[20] that person is not deprived of his ability to consent to medical treatment[21] simply because of this incapacity. The test to be applied is the same as that for any other adult.[22] The cases involving a victim with a mental impairment[23] probably all fail the test of capacity. On this basis, it is possible to view these victims as being

---

[16] T was about to die, required a blood transfusion and was under the care of a doctor in a hospital.

[17] N. 15 above at 799, PER LORD DONALDSON OF LYMINGTON MR. Butler-Sloss LJ at 801 and Staughton LJ at 805 delivered judgments consistent with this formulation. Lord Donaldson's formulation was expressly relied upon in *Re C (Adult: Refusal of Medical Treatment)* [1994] 1 All ER 819 at 823–824 PER THORPE J.

[18] *Schneider* v. *Eisovitch* [1960] 2 QB 430; *Gow* v. *Motor Vehicle Insurance Trust* [1967] WAR 55; *Richardson* v. *Schultz* (1980) 25 SASR 1; *Wilson* v. *McLeay* (1961) 106 CLR 523.

[19] The Mental Health Act 1983 s. 1(2) defines mental disorder to mean 'mental illness, arrested or incomplete development of mind, psychopathic disorder *and any other disorder or disability of mind*' (emphasis added). It is uncertain whether a victim suffering, for example, only from brain damage would fall within this definition.

[20] The Law Commission has adopted a broader definition of 'Mental Disability' including 'any *disability or disorder of the mind or brain*, whether temporary or permanent, *which results in an impairment or disturbance of mental functioning*' (emphasis added). UK Law Commission, *Mental Incapacity. Item 9 of the Fourth Programme of Law Reform: Mentally Incapacitated Adults* (Law Com No 231, 1995), pp. 35–6. This definition would encompass a broad range of individuals, including those victims identified in this study as suffering from mental incapacity.

[21] Leaving aside treatment for the mental disorder itself pursuant to the Mental Health Act 1983.

[22] *Re C (Adult: Refusal of Medical Treatment)* [1994] 1 All ER 819 itself concerned a patient suffering from chronic paranoid schizophrenia.

[23] For example: *McLeod* v. *Palardy* (1980) 4 Man R (2d) 218; *Yepremian et al* v. *Scarborough General Hospital et al* (1980) 110 DLR (3d) 513; *Roberts* v. *Johnstone* [1988] 3 WLR 1247 (also seven years old); *Roach* v. *Yates* [1938] 1 KB 256; *Brown et al* v. *University of Alberta Hospital et al* (1997) 145 DLR (4th) 63 (also an infant); *Grincelis* v. *House* (2000) 201 CLR 321; *Lusignan (Litigation Guardian of)* v. *Concordia Hospital* unreported Manitoba Queen's Bench 28 April 1997 (also an infant). In the following cases the impairment was so severe that the victim was not competent to give reliable evidence in court: *Beasley* v. *Marshall* (1996) 10 SASR 544; *Kovac* v. *Kovac* [1982] 1 NSWLR 655.

unable to consent. For example, in *Roach* v. *Yates* the trial judge describes the victim in the following terms:[24]

> As a consequence of his injuries he is suffering from traumatic dementia. He is less capable now of looking after himself than a normal child. He has a vacant expression; he does not speak spontaneously; his memory is grossly defective; he is listless and takes no interest in any matters which usually are of interest to a man in his position.

Those cases in which the victim is a minor do not always fall within the adult test of capacity to consent to medical treatment. Statute provides that a minor who is over the age of sixteen can consent effectively to medical treatment.[25] However, a child who is younger than sixteen may be able to consent to medical treatment if that child has reached a '... sufficient understanding and intelligence to be capable of making up his own mind on the matter requiring decision.'[26] In the cases in this study, there are victims of a very young age[27] who would clearly be unable to consent. There are also more borderline cases of victims who are slightly older[28] whose consent may be valid. To the extent that these older victims possess the understanding and intelligence to be capable of making their own decisions, they fall into the category of adults referred to below in which there is neither an obvious impediment to consent nor evidence of a promise to pay. This outcome may seem unjust in the light of the protection offered to minors against contractual liability.[29] However, given that contract and unjust enrichment are different events there is no logical reason why rules concerning incapacity in contract should carry over into the law of unjust

---

[24]   *Roach* v. *Yates* [1938] 1 KB 256 at 259 PER HILBERY J.

[25]   Family Law Reform Act 1969 s. 8.

[26]   *Gillick* v. *West Norfolk and Wisbech Area Health Authority* [1986] 1 AC 112 at 186 and 189 PER LORD SCARMAN. The majority of the House was generally in agreement with this proposition except for Lord Brandon and Lord Templeman who did not rest their opinions on the issue of capacity.

[27]   For example: *Arnold* v. *Teno* (1978) 83 DLR (3d) 609 ($4\frac{1}{2}$ years); *Lapensée* v. *Ottawa Day Nursery* (1986) 35 CCLT 129 ($15\frac{1}{2}$ months); *Lunnon* v. *Reagh* (1978) 25 NSR (2d) 196 (six years); *Donnelly* v. *Joyce* [1974] 1 QB 454 (six years); *Garland* v. *Clifford* (1996) 67 SASR 47 (six years); *Brown et al* v. *University of Alberta Hospital et al* (1997) 145 DLR (4th) 63 ($2\frac{1}{2}$ years).

[28]   For example: *Crane* v. *Worwood* (1992) 65 BCLR (2d) 16 (twelve years); *Goode* v. *Thompson and Anor* (2001) Aust Torts Rep ¶81–617 (twelve years); *Thornton* v. *Board of School Trustees of School District No 57 (Prince George) et al* (1976) 73 DLR (3d) 35 ($15\frac{1}{2}$ years).

[29]   The relevant principles are summarised in Goff and Jones, pp. 640–51. The basic position is that, leaving aside agreements for the supply of necessaries, or certain agreements conferring an interest in property and imposing obligations of a continuing or recurring nature, a contract will not be binding on a minor.

enrichment.[30] Minority, however, is a factor which will briefly be considered when considering any defences which may be available to the victim.

The balance of cases in which none of the above factors (i.e. minority, mental incapacity, unconsciousness) is present are more difficult, as we do not know what impact the so-called 'temporary factors' referred to by Lord Donaldson, such as confusion, fatigue, pain or drugs, may have had on the relevant victim's decision making ability.[31] It will be a matter for the evidence in each case. However, it is possible that in some of the cases, the victim did enjoy the relevant capacity. Finally, in those cases in which there is a non-contractual promise by the victim to pay the carer, absent any other evidence invalidating the victim's promise to pay, it seems that it is safe to conclude that the victim was able to consent to the intervention of the carer.

Capacity to communicate with the carer

The second part of this inquiry is directed only to those victims whom we regard as capable of consenting to the carer's intervention. It therefore excludes from its ambit those who are unconscious, of a very young age or mentally incapacitated. In those cases containing a promise to pay, there is clear evidence of an ability to communicate. The balance of cases, including those concerning older children, in which there is no promise to pay are more difficult. In these cases there seems to have been no obvious impediment to communication between the victim and the carer. However, the facts of these cases do not explicitly reveal the existence of any such communication. On this basis, all that we are able to conclude is that communication seems possible.

Tests of enrichment

This analysis will now determine whether the cases show that the victim is enriched. Although unjust enrichment jurisprudence contains cases in which judges have discussed whether a particular defendant has received a benefit or been enriched,[32] much of the development of the law on this

---

[30] Birks, pp. 432–3.

[31] *In re T (Adult: Refusal of Treatment)* [1992] 3 WLR 782 at 799 PER LORD DONALDSON MR.

[32] *Ministry of Defence* v. *Ashman* [1993] 2 EGLR 102; *Proctor & Gamble Philippine Manufacturing Corporation* v. *Peter Cremer GmbH (The Manilla)* [1988] 3 All ER 843; *Peel (Regional Municipality)* v. *Canada* (1993) 98 DLR(4th) 140.

issue has occurred in the writings of scholars. Within the boundaries of current academic debate, the following tests of enrichment are relevant: (1) an objective test of enrichment; (2) consent-based tests of enrichment; (3) necessity as an indication of enrichment; and (4) a subjective approach.

Objective test of enrichment

Although it is not always explicitly the case, orthodox unjust enrichment analysis answers the enrichment question by first identifying an objective benefit to the defendant.[33] According to Virgo: '[t]he objective test of enrichment assesses whether the defendant has received anything of value by asking whether reasonable people would have been prepared to pay money for the benefit which the defendant has received.'[34] Applying the objective test to the victim and carer cases, it is arguable that all satisfy Virgo's formulation. At the very least, it is clear that the courts regard the carer's contributions as valuable. Cases such as *Hunt* v. *Severs* and *Griffiths* v. *Kerkemeyer* show that the tortfeasor must pay corresponding amounts in damages to the victim. As will be explored below, in many cases the voluntary services provided by the carer were essential. Had the carer not intervened, the victim would have been forced to obtain the services elsewhere, possibly from a commercial provider.

Convincingly to demonstrate that the victim is enriched requires further investigation. The difficulty is that it is always open to a defendant victim to argue that in her particular circumstances, and taking into account her unique consumer choices, she is not enriched. For example, she may say that the services provided by the carer or the expenses paid on her behalf are not valuable to her, and therefore that she is not enriched. The possibility that the defendant will devalue the alleged enrichment in this way is called the problem of subjective devaluation. Subjective devaluation recognises the defendant's freedom to choose. Money is the very measure of value and cannot be subjectively devalued as its worth is universally recognised.[35] Non-money benefits are, however, valued differently by different people. Hence the possibility of subjective devaluation. Recognising her freedom of

---

[33] Even Garner, who in general favours a purely subjective approach, recognises this as the orthodox position. M. Garner, 'Benefits for Services Rendered: Commentary' in M. McInnes (ed.), *Restitution: Developments in Unjust Enrichment* (North Ryde, 1996), p. 109. Burrows states that '[t]he outer parameters of the law of restitution have been fixed by the notion of an objective benefit qualified by downward subjectivity only'. Burrows, p. 15. See also the discussion in Virgo, pp. 60–5.

[34] Virgo, p. 62.

[35] *BP Exploration Co (Libya)* v. *Hunt (No 2)* [1979] 1 WLR 783 at 780 PER ROBERT GOFF J.

choice,[36] the law permits the defendant to argue that the particular benefit is not enriching to her. In order to be certain that the victim is enriched, it is therefore necessary to overcome subjective devaluation.[37]

Subjective devaluation, and the strategies to overcome it, have been little discussed in the cases. However, they have been vigorously debated in academic writings.[38] Two relevant arguments, which operate to negate subjective devaluation, and confirm that the victim is enriched, are that the victim consents to the carer's intervention or that the intervention is necessary.

Consent-based tests of enrichment

The victim may consent to the carer's intervention. In cases of an unconscious victim, one who is very young or suffering mental impairment, it is reasonable to view the victim as being unable to consent to the carer's intervention, and therefore also unable to communicate meaningfully with the carer. These cases are therefore outside the ambit of this discussion. We are concerned only with the balance of cases, in which there seems to be no impediment to consent, and those cases in which the victim actually promises to pay the carer. The next section discusses the extent to which the benefits in question are capable of satisfying various consent-based tests of enrichment. These are: (1) free acceptance; and (2) the bargained-for benefit test.

Free acceptance   Free acceptance focuses on the fact of the victim's acceptance of the benefit and does not require that the victim has requested it. Birks describes free acceptance as occurring '... where a recipient knows that a benefit is being offered to him non-gratuitously and where he, having the opportunity to reject, elects to accept.'[39] Free acceptance defeats the

---

[36] The rationales of subjective devaluation are documented in Virgo, pp. 65–6.

[37] Birks, pp. 109–14.

[38] J. Beatson, 'Benefit, Reliance and the Structure of Unjust Enrichment' (1987) 40 *Current Legal Problems* 71 revised and expanded in J. Beatson, *The Use and Abuse of Unjust Enrichment* (Oxford, 1991), chapter 2; Birks, chapter V; P. Birks, 'In Defence of Free Acceptance' in A. Burrows (ed.), *Essays on the Law of Restitution* (Oxford, 1991) 105; A. Burrows, 'Free Acceptance and the Law of Restitution' (1988) *Law Quarterly Review* 576; Burrows, pp. 8–16; D. Byrne, 'Benefits-For Services Rendered' in M. McInnes (ed.), *Restitution: Developments in Unjust Enrichment* (North Ryde, 1996) 87; M. Garner, 'The Role of Subjective Benefit in the Law of Unjust Enrichment' (1990) 10 *Oxford Journal of Legal Studies* 42; Goff and Jones, pp. 26–7; Virgo, pp. 70–86.

[39] Birks, p. 265. A similar definition is employed by Goff and Jones: '... [the victim] will be held to have benefited from the services rendered if he, as a reasonable man, should have known that the [carer] who rendered the services expected to be paid for them, and yet did not take a reasonable opportunity open to him to reject the proffered services'. Goff and Jones, p. 18.

possibility of subjective devaluation because in accepting the benefit, the victim acknowledges the objective valuation of the benefit. It is unconscientious for the victim subsequently to appeal to any subjectivity of value and attempt to devalue the benefit.[40]

It has been argued that free acceptance is capable of demonstrating an enrichment in relation to services.[41] It is also suggested, somewhat controversially,[42] that free acceptance reveals an enrichment in relation to the carer's payment of the victim's debt. In general, an intervener who voluntarily pays the debt of another does not discharge that debt, unless the debtor subsequently ratifies or accepts the payment. It might be argued that in the case where the debtor has ratified the payment: '[i]f there was a sufficient acceptance to perfect the discharge, it would ... [be] difficult to argue that there was not also a free acceptance sufficient to give the volunteer stranger a right to restitution.'[43] For the purpose of this discussion, it is enough to know that there is at least an argument that, to the extent that the victim's ratification of the carer's payment is an acceptance, free acceptance demonstrates an enrichment in relation to the unrequested payment of the victim's debt.

In applying free acceptance to the cases in this study, it is clear that in those cases involving a promise to pay,[44] the victim accepts a benefit. In the other cases, there is insufficient evidence to reach a firm conclusion. Turning first to those cases which concern the provision of services, to the extent that we are able to infer factual information, McInnes' observation that '[e]ven if a victim had not cried out for help, consent to receive the

---

[40] P. Birks, 'In Defence of Free Acceptance' in A. Burrows (ed.), *Essays on the Law of Restitution* (Oxford, 1991) 105. *Angelopoulos* v. *Sabatino* (1995) 65 SASR 1 at 13 PER DOYLE CJ.

[41] P. Birks, 'In Defence of Free Acceptance' in A. Burrows (ed.), *Essays on the Law of Restitution* (Oxford, 1991) 105 at 132. The contrary argument is put by Beatson whose view is that in general so called pure services – those which do not result in an end product – cannot be enriching unless the services anticipate necessary expenditure. J. Beatson, 'Benefit, Reliance, and the Structure of Unjust Enrichment' in *The Use and Abuse of Unjust Enrichment* (Oxford, 1991), pp. 31–9.

[42] Burrows argues that merely by taking the view that the debtor's adoption of the payment is required to discharge the debt does not '... commit one to accepting that those courts have been applying "free acceptance" reasoning'. Burrows, p. 230.

[43] Birks, p. 290. P. Birks and J. Beatson, 'Unrequested Payment of Another's Debt' (1976) *Law Quarterly Review* 188.

[44] *Sauve* v. *Provost* (1990) 66 DLR (4th) 338; *Dziver* v. *Smith* (1983) 146 DLR (3d) 314; *Gibeault* v. *Schultz* (1978) 11 AR 584; *Redden* v. *Hector* (1980) 42 NSR (2d) 96; *Johnson* v. *Shelest* (1988) 22 BCLR (2d) 230. These cases were all concerned with services, not the payment of the victim's debt.

services could typically be inferred from [the circumstances] ...'[45] allows us to find an acceptance. Cases involving payment of the victim's debt are more difficult as the facts do not identify an acceptance, although the courts appear to regard the debt as discharged.[46]

The acceptance must be made in circumstances where the victim has opportunity to reject the benefit, but has not availed himself of this opportunity. Practically speaking, this requirement means, among other things, that the victim is able to communicate with the carer. Therefore, cases in which there is a non-contractual promise to pay are those in which the victim and carer have successfully communicated. In these cases, it is likely that there was an unused opportunity by the victim to reject the benefit. However, in the balance of cases in which there seems to have been no impediment to communication, there is insufficient evidence to be certain.

For free acceptance to be made out, the victim must accept benefits in the knowledge that they are being offered to him non-gratuitously. In those cases containing a non-contractual promise to pay, the victim knows that there is a price attached to the benefits. In the balance of the cases in which there is no promise, it is necessary to show an alternative ground on which it can be said that the victim knows that the carer expects payment. One basis lies in the nature of the benefits themselves. The services provided by the carer are onerous. They extend beyond what is regarded as a normal incident to family life or friendship.[47] If the carer does not intervene, the victim may engage a nurse or housekeeper to provide substitute services. It might therefore be argued that the victim knows that it is commercial practice to pay for these services, and therefore that the carer expects to be paid. However, the identity of the carer makes this analysis difficult. In particular, the victim may say that it is reasonable for him to assume that his friends and family intervene without any expectation of payment, whereas

---

[45] M. McInnes, 'Restitution and the Rescue of Life' (1994) 32 *Alberta Law Review* 37 at 57. McInnes extends this statement to include those cases where, due to some factor such as unconsciousness, non-consent might have been presumed. He argues that, given the desirability of rescue, even in such cases non-consent should not be presumed. This book does not adopt this extended position.

[46] For example: *Coderre* v. *Ethier* (1978) 85 DLR (3d) 621; *Rawson* v. *Kasman* (1956) 3 DLR (2d) 376. *Arnold* v. *Teno* (1978) 83 DLR (3d) 609 is also an example although it is complicated by the victim's minority.

[47] For example: *Mitchell* v. *U-Haul Co of Canada Ltd* (1986) 72 AR 91 at 131–132 PER.LOMAS J; *Hogan* v. *Gill* (1992) Aust Torts Rep ¶81–182 at 61,589 PER SHEPERDSON J; *Fairhurst* v. *St-Helens and Knowsley Health Authority* [1995] 4 PIQR Q1 at Q4 PER JUDGE DAVID CLARK QC.

an outside carer would expect remuneration. This difficulty is illustrated by the facts of *James Hardie & Co* v. *Newton*.[48] The victim had contracted mesothelioma because of the defendant's negligence. As a result, the victim was dying and was cared for at home by his wife and daughter. The trial judge found that both victim and carer wanted '...this state of affairs to prevail, if possible, until his death.'[49] Notwithstanding that by statute the victim was entitled to care '...by professionals for [which] he would not have to pay...',[50] the court recognised his right to choose his family as his carers. On such facts it might be thought that the victim would assume the carer's services to be offered non-gratuitously.[51]

Therefore, only in relation to those cases containing a promise to pay are we able confidently to say that free acceptance demonstrates enrichment. In these examples, it is unconscionable for the victim, having accepted the benefits, to appeal to a personal system of value and spending priority in order to devalue the benefits and deny that they are enriching. In the balance of the cases in this study, free acceptance does not assist in demonstrating an enrichment. There are too many unknown facts to make it a reliable method.

Bargained-for benefit   This test of enrichment looks to something more than a mere acceptance of the benefit. Burrows[52] suggests a bargained-for benefit test. In this model enrichment is made out because '...where the [victim] has "promised" to pay for a particular performance the outward appearance is that he regards that performance as beneficial, or, put in an alternative way, that he has been saved expense that he would otherwise have been willing to incur'.[53] This test therefore requires a bargain,[54] a request

---

[48] *James Hardie & Co* v. *Newton* (1997) 42 NSWLR 729.

[49] *Ibid.*, 737 PER STEIN JA.   [50] N. 48 above at 738 PER STEIN JA.

[51] The report of the case does not reveal whether Mr Newton actually believed the services to be gratuitous. He was permitted pursuant to *Griffiths* v. *Kerkemeyer* (1977) 139 CLR 161 to recover damages on account of his wife's care.

[52] A. Burrows, 'Free Acceptance and the Law of Restitution' (1988) *Law Quarterly Review* 576; Burrows, pp. 8–16.

[53] Burrows, p. 14.

[54] Burrows intends the analysis to apply a broader category of case than one in which there is a mere request. He rejects a 'request' label in favour of a 'bargained for' label, but also states that the category extends to discharged, void, unenforceable, incomplete or anticipated contracts. Burrows, p. 14. A slightly different position is taken by McKendrick who proposes (at least in the context of work done prior to the formation of a contract) that enrichment may be established

for the benefit and a promise to pay for it.[55] As with free acceptance, this discussion is capable of application only to those cases containing a promise to pay the carer and the balance of cases in which there seems to have been no impediment to meaningful communication between the victim and the carer. Those cases involving an unconscious or mentally impaired victim, or one who is very young, are excluded from this discussion.

Those cases in which the victim promised to pay the carer[56] clearly satisfy the requirement that there is a promise to pay. There are also cases in which the court has found as a matter of fact that there was no promise to pay.[57] In these cases the test is clearly not able to be satisfied. In the balance of cases, although it may be reasonable to assume otherwise, we do not know whether in fact any promise was made. On this basis, it is necessary to conclude that the bargained-for benefit test does demonstrates the existence of an enrichment in those cases containing a promise to pay the carer. On the facts of the other cases, however, it does not.

Necessity as an indication of enrichment – incontrovertible benefit

This argument relies on the evidence that the carer's intervention is necessary.[58] Birks states that '[w]here the plaintiff has conferred a benefit on the defendant which was necessary to the defendant in the sense that he would have had to seek it himself, or would have sought it had he not been deprived of the opportunity (as by absence or disability), no reasonable man would deny that the defendant had been enriched by the amount which he himself would have had to lay out'.[59] The victim is incontrovertibly enriched[60] because the benefits are so intrinsically advantageous to him that he would be unreasonable to argue otherwise.[61] This method of negating the possibility of subjective devaluation, and thereby confirming

---

by the defendant's request for the work to be done and receipt of the benefit. E. McKendrick, 'Work Done in Anticipation of a Contract which does not Materialise' in W. Cornish et al (eds.), *Restitution Past, Present & Future* (Oxford, 1998) 163, p. 177.

[55] It is not necessary that the bargain be reflected in a concluded contract.

[56] *Sauve* v. *Provost* (1990) 66 DLR (4th) 338; *Dziver* v. *Smith* (1983) 146 DLR (3d) 314; *Gibeault* v. *Schultz* (1978) 11 AR 584; *Redden* v. *Hector* (1980) 42 NSR (2d) 96; *Johnson* v. *Shelest* (1988) 22 BCLR (2d) 230.

[57] *Liffen* v. *Watson* [1940] 1 KB 556; *Kobs* v. *Merchants Hotel* (1990) 70 Man R (2d) 178 at 215 PER SMITH J.

[58] *Exall* v. *Partridge* (1799) 8 TR 308; *Craven-Ellis* v. *Cannons Ltd* [1936] 2 KB 403.

[59] Birks, p. 117.   [60] Burrows, p. 247; Virgo, 72–99.   [61] Birks, 116–17.

the presence of an enrichment, is of wide application in the cases in this study. Perhaps the only category of case to which it cannot apply are those in which the victim promises to pay the carer.[62] In the balance of the cases in which the carer's intervention is gratuitous, the necessity argument is relevant.

Turning first to those cases in which the carer provides services to the victim. In the absence of these services, the victim will probably engage a professional nurse or housekeeper to provide substitute services. The victim is saved this expenditure and is thereby enriched. For example, in *Yepremian et al v. Scarborough General Hospital et al*[63] the victim was Tony Yepremian who, as a result of his accident, required constant care. His mother provided much of this care. Morden JA stated:[64]

> If the mother did not meet them [his demands] when Tony is at home then help in the form of something akin to a paid baby sitter would have to be obtained.

In the same way, it is possible to argue that the victim is enriched by the intervention of the carer in paying the victim's debt, thus saving the victim inevitable expenditure. In order for this enrichment to be made out, we must show that the victim's debt is discharged by the carer's payment. In general, an intervener who voluntarily pays the debt of another does not discharge that debt, unless the debtor subsequently ratifies the payment. However, there is some support for an exception to this rule such that an intervener who pays another's debt in circumstances of necessity will discharge that debt.[65]

---

62 The carer does not anticipate the victim's necessary expenditure because the victim has in fact agreed to pay the carer. One exception may be the case where the cost to the victim of employing the carer is less than the market rate for the same service.

63 *Yepremian et al v. Scarborough General Hospital et al* (1980) 110 DLR (3d) 513. Other examples include: *Britliffe v. Britliffe* (1990) Aust Torts Rep ¶81–060; *D'Ambrosio v. DeSouza Lima* [1983] 60 ACTR 18; *Weinman v. Boten* (1990) 104 FLR 146; *Cavanaugh v. MacQuarrie* (1979) 62 APR 687; *Crane v. Worwood* (1992) 65 BCLR (2d) 16; *Garland v Clifford* (1996) 67 SASR 47 at 58 PER LANDER J. Practicalities of space prevent all of the cases being listed. By definition, all of the cases under consideration in which the victim recovers damages on account of the carer's intervention meet the requisite standard.

64 *Yepremian et al v. Scarborough General Hospital et al* (1980) 110 DLR (3d) 513 at 550 PER MORDEN JA with whom the rest of the Court of Appeal agreed.

65 *Owen v. Tate* [1976] 1 QB 402 at 409–410 PER LORD SCARMAN; *The 'Zuhal K' and 'Selin'* [1987] 1 Lloyd's Rep 151 at 156 PER SHEEN J; *Exall v. Partridge* (1799) 8 TR 308 at 311 PER BLANC J. Birks, p. 198; P. Birks, and J. Beatson, 'Unrequested Payment of Another's Debt' (1976) *Law Quarterly Review* 188; Goff and Jones, pp. 16–17 and pp. 476–7; Burrows, p. 239; Mitchell, pp. 20–5; Virgo, pp. 225–30.

An example is *Coderre* v. *Ethier*,[66] in which the carer intervened to pay the victim's debts. Germaine Gachot was a member of a religious order who was struck by a car and required medical and nursing care. The cost of care amounted to $70,066.65 in out-of-pocket expenses of which $64,000 was paid by the religious order. Germaine sued the wrongdoer for damages, including an amount in respect of the expenses which had been paid on her behalf. Lerner J found on the facts that Germaine had not promised to repay the order. Nor was there any evidence of an agreement between Germaine and the order that, as part of the consideration for being a member of the order, she would be taken care of in circumstances such as these.[67] Although not explicitly stated, it is clear that the judge regarded any payment obligation that Germaine may have had to the providers of her medical and nursing care as having been discharged. It was on the basis that Germaine's nursing aid services had been paid for by the order that Germaine's claim for damages in respect of them was allowed.[68] In being relieved of this liability, Germaine was enriched.

The victim is also enriched when the carer fulfils the victim's non-payment obligations to a third party, thus releasing the victim from performance. This is demonstrated by *Hall* v. *Miller*.[69] Mr Hall and his wife were both employed in the same hotel as managers. Their contracts of employment did not allocate duties between them. Prior to commencing this employment, Mr Hall was negligently injured in a car accident. As a result, he was not able to work as hard as he would have had he not been injured. In his claim for compensatory damages, it was found as fact that the Halls had received the same income as they would have received had Mr Hall been healthy.[70] Despite the fact that her contract did not specify her duties, the British Columbia Court of Appeal found that Mrs Hall had assumed 75 per cent of the burden of work to be performed, providing services to the hotel that Mr Hall was unable to provide.[71] In effect, Mrs Hall had discharged a portion of Mr Hall's obligation to their employer. In being released from this performance, Mr Hall was enriched.

The expenditure made by the carer may also reveal an enrichment. In some cases, the carer incurs expenses in coming to the assistance of the

---

[66] *Coderre* v. *Ethier* (1978) 85 DLR (3d) 621.   [67] *Ibid.*, 632 PER LERNER J.
[68] N. 66 above at 633 PER LERNER J.   [69] *Hall* v. *Miller* (1989) 41 BCLR (2d) 46.
[70] *Ibid.*, 50 PER SEATON JA who delivered the judgment of the British Columbia Court of Appeal.
[71] N. 69 above PER SEATON JA.

victim.[72] On the facts of the cases in this study, these expenses are usually travelling expenses. Two categories of expenses may be distinguished. In the first, the carer provides transport so that the victim may attend treatment. These cases do reveal an enrichment to the victim. For example, the carer in *Gibeault* v. *Schultz* drove the victim to the physiotherapist.[73] If the carer had not done so, the victim would have had to make alternative transport arrangements. The expenses incurred by the carer in driving the victim to the physiotherapist are therefore necessary, because they represent inevitable expenditure that the victim has been saved. The victim is therefore enriched.

However, in the second category, the expenses arise in the course of the carer's own travelling. The expenses are more difficult to fit into an unjust enrichment analysis. Unlike, for example, the performance of necessary services or the payment of the victim's debts, these expenses are connected more remotely to the victim. There is no enrichment of the victim, only a loss to the carer. An example is *Schneider* v. *Eisovitch*[74] in which £110 in out-of-pocket expenses was spent by Mr and Mrs Taylor in travelling to the assistance of the victim. Paull J allowed the victim to recover this amount in her claim against the tortfeasor.[75] Although the victim obtained the benefit of Mr and Mrs Taylor's presence at her bedside, this benefit is properly to be accounted for in a claim for Mr and Mrs Taylor's reasonable remuneration.[76] The costs incurred by them in travelling to France are more removed from the facts. Of themselves, the costs produced no benefit to the victim. Our difficulty is in drawing the line between the first and second type of case. Those cases which can be shown to produce only a loss to the carer, rather than an enrichment of the victim, should not be the subject of an unjust enrichment claim.

This difficulty is identified by commentators who attempt to provide some guidance, while acknowledging that there is a degree of arbitrariness

---

[72] For example: *Schneider* v. *Eisovitch* [1960] 2 QB 430; *Hunt* v. *Severs* [1994] 2 AC 350; *Wilson* v. *McLeay* (1961) 106 CLR 523; *Curator of Estates* v. *Fernandez* [1976] 16 ALR 445; *Gibeault* v. *Schultz* (1978) 11 AR 584; *Levesque* v. *Grondin* (1974) 7 NBR (2d) 98; *Veldhuizen and Stevens* v. *Blokzyl* [1977] 1 WWR 526.

[73] *Gibeault* v. *Schultz* (1978) 11 AR 584 at 588 PER DECORE DCJ. Similarly, in *Levesque* v. *Grondin* (1974) 7 NBR (2d) 98 the carer drove the victim to the physiotherapist and the victim recovered these travelling expenses. In *Veldhuizen and Stevens* v. *Blokzyl* [1977] 1 WWR 526 the carer recovered the expenses of operating his car to take the victim to treatment.

[74] *Schneider* v. *Eisovitch* [1960] 2 QB 430.   [75] *Ibid.*, 440 PER PAULL J.

[76] This benefit could have been reflected in a claim by the Taylors, or at least by the victim on their behalf, for reasonable remuneration for their services. However, no such claim was made.

to any analysis.[77] For example, McInnes argues that the '... sums expended and materials consumed in the course of intervention for the direct purpose of providing assistance'[78] are enriching to the victim. He uses the example of petrol used by the carer to drive the victim to the hospital, and argues that on his proposed test there is an enrichment of the victim. To the extent that the carer has thereby saved the victim inevitable expenditure, on the assumption that the victim would have had to be transported to the hospital in any event, the value of the petrol could be regarded as an enrichment. As we have seen, this analysis does explain some of the cases under examination.[79] However, this test might also capture cases such as *Schneider* v. *Eisovitch*, which is a case in which the expenses are not enriching.

The expenses incurred by the carer are not all expenses which would inevitably have been incurred by the victim. For example, in *Hunt* v. *Severs* the victim claimed the carer's travelling expenses incurred in visiting her while she was in hospital.[80] While it is not difficult to justify the carer's right to a reimbursement of these expenses, it seems safer to conclude that these cases are not explicable on the basis of unjust enrichment. The principle of negotiorum gestio, discussed briefly later in this chapter, may provide some answers.

Subjective tests of enrichment

Garner argues that an enrichment exists if the services are subjectively valuable to the victim.[81] He states that '[a] subjective benefit should be identified only where it is reasonable to infer that the recipient, by his or her conduct, has truly acknowledged or accepted that he or she values the services rendered by the plaintiff. At a minimum, there will need

---

[77] M. McInnes, 'Restitution and the Rescue of Life' (1994) 32 *Alberta Law Review* 37 at 66; G. Jones, *Restitution in Public and Private Law* (London, 1990), pp. 162–6.

[78] McInnes, M., 'Restitution and the Rescue of Life' (1994) 32 *Alberta Law Review* 37 at 66.

[79] *Gibeault* v. *Schultz* (1978) 11 AR 584; *Levesque* v. *Grondin* (1974) 7 NBR (2d) 98; *Veldhuizen and Stevens* v. *Blokzyl* [1977] 1 WWR 526.

[80] *Hunt* v. *Severs* [1994] 2 AC 350 at 356 PER LORD BRIDGE. Similarly, in *Shaw et al* v. *Roemer et al* (1981) 46 NSR (2d) 629 affirmed (1981) 134 DLR 590 (3d) the victim as plaintiff claimed the carer's costs of travel to visit his wife at the hospital. However, his claim failed. In *Schneider* v. *Eisovitch* [1960] 2 QB 430 the victim recovered her carer's travelling expenses in travelling to France.

[81] M. Garner, 'Benefits for Services Rendered: Commentary' in M. McInnes (ed.), *Restitution: Developments in Unjust Enrichment* (Sydney, 1996) 109, p. 112. See also M. Garner, 'The Role of Subjective Benefit in the Law of Unjust Enrichment' (1990) 10 *Oxford Journal of Legal Studies* 42 at 62–65.

to be a request for the services, and not simply an acceptance of them.'[82] The enrichment arises because, taking account of the victim's personal preferences and spending priorities, it can be reasonably inferred that the service is, as a matter of fact, valuable to the victim. The court is not concerned with identifying an objective value in the benefit. There is no room for the victim to say that, notwithstanding that others would value the intervention of the carer, he does not and that he is therefore not enriched: '... [A] subjective benefit cannot (by definition) be subjectively devalued.'[83]

This test is only capable of application in those cases where there is no impediment to the existence of meaningful communication between the victim and the carer. The question is to what extent we are able to identify a request. It is not clear from the accounts of the cases in this study whether any victim actually requests the carer's intervention.[84] In the cases in which the victim promises to pay the carer, we might infer that there was a request.[85] However, there is insufficient evidence on the facts of these cases to distinguish those examples from being mere instances of an acceptance (which on the subjective benefit approach would not be sufficient to demonstrate an enrichment) coupled with a promise to pay, rather than of a request for assistance. In the balance of cases in which there is no impediment to meaningful communication between the victim and the carer, we are likewise unable to identify any request. Therefore, in the absence of evidence of a request by the victim, Garner's subjective enrichment analysis does not show an enrichment of the victim.

---

[82] M. Garner, 'Benefits for Services Rendered: Commentary' in M. McInnes (ed.), *Restitution: Developments in Unjust Enrichment* (Sydney, 1996) 109, p. 110.

[83] *Ibid.*

[84] One of the few cases in which the court actually alludes to the possibility of a request is *Schneider* v. *Eisovitch* in which Paull J agrees with counsel for the tortfeasor that there was no request as the victim had been unconscious at the relevant time. *Schneider* v. *Eisovitch* [1960] 2 QB 430 at 437 PER PAULL J. The same observation is made in *Gow* v. *Motor Vehicle Insurance Trust* [1967] WAR 55 at 58 PER NEGUS J. In *James Hardie & Co* v. *Newton* (1997) 42 NSWLR 729 we are told that both the victim and carer wanted the carer to look after the dying victim. *James Hardie & Co* v. *Newton* (1997) 42 NSWLR 729 at 737 PER STEIN JA.

[85] A rare example of an actual request is *Einarson* v. *Keith* [1961] 36 WWR 215 at 216 PER FERGUSON J. The victim asked the carer to assist and they entered into a contract pursuant to which the carer was paid for her services. However, *Einarson* is not relevant for this unjust enrichment analysis because it concerns contractual obligations which were satisfactorily performed.

Conclusion

The most useful test of enrichment is to ask whether the victim has been incontrovertibly enriched. The necessitous nature of the carer's intervention means that in most, if not all, victim and carer cases this test will show the victim's enrichment. The only exception is in those cases in which the victim has promised to pay the carer. On these facts, one of the consent-based tests of enrichment, such as the bargained-for benefit test, allows us to find the victim's enrichment.

Valuation of the enrichment

Having identified an enrichment in the hands of the victim, it is necessary to attribute a monetary value to this enrichment. The next section examines the victim and carer cases to see if the methods of valuation applied in those cases are consistent with the carer's unjust enrichment claim against the victim. The discussion will consider: (1) services provided by the carer; (2) discharge of the victim's debt; and (3) expenses incurred by the carer.

Provision of services

The cases which are concerned with the services provided by the carer to the victim are difficult. The enrichment is a non-money benefit which must be valued. The cases show evidence of three methods of valuation. The first is the opportunity cost approach, which values the services according to the value of the activity forgone by the carer in order to assist the victim. The second is the reasonable remuneration method, which is concerned with the market value of the services provided. The carer's services are valued by reference to what it would have cost to purchase substitute services from a commercial provider. The third method of valuation is that which arbitrarily assigns value to the carer's services. It is necessary to determine the extent to which these methods of valuation are consistent with an unjust enrichment analysis.

These methods of valuation are applied by the courts in the context of the victim's tort claim against the wrongdoer. Chapter 2 records that the victim and carer cases contain two models pursuant to which the benefits provided by the carer are accounted for: (1) the 'compensate the carer' approach; and

(2) the 'needs of the victim' approach. This discussion will return to these approaches and examine the methods of valuation which are adopted by each. The discussion will then attempt to determine the consequence of these approaches for an unjust enrichment analysis.

Compensate the carer

This approach is endorsed by the House of Lords in *Hunt* v. *Severs*, and recognises that the central purpose of an award in respect of the voluntary care received by the victim is to compensate the carer:[86]

> But it is nevertheless important to recognise that the underlying rationale of the English law, as all the cases before *Donnelly* v. *Joyce* [1974] QB 454 demonstrate, is to enable the voluntary carer to receive proper recompense for his or her services... By concentrating on the plaintiff's need and the plaintiff's loss as the basis of an award in respect of voluntary care received by the plaintiff, the reasoning in *Donnelly* v. *Joyce* diverts attention from the award's central objective of compensating the voluntary carer.

The cases which adopt the 'compensate the carer' approach contain evidence of the following methods of valuation: (1) opportunity cost measure; and (2) the reasonable remuneration measure, which will each be referred to below.

Opportunity cost   The amount to be awarded for the purpose of compensating the carer is in rare cases calculated by reference to the carer's forgone income. If the purpose of the court is to effect compensation rather than restitution for the carer, this approach makes sense. The amount awarded to the victim correlates with the carer's loss. The measure of loss is the same as would have been applied had the carer directly sued the tortfeasor for his loss. An example is *Roach* v. *Yates* in which an amount was awarded to the victim on account of past care sufficient to compensate the carer. Greer LJ states:[87]

> He can get those services, and perhaps get them better than any other way, from the attendance which is being given to him by his wife and sister-in-law; but he would naturally feel that he ought to compensate them for what they have lost by giving up the work at which they were earning the sum of *3l* a week.

---

[86] *Hunt* v. *Severs* [1994] 2 AC 350 at 363 PER LORD BRIDGE.
[87] *Roach* v. *Yates* [1938] 1 KB 256 at 263 PER GREER LJ with whom the rest of the Court of Appeal agreed.

Reasonable remuneration   Many cases purport to compensate the carer by adopting a reasonable remuneration or quantum meruit measure.[88] An example is *Alexander Enterprises Limited* v. *Dobbin* in which, after a motor vehicle accident, Mr Dobbin was cared for by his common law wife Audrey House. He sued the tortfeasor for damages including an amount referable to the value of her care. In fact the claim failed. Goodridge CJN held that the services provided by Audrey were not necessary. However, the court did not dispute that on other facts the victim's claim for the value of Audrey's services would have succeeded. The court offered the following guidance as to the way in which the carer's contribution should be valued:[89]

> The principle, therefore, appears to have been accepted in Canada that a person who is the victim of a tortfeasor and who receives from another services that are rendered necessary as the result of injuries received is entitled to be compensated in an amount that is equal to the value of those services calculated, where there is no bona fide contract in existence relating to those services, on a quantum meruit basis ... the relationship to the injured party of the person rendering the services is not relevant; nor is it relevant to that liability that there is no agreement to compensate the person providing those services.

It is difficult to reconcile the reasonable remuneration approach with the notion that what is being compensated is the carer's loss. Leaving to one side the exceptional case, in which the carer's services to the victim are coincidentally services which the carer is usually employed to provide to others, such as nursing or medical services, the reasonable remuneration measure does not align with a compensatory approach. Rather, the method of calculation assigns a value which is consistent only with the identification of an enrichment or benefit received by the victim from the carer.

Needs of the victim

This approach purports to compensate the victim for loss. The provision of necessary assistance by the victim is taken to indicate the presence of

---

[88] For example: *Hunt* v. *Severs* [1994] 2 AC 350 at 363 PER LORD BRIDGE; *Cunningham* v. *Harrison* [1973] 1 QB 942 at 952 PER LORD DENNING MR with whom the rest of the Court of Appeal agreed; *A* v. *National Blood Authority* [2001] 3 All ER 289 at 391 PER BURTON J; *Joy* v. *Newell* unreported Queen's Bench Division 27 February 1998; *Parry* v. *North West Surrey Area Health Authority* unreported Queen's Bench Division 29 November 1999; *Thornton* v. *Board of School Trustees of School District No 57 (Prince George) et al* (1976) 73 DLR (3d) 35 at 55 PER TAGGART JA with whom the rest of the British Columbia Court of Appeal agreed.

[89] *Alexander Enterprises* v. *Dobbin* (1987) 63 Nfld & PEIR 1 at 16 PER GOODRIDGE CJN.

the needs of the victim which have been created by the wrongdoer, and for which compensation can be awarded.[90] Both (1) the opportunity cost; and (2) reasonable remuneration measures are used by the court to value the needs of the victim.

Opportunity cost   There is some evidence that the needs of the victim are valued according to the carer's forgone income. An example is *Donnelly* v. *Joyce*,[91] in which the victim Christopher Donnelly was injured in a road accident. Mrs Donnelly had given up her employment for more than six months to care for her son. She was awarded £147.16 in damages, an amount equal to the value of her lost wages for that six-month period.[92] There are other example cases in which forgone income comprised an element in the court's calculations.[93]

Unless the services provided by the carer are also those in respect of which the carer has forgone income,[94] this approach does not align with the court's stated objective of compensating the victim for his losses as indicated by the needs generated by the wrongdoing. Rather, the calculation is consistent with an approach which compensates the carer for his own loss.

Reasonable remuneration   The reasonable remuneration method of valuation is concerned with the market valuation of the services provided by the carer. In effect, the value is the amount that the victim will spend in obtaining substitute services on the open market. The position is stated in *Van Gervan* v. *Fenton*:[95]

---

[90] *Donnelly* v. *Joyce* [1974] 1 QB 454; *Kars* v. *Kars* (1996) 187 CLR 354.

[91] *Donnelly* v. *Joyce* [1974] 1 QB 454.

[92] *Ibid.*, 460 and 467 PER MEGAW LJ who delivered the judgment of the court. Although Mrs Donnelly claimed to have given up work for two years, recovery was only given in respect of six months.

[93] For example the following cases in which the court looked to the carer's lost income, although subject to a ceiling of the commercial rate: *Housecroft* v. *Burnett* [1986] 1 All ER 332 at 342–343 PER O'CONNOR LJ with whom the other members of the Court of Appeal agreed; *Crane* v. *Worwood* (1992) 65 BCLR (2d) 16 at 35–38 PER HUDDART J.

[94] For example in *Rosecrance* v. *Rosecrance* some of the care was provided by the victim's son. 'Dr John C Rosecrance began to provide physical therapy to the plaintiff. This was an area in which he had expertise, both academically and practically.' To the extent that the victim recovered damages for the value of this care, it might be disputed whether the measure was opportunity cost or not. *Rosecrance* v. *Rosecrance* (1996) Aust Torts Rep ¶81–374 at 63,122 PER MILDREN J.

[95] *Van Gervan* v. *Fenton* (1992) 175 CLR 327 at 333–334 PER MASON CJ, TOOHEY AND MCHUGH JJ. Later (at 334) in that judgment it is specified that, in exceptional circumstances,

Once it is recognised that it is the need for services which gives the plaintiff the right to an award of damages, it follows that the damages which he or she receives are not determined by reference to the actual cost to the plaintiff of having them provided or by reference to the income foregone by the provider of the services ... Because the market cost is ordinarily the reasonable and objective value of the need for those services, the market cost, as a general rule, is the amount which the defendant must pay as damages.

In relation to the victim's future care needs, this method of calculation is consistent with an approach which purports to compensate the victim for the loss generated by those needs, to the extent that it represents the future cost to the victim of meeting those needs. However, in relation to past gratuitous care received by the victim, it is difficult to see how this method of computation aligns with the victim's own loss. She has suffered no loss as she has not promised to pay the carer. The same objection operates for future care to the extent that it will be gratuitously provided by the carer. This method of computation thus looks to the value of the services in the hands of the victim. It is consistent with an approach which seeks to value the victim's enrichment.

What is the consequence of these different approaches?

Both the compensate the carer approach and the needs of the victim approach adopt in some cases a method of valuing the carer's services by reference to a reasonable or market valuation. These cases do not align with the proposition that what is being calculated is an amount to effect compensation for loss, whether to the victim or the carer. Rather, the measure of damages seems to reflect the value of the enrichment which has been

---

the market valuation may be either increased or decreased to ensure that the amount paid by the tortfeasor is the reasonable value of the carer's services. This approach has been confirmed by *Grincelis* v. *House* in which the High Court of Australia also makes clear that interest is to be assessed on the amount awarded. *Grincelis* v. *House* (2000) 201 CLR 321 at 327 and 330–331 PER GLEESON CJ, GAUDRON, MCHUGH, GUMMOW AND HAYNE JJ. Examples of cases applying the reasonable remuneration method of calculation include: *Cole* v. *Lawrence* (2001) 33 MVR 159 at 179 PER HULME J; *Garland* v. *Clifford* (1996) 67 SASR 47 at 58 PER LANDER J; *Goode* v. *Thompson and Anor* (2001) Aust Torts Rep ¶81–617 at 67,171 PER AMBROSE J (the award was less than the market rate as this was what was claimed. However the court recognised that ordinarily the commercial cost of a carer was relevant); *Hendrie* v. *Rusli* (2000) 32 MVR 240 at 245 PER MURRAY J (subject to a statutory maximum amount); *James Hardie & Co* v. *Newton* (1997) 42 NSWLR 729 at 738 PER STEIN JA; *Kite* v. *Malycha* (1998) SASR 321 at 351 PER PERRY J; *Sullivan* v. *Gordon* (1999) 47 NSWLR 319 at 327 PER BEAZLEY JA.

received by the victim from the carer. Although the cases do not purport to adopt an unjust enrichment model, the method of valuing the carer's contribution in these cases is consistent with an unjust enrichment analysis.

The cases which adopt an opportunity cost measure are different. When the loss to be compensated is the carer's, the opportunity cost calculation makes sense. Although it conflicts with the notion that only the victim has a cause of action against the wrongdoer, it is a purely loss-based approach. There is little room for the suggestion that the method of calculating damages reflects any enrichment of the victim. However, it is difficult to understand the opportunity cost measure when it is used to calculate an amount to compensate the victim. There is no necessary link between the cost of meeting the victim's needs and the carer's lost income.

However, it has to be remembered that these difficulties arise from cases in which the claim, on the face of things, is the claim of a victim seeking compensatory damages. In this context it will inevitably be difficult to explain how the focus can shift to the position of the carer, and different angles of approach are not wholly surprising. However, in this section of this chapter our question is whether the methods of valuing the carer's services are such as will support a claim by the carer against the victim in unjust enrichment. In this context, in which opportunity cost is irrelevant, it is sufficient that these cases afford some evidence of the value of the services approach. In addition, there is some evidence that judges in other contexts value enriching services by reference to the cost to the service provider, notwithstanding that the claim is to reverse an unjust enrichment.[96] The victim and carer cases which employ the opportunity cost method of calculation may be further examples of this phenomenon.

It must also be admitted that in some cases, the court values the carer's contribution arbitrarily, without particular reference to the opportunity cost or reasonable remuneration measure. An example is *Turnbull* v. *Hsieh* in which the victim claimed damages for the care given by her mother. On the basis that difficulties in valuation should not defeat the victim's claim, Hoyt JA fixed the damages award as an arbitrary amount.[97] There are other

---

[96] D. Byrne, 'Benefits-for Services Rendered' in M. McInnes (ed.), *Restitution: Developments in Unjust Enrichment* (North Ryde, 1996) 87, p. 107. The author cites *Pavey and Matthews Pty Ltd* v. *Paul* (1987) 162 CLR 221 at 263 PER DEANE J and *Renard Constructions (ME) Pty Ltd* v. *Minister for Public Works* (1992) 26 NSWLR 234 at 237 PER MEAGHER JA.

[97] *Turnbull* v. *Hsieh* (1990) 269 APR 33 at 41 PER HOYT JA who delivered the judgment of the New Brunswick Court of Appeal.

examples in which the amount awarded is arbitrarily determined, either because it is difficult to determine an appropriate award, or because the court has arbitrarily altered an amount calculated by reference to one of the other methods of valuation.[98] It is best to regard this category as inconclusive as to whether the method of valuation is capable of supporting an unjust enrichment analysis. At best, some cases may fall into one of the other categories.

Discharge of the victim's debt

In those cases where the carer discharges the victim's debt, the claim is in respect of money. The value of the enrichment equates to the value of the debt, being inevitable expenditure which is saved by the victim.[99] This measure is consistent both with an approach which is concerned with the carer's loss and also the victim's enrichment. The amount saved by the victim by definition equals the carer's loss.

Expenses incurred by the carer

As we have seen, those expenses incurred by the carer which anticipate the victim's inevitable expenditure are to be regarded as enrichments. The value of the enrichment in these cases is most easily determined as the amount expended by the carer. Difficulties might arise, however, if the victim argues that she would have spent less. For example, the carer's petrol cost in driving the victim to treatment might exceed the usual taxi fare for the same journey. To the extent that we can sever the value of the services provided by the carer from the expenses incurred in providing them,[100] an unjust enrichment analysis requires that the expenses be valued as the amount saved by the victim. In the above example, therefore, the surplus above the usual taxi fare would not be recoverable.

---

[98] For example: *Ruch* v. *I & H Transfer Limited* (1969) 1 NBR (2d) 379 at 382–383 PER RO-BICHAUD J. No record of the amount of time spent by the carer had been kept. Robichaud J awarded a reasonable amount. *Wheatley* v. *Cunningham* [1992] 1 PIQR Q100 at Q104 PER TUDOR-EVANS J who describes the calculation as a matter of 'impression'. *Woodrup* v. *Nicol* [1993] 2 PIQR Q104 at Q106 PER RUSSELL LJ who favoured a broad-brush approach.

[99] For example: *Rawson* v. *Kasman* (1956) 3 DLR (2d) 376; *Coderre* v. *Ethier* (1978) 85 DLR (3d) 621.

[100] D. Byrne 'Benefits-for Services Rendered' in M. McInnes (ed.), *Restitution: Developments in Unjust Enrichment* (North Ryde, 1996) 87, p. 107.

At the carer's expense

It is necessary to show that the enrichment has travelled to the victim at the expense of the carer.[101] In those cases which concern the provision of services it is clearly the carer who has assisted the victim. Similarly, where the enrichment is the discharge of the victim's debt, the relevant payment is made by the carer. In neither case is there any room for suggestion that the enrichment has not been transferred from the carer to the victim.

One question which arises, however, is whether the carer must show an exactly corresponding impoverishment.[102] The better answer is probably that she does not. It is sufficient that the enrichment has come from the carer.[103] However, even if that view were incorrect or insecure, it would remain the case that the carer does in general suffer loss by devoting herself to the victim.

Unjust factors

The 'unjust factor' is what goes to make the enrichment of the defendant unjust in the circumstances, it is the reason for restitution. For a claimant to succeed it is not sufficient simply to demonstrate enrichment at her expense. A recognised unjust factor must also be established. The victim and carer cases do not in general explicitly adopt the language of unjust enrichment.[104] It is not therefore surprising that judicial analysis in these cases does not explicitly identify the relevant unjust factors. However, close

---

[101] Birks and Mitchell pp. 529–38; P. Birks, 'At the Expense of the Claimant: Direct and Indirect Enrichment in English Law' (2000) *Oxford U Comparative Law Forum* 1 at ouclf.iuscomp.org; M. McInnes, ' "At The Plaintiff's Expense": Quantifying Restitutionary Relief' [1988] 57 *Cambridge Law Journal* 472; Virgo, pp. 105–15; Goff and Jones, pp. 37–41.

[102] This is an element in Canada where the law requires that the defendant's '. . . enrichment be matched by the plaintiff's corresponding deprivation'. M. McInnes, 'The Canadian Principle of Unjust Enrichment: Comparative Insights into the Law of Restitution' (1999) 37 *Alberta Law Review* 1, p. 20. *Rathwell* v. *Rathwell* (1978) 83 DLR (3d) 289; *Pettkus* v. *Becker* (1980) 117 DLR (3d) 257.

[103] English and Australian cases do not require a loss or minus to the claimant corresponding to the defendant's plus or enrichment. *Commissioner of State Revenue (Victoria)* v. *Royal Insurance Ltd* (1994) 182 CLR 51 at 75 and 78 PER MASON C; *Kleinwort Benson Ltd* v. *South Tyneside Metropolitan Borough Council* [1994] 4 All ER 972 at 985 PER HOBHOUSE J; *Kleinwort Benson* v. *Birmingham City Council* [1997] QB 380 at 393 PER EVANS LJ, 395 PER SAVILLE LJ and 400 PER MORRITT LJ.

[104] *Feng* v. *Graham* (1988) 44 CCLT 5 is an exception.

scrutiny of the victim and carer cases does reveal the presence of various unjust factors.

The model of liability adopted in this book separates the unjust factors into two categories.[105] The first is non-voluntary transfer. This looks to the claimant's vitiated or qualified intention in benefiting the defendant and reverses the enrichment because, by virtue of this vitiated or qualified intention, the claimant did not intend to give a benefit to the defendant. The second category of claim is that of policy motivated restitution. This is a claim made pursuant to an unjust factor which the law recognises in order to promote a particular policy objective. The policies calling for restitution are not necessarily linked to the intention of the claimant in passing enrichment to the defendant. Rather, the availability of a claim in unjust enrichment is tied to that particular policy objective.

Non-voluntary transfer

Birks and Mitchell[106] state that there are two kinds of non-voluntary transfer, deficient intent[107] and qualified intent. Cases of deficient intent occur when the claimant's intention to transfer the benefit is impaired by such factors as mistake, pressure, relational dependence or personal or transactional disadvantage.[108] Cases of qualified intent concern those instances in which the claimant did intend to transfer a benefit to the defendant, but her intention to do so was qualified. Birks and Mitchell identify the following three bases or qualifications upon which a transfer may be made and which may correspondingly fail: (a) counter-performance; (b) the coming about or continuation of some state of affairs; and (c) the application of the money or other matter transferred.[109] The facts of the victim and carer cases do not raise the issue of impaired intent. However, as the discussion below shows, there is some limited room for the application of failure of

---

[105] Birks and Mitchell pp. 543–4 and n. 89 on p. 548. This model is a recantation from that articulated in P. Birks and R. Chambers, *The Restitution Research Resource* (2nd edn., Oxford, 1997), pp. 2–3 which separated the unjust factors into three categories: (i) vitiated or qualified intention of the claimant; (ii) unconscientious receipt by the defendant; and (iii) policy motivated claims. All cases of unconscientious receipt are now to be regarded as a '. . . weak or otherwise special case of non-voluntary transfer'. Birks and Mitchell, p. 543.

[106] Birks and Mitchell pp. 543–4, 546 and 558.

[107] The category deficient intent is also said to include the case where the claimant had no intention to benefit the defendant, a state of affairs often called ignorance. *Ibid.*, pp. 544–6.

[108] N. 106 above at p. 546.　　　[109] N. 106 above at p. 561.

basis. The novel unjust factor called absence of consideration or absence of basis will also be discussed.

Failure of basis

The carer and victim may agree the terms pursuant to which the carer intervenes. Sometimes, but not always, these arrangements will have the status of contract. Chapter 2 deals with those cases in which the victim and carer have entered into a contract for care. It is generally true that, if the contract between carer and victim remains effective, there is no room for an unjust enrichment claim unless it arises independently from the contract. Prima facie, the parties have allocated risks according to their agreement, and these will not be disturbed.[110] However, if the arrangements between the parties are less formal, the law of unjust enrichment does have a role to play. This discussion returns briefly to those cases to examine any unjust enrichment liability.

The failure of counter-performance arises because the claimant has passed a benefit to the defendant on the basis of an expected exchange. Subject to a construction of the terms of their agreement, either the claimant or defendant may be in breach. The party who has been enriched at the expense of the other may have a liability to make restitution. As will be seen, this unjust factor has very little to say about the cases in this study. It is beyond the scope of this book adequately to recount the view of scholars and judges on the difficulties generated by this type of claim.[111] However, the analysis will briefly be considered.

There are examples in which the carer and victim agree that the carer is to be remunerated for his beneficial intervention, and in which the court seems to proceed on the basis that these arrangements do not have the status of contract.[112] In none of these examples has the court imposed a mechanism, as at the date of judgment, enforcing the carer's right to be

---

[110] It is a difficult question whether a non-contractual arrangement might have been held by the court to be binding in contract. There is no doubt that a determined court will hold that a valid contract exists. The point is that in the cases under examination, such as *Sauve* v. *Provost* (1990) 66 DLR (4th) 338, the court reasoned from the proposition that no contract existed. The analysis in this book does not seek to disturb that finding.

[111] A brief bibliography includes: Birks, chapter VII; Burrows and McKendrick, chapter 5; Burrows, chapter 9; Goff and Jones, chapters 19 and 20; Mason and Carter, Part IV; Virgo, chapter 12.

[112] *Dziver* v. *Smith* (1983) 146 DLR (3d) 314; *Gibeault* v. *Schultz* (1978) 11 AR 584; *Redden* v. *Hector* (1980) 42 NSR (2d) 96; *Sauve* v. *Provost* (1990) 66 DLR (4th) 338.

paid. If the analysis in this book is correct, this is because as at the date of trial, the victim is not in breach of any payment obligation. It must be remembered that these cases come to court as claims by the victim for compensation from the wrongdoer, and might therefore not record any dispute between victim and carer. However, so far as it is possible to tell, the cases contain no suggestion of a breach by the victim. In the end, however, this turns on a construction of the agreement between the carer and victim.

The victim and carer may specifically provide that no obligation to pay arises until the victim has recovered in her action against the wrongdoer. An example is *Sauve* v. *Provost*,[113] in which the victim Eileen Sauve undertook to pay her carer Carol Boulianne out of any damages recovered if her claim succeeded.[114] In order to assist calculations, Carol kept a diary of the hours that she had worked for Eileen. Granger J held that no contractual obligation existed, but that Eileen was morally bound to perform her promise to pay Carol, and for this reason allowed Eileen's claim against the wrongdoer. Although he confirmed the existence of Eileen's obligation to pay, the judge did not go so far as to impose a mechanism implementing this obligation:[115]

> The agreement between Mrs Sauve and Carol Boulianne is evidenced by the fact that Carol Boulianne kept a diary of the hours which she worked between June 2, 1986 and August 1, 1986. Any obligation on Mrs Sauve to pay Carol Boulianne can be characterised as merely a moral and not a legal obligation . . .
> I find that the plaintiff is under an obligation to repay Carol Boulianne for the domestic services rendered, as she agreed Carol Boulianne would be paid if she recovered moneys from the defendant for her injuries. The fact that the obligation to repay was contingent does not make it unreasonable in the circumstances that payment should be made. In my opinion, therefore, Carol Boulianne is entitled to be paid $3,250 for her services and Mrs Sauve is entitled to recover these expenses from the defendants.

The terms of the agreement between Eileen and Carol did not require that Eileen pay Carol at any time prior to trial. There was no breach of their

---

[113] *Sauve* v. *Provost* (1990) 66 DLR (4th) 338. Other examples of this type of arrangement include the following cases although it is less clear whether or not the court assumed that the arrangements between the parties were non-contractual: *Hasson* v. *Hamel* (1977) 78 DLR (3d) 573; *Johnson* v. *Shelest* (1988) 22 BCLR (2d) 230.

[114] *Sauve* v. *Provost* (1990) 66 DLR (4th) 338 at 345–346 PER GRANGER J.

[115] *Ibid.*, 345 PER GRANGER J.

understanding because Eileen's obligation to pay Carol did not arise until Eileen had recovered damages, if any, in litigation against the wrongdoer. Therefore, it is not safe to conclude that Eileen was unjustly enriched by virtue of a failure of basis.

Absence of basis

Recent judicial statements suggest that a claimant may sue in unjust enrichment on the ground not of a failure of basis but rather on an absence of basis.[116] In this context, the absence in question refers to the basis for the transfer. The enrichment is unjust because there is *no* basis for the transfer. The typical example is an interest rate swap agreement. Let us assume that the swap contract has now been declared void ab initio. The swap transaction may in fact be completed and both parties obtained what they bargained for. To this extent, there is no failure of contractual reciprocation. However, because the swap agreement is void there was in fact no legal basis for the transfer. The transaction is a nullity.

Academics have criticised the inclusion of absence of basis in the list of unjust factors[117] and there are powerful arguments against its recognition. Apart from the fact that there appears to be little authority in the common law for this radical approach, the recognition of this unjust factor would have serious consequences for the structure of the law of unjust enrichment.[118] In particular, absence of basis forces an artificial dichotomy so that cases fall either into the failure of basis or absence of basis category.

---

[116] *Woolwich Building Society* v. *IRC (No 2)* [1993] AC 70 at 166 PER LORD GOFF and 197 PER LORD BROWNE-WILKINSON; *Westdeutsche Landesbank Girozentrale* v. *Islington London Borough Council* [1994] 4 All ER 890 at 925–930 PER HOBHOUSE J and [1994] 1 WLR 938 at 945 PER DILLON LJ in the Court of Appeal phase. In the House of Lords phase Lord Goff recognised the force of academic criticisms of absence of consideration and favoured the application of failure of consideration. *Westdeutsche Landesbank Girozentrale* v. *Islington London Borough Council* [1996] AC 669 at 682–683 PER LORD GOFF. *Guinness Mahon & Co Ltd* v. *Kensington and Chelsea Royal London Borough Council* [1998] 2 All ER 272.

[117] P. Birks, 'No Consideration: Restitution after Void Contracts' (1993) 23 *University of Western Australia Law Review* 195; A. Burrows, 'Swaps and the Friction Between Common Law and Equity' [1995] *Restitution Law Review* 15; W. Swadling, 'Restitution for No Consideration' [1994] *Restitution Law Review* 73; Virgo, pp. 403–8.

[118] N. 106 above, pp. 567–8; T. Krebs, 'In Defence of Unjust Factors' (2000) *Oxford U Comparative Law Forum* 3 at ouclf.iuscomp.org; P. Birks, 'Private Law' in P. Birks and F. Rose (eds.), *Lessons of the Swaps Litigation* (Oxford, 2000) 1, at pp. 19–20; E. McKendrick, 'The Reason for Restitution' in P. Birks and F. Rose (eds.), *Lessons of the Swaps Litigation* (Oxford, 2000) 84, at pp. 106–8.

This leaves no room for the other unjust factors, such as mistake and compulsion, which have been hitherto widely accepted.[119]

It might erroneously be thought that absence of consideration or basis would be of wide application to the cases in this study. Leaving to one side the cases in which the carer and victim have agreed that the carer will be paid, the victim in all cases provides no consideration or counter performance for the benefits conferred by the carer. However, this view fundamentally misunderstands the meaning of absence of basis. As noted above, the unjust factor does not refer to the presence or absence of any counter-performance. Rather, it is concerned with the basis of the transfer. It is difficult to identify the nullity or absence of basis for the carer's contribution.[120]

The clearest example concerns those cases in which it is a reasonable inference that the carer intended his intervention to be by way of gift such as *Hasson* v. *Hamel*.[121] The carer assisted without any intention of obtaining remuneration or reward. Vera Hasson was injured in a car accident and was for a time completely incapacitated. She was looked after by her daughter, Mrs Oostenbrug, a registered nurse. Despite her professional qualifications, Mrs Oostenbrug gave evidence which showed that she intended that her mother should have the benefit of her care as a gift. Zalev Co Ct J noted:[122]

> I have found as a fact that Mrs Hasson did not contract with her daughter to pay for these services, nor does her undertaking to pay her for them create any legal liability . . . Mrs Oostenbrug has no right to sue Mrs Hamel to recover the amount I have assessed or any amount. She told Mr Knight in cross examination that she would have done the work even without her mother's promise to pay, which was made at least a month after the accident. She said that she did it not for the money but because it was her mother, and that *whatever happened in this action, her mother was under no obligation to repay her*.

---

[119] Birks and Mitchell suggest that one way of accommodating absence of basis may be to view it as an example of policy motivated restitution where the policy behind the nullity justifies the claim. N. 106 above, p. 567; P. Birks, 'Private Law' in P. Birks and F. Rose (eds.), *Lessons of the Swaps Litigation* (Oxford, 2000) 1, pp. 18–19.

[120] This is in part because the cases of nullity which have hitherto been judicially considered are those in which the transfer occurs pursuant to a contract subsequently declared void ab initio. There are very few examples of carers who intervene pursuant to a contract for care.

[121] *Hasson* v. *Hamel* (1977) 78 DLR (3d) 573. The following are also examples although the victim's claim in each failed: *Michols* v. *McWilliams* (1980) 24 AR 102; *Martorana* v. *Lee* (1994) 17 Alta LR (3d) 409; *Johns* v. *Prunell* [1960] VR 208; *McGregor v Rowley* (1928) SASR 67.

[122] *Hasson* v. *Hamel* (1977) 78 DLR (3d) 573 at 582 PER ZALEV CO CT J (emphasis added).

McKendrick explains that '... if we use consideration to mean "basis", then there is no absence of consideration for a gift. A gift is often given to reflect friendship or love.'[123] It does not make sense to talk about the basis of Mrs Oostenbrug's intervention having failed. Of course, it is possible to make a cynical argument and take the example of a carer who believes that he holds the victim in love and affection, and on this basis lends assistance. Subsequently she discovers that she did not actually feel this way when she intervened. Although it later turned out that there was no basis for her transfer, the better view is that she was mistaken.[124]

Utility of the non-voluntary transfer unjust factors

The evidence indicates that none of the cases in this study disclose a claim for the carer in unjust enrichment founded on a failure of basis. Quite simply, the facts of the cases do not support the application of this unjust factor. In few cases do the victim and carer actually agree a basis for the carer's intervention. Those rare cases in which the victim has promised to pay the carer do not in general disclose any failure of basis sufficient to generate a claim. In none of these examples has the court imposed a mechanism, as at the date of judgment, enforcing the carer's right to be paid. This is because as at the date of trial, the victim is not in breach of any payment obligation.

Neither does absence of basis command clear support. For one thing the existence of the unjust factor is not sufficiently settled. In addition, as demonstrated above, properly understood it is difficult to see how the basis of the carer's intervention could fail. Assuming, as suggested by the evidence, the carer intervenes out of love and affection, the basis of the carer's assistance is not likely to fail.

Finally, as is explored in chapter 6, neither of these unjust factors can explain the apparently contingent nature of the carer's right to share in the fund. The question of enrichment is determined at the moment of receipt. If the carer's entitlement is generated by unjust enrichment, it arguably arises at the moment the victim receives services from the carer. However, the carer's entitlement to share in the victim's damages is not expressed to be in satisfaction of any pre-existing obligation to the carer, and is not

---

[123] E. McKendrick, 'The Reason for Restitution' in P. Birks and F. Rose (eds.), *Lessons of the Swaps Litigation* (Oxford, 2000) 84, p. 107.

[124] There is already authority supporting the right to claim back the value of a gift in unjust enrichment. Other unjust factors are able to do this work. *Lady Hood of Avalon* v. *Mackinnon* [1909] 1 Ch 476; *Louth* v. *Diprose* (1992) 175 CLR 621.

visible until the victim is successful in her claim against the wrongdoer. It is therefore difficult to explain the carer's entitlement to share in the fund as being generated by these unjust factors.

Conclusion

An unjust enrichment analysis predicated either on failure of basis or absence of basis takes us no further in understanding the carer's right to share. While theoretically possible, there is little evidence in support of either analysis. The carer's right to share in the fund of damages is not convincingly explicable on either ground.

Policy motivated claims

As has been said, the second type of unjust factor is policy based. This is a claim made pursuant to an unjust factor which the law recognises in order to promote a particular policy objective. The claim is not based on any deficiency or qualification to the claimant's intention. This discussion examines whether, according to the existing unjust factors, the carer holds a policy motivated unjust enrichment claim. It must be remembered that the task of this book is first, to explain why the carer is entitled to share in the victim's damages and secondly, to shed some light on the fact that in some cases this right to share is proprietary. The form of the carer's participation is dealt with in chapter 9. At this point, all we are trying to understand is the basis for the carer's right to participate. As such, it is helpful to notice that the courts have in some cases given policy reasons in support of a mechanism giving the carer access to the victim's damages. It is possible that the policy motivations identified by the judges will help explain the basis for the carer's right to share and provide the foundation for a policy motivated unjust enrichment analysis.

Policy justifications for the carer's right to participate

The policy rationales given in favour of the carer's access are separate from those given in support of the victim's entitlement to claim damages. As is set out in chapter 2, the victim is entitled to sue the wrongdoer for loss including an amount calculated by reference to the value of the carer's contribution. There are various policy reasons which are invoked in support of the victim's right to sue for the value of services provided and expenses paid by the carer.[125] However, the victim's right to sue the wrongdoer is logically distinct from the carer's right to share in the fund, and the reasons given in support of the victim's ability to claim from the wrongdoer are not the concern of this discussion. Of interest are the reasons given in support of the carer's access to the victim's damages.

There are two difficulties encountered in identifying these policy rationales. The first is that judges do not always separate a discussion of the reason given for the mere existence of a mechanism implementing the carer's right to participate, from the reason that a particular form of mechanism is imposed. An example of this type of reasoning occurs in *Thomson* v. *MacLean*. The judge collapsed his inquiry of the threshold question as to whether or not the carer should be entitled to participate, into the secondary question of the applicability of a trust. He imposed a trust of the damages without turning his mind to whether a personal obligation to pay the carer may have been appropriate. The form of the carer's access to the fund is the subject of chapter 9. The case is referred to here only as an example in which the reason given in support of the imposition of a trust is best seen as a rationale for the imposition of a mechanism per se rather than as the rationale for the recognition of a trust:[126]

> ... the expedient has been adopted in the Nova Scotia cases of impressing such awards with a trust in favour of the party who actually rendered the services. In other cases it has been determined that the issue is not one that arises between a plaintiff and tortfeasor and that it is for the plaintiff to do as the plaintiff sees fit with damages recovered under this head. (See *Donnelly* v. *Joyce*, [1973] 3 All ER 475, and *Hasson* v. *Hamel* (1977) 78 DLR (3d) 573, but for an opposite view see *Coderre* v. *Ethier* (1978), 85 DLR (3d) 621) ... [next paragraph] ... Although the approach may lack something in terms of pure logic, I think that where all the facts are before the court and no dispute

---

[125] The victim's ability to claim has been justified on various policy grounds. For example, because the wrongdoer should not benefit from the carer's intervention which is cited in *Rawson* v. *Kasman* (1956) 3 DLR (2d) 376 at 378 PER SCHROEDER JA with whom the other members of the court agreed on this issue. In *Thomas* v. *Eyles* (1998) 28 MVR 240 Priestley JA at 257 stated '... where a favour is done to a disabled person, whether by a relative or a stranger, where the favour consists of the gratuitous provision (that is, a gift) of funds, services or goods, then the plaintiff should reap the benefit rather than the tortfeasor defendant'. Another view is that the victim's claim is justified because the care is reasonably necessary and caused by the wrongdoer's negligence, as cited in *Schneider* v. *Eisovitch* [1960] 2 QB 430 at 440 PER PAULL J.

[126] *Thomson* v. *MacLean* (1983) 57 NSR (2d) 436 at 438 PER BURCHELL J.

as to entitlement is raised between the plaintiff and the person performing the non-contracted services, it is expedient and just to adopt the trust approach . . .

The second difficulty is related to the first. In many of the cases in which the carer is granted access to the fund, there is no coherent justification cited in support of the imposition of a mechanism.[127] Rather, the court is silent, and merely asserts that the carer is entitled to participate in the damages won by the victim. In these circumstances, all that can be recorded is the fact of the carer's access to the fund. It is dangerous to hypothesise about the factors which may have weighed on the mind of the judge in permitting the carer access.

These qualifications having been given, the discussion will document the reasons which have been invoked by the courts in support of the carer's right to share in the fund. Broadly speaking, these fall into the following categories which are dealt with below: (1) the necessitous nature of the carer's intervention; (2) the carer's right to reasonable remuneration; (3) the risk that the victim will accumulate in respect of his loss; and (4) miscellaneous reasons.

The necessitous nature of the carer's intervention   There is some authority that the carer's access to the fund is given in recognition of the necessitous and onerous nature of the carer's intervention. The court seems to link the availability of a mechanism to a qualitative judgment about the assistance provided by the carer.[128]

An example is *Coderre* v. *Ethier* in which the victim recovered damages subject to a direction to pay the carer. The victim Germaine Gachot was a member of a religious order who had been injured in a traffic accident and consequently required amputation of her left leg immediately below the hip joint. In addition, her arms and right leg were partially paralysed. The prognosis at trial was that '. . . she will be a bed patient requiring constant attention permanently. She is presently confined and treated in a nursing home. She is mentally alert and can converse but because of her pain and

---

[127] Examples include the following cases in which a trust was imposed: *Grover* v. *Lowther* (1982) 52 NSR (2d) 22 at 41 PER GRANT J; *Scarff* v. *Wilson* (1986) 39 CCLT 20 at 67 PER CUMMING J.

[128] *Crane* v. *Worwood* (1992) 65 BCLR (2d) 16; *Coderre* v. *Ethier* (1978) 85 DLR (3d) 621; *Cunningham* v. *Harrison* [1973] 1 QB 942.

discomfort she is unable to read except for short periods.'[129] As a result of her helplessly disabled condition, she required nursing care for twenty-four hours a day. The victim incurred an obligation to pay $64,000 for this nursing assistance in the period prior to trial. This amount, together with other related expenses, was paid on her behalf by the religious order of which she was a member.

The victim sued the wrongdoer for damages, including an amount calculated by reference to the medical and nursing expenses paid on her behalf by the religious order. The judge allowed her claim on the basis that the tortfeasor's liability should not be reduced by the fact that the expenses were paid by the religious order. However, he put a condition on her award. Citing as his reason the magnitude of the nursing services paid for by the religious order, he directed the victim to pay the requisite portion of her damages to the religious order:[130]

> These expenses, along with the other expenses, were paid by the religious order of which she is a member. She is under no obligation to repay them nor was there evidence of an agreement that as part of the consideration for being a member of this order she would be taken care of in circumstances such as these. However, out-of-pocket expenses paid by any third party in the way of philanthropy, sympathy or other compassionate grounds accrue no benefit to the tortfeasor: . . . *In view of the magnitude of the nursing aid services* paid for by the order, any of the expenditures listed in ex. 13 which were made by other than the plaintiff Gachot directly should be subject to an undertaking and a direction by the plaintiff, Gachot, to return them to the gratuitous donors.

Some evidence of this approach is also present in *Cunningham* v. *Harrison*.[131] This case concerned the victim Mr Cunningham who had been rendered tetraplegic through the negligence of the tortfeasor. The victim had entered into a contract for care with his wife pursuant to which he was obligated to pay her £2,000 per annum in respect of her nursing services. He commenced proceedings against the tortfeasor claiming damages which included an amount on account of his future care. Sadly, his wife had committed suicide three days before trial. In consequence, the claim in respect of the cost of Mr Cunningham's future care was framed, not by

---

[129] *Coderre* v. *Ethier* (1978) 85 DLR (3d) 621 at 632 PER LERNER J.
[130] *Ibid.*, 632–633 PER LERNER J (emphasis added).
[131] *Cunningham* v. *Harrison* [1973] 1 QB 942.

reference to his contract with his wife, but by reference to the cost of a commercial care provider. Although not strictly required by the facts of the case, Lord Denning MR discussed what would have been the case had Mrs Cunningham not died, and had Mr Cunningham made a claim against the tortfeasor in respect of the value of her future care.

Lord Denning MR held that the victim's ability to claim damages from the wrongdoer arises independently of a contract to pay the carer, and further held, *obiter*, that if the victim had recovered these damages they would have been held in trust for the carer. Lord Denning MR proposed a trust of the damages, and justified the imposition of a mechanism in favour of the carer on the various grounds.[132] One of his reasons for permitting the carer to share in the fund was that the carer's intervention was necessitous:[133]

> It seems to me that when a husband is grievously injured – and is entitled to damages – then it is only right and just that, if his wife renders services to him, instead of a nurse, he should recover compensation for the value of the services that his wife has rendered. It should not be necessary to draw up a legal agreement for them. On recovering such an amount, the husband should hold it on trust for her and pay it over to her. She cannot herself sue the wrongdoer (see *Best* v. *Samuel Fox & Co. Ltd.* [1952] AC 716); but she has rendered services necessitated by the wrong-doing, and should be compensated for it.

The carer's right to reasonable remuneration   The carer's participation in the fund has also been justified by some judges on the basis that the carer is entitled to reasonable remuneration for any services rendered and expenses paid.[134] The overwhelming pattern in the victim and carer cases is that in those cases where the carer participates in the fund, the carer's right to share is not justified on the basis of a pre-existing right of the carer to claim an amount from the victim.[135] The carer's entitlement is not said to be in satisfaction of an antecedent debt owed by the victim to the carer. A superficial reading of the cases therefore seems to suggest that, it is not until the victim has successfully sued the wrongdoer, that a portion of the

---

[132] As the quote states, his other reasons for granting the carer access to the fund were that: (1) the carer should be compensated; and (2) the carer had no direct claim.

[133] N. 131 above, p. 952 PER LORD DENNING MR with whom Orr LJ at 955 and Lawton LJ at 958 agreed.

[134] *Hunt* v. *Severs* [1994] 2 AC 350; *Cunningham* v. *Harrison* [1973] 1 QB 942.

[135] These arguments are described more fully in chapter 6.

damages won by the victim is identified by the court to be for the benefit of the carer.

Those cases in which the carer's participation in the fund is said to be justified by the carer's entitlement to remuneration exemplify the above pattern. As will be outlined in chapter 6, these cases do not assist our understanding of the carer's right to share in the fund. Even though the carer's participation is justified on the basis of the carer's right to remuneration, we are no further to understanding the reason for this right to be paid. All that these decisions do is to restate the conclusion that the carer is entitled to participate in the fund, without explaining why the carer has a right to do so.

An example of this type of reasoning is that given in support of a trust of the victim's damages in *Hunt* v. *Severs* and also in *Cunningham* v. *Harrison*. Although on the particular facts of *Hunt* v. *Severs* a trust was not imposed, their Lordships nonetheless identified two reasons which, on other facts, would in their view support a trust. First, to enable the voluntary carer to receive proper recompense for her services and secondly, in order to harmonise the relevant law in England and Scotland. The second of these arguments is discussed below. This discussion is concerned with the first reason, namely that the carer is entitled to participate in the fund because the underlying reason for this type of award to the victim is to enable the carer to receive reasonable recompense for services given to the victim. Lord Bridge stated:[136]

> Thus, in both England and Scotland the law now ensures that an injured plaintiff may recover the reasonable value of gratuitous services rendered to him by way of voluntary care by a member of his family. Differences between the English common law route and the Scottish statutory route to this conclusion are, I think, rarely to be likely to be of practical importance, since in most cases the sum recovered will simply go to swell the family income. But it is nevertheless important to recognise that the underlying rationale of the English law, as all of the cases before *Donnelly* v. *Joyce* [1974] QB 454 demonstrate, is to enable the voluntary carer to receive proper recompense for his or her services and I would think it appropriate for the House to take the opportunity so far as possible to bring the law of the two countries into accord by adopting the view of Lord Denning MR in *Cunningham* v. *Harrison* [1973] QB 942 that in England the injured plaintiff who recovers damages under this head should hold them on trust for the voluntary carer.

---

[136] *Hunt* v. *Severs* [1994] 2 AC 350 at 363 PER LORD BRIDGE.

The difficulty with the above passage is that it does not tell us on what basis the carer's right to recompense is given. The reasoning does not disclose any more information than the fact of the conclusion that the carer is entitled to participate in the fund. Statements of this nature do no more than emphasise the apparently contingent nature of the carer's entitlement. No information is given about when the carer's right to compensation arises nor about the event or policy rationale underpinning the carer's entitlement.

Similar reasoning is present in some Australian cases, a fact made even more surprising by that jurisdiction's commitment to denying the carer's entitlement to share in the fund.[137] Despite the seemingly absolute rule that damages on account of the carer's intervention '... [belong] to the injured person beneficially. There is no legal obligation to pay them over to a carer, nor is there any equitable obligation involving any element of trust'[138] the carer in particular cases obtains access to the victim's damages.[139] We will return to these cases in chapters 8 and 9. At this point, all that must be observed is that payment is often made to a carer on the basis that a moral obligation to do so binds the victim and evidence that, had the victim been mentally capable and in control of the fund, the victim would have paid the carer.[140] Once again, such statements do no more than identify the conclusion that the victim must share her damages with the carer. No satisfying reason is given for the carer's access.

---

[137] *Griffiths* v. *Kerkemeyer* (1977) 139 CLR 161; *Kars* v. *Kars* (1996) 187 CLR 354; *Grincelis* v. *House* (2000) 201 CLR 321.

[138] *Re B* [2000] NSWSC 44 PER YOUNG J.

[139] The cases involve the protective jurisdiction of the court and a claim by the carer for payment out of the fund of damages administered on behalf of a severely incapacitated victim. Examples include: *Re B* [2000] NSWSC 44 PER YOUNG J; *Re DJR and the Mental Health Act 1958* [1983] 1 NSWLR 557; *Goode* v. *Thompson and Anor* (2001) Aust Torts Reports ¶81–617; *In the Matter of GDM and the Protected Estates Act 1983* (1992) Aust Torts Rep ¶81–190; *Re N* (2001) 33 MVR 237; *Jones* v. *Moylan [No 2]* (2000) 23 WAR 65; *Re ES and the Mental Health Act 1958* [1984] 3 NSWLR 341; *Beasley* v. *Marshall (No 4)* (1986) 42 SASR 407; *W* v. *Q* (1992) 1 Tas R 301; *Marinko & Anor* v. *Masri* (2000) Aust Torts Rep ¶81–581.

[140] *Re B* [2000] NSWSC 44 PER YOUNG J; *Re DJR and the Mental Health Act 1958* [1983] 1 NSWLR 557 at 564–565 PER POWELL J; *Re N* (2001) 33 MVR 237 at 237–238 PER YOUNG J. In some cases there is emphasis on the fact that payment to the carer will benefit the victim: *Jones* v. *Moylan [No 2]* (2000) 23 WAR 65 at 85 PER MCKECHNIE JJ; *Re B* [2000] NSWSC 44 PER YOUNG J; *Re ES and the Mental Health Act 1958* [1984] 3 NSWLR 341 at 343 PER POWELL J. In *Re N* (2001) 33 MVR 237 Young J at 238 expresses these requirements to be in the alternative. Payment to the carer is permitted where '... (a) it can be seen to be for the benefit of the person; or (b) it is more likely than not that had that person remained fully capable, that person would have made the payment herself'.

The victim will accumulate in respect of the same loss   The victim receives services from the carer. In other cases, the carer pays those of the victim's debts which are incurred as a result of his injuries. The victim's claim against the wrongdoer arises by operation of law. The wrongdoer's liability to make good the victim's loss is unaffected by the carer's intervention. There is thus a risk that, by virtue of the fact that the victim holds a right to sue the wrongdoer, which is not reduced by the value of the carer's intervention, the victim will accumulate in respect of the same loss. In some cases, a mechanism requiring the carer to pay the victim is justified on the basis that it reverses this accumulation.[141] We will return to this policy rationale in chapter 8. It will be argued that such arguments, justifying the carer's entitlement, form part of a body of evidence revealing a novel unjust factor called the policy against accumulation.

Miscellaneous reasons   This section will briefly document various other reasons which have been cited by some judges in support of the carer's access to the fund of damages. They are recorded here only in the interests of completeness. It is not intended to discuss any of these in depth.

The first is that the carer has no direct claim against the wrongdoer. Lord Denning MR in *Cunningham* v. *Harrison* cites in support of the carer's access to the victim's damages the fact that the carer could not 'herself sue the wrongdoer'.[142] This merely restates the problem identified at the start of this book. It is prima facie impossible to explain why someone with no claim of her own should be given an interest in the damages won by another person. In *Hunt* v. *Severs* the House of Lords assumed that the carer has no direct claim against the tortfeasor.[143] Chapter 5 will confirm this conclusion. It is very difficult to explain why the absence of the carer's direct claim should justify the creation of an indirect claim for the carer expressed as a right to share in the proceeds of the victim's suit. In the absence of a direct claim in tort, the carer's suit against the tortfeasor seems likely to be achieved via the enactment of legislation conferring a right to claim.

---

[141] For example: *Feng* v. *Graham* (1988) 25 BCLR (2d) 116; *Hunt* v. *Severs* [1994] 2 AC 350. Although not a case in which a mechanism was imposed, support is also present in *Donnelly* v. *Joyce* [1974] 1 QB 454. See also *In the Matter of GDM and the Protected Estates Act 1983 (NSW)* (1992) Aust Torts Rep ¶81–190.

[142] *Cunningham* v. *Harrison* [1973] 1 QB 942 at 952 PER LORD DENNING MR.

[143] *Hunt* v. *Severs* [1994] 2 AC 350 at 358 PER LORD BRIDGE.

The other reason cited in support of the carer's access to the fund is that given by Burchell J in *Thomson* v. *MacLean*.[144] The judge justified the carer's access on the basis that as 'no dispute as to entitlement [was] raised between the plaintiff and the person performing the non-contracted services, it is expedient and just to adopt the trust approach'. With respect, the judge was correct when commenting that this approach lacked 'something in terms of pure logic'.[145] It does not merit further discussion.

Conclusion

The purpose of the above discussion has been to document the reasons which are invoked by courts in support of the carer's right to share in the victim's damages. The following reasons are given: (1) the necessitous nature of the carer's intervention; (2) the carer's right to reasonable remuneration; (3) the risk that the victim will be accumulate in respect of her loss; and (4) miscellaneous other reasons. Of these reasons, only two are capable of informing our understanding of the carer's right to share in the fund. Those judges who cite the carer's right to reasonable remuneration or various miscellaneous reasons do little to assist our understanding of the carer's apparently contingent right. In the end, only arguments that the carer's access is predicated on (1) the risk that the victim accumulate in respect of her loss; or (2) the necessitous nature of the carer's intervention, carry our analysis forward.

As is argued in chapter 8, there is a policy motivated unjust factor disclosed in those cases which cite the risk that the victim will accumulate in respect of loss when justifying the carer's right to share in the fund. This unjust factor is the policy against accumulation. It is of wide significance, and arguably applies whenever a claimant receives a benefit from another party and receives, or has the right to receive, in respect of the *same debt or damage* from a third party.[146] However, it must be conceded that the policy against accumulation is a novel unjust factor and has been little discussed. On the basis that necessity is an unjust factor discussed in most unjust enrichment books, the application of necessity to the victim and carer cases

---

[144] *Thomson* v. *MacLean* (1983) 57 NSR (2d) 436 at 438 PER BURCHELL J.

[145] *Ibid.*

[146] S. Degeling, 'The Policy Against Accumulation as an Unjust Factor' in E. Schrage, *Unjust Enrichment and the Law of Contract* (The Hague, 2001), pp. 167–92. S. Degeling, 'A New Reason for Restitution: The Policy Against Accumulation' (2002) 22 *Oxford Journal of Legal Studies* 435.

will conclude this examination of the unjust factors. The role of the policy against accumulation will be deferred until chapter 8.

The necessitous nature of the carer's intervention

In some cases the carer's access to the fund is given in recognition of the necessitous and onerous nature of the carer's intervention. The question is therefore whether there is some support in the victim and carer cases for the recognition of a policy-based unjust factor linked to the necessitous nature of the carer's intervention. Stated more precisely, the policy motivation for recovery is that necessitous intervention, such as that provided by the carer, should be encouraged. The purpose of this discussion is to determine whether an unjust enrichment analysis predicated on this policy motivated unjust factor is capable of accounting for the carer's participation in the victim's damages. This discussion will proceed as follows: (1) a consideration of necessity as a policy-based reason for restitution; (2) an application to the victim and carer cases; and (3) an evaluation of the utility of necessity as an unjust factor.

Necessity as an unjust factor

Necessity is a policy motivated unjust factor. It is not concerned with the intention of the claimant in transferring a benefit to the defendant, but rather gives recovery in recognition of the fact that it is in the public interest to encourage necessitous interventions. In order to encourage intervention in an emergency, the intervener is allowed a claim in respect of any benefit conferred.

It must be conceded that as yet there is no case authoritatively recognising necessity as an unjust factor.[147] The common law is generally reluctant to allow recovery to a person who intervenes in an emergency. The classic

---

[147] Some support is provided by *Mollgaard* v. *ARCIC*, a decision of the New Zealand High Court. For the purpose of determining a severely disabled claimant's entitlement to financial relief under the Accident Rehabilitation and Compensation Insurance Act 1992 (New Zealand) the court was asked to consider whether the claimant had incurred a liability to his carer for services provided. The question was answered in the affirmative, one of the reasons being that the carer had provided a necessitous intervention, giving rise to a potential liability in unjust enrichment. *Mollgaard* v. *ARCIC* [1999] 3 NZLR 735 at 742–743 PER HAMMOND J who delivered the judgment of the court.

expression of this hostility is the decision of the Court of Appeal in *Falcke* v. *Scottish Imperial Insurance Company*.[148] Bowen LJ stated:[149]

> The general principle is, beyond all question, that work and labour done or money expended by one man to preserve or benefit the property of another do not according to English law create any lien upon the property saved or benefited, nor, even if standing alone, create any liability to repay the expenditure. Liabilities are not to be forced upon people behind their backs any more than you can confer a benefit upon a man against his will.

However, it may be argued that *Falcke* is not the last word on this matter.[150] First, the objection that liability cannot be placed on a man behind his back is clearly spurious. All liabilities arising in unjust enrichment are by definition imposed without the consent of the defendant.[151] Secondly, the principle for which *Falcke* is authority must not be overstated. It was not itself on the facts a case of an emergency necessitating intervention to assist another person. Rather, the intervener acted in his own interests.[152] Thirdly, it is inconsistent with the categories of case in which the intervener's right to claim is well established. Where there is a pre-existing contractual obligation between the claimant and defendant, the doctrine of agency of necessity permits the claimant in some circumstances to recover from his principal his expenses incurred in protecting the principal's property from loss or damage. This right of reimbursement is said not to arise from any agreement between

---

[148] *Falcke* v. *Scottish Imperial Insurance Company* (1886) 34 Ch D 234.

[149] *Ibid.*, 248 PER BOWEN LJ.

[150] Birks, 193–202; Burrows, chapter 8; D. Friedmann, 'Valid, Voidable, Qualified, and Non-existing Obligations: An Alternative Perspective on the Law of Restitution' in A. Burrows (ed.), *Essays on the Law of Restitution* (Oxford, 1991); Goff and Jones, chapter 17; G. Jones, *Restitution in Public and Private Law* (London, 1991), chapter 4; G. B. Klippert, *Unjust Enrichment* (Toronto, 1983), chapter 4; Maddaugh and McCamus, chapter 28; J. D. McCamus, 'Necessitous Intervention: The Altruistic Intermeddler and the Law of Restitution' (1979) 11 *Ottawa Law Review* 297; M. McInnes, 'Restitution and the Rescue of Life' (1994) 32 *Alberta Law Review* 37; Mitchell, chapter 8; Mason and Carter, Part III; F. Rose, 'Restitution for the Rescuer' (1989) 9 *Oxford Journal of Legal Studies* 167.

[151] If this objection were true, one might also call into question any other liability arising outside the realm of consent including, for example, liability in tort.

[152] Emanuel was the owner of the ultimate equity of redemption on a life insurance policy which he had mortgaged a number of times. He paid the outstanding premiums on the policy to prevent it lapsing. Emanuel claimed a lien entitling himself to repayment of these premiums in priority to the mortgagees. He failed. For our analysis, the crucial fact is that he paid in his own interest, not in the interest of the mortgagees. *Falcke* v. *Scottish Imperial Insurance Company* (1886) 34 ChD 234 at 251 PER BOWEN LJ.

the agent and principal but rather from the state of emergency itself.[153] Even in the absence of a pre-existing relationship between the claimant and defendant, the claimant is in some cases entitled to recover. For example, those who intervene to bury a body which it is not their responsibility to bury may recover their reasonable expenses.[154] Similarly, in the context of a parish's duty to provide for its poor, a doctor attending a seriously injured patient has been able to recover from the parish responsible.[155]

Proponents of necessity argue that these pockets of recovery[156] form the basis of a more generalised right to recover for the emergency intervener. The law is not yet decided and any analysis of the issue leans heavily on the writings of scholars.[157] It is beyond the scope of this book to do more than briefly summarise the model for recovery on the ground of necessity which has been proposed. Burrows and McKendrick isolate three core requirements to be established in an unjust enrichment claim based on necessity.[158] First, there must be an emergency, generating the state of

---

[153] *Prager* v. *Blatspiel, Stamp and Heacock Ltd* [1924] 1 KB 566; *China Pacific SA* v. *Food Corporation of India* [1982] AC 939; *Burns Philp & Co Ltd* v. *Gillespie Brothers Pty Ltd* (1947) 74 CLR 148.

[154] The so-called 'funeral cases' such as *Jenkins* v. *Tucker* (1788) 1 Hy Bl 90; *Ambrose* v. *Kerrison* (1851) 10 CB 776.

[155] *Tomlinson* v. *Bentall* (1826) 5 B & C 738.

[156] Other examples include: *In re F. (Mental Patient: Sterilisation)* [1990] 2 AC 1 (agency of necessity); *In re Rhodes* (1890) 44 Ch D 94 (necessaries to an incapax); *Great Northern Railway* v. *Swaffield* (1874) LR 9 Ex 132 (bailees preserving property of bailor); *In re Berkeley Applegate (Investment Consultants)* [1989] Ch 32 (liquidator/trustee doing more than is strictly required of his position).

[157] Birks, pp. 304–8; Burrows, pp. 242–9; Burrows and McKendrick, chapter 9; J. Dawson, 'Rewards for the Rescue of Human Life?' in *The Good Samaritan and the Law* (New York, 1966), pp. 63–89; Goff and Jones, chapter 17; Maddaugh and McCamus, chapter 28; Mason and Carter, pp. 239–54; J. D. McCamus, 'Necessitous Intervention: The Altruistic Intermeddler and the Law of Restitution' (1979) 11 *Ottawa Law Review* 297; M. McInnes, 'Restitution and the Rescue of Life' (1994) 32 *Alberta Law Review* 37; F. Rose, 'Restitution for the Rescuer' (1989) 9 *Oxford Journal of Legal Studies* 167.

[158] Burrows and McKendrick, pp. 474–5. Broadly speaking, the other models which have been proposed are consistent with this analysis. For example, Birks and Mitchell propose the following elements: (1) likelihood of great imminent harm to the claimant or his property; (2) impracticable for the claimant to communicate directly with the defendant. Subject to the limit of public interest, recovery should be denied where intervention is contrary to the known wishes of the assisted person; (3) the claimant must be an appropriate person to intervene in the circumstances; (4) claimant should be able to recover only in respect of reasonably incurred expenses; and (5) it is a bar to recovery if the claimant acted for his own benefit and only incidentally benefited the defendant. It should be noted that this model is a new development so far as the Birksian analysis goes. In earlier work it was controversially proposed that an unjust factor called moral compulsion might account for these cases. Moral compulsion seems no longer to be a viable analytical tool. Birks, pp. 193–202. See now P. Birks and Mitchell, pp. 580–3. Other formulations include those given by Goff and Jones, pp. 473–6; Virgo, pp. 304–5.

necessity, pursuant to which the defendant, his property or those for whom he is legally responsible will be affected. Secondly, although the issue is not resolved, it seems that it must be impossible or impractical for the intervener to obtain instructions from the defendant. Thirdly, the claimant must be an appropriate person to intervene.

It is of course also possible that the cases in this analysis are not properly to be accounted for via an unjust enrichment analysis, and instead fall under some other head of obligation such as unjust sacrifice.[159] The gist of an unjust sacrifice claim is that, in receiving services from the carer, the victim has incurred an obligation to pay the carer. The carer's claim in unjust sacrifice is compensatory. It is not concerned with reversing an enrichment of the victim. Both judicial and academic discussion have yet to authoritatively determine whether the law recognises or ought to recognise unjust sacrifice as a source of rights and obligations. It has been noted in this discussion for the sake of completeness only. This chapter is concerned only with the possible claim for the carer in unjust enrichment. Unjust sacrifice, to the extent that it exists, belongs outside the boundaries of the law of unjust enrichment. Brief mention will be made of the principle of negotiorum gestio at the end of this chapter.

Application to the victim and carer cases

As has been stated, the core elements of a policy motivated claim based on necessity are that: (1) there must be an emergency generating the state of necessity; (2) it must be impossible or impractical for the intervener to obtain instructions from the defendant; and (3) the claimant must be an appropriate person to intervene. Each of these will be applied to the victim and carer cases.

Emergency generating necessity

Judicial discussion of the state of necessity which arises from an emergency is given by Lord Goff in *In re F. (Mental Patient: Sterilisation)*.[160] The case

---

[159] J. Beatson, *The Use and Abuse of Unjust Enrichment* (Oxford, 1991), pp. 23–4; G. Muir, 'Unjust Sacrifice and the Officious Intervener' in P. Finn (ed.), *Essays on Restitution* (1990) 297; S. Stoljar, 'Unjust Enrichment and Unjust Sacrifice' (1987) 50 *Modern Law Review* 603.

[160] *In re F. (Mental Patient: Sterilisation* [1990] 2 AC 1. Applied in *R v. Bournewood Community and Mental Health N.H.S. Trust ex parte L* [1998] 3 All ER 289 at 298 and 301 PER LORD GOFF with whom Lord Lloyd, Lord Nolan and Lord Hope agreed. Lord Steyn at 307 also applied the formulation identified by Lord Goff in *In re F*.

concerned the proposed sterilisation of F, a mentally handicapped woman, without her consent. F's mother and the local health authority brought an action to determine the lawfulness of this surgery. Although the case was not an action in unjust enrichment, we are able to derive much assistance from Lord Goff's consideration of the nature and extent of the principle of necessity. In the course of his opinion, he states that the principle of necessity, often but not exclusively associated with an emergency, might possibly provide justification for such medical treatment. In relation to that principle he states:[161]

> In truth, the relevance of an emergency is that it may give rise to a necessity to act in the interests of the assisted person, without first obtaining his consent. Emergency is however not the criterion or even a pre-requisite; it is simply a frequent origin of the necessity which impels intervention. The principle is one of necessity, not of emergency.

The underlying premise of Lord Goff's approach is that, where legal consequences flow from consent, the same or similar consequences may flow from necessity. Necessity thus displaces the need for consent. When one person works for the benefit of another, and seeks to claim in respect of that work, we look first to see if the provider of services has a consent based claim, a claim in contract. However, a non-contractual claim becomes possible in circumstances of necessity. It is the necessity which calls for and justifies the provider's intervention.

Although the intervention of the carer is undoubtedly necessary, it is not clear that in all cases the circumstances constitute a state of crisis sufficient to attract the principle of necessity. It is necessary to define the scope of the emergency. Goff and Jones[162] ask whether the need of the victim is '...great enough and immediate enough...' to justify the carer's intervention. This involves a consideration of the consequences which would follow if the carer had not acted. If the consequences are sufficiently serious, then the principle of necessity applies and the carer's intervention is justified. This involves a detailed examination of the facts in any particular case. Burrows[163] says that the following might be examples of cases in which the intervener's actions are justified: the actions of a passer by who dives into a lake to save a drowning child or the actions of a person who repairs serious storm damage to the roof of his neighbour while the neighbour is away. However, these

---

[161] *Ibid.*, 75 PER LORD GOFF.   [162] Goff and Jones, p. 474.   [163] Burrows, p. 231.

examples do not define exhaustively the situations in which the principle is relevant. The barrier for the carer's claim is to demonstrate that his intervention is of the same genre as those examples identified by Burrows. As was emphasised by Lord Goff in *In re F. (Mental Patient: Sterilisation)*[164] the crucial element is that there are circumstances of necessity.

Some of the cases under examination here are explicable as cases where the carer intervenes in a situation of necessity. The factual ingredients which go to demonstrate the necessity vary from case to case. In all cases, the victim has been injured and consequently suffers some degree of incapacity. The cases include victims who are unconscious or supported by a ventilator,[165] or suffering paralysis,[166] while in others the injuries are more general.[167] In other cases, the necessity is not created simply by the need for services. It is this need for assistance combined with the victim's mental incapacity,[168] young age[169] or combined with an environment of financial difficulty preventing the victim from engaging a professional carer, such as a nurse or housekeeper, thus making the intervention of a family member more imperative.[170]

---

[164] *In re F. (Mental Patient: Sterilisation)* [1990] 2 AC 1 at 75 PER LORD GOFF.

[165] *Schneider* v. *Eisovitch* [1960] 2 QB 430; *Gow* v. *Motor Vehicle Insurance Trust* [1967] WAR 55; *Richardson* v. *Schultz* (1980) 25 SASR 1; *Wilson* v. *McLeay* (1961) 106 CLR 523; *Lankenau* v. *Dutton* (1989) 56 DLR (4th) 364.

[166] For example: *Hunt* v. *Severs* [1994] 2 AC 350 (paraplegia); *Thornton* v. *Board of School Trustees of School District No 57 (Prince George) et al* (1978) 83 DLR (3d) 480 (paraplegia); *Griffiths* v. *Kerkemeyer* (1977) 139 CLR 161 (quadriplegia); *Burford* v. *Allen* (1992) Aust Torts Rep ¶81–184 (most serious paraplegia consistent with life).

[167] For example: *Kars* v. *Kars* (1996) 187 CLR 354 (back injury); *Marin* v. *Varta* (1983) 218 Sask R 173 (impaired vision); *Thomson* v. *MacLean* (1983) 57 NSR (2d) 436 (ankle injury).

[168] For example: *McLeod* v. *Palardy* (1980) 4 Man R (2d) 218; *Yepremian et al* v. *Scarborough General Hospital et al* (1980) 110 DLR (3d) 513; *Roberts* v. *Johnstone* [1988] 3 WLR 1247 (also seven years old); *Roach* v. *Yates* [1938] 1 KB 256; *Brown et al* v. *University of Alberta Hospital et al* (1997) 145 DLR (4th) 63 (also an infant); *Grincelis* v. *House* (2000) 201 CLR 321; *Lusignam (Litigation Guardian of)* v. *Concordia Hospital* unreported Manitoba Queen's Bench 28 April 1997 (also an infant); *Altmann* v. *Dunning* [1995] 2 VR 1; *Clark* v. *Kramer* [1986] WAR 54; *Goldfinch* v. *Scannell* [1993] 2 PIQR Q143; *Fitzgerald* v. *Ford* [1996] 5 PIQR 73; *Lefebvre* v. *Kitteringham* (1985) 39 Sask R 308.

[169] For example: *Scarff* v. *Wilson* (1987) 39 CCLT 20 (five years); *Turnbull* v. *Hsieh* (1990) 269 APR 33 (five years); *Donnelly* v. *Joyce* [1974] 1 QB 454 (six years); *D'Ambrosio* v. *DeSouza Lima* [1983] 60 ACTR 18 (six years); *Arnold* v. *Teno* (1978) 83 DLR (3d) 609 ($4\frac{1}{2}$ years); *Lapensée* v. *Ottawa Day Nursery* (1986) 35 CCLT 129 ($15\frac{1}{2}$ months); *Lunnon* v. *Reagh* (1978) 25 NSR (2d) 196 (six years); *Garland* v. *Clifford* (1996) 67 SASR 47 (six years); *Brown et al* v. *University of Alberta Hospital et al* (1997) 145 DLR (4th) 63 ($2\frac{1}{2}$ years).

[170] For example: *Grover* v. *Lowther* (1982) 52 NSR (2d) 22; *Johnson* v. *Shelest* (1988) 2 BCLR (2d) 230; *Benstead* v. *Murphy* (1994) 23 Alta LR (3d) 251.

The existence of this state of emergency is reflected in the judicial language employed to describe the circumstances of each victim. In some cases this is expressed as a recognition of the fact that if the carer had not intervened, a professional care giver would have had to be employed by or on behalf of the victim,[171] or that the services were necessary, essential, or were referable to the victim's need.[172] It should be noted that the use of 'essential' in these cases was used to describe the extreme need, as a matter of fact, of the victim. It is not suggested that the standard for recovery in unjust enrichment is that the care should be essential. What is required is that there is a state of necessity justifying the carer's intervention.

One factor which creates difficulty for this unjust factor is the time frame over which the emergency occurs. Beyond doubt are those cases in which there is an immediate emergency. The easiest case is when the carer intervenes in the period between the accident and trial. Particularly when the financial circumstances of the victim are such that the victim cannot afford to hire a commercial provider, the facts will probably disclose the requisite urgency.[173] If not for the assistance of a friend or relative in this interim period, the victim may be left to cope alone or in some instances to rely on whatever services the state may be able to provide. It is not until the victim has been put in funds by an award of damages that the victim can afford to pay a commercial provider.

---

[171] For example: *Britliffe* v. *Britliffe* (1990) Aust Torts Rep ¶81–060, at 68,281 PER HOPE JA with whom the rest of the Court of Appeal agreed; *Weinman* v. *Boten* (1990) 104 FLR 146 at 157 PER MILES CJ AND JENKINSON J; *Lankenau* v. *Dutton* (1989) 56 DLR (4th) 364 at 368 PER SPENCER J; *Gerow* v. *Reid* (1989) 225 APR 34 at 42 PER GRANT J; *Yepremian et al* v. *Scarborough General Hospital et al* (1980) 110 DLR (3d) 513 at 550 PER MORDEN JA; *Crane* v. *Worwood* (1992) 65 BCLR (2d) 16 at 23 PER HUDDART J.

[172] For example: **'Necessary'** *Hunt* v. *Severs* [1994] 2 AC 351 at 355 PER LORD BRIDGE; *Turnbull* v. *Hsieh* (1990) 269 APR 33 at 39 PER HOYT JA; *Mitchell* v. *U-Haul Co of Canada Ltd* (1986) 73 AR 91 at 132 PER LOMAS J; *Shaw et al* v. *Roemer et al* (1981) 46 NSR (2d) 629 at 682 PER RICHARD J affirmed (1981) 134 DLR 590 (3d); *Roach* v. *Yates* [1938] 1 KB 256 at 263 PER GREER LJ; *Daly* v. *General Steam Navigation Co Ltd* [1980] 3 All ER 696 at 699 PER BRIDGE LJ. **'Need'** *Malat* v. *Bjornson (No 2)* [1979] 4 WWR 673 at 705 PER RUTTAN J; *Feng* v. *Graham* (1988) 44 CCLT 52 at 66 PER WALLACE JA; *Millett* v. *McDonald's Restaurants of Canada Limited* (1984) 29 Man R (2d) 83 at 99 PER WILSON J; *Donnelly* v. *Joyce* [1974] 1 QB 454 at 462 PER MEGAW LJ; *Valois* v. *Long* (1984) 146 APR 191 at 204 PER DAIGLE J varied on other grounds (1986) 167 APR 434; *Roberts* v. *Johnstone* [1988] 3 WLR 1247 at 1251 PER STOCKER LJ. **'Essential'** *Kobs* v. *Merchants Hotel et al* (1990) 62 Man R (2d) 210 at 215 PER SMITH J approved (1990) 70 Man R (2d) 178.

[173] For example: *Grover* v. *Lowther* (1982) 52 NSR (2d) 22; *Johnson* v. *Shelest* (1988) 2 BCLR (2d) 230; *Benstead* v. *Murphy* (1994) 23 Alta LR (3d) 251.

However, it is difficult to see how the state of crisis which may have existed in the weeks and months immediately following the victim's injury can continue indefinitely into the future. It might be argued that once the victim's claim for damages in tort has been decided, and damages awarded, the necessity compelling the carer's intervention has ceased. Having received compensation, the victim is in a position to make permanent arrangements for care given by commercial providers. Although Lord Goff does seem to contemplate that the principle of necessity might apply to a situation over a period of time,[174] it seems doubtful that the state of necessity could continue indefinitely. As Lord Goff emphasises, '... it would be an unusual use of language to describe the case as one of "permanent emergency" – if indeed such a state of affairs can properly be said to exist.'[175]

This problem of timing is brought into sharp relief in those awards on account of the future care of the victim. In those cases in which the carer is given access to the fund containing damages on account of future care, it is difficult to see how the state of necessity will continue. The victim, having received damages, will then be in a position to make arrangements for care given by commercial care providers. It is difficult to see how the state of crisis which may have existed in the weeks and months immediately following the victim's injury can continue indefinitely into the future.

Impossible or impractical for the carer to obtain instructions

To establish necessity the carer must not, as a matter of practicality, be able to communicate rationally with the victim in order to obtain instructions. In the absence of these instructions, it is said that a state of necessity exists pursuant to which the carer intervenes. As is explored below, it is unlikely that this element of a policy motivated claim based on necessity will be established in any but a few of the victim and carer cases. The primary difficulty is that, contrary to the legal requirements, many victims do seem to be in a position to communicate with their carers. Even in the case of those victims who seem not to be able to give instructions, it is doubtful that such an inability to communicate will continue indefinitely.

---

[174] 'When the state of affairs is permanent, or semi-permanent, action properly taken to preserve the life, health or well-being of the assisted person may well transcend measures such as surgical operation or substantial medical treatment and may extend to include such humdrum matters as routine medical or dental treatment, even simple care such as dressing and undressing and putting to bed.' *In re F. (Mental Patient: Sterilisation)* [1990] 2 AC 1 at 76 PER LORD GOFF.
[175] *In re F. (Mental Patient: Sterilisation)* [1990] 2 AC 1 at 75 PER LORD GOFF.

At its most strict, the requirement that the victim not be able effectively to communicate with the carer means that only those victims suffering severe impairment will satisfy the test. These cases will include a minor who is not yet at the age of reason, an unconscious victim or a victim experiencing mental incapacity. The cases in this study encompass those in which there are victims who are minors of a very young age[176] and those who are mentally incapable of consenting to the carer's intervention.[177] In these cases it is arguable that the carer is unable to obtain rational instructions from the victim thus satisfying this element of liability.

However, the above categories do not explain those cases in which the victim is paralysed or otherwise incapacitated. In these cases, it is necessary to define more precisely what is meant by the carer's inability to obtain rational instructions from the victim. A helpful authority is *In re T. (Adult: Refusal of Treatment)*[178] which was discussed earlier in this chapter. An application was brought by T's father for a declaration that it would not be unlawful for the hospital to administer a blood transfusion to T without her consent. At the time of the application T was sedated and on a ventilator. Lord Donaldson MR identified the factors which may be operating on the mind of the victim following a traumatic accident:[179]

> An adult patient may be deprived of his capacity to decide either by long term mental incapacity or retarded development or by temporary factors such as unconsciousness, confusion or the effects of fatigue, shock, pain or drugs.

It is these so-called 'temporary factors' which are relevant. In those cases under examination where the victim is paralysed or otherwise incapacitated, the victim may well have been suffering from the effects of confusion, fatigue, shock, pain or drugs. In the same way as those victims who suffer mental impairment, are unconscious or very young, these victims are unable to rationally communicate with the carer. In this way, the test for liability might be satisfied.

---

[176] For example: *Scarff* v. *Wilson* (1986) 39 CCLT 20 (five years); *Turnbull* v. *Hsieh* (1990) 269 APR 33 (five years); *Donnelly* v. *Joyce* [1974] 1 QB 454 (six years); *D'Ambrosio* v. *DeSouza Lima* [1983] 60 ACTR 18 (six years).

[177] For example: *Altmann* v. *Dunning* [1995] 2 VR 1; *Clark* v. *Kramer* [1986] WAR 54; *Goldfinch* v. *Scannell* [1993] 2 PIQR Q143; *Fitzgerald* v. *Ford* [1996] 5 PIQR 73; *Lefebvre* v. *Kitteringham* (1985) 39 Sask R 308.

[178] *In re T (Adult: Refusal of Treatment)* [1992] 3 WLR 782.

[179] *Ibid.*, 799 PER LORD DONALDSON MR. Butler-Sloss LJ at 801 and Staughton LJ at 805 delivered judgments consistent with this formulation.

Even if an extended view is taken of the cases so that these temporary factors are acknowledged, a problem remains. The inability of a victim to communicate with the carer is, at the minimum, likely to exist in the period immediately following the injury. Over the longer term, however, the capacity of the victim to give rational instructions might improve. For example, a child will grow up and, absent any other debilitating factors, will be able to communicate with the carer. In these cases it seems likely that the situation of necessity will end. To the extent that a state of necessity is capable of continuing over a period of time,[180] those victims who remain unable to rationally communicate with the carer may still be regarded as being affected by necessity. In these latter cases, the carer may still be regarded as a necessitous intervener. However, for other victims and carers it is not likely that this will continue to be the case. This presents a problem for this unjust factor in those cases which award the victim damages including an amount in respect of the carer's future contribution.[181]

The claimant must be an appropriate person to intervene

Burrows and McKendrick say in relation to this last requirement that '[i]n deciding whether or not the plaintiff is an appropriate person to intervene the courts will inquire into the motives which prompted the plaintiff to intervene, whether or not he had an intention to charge for his intervention, and the qualifications which he possessed which made him an appropriate person to intervene'.[182] The carer is a friend or relative of the victim who in most cases has no professional qualifications or training.[183] However, it is clear from the facts of the victim and carer cases that the carer is acting in the best interests of the victim. The carer's intervention occurs in the context of the relationship of love and affection which exists between the victim and carer. In general, the cases contain no suggestion that the carer is acting completely out of self-interest.

There are, however, cases of mixed motives. This objection is particularly relevant when the carer provides housekeeping services. It is not hard to see

---

[180] *In re F. (Mental Patient: Sterilisation)* [1990] 2 AC 1 at 76 PER LORD GOFF.

[181] For example: *Hunt* v. *Severs* [1994] 2 AC 350; *Roach* v. *Yates* [1938] 1 KB 256; *Taylor* v. *Bristol Omnibus Co* [1975] 1 WLR 1054.

[182] Burrows and McKendrick, p. 474.

[183] There are rare exceptions such as *Greenaway* v. *CPR Co et al* [1925] 1 DLR 992 in which the carer coincidentally happened to be professionally trained. In that case the victim's claim on account of past care provided by her daughter for nursing services failed. Her daughter was a nurse.

this difficulty when the carer and victim live in the same household. There is an element of self-interest, because the carer also benefits from the meals she cooks and cleaning that she performs.[184] The objection extends to other cases in which the assistance is not household help. In *Hall* v. *Miller*[185] Mrs Hall assumed a portion of Mr Hall's employment duties, with the result that the family income was unaltered, despite his infirmity. To the extent that Mrs Hall also benefited from the sustained level of income, she was not acting solely in the best interests of the victim. It maybe inferred from the facts that her own self-interest may also have been operating in her decision to assist her husband.

It is not clear whether the existence of these mixed motives is fatal to the carer's restitutionary claim. In relation to this issue, both Rose[186] and McInnes[187] have recourse to authorities concerning maritime salvage[188] as the basis for the view that '... where a plaintiff acts from mixed motives, he may be able to recover if he acts *primarily* for the defendant's benefit or possibly even if he could merely show that the defendant derived *a* benefit from his acts'.[189] On this basis, it seems that the carer's claim is not precluded by mixed motives. The existence of these mixed motives does not detract from the conclusion that the carer, as a person who is close to the victim, is an appropriate person to intervene.

Payment of the victim's debts

In some cases, the victim's enrichment lies in being relieved of paying certain expenses which are paid by the carer. In general, an intervener who pays the debt of another does not discharge that debt unless the debtor subsequently ratifies the payment. However, there is growing support, both judicial and academic, for the view that when the payment is made under circumstances of necessity, the intervener's payment will discharge the victim's debt.[190] The

---

184 Examples include: *Benstead* v. *Murphy* (1994) 23 Alta LR (3d) 251; *Crane* v. *Worwood* (1992) 65 BCLR (2d) 16; *Feng* v. *Graham* (1988) 44 CCLT 52.
185 *Hall* v. *Miller* (1989) 41 BCLR (2d) 46.
186 F. Rose, 'Restitution for the Rescuer' (1989) 9 *Oxford Journal of Legal Studies* 167 at 196–8.
187 M. McInnes, 'Restitution and the Rescue of Life' (1994) 32 *Alberta Law Review* 37 at 60.
188 *The Winson* [1982] AC 939 at 966 PER LORD SIMON and at 962–963 PER LORD DIPLOCK.
189 N. 186 above at 196–7.
190 *Owen* v. *Tate* [1976] 1 QB 402 at 409–410 PER LORD SCARMAN; *The 'Zuhal K' and 'Selin'* [1987] 1 Lloyd's Rep 151 at 158 PER MR JUSTICE SHEEN; *Exall* v. *Partridge* (1799) 8 TR 308 at 311 PER BLANC J. Birks, p. 198; P. Birks and J. Beatson, 'Unrequested Payment of Another's

same argument applies when the carer intervenes to fulfil other obligations of a victim owed to a third party. It is arguable that these obligations of the victim are also discharged. The payment of the victim's debt, or fulfilment of the victim's other obligations, are thus a special application of the principles under discussion. These are additional examples of necessitous intervention which is not requested by the victim.

The facts of the cases do provide some evidence of a situation of necessity. In the cases where the carer has paid the victim's expenses[191] there is clearly a situation of necessity, as in each case the victim was injured requiring medical attention. In this situation it is often the case that the victim will be physically incapable of managing her day-to-day life and affairs, includ-ing the payment of her bills, medical or otherwise. This situation may be exacerbated by the victim's inability to pay. An example is the case of the injured nun Germaine Gachot. It is a reasonable inference that she did not have the personal resources to pay for her medical care. The judge identi-fied the payment of her expenses as having been made out of philanthropy, sympathy or other compassionate grounds.[192]

Hall v. *Miller*[193] is a case in which the victim is enriched by the carer's performance of his obligations to a third party. At the time of the carer's intervention, Mr Hall's incapacity had to a large degree been reversed. He had recovered from his injuries sufficiently well to seek other employment. Any necessity on the facts of this case lies in the fact that, if Mrs Hall had not assumed a portion of his obligations to their employer, Mr Hall would have remained unemployed.[194] He could not perform his contracted duties without her assistance.

Utility of necessity as an unjust factor

As demonstrated by the above discussion, it seems unlikely that a policy motivated analysis tied to the existence of a state of necessity satisfactorily can explain the carer's entitlement to share in the victim's damages. The first barrier is that the facts of the victim and carer cases do not actually reveal

---

Debt' (1976) *Law Quarterly Review* 188; Goff and Jones, pp. 16–17 and pp. 476–7; Burrows, p. 239; Mitchell, pp. 20–5; Virgo, pp. 225–30.

[191] *Coderre* v. *Ethier* (1978) 85 DLR (3d) 621; *Rawson* v. *Kasman* (1956) 3 DLR (2d) 376.

[192] *Coderre* v. *Ethier* (1978) 85 DLR (3d) 621 at 632 PER LERNER J.

[193] *Hall* v. *Miller* (1989) 41 BCLR (2d) 46.

[194] *Ibid.*, 48 PER SEATON JA who delivered the judgment of the British Columbia Court of Appeal.

the elements of the unjust factor. Although in a few rare cases all of the requirements may be met, it is difficult to see how the carer could successfully argue that the state of crisis which may have existed immediately following the victim's accident will continue far into the future. Similarly, even if it is possible to argue that the carer is unable rationally to communicate with the carer, it is unlikely that over time the victim's ability to communicate would not improve.

The second barrier to the analysis is a structural objection, which will be more fully explored in chapter 6. Put simply, the difficulty is that the carer's entitlement is not visible at the moment of the victim's receipt of the relevant enrichment. A necessity-based claim for the carer must arise at the moment of the defendant's receipt. Taken literally, this is the moment when the victim receives assistance from the carer. However, the carer's entitlement becomes visible only later in time, when the victim has successfully won damages from the victim. This logically takes us to the third barrier, which is that the carer apparently has a contingent entitlement to share in the damages won by the victim. The application of necessity as an unjust factor does not remove either of these difficulties. The carer's entitlement does not become visible until the victim has been successful in his suit and is not given on the basis of a prior right to be paid.

Conclusion

Although in some cases the court links the carer's participation to the necessitous and onerous nature of his intervention, it is clear that an unjust enrichment analysis predicated on necessity takes us little further in understanding the carer's right to share. It also suffers from an additional defect. The criticisms identified above relate to the use of necessity as an unjust factor. Even if the unjust enrichment analysis is abandoned, and reference is had merely to necessity as a general policy consideration which the courts have considered relevant when imposing a mechanism in favour of the carer, the identification of necessity as a policy rationale fails to assist. As has been shown, it fails to illuminate the apparently contingent nature of the carer's right to share. It does not explain why the carer's right becomes visible only when the victim has won damages from the wrongdoer.

Defences

The final element of an unjust enrichment claim is that there must be no defence available. The primary defence to an unjust enrichment claim is change of position, and this is discussed below. In addition, the more specialised defence of incapacity will be considered on the basis that, as we have discovered, many victims suffer some degree of incapacity.

Change of position

The defence of change of position is a general defence which applies to all claims founded in unjust enrichment. It operates to allow a defendant to set against the value received amounts expended on the faith of the receipt. A defendant who successfully raises change of position will persuade a court that it would be inequitable to force her to make restitution of the enrichment received, or at least to make restitution in full.[195]

Outline of the defence

The foundation of our modern understanding of the defence of change of position lies in the decision of the House of Lords in *Lipkin Gorman* v. *Karpnale Ltd*.[196] Lord Goff stated the elements of the defence as follows:[197]

> ... the defence is available to a person whose position has so changed that it would be inequitable in all circumstances to require him to make restitution, or alternatively to make restitution in full. I wish to stress however that the mere fact that the defendant has spent the money, in whole or in part, does not of itself render it inequitable that he should be called upon to repay, because the expenditure might in any event have been incurred by him in the ordinary course of things.

Recognition of the defence was a welcome development but, as acknowledged by Lord Goff himself, the formulation given in *Lipkin Gorman* was not very detailed, and it was envisaged that change of position would develop on a case-by-case basis.[198] The exact scope of the defence is thus

---

[195] *Lipkin Gorman* v. *Karpnale* [1991] 2 AC 548 at 580 PER LORD GOFF; *Dextra Bank and Trust Company Limited* v. *Bank of Jamaica* [2002] 1 All ER (Comm) 193 at 204–205 PER LORD BINGHAM AND LORD GOFF delivering the advice of the Privy Council.

[196] *Lipkin Gorman* v. *Karpnale* [1991] 2 AC 548.   [197] *Ibid.* at 580 PER LORD GOFF.

[198] N. 196 above at 580 PER LORD GOFF.

still subject to debate[199] and is emerging via a gradually developing case law.[200]

Change of position thus allows the defendant to subtract from the value of the enrichment received the value of certain disenrichments or reductions in wealth which would not have occurred but for the enrichment. In this way, the value which the defendant is obligated to return to the claimant by way of restitution is reduced. The overriding objective of the defence is to recognise that, on certain facts, it would be inequitable to require the defendant to make restitution. In applying this defence three key elements merit attention: (1) to identify those outgoings or disenrichments which will qualify for the defence; (2) to clarify whether the enrichment must actually be received prior to the disenrichment; and (3) to determine the relevance of fault to the application of the defence.

The first task is to identify those outgoings which will qualify for the application of change of position. There must be some causal connection between receipt of the enrichment and the change of position. The defendant must rely on the validity of the receipt.[201] In proving detrimental reliance, it seems that it is not necessary that a particular item of expenditure be cited as proof of change of position. In a case involving a series of periodic overpayments, the defendants were permitted to raise an increased general level of expenditure as relevant disenrichment.[202] In addition to a

---

[199] P. Birks, 'Change of Position and Surviving Enrichment' in W. Swadling (ed.), *The Limits of Restitutionary Claims* (London, 1997), pp. 36–63; Birks and Mitchell, pp. 610–15 and p. 630; R. Chambers, 'Change of Position on the Faith of the Receipt' [1996] *Restitution Law Review* 100; E. Fung and L. Ho, 'Change of Position and Estoppel' (2001) 117 *Law Quarterly Review* 14; E. Fung and L. Ho, 'Establishing Estoppel After the Recognition of Change of Position' [2001] *Restitution Law Review* 52; Goff and Jones, pp. 818–28; M. Jewell, 'The Boundaries of Change of Position – A Comparative Study' [2000] *Restitution Law Review* 1; P. Key, 'Change of Position' (1995) 58 *Modern Law Review* 505; R. Nolan, 'Change of Position' in P. Birks (ed.), *Laundering and Tracing* (Oxford, 1995), pp. 136–89; Virgo, pp. at 709–30.

[200] *Scottish Equitable* v. *Derby* [2001] 3 All ER 818; *Amoco (UK) Exploration Co* v. *Imperial Chemical Industries plc* unreported 30 July 1999 noted Mitchell [2000] *Restitution Law Review* 332; *South Tyneside Metropolitan BC* v. *Svenska International* [1995] 1 All ER 545; *Dextra Bank & Trust Company Limited* v. *Bank of Jamaica* [2002] 1 All ER (Comm) 193; *National Bank of New Zealand* v. *Waitaki International Processing Ltd* [2000] 2 NZLR 1; *RBC Dominion Securities Inc.* v. *Dawson* (1994) 111 DLR (4th) 230; *Gertsch* v. *Atsas* [1999] NSWSC 898; *Phillip Collins Ltd* v. *Davis* [2000] 3 All ER 806; *National Westminster Bank plc* v. *Somer International (UK) Ltd* [2002] 1 All ER 198.

[201] *Scottish Equitable* v. *Derby* [2001] 3 All ER 818 at 827–828 PER ROBERT WALKER LJ; *Amoco (UK) Exploration Co* v. *Imperial Chemical Industries plc* unreported 30 July 1999.

[202] *Phillip Collins Ltd* v. *Davis* [2000] 3 All ER 806 at 829–830 PER JONATHAN PARKER J; *Scottish Equitable* v. *Derby* [2001] 3 All ER 818 at 827–828 PER ROBERT WALKER LJ.

causal relationship between the enrichment and the change of position, the defence will apply only if the expenditure is extraordinary. As emphasised by Lord Goff, if the expenditure might in any event have been incurred by the defendant in the ordinary course of things, then the defence will not be available.[203]

The second issue is one of timing. It is not necessary that the enrichment has in fact been received prior to the change of position. On the facts of *Lipkin Gorman* the claimant was permitted to aggregate its net payments against receipts. This meant, in effect, that the defendant casino incurred some losses prior to receiving the stake in respect of which the loss was incurred. More recent authority affirms that the change of position defence can succeed '... where the alleged change occurs before receipt of the money'.[204] In *Dextra Bank & Trust Company Limited* v. *Bank of Jamaica*[205] the Privy Council clarified this issue. Although speaking only *obiter*, Lord Bingham and Lord Goff unequivocally confirmed that anticipatory expenditures will qualify for the defence of change of position:[206]

> ... it is difficult to see what relevant distinction can be drawn between (1) a case in which the defendant expends on some extraordinary expenditure all or part of a sum of money which he has received from the plaintiff, and (2) one in which the defendant incurs such expenditure in the expectation that he will receive the sum of money from the plaintiff, which he does in fact receive ... It is true that, in the second case, the defendant relied on the payment being made to him in the future (as well as relying on such payment, when

---

[203] N. 196 above at 580 PER LORD GOFF; *RBC Dominion Securities Inc* v. *Dawson* (1994) 111 DLR (4th) 230; *Gertsch* v. *Atsas* [1999] NSWSC 898; *Scottish Equitable* v. *Derby* [2001] 3 All ER 818; *Phillip Collins Ltd* v. *Davis* [2000] 3 All ER 806.

[204] *South Tyneside Borough Council* v. *Svenska International* [1995] 1 All ER 545 at 565 PER CLARKE J. On the facts of *Svenska* the claimant was not in the end entitled to assert this defence as the underlying transaction pursuant to which the payments were made was null and void. '... if a net payee can show that it has altered its position in good faith after receipt of money under a swap from the net payer it might in principle be entitled to rely on the defence of change of position. What it cannot do is rely on the supposed validity of the transaction because the transaction is and has always been void.' *South Tyneside Borough Council* v. *Svenska International* [1995] 1 All ER 545 at 567 PER CLARKE J. The Privy Council has subsequently referred to the decision of Clarke J and noted that '... the exclusion of anticipatory reliance in that case depended on the exceptional facts of the case; though it is right to record that the decision of Clarke J has been the subject of criticism'. *Dextra Bank and Trust Company Limited* v. *Bank of Jamaica* [2002] 1 All ER (Comm) 193 at 205 PER LORD BINGHAM AND LORD GOFF.

[205] *Dextra Bank & Trust Company Limited* v. *Bank of Jamaica* [2002] 1 All ER (Comm) 193.

[206] *Ibid.*, 204–205 PER LORD BINGHAM AND LORD GOFF.

made, being a valid payment); but, provided that his change of position was in good faith, it should provide, pro tanto at least, a good defence because it makes it inequitable to make the defendant to make restitution, or restitution in full.

The final element is to determine the role of fault in the application of the defence – in particular, whether the fault of the defendant will preclude reliance on the defence. In his original formulation of the defence articulated in *Lipkin Gorman*, Lord Goff stated that '... the defence is not open to one who has changed his position in bad faith, as where the defendant has paid away the money with knowledge of the facts entitling the plaintiff to restitution; and it is commonly accepted that the defence should not be open to a wrongdoer'.[207] The requirement of good faith was again highlighted in *Dextra*. Their Lordships regarded '... good faith on the part of the recipient as a sufficient requirement in this context...'[208] and rejected the notion that good faith should be assessed by examining the relative fault of the parties. Bad faith has been interpreted to mean dishonesty[209] and usually means something more than mere carelessness.

The limitation as to wrongdoers is also subject to variable interpretation. Birks and Mitchell[210] argue that this exclusion simply reflects the fact that a claim to recover a gain made as a result of wrongdoing, and therefore not a claim in unjust enrichment, is not susceptible to the defence. Virgo[211] takes a more literal interpretation, suggesting that some wrongdoers are not entitled to rely on the defence and that the court should have regard to the nature of the wrong committed in deciding this issue.

Application to the victim and carer cases

The question is whether the victim might be entitled to raise the defence of change of position. It seems likely that the question will be answered in the affirmative. The core configuration in the victim and carer cases is of the victim who receives gratuitous services from the carer. In such circumstances, as we have seen, it is likely that the victim has thereby been factually relieved of the need to engage a commercial care provider. In this

---

[207] N. 196 above at 580 PER LORD GOFF.

[208] N. 205 above at 207 PER LORD BINGHAM AND LORD GOFF.

[209] Birks and Mitchell, p. 613. Virgo suggests a higher threshold than dishonesty, suggesting that bad faith is an uncertain standard but would clearly exclude the defendant that has 'committed fraud or duress or had been participating in an illegal transaction'. Virgo, pp. 720–1.

[210] Birks and Mitchell, p. 613.   [211] Virgo, p. 721.

way, the victim may have greater financial resources available to spend, thus raising the possibility of change of position. In establishing the defence two primary difficulties will be faced by the victim. First, to establish a sufficient causal connection between the benefits provided by the carer and the relevant outgoings. Secondly, to persuade the court that these outgoings are sufficiently extraordinary.

Turning first to the issue of causation. As we have seen, the key is to identify expenditure which would not have happened, but for receipt of the relevant enrichment. On the basis that the carer's intervention has freed financial resources which might otherwise be deployed to pay medical expenses or meet the cost of care, it seems it will be relatively easy to establish the necessary causal connection.

More difficult will be to demonstrate that the outgoings would not have been incurred by the victim in the ordinary course of things. It is easy to construct facts in which the victim does incur extraordinary expense, for example takes a holiday which would otherwise be unaffordable. In Gertsch v Atsas,[212] the court weighed up the advantages and disadvantages accruing to the defendant from the receipt of money paid under a bequest. The recipient was entitled to set against her receipt, income which would have been earned had she not, on the faith of the legacy, given up her employment and pursued university education.[213] Such extraordinary expenditure therefore qualifies for the defence. However, it is also likely that the victim will incur an increased level of expenditure on day-to-day items. So long as the causal connection between receipt of the enrichment and the relevant expenditure is established, the defence will be available to '... the person who lives at a higher standard of living because more money is available but would not have done so but for the windfall'.[214]

The additional requirements of the defence are that it is not available to a recipient who has changed her position in bad faith or is a wrongdoer. The qualification concerning wrongdoers is unlikely to cause difficulty in the victim and carer example. However, a possible complication arises on the ground of good faith in those rare cases where the victim has promised to pay the carer. In these cases, even though the arrangements between the parties may not have the formal status of contract, it is nonetheless the case that the victim has agreed to pay for care. In such circumstances, it seems

---

[212] Gertsch v. Atsas [1999] NSWSC 898.   [213] Ibid., para. 98 PER FOSTER AJ.

[214] RBC Dominion Securities Inc v. Dawson (1994) 111 DLR (4th) 230 at 239–240 PER CAMERON JA who delivered the judgment of the Newfoundland Court of Appeal.

unlikely that the victim would be entitled to set against the value of the carer's claim any relevant disenrichments since, by virtue of the agreement to pay, the victim has '...knowledge of the facts entitling the plaintiff to restitution'.[215]

Incapacity

The role of defences in unjust enrichment has become more prominent as the grounds of claim have expanded. While the carer's claim is as vulnerable as any other to a defence raised by the victim, a defence arising from the victim's incapacity is particularly relevant. As was discussed at the start of this chapter, many victims suffer some degree of incapacity. In particular, there are victims who suffer mental impairment[216] or are of a very young age.[217] The question is whether this incapacity allows them to escape restitutionary liability to the carer.

The speech of Lord Goff in *Westdeutsche Landesbank Girozentrale* v. *Islington London Borough Council* touches on the incapacity defence in an unjust enrichment claim, although the incapacity in that case arose as a result of the ultra vires nature of the transaction which had been entered into by Islington LBC. However, Lord Goff's speech is helpful for this analysis, because he articulates the policy imperative that a claim in unjust enrichment should not be permitted if it would indirectly enforce a contract which is otherwise invalid by reason of the defendant's incapacity. Speaking of the decision of the House of Lords in *Sinclair* v. *Brougham* [1914] AC 398, he said that he himself inclined against the view that the personal claim in restitution would indirectly enforce the ultra vires contract. However, he nonetheless defended the need to ask the question whether on other facts incapacity might affect an unjust enrichment claim:[218]

I recognise that nowadays cases of incapacity are relatively rare, though the swaps litigation shows that they still can occur. Even so, the question could still arise whether, in the case of a borrowing contract rendered void because

---

[215] N. 196 above at 580 PER LORD GOFF.

[216] For example: *McLeod* v. *Palardy* (1980) 4 Man R (2d) 218; *Yepremian et al* v. *Scarborough General Hospital et al* (1980) 110 DLR (3d) 513; *Roberts* v. *Johnstone* [1988] 3 WLR 1247 (also seven years old); *Roach* v. *Yates* [1938] 1 KB 256.

[217] For example: *Arnold* v. *Teno* (1978) 83 DLR (3d) 609 ($4\frac{1}{2}$ years); *Lapensee* v. *Ottawa Day Nursery* (1986) 35 CCLT 129 ($15\frac{1}{2}$ months); *Lunnon* v. *Reagh* (1978) 25 NSR (2d) 196 (six years); *Donnelly* v. *Joyce* [1974] 1 QB 454 (six years).

[218] *Westdeutsche Landesbank Girozentrale* v. *Islington London Borough Council* [1996] AC 669 at 688 PER LORD GOFF.

it was ultra vires the borrower, it would be contrary to public policy to allow a personal claim in restitution. Such a question has arisen in the past in relation not only to associations such as the Birkbeck Permanent Building Society, but also in relation to infants' contracts. Moreover, there is a respectable body of opinion that, if such a case arose today, it should still be held that public policy would preclude a personal claim in restitution, though not of course by reference to an implied contract. That was the opinion expressed by Leggatt, LJ in the Court of Appeal in the present case [1994] 1 W.L.R. 938, 952E–F, as it had been by Hobhouse J; and the same view has been expressed by Professor Birks (see *An Introduction to the Law of Restitution* (1985), p. 374). I myself incline to the opinion that a personal claim in restitution would not indirectly enforce the ultra vires contract...

Minors

Minors have limited contractual capacity to contract for necessaries.[219] The cases in this study are however primarily concerned with benefits which have been conferred outside of contract. We must come to some view about whether, in the same way as a contract for necessaries, the minor should be required to make restitution or whether the incapacity prevents the carer's claim.

The model of liability in unjust enrichment which has been adopted in this book is that which is sensitive to the need to create and maintain an accurate taxonomy. Logic therefore dictates that, given that contract and unjust enrichment are different events, there is no particular reason why a defence which is not available in relation to one generic class of event should be unavailable in another. Thus, the mere fact that a minor must pay for necessaries should not mean that the minor is liable to make restitution in respect of the same benefits conferred outside of a contractual relationship.

However, the reasons underpinning the minor's contractual liability to pay for necessaries are also present in the victim and carer cases. Lord Goff's objection that the unjust enrichment claim should not indirectly enforce an unenforceable contract therefore cannot apply. The benefits in most cases in this study are necessary.[220] The victim's injuries necessitate the services

---

[219] *Nash* v. *Inman* [1908] 2 KB 1; Minors Contracts Act 1987 s. 3 (1) and (2); Goff and Jones, pp. 640–51; Virgo, pp. 758–60.

[220] Perhaps the only exception to this statement are the expenses incurred by the carer in attending the victim. It is difficult to see how these expenses, as opposed to the services rendered by the carer, are capable of generating any enrichment for the victim. *Schneider* v. *Eisovitch* [1960] 2 QB 430; *Wilson* v. *McLeay* (1961) 106 CLR 523.

provided by the carer. In the same way, the debts discharged by the carer's payment arise out of the victim's injury. For this reason, it might be argued that the victim's incapacity should provide no defence to the carer's unjust enrichment claim.[221]

Mental incapacity

The parallel argument is that the mentally incapacitated victim should likewise be required to reverse her unjust enrichment. This also relies on the quality of the benefits as necessaries in denying the victim a defence to the carer's claim.[222]

Conclusion

This discussion has only dealt with clear cases of incapacity arising from mental impairment or minority. The vast majority of cases in this study, however, concern victims who, while they suffer debilitating illness and injury, do not fall into either of these categories. Although the analysis of Lord Donaldson MR in *In re T. (Adult: Refusal of Treatment)*[223] provides some assistance in determining whether the victim is capable of consenting to the carer's intervention, it is still a question to be determined on the facts of each case. It seems reasonable to argue that, by analogy with minors and the mentally impaired, those victims suffering the effects of shock, pain and drugs will likewise have no defence of incapacity to the carer's unjust enrichment claim.

Claim in negotiorum gestio

An alternative basis of claim which some would argue should be available to the carer is the principle of negotiorum gestio. Strictly speaking, this

---

[221] Birks, pp. 433–7; Burrows and McKendrick, pp. 892–900; Virgo, pp. 758–60.

[222] *Williams* v. *Wentworth* (1842) 5 Beav 325 at 329 PER LORD LANGDALE MR. Goff and Jones, pp. 636–7; Virgo, p. 736. The intervener in *In Re Rhodes* (1890) 44 Ch D 94 would have been successful in his claim against the incapax had it not been erroneously thought that it was necessary for him to show an intention to charge. Irrespective of whether we agree with that analysis, once it is accepted that this is a matter going to the intervener's right to claim, but not to a defence available to the incapax, this case is also authority for the victim's liability to make restitution. Burrows, pp. 456–7.

[223] *In re T (Adult: Refusal of Treatment)* [1992] 3 WLR 782 at 799 PER LORD DONALDSON MR.

principle should not appear in a consideration of the carer's unjust enrichment claim, as it is a source of rights and obligations consonant only with a compensatory rather than a restitutionary response. However, commentators suggest that the cases which are taken as evidence of the existence of an unjust enrichment claim for the intervener might also be explained in terms of negotiorum gestio.[224] It is for this reason that this brief discussion appears in this chapter. The following analysis is included only in the interests of completeness. It is not intended to conduct an in depth assessment of the existence or utility of negotiorum gestio. The question whether the common law does or does not recognise negotiorum gestio requires a book of its own.

In many civilian systems, it is on this basis that the claim of the carer would be considered. Negotiorum gestio is the conduct of another's affairs without any mandate to do so. Roman law and roman-based systems allow such uninvited interveners to recover their expenses, provided the intervention is useful and not officiously given. This claim is not founded on contract or unjust enrichment. It is a claim for recompense of the carer's expenses, and in some cases, compensation for the time and effort employed in assisting the victim.[225]

The common law does not officially recognise negotiorum gestio as a basis for recovery.[226] However, scholars argue that there is some evidence for an emerging common law doctrine of negotiorum gestio.[227] It may be that development of the common law will provide a remedy to the carer as gestor on this basis. At least in those cases in which the carer has incurred expenses in coming to the assistance of the victim, and in which we have had difficulty identifying an enrichment in the hands of the victim, the principle of negotiorum gestio would seem to be applicable. For example, the £110 spent by Mr and Mrs Taylor in coming to the assistance of Betty Schneider

---

[224] S. Stoljar, 'Negotiorum Gestio' in *The International Encyclopaedia of Comparative Law* vol. X (London, 1984) 10; S. Stoljar, *The Law of Quasi Contract* (2nd edn., Sydney, 1989), chapter 7; P. Birks, 'Negotiorum Gestio and the Common Law' (1971) 24 *Current Legal Problems* 110; G. Muir, 'Unjust Sacrifice and the Officious Intervener' in P. Finn (ed.), *Essays on Restitution* (Sydney, 1990) 297.

[225] S. Stoljar, 'Negotiorum Gestio' in *The International Encyclopaedia of Comparative Law* vol. X (London, 1984) 10, pp. 41–3.

[226] *Ibid.*, p. 33.

[227] P. Birks, 308; P. Birks, 'Negotiorum Gestio and the Common Law' (1971) 24 *Current Legal Problems* 110; S. Stoljar, 'Negotiorum Gestio' in *The International Encyclopaedia of Comparative Law* vol. X (London, 1984) 10, pp. 35–6. For a contrary view, L. Aitken, 'Negotiorum Gestio and the Common Law: A Jurisdictional Approach' (1988) 11 *Sydney Law Review* 566.

might be recoverable on this basis.[228] Additionally, a negotiorum gestio analysis is consistent with those cases in which the carer's contribution includes, in part, the management of the victim's life and affairs.[229]

Conclusion

This chapter demonstrates that the victim is often unjustly enriched at the carer's expense. The key to understanding this lies in the injuries and incapacity suffered by all of the victims in this study. Although in particular cases the claim may fail, it seems that in every case the victim is likely to have been incontrovertibly enriched. More difficult is the identification of an unjust factor. In some cases it might successfully be argued that the carer intervenes in circumstances of necessity. However, necessity cannot explain every case, and the other unjust factors garner little support. Chapter 8 argues that the law of unjust enrichment includes a novel policy motivated unjust factor called the policy against accumulation. As will be shown, this unjust factor provides a more secure basis on which to rest the carer's unjust enrichment claim.

This chapter has not properly addressed the question whether the carer's unjust enrichment claim is capable of explaining the carer's right to participate in the victim's damages and further, the fact that in some cases this right is proprietary. The purpose of this chapter has only been to show that on some facts the victim is unjustly enriched at the carer's expense. The consequence of this conclusion will be dealt with in later chapters.

---

[228] For example: *Schneider* v. *Eisovitch* [1960] 2 QB 430; *Wilson* v. *McLeay* (1961) 106 CLR 523.
[229] For example: *D'Ambrosio* v. *DeSouza Lima* [1983] 60 ACTR 18 at 20 PER BLACKBURN CJ; *Treonne Wholesale Meats* v. *Shaheen* (1988) 12 NSWLR 522.

5

The carer's claim in tort

Analogies with the position of rescuers, and developments in the law relating
to recovery of purely economic loss, suggest that the carer might hope to
have a cause of action in tort against the wrongdoer. There are in fact some
cases in which the carer has pursued her own claim.[1] However, this chapter
will conclude that they are unreliable and confirm the assumption made in
Hunt v. *Severs* that the carer in general has no such action:[2]

> The voluntary carer has no cause of action of his own against the tortfeasor.
> The justice of allowing the injured plaintiff to recover the value of the services
> so that he may recompense the voluntary carer has been generally recognised,
> but there has been difficulty in articulating a consistent juridical principle to
> justify this result.

A possible claim in negligence?

The carer's action can only lie in negligence. There is no purpose in pursuing
the limited potential of the old cause of action called actio per quod consortium et servitium amisit which is occasionally mentioned in this context.[3]
In most jurisdictions it has been abolished and it is of limited utility to this
analysis.[4]

---

[1] For example: *Kiddell* v. *Kulczycki* [1977] 3 WWR 216; *Lang* v. *Ballash* (1989) 72 Alta LR (2d)
306; *Mills* v. *British Rail Engineering Limited* [1992] PIQR Q130; *Riordon* v. *Palmer* (1989) 226
APR 326; *Roberts* v. *Bailey* (1975) 10 NBR (2d) 212; *Stevens et al* v. *Kachman* (1978) 10 AR 192;
Stewart et al v. *Mayer* (1990) 243 APR 298; *Veivers* v. *Connolly* (1994) Aust Torts Rep ¶81–309.
[2] *Hunt* v. *Severs* [1994] 2 AC 350 at 358 PER LORD BRIDGE with whom the other members of
the House agreed. The Law Commission has rejected the enactment of a statutory claim for the
carer. UK Law Commission, *Damages for Personal Injury: Medical, Nursing and Other Expenses;
Collateral Benefits* (Law Com No 262, 1999), para. 3.53.
[3] For example: *Caltex Oil (Australia) Pty Ltd* v. *The Dredge 'Willemstad'* (1976) 136 CLR 529 at
575 PER STEPHEN J; *Kirkham* v. *Boughey* [1958] 2 QB 338 at 342 PER DIPLOCK J.
[4] Abolished in England by the Administration of Justice Act 1982, s. 2. Abolished in the Australian
Capital Territory: Law Reform (Miscellaneous Provisions) Act 1955 s. 32, inserted by Law Reform

The loss experienced by the carer is purely economic loss, in the sense that it does not flow from injury to the carer or to her property. For example, the carer frequently forgoes income and incurs expenses, such as travelling costs, when intervening to assist the victim. The cases also show evidence that the carer suffers financial loss when meeting obligations, such as the victim's obligation to pay for medical treatment. These facts are important because, as will be discussed later in this chapter, there is in general no recovery for purely economic loss unless the facts fall within the pocket[5] of cases identified with the decision of the House of Lords in *Hedley Byrne & Co Ltd* v. *Heller & Partners*.[6] The following discussion will briefly set out the categories of case in which the recovery of economic loss has been permitted. These are: (1) economic loss consequent on physical injury to the person; and (2) economic loss consequent on damage to property. The discussion will then investigate possible claims for the carer pursuant to the rule in *Hedley Byrne & Co Ltd* v. *Heller & Partners*, or via the recognition of a novel category of claim.

Physical injury to the person

Pure economic loss is recoverable where it flows from negligently caused physical injury to the claimant. However, where this loss is a result of negligent physical injury to another person such as the victim, the claimant carer apparently has no claim for her own economic loss flowing from the victim's physical injuries. Each of these situations will be dealt with in turn.

(Miscellaneous Provisions) Act (No 2) 1991 s. 5; New South Wales: Law Reform (Marital Consortium) Act 1984 s. 3; Tasmania: Common Law (Miscellaneous Actions) Act 1986 s. 3; Western Australia: Law Reform (Miscellaneous Provisions Act) 1941 s. 3 inserted by the Acts Amendment (Actions for Damages) Act 1986 s. 4(1). It seems that where a wife is injured in a motor vehicle accident, the action is also excluded in Victoria: Transport Accident Act 1986 s. 93(1); and the Northern Territory: Motor Accidents (Compensation) Act 1979 s. 5. Abolished in: British Columbia: Family Relations Act RSBC 1979, c121, s. 75; Manitoba: Equality of Status Act RSM 1987, cE130, s. 1(1)(c); New Brunswick: An Act Respecting Compliance of the Laws of the Province with the Canadian Charter of Rights and Freedoms, 1985, SNB 1985, c. 41, s. 4; Ontario: Family Law Reform Act, RSO 1980, c. 152, s. 69(3) as amended by Family Law Act 1986 SO 1986, c. 4, s. 71(4); Saskatchewan: Equality of Status of Married Persons Act, SS 1984–85–86, c. E-10.3, s. 6.

[5] J. Stapleton, 'Duty of Care and Economic Loss: A Wider Agenda' (1991) 107 *Law Quarterly Review* 249; J. Stapleton, 'In Restraint of Tort' in P. Birks (ed.), *The Frontiers of Liability, Volume 2* (Oxford, 1994); J. Stapleton, 'Duty of Care: Peripheral Parties and Alternative Opportunities for Deterrence' (1995) 111 *Law Quarterly Review* 301.

[6] *Hedley Byrne & Co Ltd* v. *Heller & Partners* [1964] AC 465.

Physical injury suffered by the carer

Economic or financial losses are recoverable where they are the result of physical injury to the claimant. It is well established that a personal injury claimant may, subject to the satisfaction of the other elements of liability, successfully claim from the wrongdoer the value of income lost as a result of the claimant's injuries.[7] There will also be a claim for estimated future income loss, subject to adjustment for factors such as the future employment prospects for the claimant, the vicissitudes of life and the use of an appropriate multiplier.[8]

The cases in this study do not in general concern carers who have themselves suffered negligently inflicted injury. Rather, it is the victim who is incapacitated. There are rare examples of cases in which the tortfeasor's negligence also causes the carer to suffer physical injury.[9] However, the injury to the carer in these cases is not productive of economic loss relevant to this discussion. The economic loss flows only from injury to the victim. For example, in *Kiddell* v. *Kulczycki*,[10] the car containing both Colin and Jean Kiddell collided with the defendant's vehicle. Jean Kiddell was rendered a quadriplegic, and suffered a lengthy period of post-traumatic amnesia. Her husband sustained minor whiplash, but was able to visit his wife during her period of hospitalisation. He successfully claimed damages, including an amount representing his financial costs incurred in visiting his wife during the five months that she was in hospital.[11] His economic loss was a result only of his wife's injuries. Such amounts are therefore not recoverable as financial losses flowing from the carer's own physical injuries.

Physical injury suffered by the victim

There is said to be no duty of care owed to a claimant pursuant to which the claimant can sue the wrongdoer for economic loss resulting from physical injury to a third party. For example, it would ordinarily be thought that the carer could have no claim for economic loss flowing from an injury to the victim. *Kirkham* v. *Boughey* is such an example where the carer's claim was denied.[12] Thomas and Nora Kirkham had been living in Nigeria but

---

[7] *Phillips* v. *L & SW Ry* (1879) 5 CPD 280.   [8] Clerk and Lindsell, pp. 1570–8.
[9] For example: *Kiddell* v. *Kulczycki* [1977] 3 WWR 216; *Benstead* v. *Murphy* (1994) 23 Alta LR (3d) 251, although in this case the suit was brought by the victim Wendy Benstead.
[10] *Kiddell* v. *Kulczycki* [1977] 3 WWR 216.   [11] *Ibid.*, 246 PER WRIGHT J.
[12] *Kirkham* v. *Boughey* [1958] 2 QB 338.

were visiting England. Nora Kirkham was injured in a car accident and hospitalised for a period of almost five months. Her husband Thomas did not return to his employment in Nigeria, but stayed in England to care for his children and also because he was anxious about his wife's condition.[13]

Thomas sued the wrongdoer, claiming damages for his lost earnings during this period.[14] He submitted that he was entitled to receive a sum representing the difference between the amount that he in fact earned during the period of his wife's incapacity, and the amount that he would have earned had he returned to his more highly paid job in Nigeria. This part of his claim failed. Diplock J stated that, leaving aside any claim which Thomas Kirkham may have had against the negligent driver of the car based on his '... right, in the nature of a proprietary right, to consortium...',[15] no duty of care was owed to him in respect of his forgone income:[16]

> But the disputed item of damages does not fall under either of these heads. It is not claimed as damages for loss of consortium; indeed, the particulars do not suggest that the loss of wages was due to any other cause than the husband's own injuries. Mr Harington repudiates the suggestion that his right to these damages is based on loss of consortium. He submits that, provided I am satisfied that the husband acted reasonably, he must be put in as good a position, so far as money can do it, as if the wrong had not been done to him. But this submission begs the question: what was the wrong done to him? If the husband had not been present at the time of the accident the wrong would have been limited to the injury to his quasi-proprietary right to the consortium of his wife, and it is conceded that the disputed head of damages, as contrasted for the claim for domestic assistance, cannot be claimed under this head. Does it make any difference that in this case the husband was present at the accident and sustained personal injuries himself? While he is, of course, entitled to recover those damages which flow from his own injuries, I do not see how this can enlarge the measure of his damages for the quite separate wrong to his quasi-proprietary interest in the consortium of his wife.

[13] The trial judge held that this was a reasonable course of action for Thomas to follow. *Ibid.*, 341 PER DIPLOCK J.

[14] He also successfully claimed damages in respect of his expenses incurred in visiting his wife in hospital and the costs of domestic help and looking after his children. N. 12 above at 340 PER DIPLOCK J.

[15] N. 12 above at 342 PER DIPLOCK J. However, this would have provided no avenue of redress for the care given by Mr Kirkham as this cause of action was directed only at the loss of the comfort and services of his wife.

[16] N. 12 above at 342–343 PER DIPLOCK J.

Injury to property

Economic loss is recoverable where it flows from damage to the claimant's own property.[17] In order to recover, the claimant must have a proprietary or a possessory interest in the property negligently damaged by the defendant.[18] Recovery may also be allowed where the loss flows from damage to the property of a third party. In this category, the facts must fall within a specialised exception known as the general average exception.[19] This is an exception to the general requirement that the claimant must have had an interest in the property damaged by the defendant's negligence.

It is immediately obvious that the facts of the victim and carer cases do not involve economic loss flowing from the property of the carer, or damage to a ship on which the carer's cargo is being carried. The carer can therefore have no viable claim for his economic loss generated by the care provided to the victim on the basis that the loss flows from damage to her property.

Remaining possibilities for the carer

The discussion so far shows that the carer will never be able to build a satisfactory claim on the foundation of damage to person or property. It follows that a claim for the carer's economic losses must rest either on *Hedley Byrne & Co Ltd* v. *Heller & Partners* as now understood, or must take the form of a novel claim. Each of these possibilities will be reviewed in the next section which deals with the possible duty of care owed by the tortfeasor to the carer. It is best to state at the outset that this chapter will consider only the possible duty of care which may be owed to the carer. In order for the carer's claim to succeed, the other elements of liability will of course have to be established: breach of duty, causation, remoteness of damage and the possibility of any defences available to the tortfeasor. Although these additional requirements are important, the threshold difficulty for the carer will be to establish the existence of a duty of care, and it is on this issue alone that the discussion will focus.

---

[17] *Marc Rich & Co AG* v. *Bishop Rock Marine Co Ltd* [1996] 1 AC 211. In that case the owner of cargo aboard the *Nicholas H* claimed a portion of its loss from the classification society which had certified the vessel seaworthy just prior to the vessel sinking a few days later. A majority of the House of Lords refused the cargo owner's claim, but did not dispute the general entitlement of the owner of goods to bring such a claim.

[18] *Candlewood Navigation Corporation Ltd* v. *Mitsui OSK Lines Ltd* [1986] AC 1.

[19] *Morrison Steamship Co Ltd* v. *Greystoke Castle (Cargo Owners)* [1947] AC 265.

Duty of care

The inquiry as to whether the defendant owes a duty of care conceptually is divided into two questions. The first asks whether the claimant belongs to the class of persons to whom a duty of care is in general owed by the defendant. This duty of care is described as the notional duty of care, and applies to a general category of relationship and damage.[20] The question is whether the facts of the victim and carer cases fall into a general category of case in which it has already been determined that a duty of care exists. The category of potential application in the victim and carer cases is that arising pursuant to the decision of the House of Lords in *Hedley Byrne*. The second question determines whether a duty of care, sometimes called the factual duty of care or the duty to a particular claimant, exists on the facts of the case. The purpose of this inquiry is to discover whether, on the facts of the case, a duty of care should properly be owed by the defendant to the claimant. Even if the case under consideration does not fall adequately within an established category, this is not fatal to the existence of a duty of care. The law has developed a so-called 'universal test of notional duty', which is said to be capable of application across a variety of categories of case in order to determine whether a duty of care exists.[21] As is set out on pp. 125–36 below, it is sometimes possible to establish a novel category of claim.

The following discussion will identify any duty of care owed by the tortfeasor to the carer in respect of the economic loss suffered by the carer. The discussion will deal with the possible duty of care arising pursuant to: (1) the principle associated with *Hedley Byrne & Co Ltd* v. *Heller & Partners*[22]; and (2) the existence of a novel claim. There will also be brief reference to the position in Australia and Canada.

---

[20] Clerk and Lindsell, pp. 276–80.

[21] 'What emerges is that, in addition to the foreseeability of damage, necessary ingredients in any situation giving rise to a duty of care are that there should exist between the party owing the duty and the party to whom it is owed a relationship characterised by the law as one of "proximity" or "neighbourhood" and that the situation should be one in which the court considers it fair, just and reasonable that the law should impose a duty of a given scope on the one party for the benefit of the other.' *Caparo Industries plc* v. *Dickman* [1990] 2 AC 605 at 617–618 PER LORD BRIDGE. Refer to *Donoghue* v. *Stevenson* [1932] AC 562; *Dorset Yacht Co Ltd* v. *Home Office* [1970] AC 1004; *Anns* v. *Merton London Borough Council* [1978] AC 728; *Murphy* v. *Brentwood District Council* [1991] 1 AC 398; *Marc Rich & Co AG* v. *Bishop Rock Marine Co Ltd* [1996] 1 AC 211; *Mulcahy* v. *Ministry of Defence* [1996] 2 All ER 758.

[22] *Hedley Byrne & Co Ltd* v. *Heller & Partners* [1964] AC 465; *Williams* v. *Natural Life Health Foods Ltd* [1998] 1 WLR 830.

Hedley Byrne & Co Ltd *v.* Heller & Partners

Strictly speaking, *Hedley Byrne & Co Ltd* v. *Heller & Partners* confirms the existence of a duty of care in tort owed to a claimant who has suffered pure economic loss resulting from the defendant's negligent misstatement. The facts of the victim and carer cases are clearly beyond the scope of this principle. However, recent decisions give limited support for the view that this category may also include the economic loss experienced as a result of the negligent provision of services.[23] *Hedley Byrne* will briefly be recounted in order to lay the foundation for the discussion of the expanded version of the rule which appears below on pp. 118–24.

The decision

The facts of *Hedley Byrne* are as follows. Hedley Byrne & Co was an advertising agency. It had placed on credit terms orders for advertising time on television, and in certain newspapers, on behalf of its client Easipower Ltd. Hedley Byrne was liable for the cost of this advertising but intended to pass the cost to Easipower. Concerned about the credit worthiness of Easipower, Hedley Byrne obtained a bankers' reference from Heller & Partners, which reported the satisfactory financial condition of Easipower. Although the reference was expressed to be 'without responsibility', Hedley Byrne relied on the reference and refrained from cancelling the advertising orders, believing it could pass these costs to Easipower. Unfortunately, the reference was inaccurate and Easipower went into liquidation. As a result, Hedley Byrne suffered economic loss measured by the value of the advertising contracts it had entered into on Easipower's behalf. Hedley Byrne instituted proceedings claiming damages in respect of this loss from Heller & Partners.

Hedley Byrne's claim failed. The House of Lords held that the disclaimer weighed against the finding that a duty of care was owed. However, their Lordships held that in general, the maker of a negligent statement owes a duty of care to a person who suffers economic loss in reliance on that statement. Different members of the House formulated the requirements for showing the existence of a duty of care in slightly differing terms. However,

---

[23] Such as that caused by the solicitor to the intended beneficiaries of his client's estate in *White* v. *Jones* [1995] 2 AC 207 and the employer in *Spring* v. *Guardian Assurance plc* [1995] 2 AC 296 who provided a reference on behalf of his employee.

all required that there be a special relationship between the parties giving rise to a duty to take care when making statements:[24]

> ... where it is plain that the party seeking information or advice was trusting the other to exercise such a degree of care as the circumstances required, where it was reasonable for him to do that, and where the other gave the information or advice when he knew or ought to have known that the inquirer was relying on him.

The cases suggest two formulations of this special relationship. On one view, what is required is that there is an assumption of responsibility by the defendant, for a matter in the affairs of the claimant, combined with reliance by the claimant on this assumption.[25] The other view is that the necessary relationship:[26]

> ... between the maker of the statement or giver of advice ('the adviser') and the recipient who acts in reliance upon it ('the advisee') may typically be held to exist where (1) the advice is required for a purpose, whether particularly specified or generally described, which is made known, either actually or inferentially, to the adviser at the time when the advice is given; (2) the adviser knows, either actually or inferentially, that his advice will be communicated to the advisee, either specifically or as a member of an ascertainable class, in order that it should be used by the advisee for that purpose; (3) it is known either actually or inferentially, that the advice so communicated is likely to be acted upon by the advisee for that purpose without independent inquiry, and (4) it is so acted upon by the advisee to his detriment. That is not, of course, to suggest that these conditions are either conclusive or exclusive, but merely that the actual decision in the case does not warrant any broader propositions.

Expanded interpretation of *Hedley Byrne*

Recent cases have provided the foundation for judicial development of the outer limits of a claim in this category of case, to include liability for

---

[24] *Hedley Byrne & Co Ltd* v. *Heller & Partners* [1964] AC 465 at 486 PER LORD REID. See also 503 PER LORD MORRIS, although he in effect required that the relationship arise because of the special skill held by the defendant on which the claimant reasonably relied, 511 PER LORD HODSON, 528–529 PER LORD DEVLIN and 539 PER LORD PEARCE.

[25] The assumption of responsibility test was cited with approval in *Smith* v. *Eric Bush* [1990] 1 AC 831 at 846 PER LORD JAUNCEY; *Henderson* v. *Merrett Syndicates Ltd* [1995] 2 AC 147 at 180–181 PER LORD GOFF; *White* v. *Jones* [1995] 2 AC 207 at 268 PER LORD GOFF, 274 PER LORD BROWNE-WILKINSON and 293 PER LORD NOLAN; *Spring* v. *Guardian Assurance plc* [1995] 2 AC 296 at 318 PER LORD GOFF.

[26] *Caparo Industries plc* v. *Dickman* [1990] 2 AC 605 at 638 PER LORD OLIVER.

negligently provided services.[27] It has been argued that the distinction between negligent words and negligent deeds is not helpful, and that instead the law should develop sensitivity to the difference between purely economic loss and physical damage.[28] These cases have extended liability for pure economic loss to include loss generated by the negligent provision of services. It is possible that these may also be applied to allow recovery for the carer. Although the evidence for this view is limited, the arguments will be briefly canvassed here dealing with (1) the notional duty of care; and (2) the duty of care which may exist on the particular facts of the victim and carer cases.

Notional duty of care   Two approaches to liability are present in the cases. The first is that taken by Lord Goff in *Spring* v. *Guardian Assurance plc*.[29] His Lordship held that liability rests upon the existence of a special relationship between the parties. The special relationship depends upon an assumption or undertaking of responsibility by the defendant towards the claimant, coupled with the reliance by the claimant on the exercise by the defendant of due care and skill.[30] The other approach is that favoured by Lords Slynn and Woolf, who approached the matter pragmatically by first determining whether there was proximity between the claimant and defendant and then whether it would be reasonable to impose a duty of care.[31] Recent cases indicate greater acceptance of the test proposed by Lord Goff.[32] For the

---

[27] *Henderson* v. *Merrett Syndicates Ltd* [1995] 2 AC 147; *White* v. *Jones* [1995] 2 AC 207; *Spring* v. *Guardian Assurance plc* [1995] 2 AC 296; *Williams* v. *Natural Life Health Foods Ltd* [1998] 1 WLR 830.

[28] Stapleton, J., 'Duty of Care and Economic Loss: A Wider Agenda' (1991) 107 *Law Quarterly Review* 249. This view is also present in judicial statements: *Henderson* v. *Merrett Syndicates Ltd* [1995] 2 AC 147 at 178 PER LORD GOFF; *Spring* v. *Guardian Assurance plc* [1995] 2 AC 296 at 318 PER LORD GOFF with whom Lord Lowry agreed.

[29] *Spring* v. *Guardian Assurance plc* [1995] 2 AC 296.

[30] *Ibid.*, 318 PER LORD GOFF. *Henderson* v. *Merrett Syndicates Ltd* [1995] 2 AC 147 at 180–181 PER LORD GOFF; *White* v. *Jones* [1995] 2 AC 207 at 268 PER LORD GOFF, 274 PER LORD BROWNE-WILKINSON and 293 PER LORD NOLAN. The assumption of responsibility test was also cited with approval in *Smith* v. *Eric Bush* [1990] 1 AC 831 at 846 PER LORD JAUNCEY. Clerk and Lindsell, pp. 343–7.

[31] *Spring* v. *Guardian Assurance plc* [1995] 2 AC 296 at 339 PER LORD SLYNN and 342 PER LORD WOOLF.

[32] In *Williams* v. *Natural Life Health Foods Ltd* [1998] 1 WLR 830 at 834 Lord Steyn, with whom the rest of the House agreed, was of the view that '... the governing principles are as stated by the leading speech of Lord Goff of Chieveley in *Henderson* v. *Merrett Syndicates Ltd*'. See also *McFarlane* v. *Tayside Health Board* [2000] 2 AC 59 at 77 PER LORD STEYN, to the extent that the claim was made pursuant to *Hedley Byrne*.

purpose of this discussion, the difference between these approaches is not relevant. It has been argued that the approaches are '... mutually supportive rather than exclusive in their application'.[33]

White v. *Jones*[34] deals with recovery in respect of services. The case concerned the position of the children of the testator Mr Barratt. Prior to his death, Mr Barratt and his two daughters had quarrelled. Mr Barratt made a will which did not name his daughters as beneficiaries. Mr Barratt and his daughters were later reconciled, and he instructed his solicitor Jones to prepare the documents necessary to amend his will. Jones delayed carrying out his client's instructions, and Mr Barratt died without ever having formally made the amendments. His daughters sued Jones, claiming the sum each would have received had a new will been drawn up and executed by Mr Barratt.

The daughters succeeded in their claim. A majority of the House of Lords held that, pursuant to the rule in *Hedley Byrne*, the daughters as intended beneficiaries were owed a duty of care by the solicitor.[35] The crucial fact, relied upon by both Lord Goff and Lord Browne-Wilkinson, was that the solicitor had assumed responsibility for drawing up the will. This assumption of responsibility established the necessary relationship between Mr Barratt's daughters and the solicitor Jones:[36]

> The Law of England does not impose any general duty of care to avoid negligent misstatements or to avoid causing pure economic loss even if economic damage to the plaintiff was foreseeable. However, such a duty of care will arise if there is a special relationship between the parties. Although the categories of cases in which such special relationship can be held to exist are not closed, as yet only two categories have been identified, viz. (1) where there is a fiduciary relationship and (2) where the defendant has voluntarily answered a question or tenders skilled advice or services in circumstances where he

---

[33] Clerk and Lindsell, pp. 346–7. In *McFarlane* v. *Tayside Health Board* [2000] 2 AC 59 Lord Slynn at 76 acknowledged the existence of these two tests and on the facts held that neither was satisfied. '... I consider that it is not fair, just or reasonable to impose on the doctor or his employer liability for the consequential responsibilities, imposed on or accepted by the parents to bring up a child. The doctor does not assume responsibility for those economic losses.' See also J. Davies, 'Tort' in P. Birks (ed.), *English Private Law, Volume II* (Oxford, 2000), p. 459.

[34] *White* v. *Jones* [1995] 2 AC 207. Applied in *Carr-Glynn* v. *Frearsons* [1999] Ch 326; *Esterhuizen* v. *Allied Dunbar Assurance plc* [1998] 2 FLR 668; *Gorham* v. *British Telecommunications plc* [2000] 1 WLR 2129; *Horsfall* v. *Haywards* [1999] 1 FLR 1182.

[35] *White* v. *Jones* [1995] 2 AC 207 at 268 PER LORD GOFF, 274 PER LORD BROWNE-WILKINSON and 294–295 PER LORD NOLAN. Lord Keith and Lord Mustill dissented.

[36] *Ibid.* at 274 PER LORD BROWNE-WILKINSON.

knows or ought to know that an identified plaintiff will rely on his answers or advice. In both these categories the special relationship is created by the defendant voluntarily assuming to act in the matter by involving himself in the plaintiff's affairs or by choosing to speak.

If we accept that liability for economic loss pursuant to *Hedley Byrne* accrues when one party undertakes responsibility for the claimant's affairs, and this is reasonably relied upon by the claimant,[37] the possibility arises that the rule might also apply in other relationships. By analogy with *White* v. *Jones*, the claimant may allege an independent duty of care owed by the wrongdoer.[38] Particularly relevant to this discussion are the cases concerning damages for the loss occasioned by the wrongful birth of a child. As will be seen, there are strong factual analogies between the position of the carer and that of the parents in these cases. In both categories, pure economic loss is sustained by the provision of additional caring services and the incurring of additional expenses.

An example is the decision of the House of Lords in *McFarlane* v. *Tayside Health Board*.[39] The House was asked to award damages to Mr and Mrs McFarlane following the birth of their daughter Catherine, a healthy but unplanned child. Mr McFarlane had undergone a vasectomy operation and was subsequently informed that his sperm counts were negative.

---

[37] *Williams* v. *Natural Life Health Foods Ltd* [1998] 1 WLR 830 at 837 PER LORD STEYN with whom the rest of the House agreed.

[38] An argument of this nature was unsuccessfully made by the claimant in *Goodwill* v. *British Pregnancy Advisory Service*. The Advisory Service performed a vasectomy on Mr Mackinlay who then commenced a relationship with Ms Goodwill. His vasectomy underwent a spontaneous reversal and Ms Goodwill fell pregnant. She sued the Advisory Service for damages. The matter came before the Court of Appeal as an application to strike out the claim on the basis that the particulars disclosed no reasonable cause of action. The court agreed, holding that there was no duty of care. The Court of Appeal did not deny that the rule in *Hedley Byrne* was capable of application in this type of case. Rather, the claimant's claim was struck out because she had no 'special relationship' with the defendant. *Goodwill* v. *British Pregnancy Advisory Service* [1996] 2 All ER 161 at 167–169 PER PETER GIBSON LJ with whom Thorpe LJ agreed. Similarly, in *Williams* v. *Natural Life Health Foods Ltd*, the House of Lords denied recovery against the director of a company which had provided negligent advice. There was no evidence that the director, as opposed to the company, had assumed responsibility to the claimants. *Williams* v. *Natural Life Health Foods Ltd* [1998] 1 WLR 830 at 838 PER LORD STEYN with whom the rest of the House agreed.

[39] *McFarlane* v. *Tayside Health Board* [2000] 2 AC 59. The case came to the House from Scotland and it was accepted that the law of England and the law of Scotland '... should be the same in respect of the matters which [arose] on this appeal'. *McFarlane* v. *Tayside Health Board* [2000] 2 AC 59 at 68 PER LORD SLYNN.

Unfortunately, this advice was incorrect, and Mrs McFarlane became pregnant. The McFarlanes claimed damages on account of their costs in bringing up an unplanned child. In addition, Mrs McFarlane claimed on account of her own pain and suffering following the pregnancy and birth of Catherine.[40] All members of the House denied the claim in respect of the costs of maintaining Catherine.[41] Of interest is the way that the claim was framed. Counsel for the McFarlanes seized on the fact that it was as a result of allegedly negligent advice[42] about Mr McFarlane's sperm count that Catherine was conceived. In its narrowest form, the claim was thus for damages on account of economic loss brought under the extended *Hedley Byrne* principle.[43] The loss did not flow from any personal injury to Catherine's mother. Included in the claim were amounts on account of the parents' financial detriment in terms of wage loss, medical costs at birth and the costs of rearing Catherine.[44] As has been said, the claim was ultimately not successful, a strong policy theme being that the birth of a healthy child can never be regarded as anything but beneficial. However, the case is nonetheless helpful as it concedes the possibility that, had Catherine *not* been born healthy, a direct duty of care might have been owed to Catherine's parents in respect of their purely economic loss.

It is on this foundation that subsequent cases *have* allowed recovery for the extra costs associated with bringing up a disabled child.[45] An example is *Parkinson* v. *St James NHS Trust*.[46] Angela Parkinson claimed damages following a negligently performed sterilisation operation. As a result of the

---

[40] All members of the House, except Lord Millett, allowed Mrs McFarlane's claim for damages on account of her own pain, suffering, discomfort and inconvenience flowing from the unplanned pregnancy and birth.

[41] N. 39 above at 76 PER LORD SLYNN, 83 PER LORD STEYN, 97 PER LORD HOPE, 106 PER LORD CLYDE and 113–114 PER LORD MILLETT.

[42] The defenders did not admit negligence and this issue remained to be tried when the matter came before the House. N. 39 above at 106 PER LORD MILLETT.

[43] Lord Millett made the point that it should not matter whether the claim arises '. . . from the negligent supply of incorrect information or from the negligent performance of the operation itself'. N. 39 above at 108–109 PER LORD MILLETT. See similar remarks at 83–84 PER LORD STEYN. Lord Hope at 96–97 seems to deny recovery by applying the criteria explicitly associated with the existence of a novel claim. Having decided that the costs of bringing up Catherine were foreseeable, he states that the additional requirements that '. . . [t]here must be a relationship of proximity between the negligence and the loss . . . and the attachment of liability for the harm must be fair, just and reasonable'. N. 39 above at 95 PER LORD HOPE.

[44] N. 39 above at 65 in the summary of counsel's arguments.

[45] *Lee* v. *Taunton and Somerset NHS Trust* [2001] 1 FLR 419; *Parkinson* v. *St James NHS Trust* [2001] 3 WLR 376; *Rand* v. *East Dorset Health Authority* [2000] *Lloyd's Rep Med* 181.

[46] *Parkinson* v. *St James NHS Trust* [2001] 3 WLR 376.

failure of this operation, she conceived a child who was subsequently born with severe disabilities. Citing as his reason *inter alia* that '... there is no difficulty in principle in accepting the proposition that the surgeon should be deemed to have assumed responsibility for the foreseeable and disastrous economic consequences of performing his services negligently' Brooke LJ allowed recovery of the special costs of bringing up a child with a serious disability.[47] The surgeon owed a direct duty of care to Angela Parkinson in respect of her own economic loss.

These wrongful birth cases show how *White* v. *Jones* might provide a basis for the future recognition of the carer's direct claim. It might be argued that an analogy exists between the position of the parties in *White* v. *Jones* and the tortfeasor and carer. In *White* v. *Jones*, the solicitor was held to owe a duty of care not only to the client, but also to his client's intended beneficiaries. The duty of care owed to the beneficiaries was a duty owed to them directly. In the same way, it is clear on the facts of the cases in this study that the wrongdoer owes a duty of care to the victim. However, by analogy with *White* v. *Jones*, the wrongdoer may owe an independent duty of care to the carer. As exemplified by the wrongful birth cases when the child is born disabled, it is possible to claim for the extra expense and care necessary to bring up that child. It is arguable that the carer stands in an analogous position.[48]

Application to the victim and carer cases   This section briefly identifies whether the victim and carer cases fall into the extended view of *Hedley Byrne* liability. There are examples in which the carer has suffered economic loss as a result of the negligent provision of services to the victim. An example is *Wipfli* v. *Britten*.[49] Mrs Wiplfli was pregnant and under the care

---

[47] In giving reasons for his conclusion, Brooke LJ also noted that tests of foreseeability and proximity were satisfied and that an award of damages would be '... fair, just and reasonable'. *Ibid.* at 391 PER BROOKE LJ.

[48] The link between the wrongful birth and victim and carer cases is further strengthened by recognition of the fact that the parents' economic loss is in part occasioned by the provision of care to their child. This was emphasised by *Lee* v. *Taunton and Somerset NHS Trust*. In valuing the parents' care of their severely disabled child, Toulson J referred to *Housecroft* v. *Burnett* [1986] 1 All ER 332 (a victim and carer case) as a model '... for assessing the appropriate amount of compensation'. *Lee* v. *Taunton and Somerset NHS Trust* [2001] 1 FLR 419 at 433 PER TOULSON J.

[49] *Wipfli* v. *Britten* (1984) 13 DLR (4th) 169. *Veivers* v. *Connolly* (1994) Aust Torts Rep ¶81–309 is another example although, as will be seen later in this discussion, this case falls more naturally into the 'novel case' category.

of a doctor. The doctor's ante natal care of Mrs Wipfli was negligent, and he failed to detect that she was carrying twins. Mrs Wipfli required a caesarean section in order to deliver her apparently sole infant. As a result of the length of her pregnancy (the length not being harmful to a sole foetus), and the combination of drugs administered to her during the procedure, the undetected child Joseph Wipfli was born with cerebral palsy. Joseph and his parents sued the negligent doctor.

Mr and Mrs Wipfli and Joseph claimed for the cost of Joseph's future care. Although Joseph's care was primarily to be provided in an institution, an amount was awarded for the cost of caring for Joseph at home on the weekends and at other times. Importantly, there was no claim in respect of a physical injury to Mrs Wipfli.[50] The only relevant physical injury was that suffered by Joseph. The case is referred to here only as an illustration of a rare combination of facts in which it might be possible to construct a duty of care to the carer arising from the defendant's assumption of responsibility to the carer. Applying Lord Browne-Wilkinson's test in *White* v. *Jones*, it could be argued that the doctor had answered a question, or tendered skilled advice or services, in circumstances where he knows or ought to know that an identified claimant, Mrs Wipfli, would rely on his answers or advice. Mrs Wipfli was obviously proximate to the doctor. An argument may be made that on facts such as these the doctor owed her a direct duty of care which would have allowed her to sue for losses as carer.

Conclusion

The purpose of this section has been to determine whether the duty of care identified in *Hedley Byrne* has any possible application to the victim and carer cases. The strict application of the rule clearly does not. However, there are examples in which the expanded view of *Hedley Byrne* is relevant. By analogy with *White* v. *Jones*, the carer may have an avenue of redress. The difficulty is that such cases do not relate to the particular relationship between the carer and the tortfeasor. The law recognises no general category of relationship and damage between the tortfeasor and carer.[51] The applicability of this framework will be fortuitous.

---

[50] This is important because it might otherwise be difficult to separate this case from the principles referred to in n. 8 above which allow recovery for financial losses flowing from the claimant's (ie the carer's) own injury.

[51] This point is made in the wrongful birth cases. In identifying a direct claim for the parents, the courts have been at pains to emphasise the distinction between the parents' direct claim for their

Novel claim in negligence

This section asks whether it is possible to identify a novel category of claim in the law of negligence for the carer. It is possible that the existing law allowing recovery of damages on account of pure economic loss caused by a negligent misstatement will provide the basis for a claim by the carer. However, it will only ever rarely be the case that the carer falls within the ambit of this type of claim. As has been argued, if the carer recovers pursuant to this ground of claim, or indeed any other ground in which recovery for economic loss is permitted, this will be a fortuitous occurrence.[52] Recovery in these cases does not establish the existence of a unique duty of care owed by the tortfeasor to the carer reflecting the particular relationship of the parties.

The purpose of the following discussion is therefore to set out the method by which a duty of care owed by the tortfeasor directly to the carer might be identified. In doing so, it will be necessary to refer to analogous categories of claim such as the rules permitting a rescuer to recover for injuries sustained during a rescue[53] and those which permit recovery for a claimant suffering psychiatric injury.[54] In both of these categories, the law has recognised the harm suffered by another person as a result of the injury caused to the

own pure economic loss, and the claim by the victim for the services of the carer, noting that in the victim and carer cases the carer has no direct claim. In *McFarlane* and the cases identified at n. 45 above it is the wrongfully born child who has no direct claim against the tortfeasor. Only the parents, or carers, are able to claim for their own loss.

[52] For example, economic loss flowing from damage to the carer's property, consequent upon the carer's own physical injury or by analogy with the wrongful birth cases.

[53] *Brandon* v. *Osborne Garrett and Company Limited* [1924] 1 KB 548; *Cutler* v. *United Dairies (London) Limited* [1933] 2 KB 297; *Haynes* v. *Harwood* [1935] 1 KB 146; *Hyett* v. *Great Western Railway Company* [1948] 1 KB 345; *Baker* v. *TE Hopkins & Son Ltd* [1959] 1 WLR 966; *Videan* v. *British Transport Commission* [1963] 2 QB 650; *Chadwick* v. *British Railways Board* [1967] 1 WLR 912; *Attorney General for Ontario et al* v. *Crump* (1976) 74 DLR (3d) 345; *Harrison* v. *British Railways Board & Others* [1981] 3 All ER 679; *Crossley* v. *Rawlinson* [1982] 1 WLR 369; *Ogwo* v. *Taylor* [1988] 1 AC 431; *McFarlane* v. *EE Caledonia Ltd* [1994] 2 All ER 1; *Jeffrey* v. *Commodore Cabaret Ltd* (1995) 128 DLR (4th) 535; *Frost* v. *Chief Constable of South Yorkshire Police* [1999] 2 AC 455; *Greatorex* v. *Greatorex* [2000] 1 WLR 1970.

[54] *Bourhill* v. *Young* [1943] AC 92; *McLoughlin* v. *O'Brien* [1983] 1 AC 410; *Jaensch* v. *Coffey* (1984) 155 CLR 549; *Alcock* v. *Chief Constable of the South Yorkshire Police* [1992] 1 AC 310; *McFarlane* v. *EE Caledonia Ltd* [1994] 2 All ER 1; *Page* v. *Smith* [1995] 2 All ER 736; *Vernon* v. *Bosley (No 1)* [1997] 1 All ER 577; *Frost* v. *Chief Constable of South Yorkshire Police* [1999] 2 AC 455; *Hunter* v. *British Coal Corporation* [1999] QB 141; *W* v. *Essex County Council* [2000] WLR 601. N. Mullaney and P. Handford, *Tort Liability for Psychiatric Damage: The Law of Nervous Shock* (North Ryde, 1993); UK Law Commission, *Liability for Psychiatric Illness* (Law Com No 249, 1998).

victim. As was stated in the Court of Appeal phase of *Frost* v. *Chief Constable of South Yorkshire Police*:[55]

> Since *Bourhill* v. *Young* [1943] AC 92, it has been recognised that the ambit of persons affected by the negligence may extend beyond those actually subject to physical impact, particularly to rescuers. 'There indeed may be no one injured in a particular case by actual impact; but still a wrong may be committed to anyone who suffers a nervous shock or is injured in an act of rescue': per Lord Wright, at pp. 108–109.

The difference between the position of the rescuer, or person suffering from psychiatric injury, and the carer, is of course that the harm suffered by the carer is economic, whereas in the case both of the rescuer and the sufferer of psychiatric injury, the harm falls broadly into the category described as personal injury. Despite this difference, these categories are important because, as will be discussed below, these provide a basis from which an incremental development in the law of negligence might proceed.[56] The House of Lords has developed a three-stage approach to identify a novel category of claim in the law of negligence:[57]

---

[55] *Frost* v. *Chief Constable of South Yorkshire Police* [1998] QB 254 at 264 PER ROSE LJ.

[56] *Murphy* v. *Brentwood District Council* [1991] 1 AC 398 at 461 PER LORD KEITH endorsing the oft quoted dictum of Brennan J: 'It is preferable, in my view, that the law should develop novel categories of negligence incrementally and by analogy with established categories, rather than by a massive extension of a *prima facie* duty of care restrained only by identifiable considerations which ought to negative, or to reduce the limit or scope of the duty.' *Sutherland Shire Council* v. *Heyman* (1984–1985) 157 CLR 424 at 481 PER BRENNAN J. Similar sentiments are evident in the following statement of Dawson J: 'Where a new category is suggested, regard should be had in the first place to the established categories which may be helpful by way of analogy in determining whether to recognise a duty of care. That is how incremental development takes place. The process is affected by relevant policy considerations, such as the need to avoid indeterminate liability or the placing of impediments in the way of ordinary commercial activity. It is also important that the tort of negligence should not be regarded as providing an all-enveloping remedy, supplanting "other torts, contractual obligations, statutory duties or equitable rules in relation to every kind of damage, including economic loss". In the end, policy considerations will set the outer limits of the tort.' *Hill (Trading as RF Hill & Associates)* v. *Van Erp* (1995–1997) 188 CLR 159 at 178–179 PER DAWSON J.

[57] *Caparo Industries plc* v. *Dickman* [1990] 2 AC 605 at 617–618 PER LORD BRIDGE. This three-stage approach has been confirmed by the House of Lords in *Marc Rich & Co AG* v. *Bishop Rock Marine Co Ltd* [1996] 1 AC 211 at 235 PER LORD STEYN who delivered the judgment of the majority of the House. The dissenting opinion was delivered by Lord Lloyd who (at 219–220) did not dispute the three elements to be established by the claimant. For a critical examination of judicial techniques in identifying a duty of care, refer to the work of Jane Stapleton: 'Duty of Care: A Wider Agenda' (1991) 107 *Law Quarterly Review* 249; 'In Restraint of Tort' in P. Birks (ed.), *The Frontiers of Liability, Volume 2* (Oxford, 1994); 'Tort, Insurance and

What emerges is that, in addition to the foreseeability of damage, necessary ingredients in any situation giving rise to a duty of care are that there should exist between the party owing the duty and the party to whom it is owed a relationship characterised by the law as one of 'proximity' or 'neighbourhood' and that the situation should be one in which the court considers it fair, just and reasonable that the law should impose a duty of a given scope on the one party for the benefit of the other.

These elements will be dealt with in the following sequence: (1) foreseeability of damage; (2) proximity; and (3) fair, just and reasonable to impose a duty of care.

Foreseeability of damage

The question to be asked is whether the tortfeasor ought reasonably to have foreseen that her act or omission was liable to cause economic harm to the category of persons we describe as the carer. This involves three elements. First, an understanding of what is meant by 'reasonable foreseeability'; secondly, the kind of harm which must be foreseen; and thirdly, the definition of the category of person to whom the duty is said to be owed. The paradigm statement of what is reasonably foreseeable is that given in *Donoghue* v. *Stevenson*:[58]

> The rule that you are to love your neighbour becomes in law, you must not injure your neighbour; and the lawyer's question, Who is my neighbour? receives a restricted reply. You must take care to avoid acts and omissions which you can reasonably foresee would be likely to injure your neighbour. Who, then, in law is my neighbour? The answer seems to be – persons who are so closely and directly affected by my act that I ought reasonably to have them in contemplation as being so affected when I am directing my mind to the acts or omissions which are called into question.

What must be foreseen is the kind of harm suffered by the potential claimant, although it is not necessary to foresee the precise means by which this harm

Ideology' (1995) 58 *Modern Law Review* 820; 'Duty of Care: Peripheral Parties and Alternative Opportunities for Deterrence' (1995) 111 *Law Quarterly Review* 301; 'Duty of Care Factors: A Selection from the Judicial Menus' in P. Cane and J. Stapleton (eds.), *The Law of Obligations. Essays in Celebration of John Fleming* (Oxford, 1998) 59. See also C. Witting, 'Justifying Liability to Third Parties for Negligent Misstatements' (2000) 20 *Oxford Journal of Legal Studies* 615; C. Witting, 'Distinguishing Between Property Damage and Pure Economic Loss in Negligence: A Personality Thesis' (2001) 21 *Legal Studies* 481.
58 *Donoghue* v. *Stevenson* [1932] AC 562 at 580 PER LORD ATKIN.

results.[59] On the facts of the cases in this study, the carer must show that it is reasonably foreseeable to the tortfeasor that, in the event that the victim is injured, the carer will suffer economic loss. In the end, the answer to this question is ultimately a matter of judgment. What is reasonably foreseeable is in part a product of the age and society in which the tortfeasor and the carer find themselves. In an environment of privatised health care and economic uncertainty, it might be thought very likely that if a member of the carer's family is injured, the carer will step in and provide necessary services to that victim. The rescue cases are of some assistance here. One of the reasons why the rescuer is permitted to recover damages from the wrongdoer in respect of her physical injuries is precisely because it is foreseeable that, if the tortfeasor creates a situation of peril, a rescuer may intervene:[60]

> In the ordinary way, such a person, who is a volunteer, cannot recover if he has freely and voluntarily entered the area of danger. This is not something that the tortfeasor can reasonably foresee, and the plaintiff may also be met with a defence of volenti non fit injuria. However, if he comes as a rescuer, he can recover. This is because the tortfeasor who has put A in peril by his negligence must reasonably foresee that B may come to rescue him, even if it involves risking his own safety.

In the same way, the carer might argue that if the wrongdoer must foresee that individuals may intervene to rescue the victim from a situation of peril, the wrongdoer should also be able to foresee that the victim may suffer injury and require care. It is foreseeable that the carer may intervene after the accident to provide nursing and other assistance to the victim.

Proximity between the parties

The requirement that there be proximity between the parties was considered in *Hill (Trading as RF Hill & Associates)* v. *Van Erp*. Dawson J stated that:[61]

---

[59] The claimant must show the existence of a duty in respect of the kind of loss which he has suffered. *South Australia Asset Management Corp* v. *York Montague Ltd* [1996] 3 All ER 365 at 371 PER LORD HOFFMANN with whom the other members of the House agreed.

[60] *McFarlane v EE Caledonia Ltd* [1994] 2 All ER 1 at 10 PER STUART-SMITH LJ. McGowan and Ralph Gibson LJJ agreed. There are other examples: *Baker* v. *TE Hopkins & Son Ltd* [1959] 1 WLR 966 at 973 PER MORRIS LJ; *Videan* v. *British Transport Commission* [1963] 2 QB 650 at 669 PER LORD DENNING MR; *Chadwick* v. *British Railways Board* [1967] 1 WLR 912 at 921 PER WALLER J; *Harrison* v. *British Railways Board and Others* [1981] 3 All ER 679 at 684 PER BOREHAM J; *Frost* v. *Chief Constable of South Yorkshire Police* [1999] 2 AC 455 at 508–509 PER LORD HOFFMANN.

[61] *Hill (trading as RF Hill & Associates)* v. *Van Erp* (1995–1997) 188 CLR 159 at 177–178 PER DAWSON J.

... the requirement of proximity is at least a useful means of expressing the proposition that in the law of negligence reasonable foreseeability of harm may not be enough to establish a duty of care. Something more is required and it is described as proximity. Proximity in that sense expresses the result of a process of reasoning rather than the process itself, but it remains a useful term because it signifies that the process of reasoning must be undertaken. But to hope that proximity can describe a common element underlying all those categories of case in which a duty of care is recognised is to expect more of the term than it can provide.

It is very difficult to define precisely this element of duty of care other than to note that 'it is no more than a label which embraces not a definable concept but merely a description of the circumstances from which, pragmatically, the courts conclude that a duty of care exists'.[62] In determining whether there is proximity between the carer and the tortfeasor, it is helpful to examine the requirement of proximity in two analogous categories, that of the rescuer and the sufferer of psychiatric harm.

In the case of the rescuer, the element of proximity is satisfied by the definition of who is a rescuer. A rescuer is someone who answers the call of danger and goes to give relief. The important factual requirement is that there must be a close connection between the act of the claimant rescuer and the peril experienced by the victim. The rescuer has been described as follows:[63]

(X) Whether a particular plaintiff is a rescuer is, in each case, a question of fact to be decided in the light of all of the circumstances of the case. Among the factors to be considered, although none is in itself decisive, are the following: the character and extent of the initial accident caused by the tortfeasor; whether that incident has finished or is continuing; whether there is any danger, continuing or otherwise, to the victim or to the plaintiff [the rescuer]; the character of the plaintiff's conduct, in itself and in relation to the victim; and how proximate, in time and place, the plaintiff's conduct is to the incident.

The application of this test means that not all of those who render assistance in an emergency are classified as rescuers. An example is the case of the would-be rescuer in *McFarlane* v. *EE Caledonia Ltd*.[64] The claimant was on

---

[62] *Caparo Industries plc* v. *Dickman* [1990] 2 AC 605 at 633 PER LORD OLIVER; *Stovin* v. *Wise* [1996] 3 All ER 801 at 808 PER LORD NICHOLLS.

[63] N. 55 above at 265 PER ROSE LJ.

[64] *McFarlane* v. *EE Caledonia Ltd* [1994] 2 All ER 1.

board the vessel *The Tharos* which went to the assistance of those aboard the oil rig Piper Alpha which was on fire. Even though the claimant was aboard the rescue vessel, the Court of Appeal held that he was not a rescuer. Stuart-Smith LJ stated that '[t]he plaintiff was never actively involved in the operation beyond helping to move blankets with a view to preparing the heli-hangar to receive casualties and encountering and perhaps assisting two walking injured as they arrived on the *Tharos*'.[65] A similar argument may be made about the carer. Even though both the carer and the rescuer intervene to assist the victim, the situation of the carer is distinguishable because unlike the rescuer, the carer by definition intervenes when the immediate cause of the accident has passed. In contrast, the rescuer acts almost as the accident continues. It might be argued that the proximity between the rescuer and the accident, which justifies recovery by the rescuer, is absent in the case of the carer.

It is therefore necessary to identify a category of case in which there is loss suffered by a person in the factual matrix other than the victim, and in which this loss does not occur at the time that the negligence occurs, but is experienced later. An example are the cases which allow recovery for psychiatric damage. Even though the loss suffered by the casualty of psychiatric injury is a type of personal injury, and the loss experienced by the carer is financial, there are important similarities between the two examples. The discussion of the principles regulating liability for psychiatric injury centres around the classification of the claimant as either a primary or a secondary victim.[66] The consequence of this classification is that, in the case of the primary victim, it is very easy to satisfy the requirement of proximity. In the case of the secondary victim, it will be more difficult to satisfy the test of proximity although this is still possible. The primary and secondary victim may be differentiated in the following way:[67]

---

[65] *Ibid.*, 13 PER STUART-SMITH LJ.

[66] *Page* v. *Smith* [1995] 2 All ER 736 at 755 PER LORD LLOYD with whom Lord Ackner and Lord Browne-Wilkinson concurred; *Alcock* v. *Chief Constable of South Yorkshire Police* [1992] 1 AC 310; *Frost* v. *Chief Constable of South Yorkshire Police* [1999] 2 AC 455; 'The categorisation of those claiming . . . as primary or secondary victims . . . is not as I read the cases finally closed. It is a concept still to be developed in different factual situations . . .' *W* v. *Essex County Council* [2000] 2 WLR 601 at 607 PER LORD SLYNN; N. Mullany and P. Handford, *Tort Liability for Psychiatric Damage: The Law of Nervous Shock* (North Ryde, 1993); M. Napier and K. Wheat, *Recovering Damages for Psychiatric Injury* (London, 1995); UK Law Commission, *Liability for Psychiatric Illness* (Law Com No 249, 1998).

[67] *Page* v. *Smith* [1995] 2 All ER 736 at 755 PER LORD LLOYD with whom Lord Ackner and Lord Browne-Wilkinson concurred.

... [Referring to the speech of Lord Oliver in *Alcock* v. *Chief Constable of South Yorkshire Police*] he referred to those who are involved in an accident as the primary victims, and to those who are not directly involved, but who suffer from what they see or hear, as the secondary victims (see [1991] 4 All ER 907 at 925, [1992] 1 AC 310 at 410–411). This is, in my opinion, the most convenient and appropriate terminology.

According to this analogy, the carer is the secondary victim. In order to recover for psychiatric injury, the secondary victim must establish the following three elements which are associated with the decision of Lord Wilberforce in *McLoughlin* v. *O'Brien*.[68] That case concerned a claim brought by a mother who had experienced a psychiatric illness after seeing her injured family in hospital some two hours after the motor vehicle accident in which her family had been injured. At the time that the mother saw her family, they were in a similar state to that which they would have been in at the scene of the accident as they were covered in oil and mud, and in great pain. Mrs McLoughlin recovered damages on account of nervous shock. Lord Wilberforce articulated the following requirements. First, the secondary victim must be close to the accident in time and space. Secondly, the shock must be experienced by seeing or hearing the event or its immediate aftermath. Thirdly, there must be a close relationship between the secondary victim and the primary victim.[69]

The importance of these cases for this analysis lies in the fact that the courts allow recovery for those secondary victims, who have a close tie of love and affection to the primary victim, and who do not experience the accident itself but merely witness its aftermath. The same might be said of the carer. By definition the carer is a person with a close emotional tie to the victim, who will probably not witness the accident but must nonetheless deal with its aftermath. In this way, the carer might argue that there is the

---

[68] *McLoughlin* v. *O'Brien* [1983] 1 AC 410. The House of Lords in *Alcock* endorsed Lord Wilberforce's analysis, particularly his requirement that proximity required 'not only an element of physical proximity to the event but a close temporal connection between the event and the plaintiff's perception of it combined with a close relationship of affection between the plaintiff and the primary victim'. *Alcock* v. *Chief Constable of South Yorkshire Police* [1992] 1 AC 310 at 411 PER LORD OLIVER.

[69] These elements have been approved in *Page* v. *Smith* [1995] 2 All ER 736 at 767–768 PER LORD LLOYD; *Vernon* v. *Bosley (No 1)* [1997] 1 All ER 577 at 583 PER STUART-SMITH LJ, 603 PER EVANS LJ and 608–609 PER THORPE LJ; *Alcock* v. *Chief Constable of South Yorkshire Police* [1992] 1 AC 310; *Frost* v. *Chief Constable of South Yorkshire Police* [1999] 2 AC 455.

necessary proximity between herself and the tortfeasor, so as to establish the tortfeasor's liability to the carer.

Fair, just and reasonable to impose a duty of care

The third element which must be satisfied when establishing the existence of a novel duty of care is that it is fair, just and reasonable that a duty of care be imposed.[70] This discussion will first examine the policy factors said to justify recovery by the rescuer, noting that the same influences are observable in the case of the carer. We will then briefly deal with the policy factors which are said to mitigate against the recovery of purely economic loss. It will be argued that, whether or not these are considerations relevant to the imposition of liability for economic loss, they are absent when dealing with the carer's claim.

The judgment of Cockburn CJ in *Scaramanga* v. *Stamp*[71] provides a touchstone for claims by rescuers. The steamship *Olympias* was en route from Cronstadt to Gibraltar. Nine days out the *Arion* was sighted in distress. The favourable weather conditions would have permitted the crew of the *Arion* merely to have been taken aboard the *Olympias*, thus ensuring that the *Arion's* crew was safe. However, the master of the *Arion* wished to save not only the *Arion's* crew, but also its cargo. He paid the master of the *Olympias* l 1,000 to tow his ship into port. Unfortunately, the *Olympias* ran aground and, along with its cargo, was lost.

The claimants were the owners of the lost goods. They sued the owners of the *Olympias* claiming the value of the goods. Argument centred around whether the deviation of the *Olympias* from her designated course, in order to tow the *Arion* into port, was justified. The crucial fact was that the deviation was not for the purpose of saving the lives of the captain and crew of the *Arion*, but merely for saving the ship and its cargo. The question for decision was ultimately whether 'when deviation has taken place with the object, not of saving life, but of saving property alone the shipowner will be exempt from liability to a goods owner whose goods have been lost through the deviation'.[72] The Court of Appeal rejected the arguments of the owner of the *Olympias* and the owner of the goods succeeded in his claim.[73] In

---

[70] *Marc Rich & Co AG* v. *Bishop Rock Marine Co Ltd* [1996] 1 AC 211.
[71] *Scaramanga* v. *Stamp* (1880) 5 CPD 295.   [72] *Ibid.*, 299 PER COCKBURN CJ.
[73] N. 71 above at 306 PER COCKBURN CJ and 307 PER BRAMWELL LJ. Brett and Cotton LJJ concurred in the judgment given by Cockburn CJ.

the course of his deliberations, Cockburn CJ identified the following policy rationale which has been used[74] to justify the recovery of damages by a rescuer who is injured as a consequence of the act of rescue:[75]

> The impulsive desire to save human life when in peril is one of the most beneficial instincts of humanity, and is nowhere more salutary in its results than in bringing help to those who, exposed to destruction from the fury of winds and waves, would perish if left without assistance. To all who have to trust themselves to the sea, it is of the utmost importance that the prompting of humanity in this respect should not be checked or interfered with by prudential considerations as to injurious consequences, which may result to a ship or cargo from the rendering of the needed aid.

The same motivation often underlies the intervention by the carer. A duty of care owed by the tortfeasor to the carer might be justified because the conduct of the tortfeasor has placed the victim in a situation of need to which the carer has responded. The following formulation of principle relating to the duty of care owed by a tortfeasor to the rescuer is that given by Lord Denning MR in *Videan* v. *British Transport Commission*.[76] The same arguments apply in relation to the carer:

> Whoever comes to the rescue, the law should see that he does not suffer for it. It seems to me that, if a person by his fault creates a situation of peril, he must answer for it to any person who attempts to rescue the person who is in danger. He owes a duty to such a person above all others. The rescuer may act instinctively out of humanity or deliberately out of courage. But whichever it is, so long as it is not wanton interference, if the rescuer is killed or injured in the attempt, he can recover damages from the one whose fault has been the cause of it.

The obvious objection to be made to this argument is that the loss compensated by an award of damages to the rescuer is in respect of a personal injury, whereas the loss experienced by the carer is financial. However, it is important to realise that the barriers said to operate in limiting the existence of a duty of care in economic loss cases are not present in the victim and carer cases. These barriers are that recognising a duty of care will:

---

[74] *Brandon* v. *Osborne Garrett and Company Limited* [1924] 1 KB 548 at 554 PER SWIFT J; *Haynes* v. *Harwood* [1935] 1 KB 146 at 165 PER MAUGHAM LJ; *Frost* v. *Chief Constable of South Yorkshire Police* [1999] 2 AC 455 at 498 PER LORD STEYN.

[75] N. 71 above at 304 PER COCKBURN CJ.

[76] *Videan* v. *British Transport Commission* [1963] 2 QB 650 at 669 PER LORD DENNING MR.

create indeterminate liability; place impediments in the way of ordinary commercial activity; and create the possibility that the tort of negligence will become an all-enveloping remedy, supplanting 'other torts, contractual obligations, statutory duties or equitable rules in relation to every kind of damage, including economic loss'.[77] This analysis will not deal with the more fundamental question of whether these are valid factors to the imposition of liability for purely economic loss. Whether or not valid considerations, the following discussion argues that each of these objections is absent from the carer's claim.

Indeterminate liability is more easily understood following the work of Jane Stapleton, who argues that the indeterminacy argument contains two objections to the imposition of liability.[78] She separates the problem of multiple claims from that of the indeterminacy of each claim. In relation to multiple claims, the liability of the wrongdoer may be indeterminate in the sense that the one loss may be multiplied across a number of claimants all of whom suffer. For example, 'economic loss can "ripple" down a chain of parties; for example, the loss of profits which D causes P may in turn cause loss of profits to P's supplier and in turn to that supplier's suppliers'.[79] However, this objection is easily met in the case of the carer. It is true that intervention by the carer may cause loss to others, for example the company which employs the carer is deprived of her skills while she looks after the victim. However, it is easy to separate these losses from those experienced by the carer. It is the carer alone who is in a relationship with the victim. In any event, even if the other claims are permitted, it is possible that the requirements of causation and remoteness will operate to limit them.

The argument that the quantum of each claim is indeterminate is also inapplicable to the carer. Chapter 2 records that the victim and carer cases show evidence of different methods used to quantify the carer's loss. Some cases look at the income forgone by the carer, while others place a market value on the services provided by the carer. Whichever measure is favoured, the indeterminacy objection does not arise, because each of these measures is concerned with an objectively identifiable phenomenon. By way of contrast, a measure of damages relating to anticipated lost profit may suffer

---

[77] *Hill (Trading as RF Hill & Associates)* v. *Van Erp* (1995–1997) 188 CLR 159 at 179 PER DAWSON J.

[78] J. Stapleton, 'Duty of Care and Economic Loss: A Wider Agenda' (1991) 107 *Law Quarterly Review* 249 at 254–6.

[79] *Ibid.*, p. 255.

from a problem of indeterminacy. The calculation of profit depends on various factors, some of which may be beyond the control of the defendant. In these circumstances, it may be 'unfair to ask the defendant to take into account the commercial expectations of people with whom he or she is not in privity'.[80]

The second objection to the imposition of liability for economic loss is that it will place impediments in the way of ordinary commercial activity. It is rare for the carer and victim to enter into a contract setting out the terms on which the carer will intervene.[81] Although not theoretically impossible, it seems unlikely that the relationship between victim and carer will be often reduced to contract. Indeed, there are judicial statements to the effect that this relationship is properly not one to be regulated within the domain of contract.[82] The point is that, given the rarity of such contracts, it is unlikely that this objection to recovery for purely economic loss will be of much practical importance. The provision of care by one family member to another is unlikely ever to be an area of significant commercial activity.

The remaining objection is that imposing liability for economic loss will artificially enlarge tort's domain, to include matters properly regulated by other sources of obligation. It is unlikely that legislation[83] will provide redress for the carer, and it might be argued that absent a mechanism pursuant to which the carer obtains access to the victim's damages, there is no tort remedy for the carer. The situation of the carer is in this sense more analogous to that of the disappointed beneficiaries in *White* v. *Jones*.[84] One of the factors motivating Lord Goff in identifying a duty of care owed by the negligent solicitor was a lacuna in the law so that, if the duty of care in that

---

[80] N. 78 above at 255.

[81] Examples include: *Haggar* v. *de Placido* [1972] 2 All ER 1029 and *Cunningham* v. *Harrison* [1973] 1 QB 942.

[82] For example: *Housecroft* v. *Burnett* [1986] 1 All ER 332 at 343 PER O'CONNOR LJ with whom Slade and Bristow LJJ agreed. *Hunt* v. *Severs* [1993] QB 815 at 831 PER SIR THOMAS BINGHAM MR who delivered the judgment of the Court of Appeal.

[83] The Law Commission has rejected the statutory enactment of a direct claim against the wrong-doer for private providers of gratuitous care. UK Law Commission, *Damages for Personal Injury: Medical, Nursing and Other Expenses; Collateral Benefits* (Law Com No 262, 1999), para. 3.53. The reasons for the rejection of the carer's claim were ultimately practical concerns: (1) it would involve another party in the litigation, thus creating further complication and expense; (2) it was thought unlikely that carers would actually exercise such a right; and (3) it was thought un-acceptable to provide for claims on account of future care when there was no reliable guarantee that such care would actually be provided.

[84] *White* v. *Jones* [1995] 2 AC 207.

case were not recognised, the beneficiaries suffering the loss would have had no claim, and the only entity with a claim would have been the testator's estate, which had suffered no loss.[85] Thus, far from being regulated by other sources of obligation, the carer has limited avenues of redress. Recognition of a direct claim for the carer is unlikely to artificially enlarge tort's domain.

This and the preceding chapters have been concerned with identifying the direct claims which may be held by the carer. As will be seen, on certain facts it is possible that the carer will have a claim in unjust enrichment. Similarly, it is theoretically possible that the carer may be the beneficiary of a contractual obligation pursuant to which he is entitled to be paid for his services. However, the doctrine of election[86] mediates between the various rights and remedies which may be available to the carer. Particularly where it is doubted whether the carer has any claim at all, let alone that he may have multiple claims, this does not seem to be a convincing reason for denying the existence of a duty of care. Whether the carer is entitled to recover pursuant to more than one source of obligation is of course a separate inquiry.

Conclusion

The requirements for the recognition of a novel claim in negligence are: (1) foreseeability of damage; (2) proximity; and (3) that it is fair, just and reasonable to impose a duty of care. The discussion has shown that it is possible to meet these requirements so as to provide a direct ground of claim for the carer. In addition, it seems arguable that the policy objections to the recognition of liability to make good purely economic loss do not apply to the victim and carer cases. It must, however, be admitted that on the present state of the law, no duty of care is owed by the tortfeasor to the carer. The assumption made by Lord Bridge in *Hunt* v. *Severs*, that the carer has no claim of her own is correct, and it seems unlikely that a claim will in the future be conferred by statute.

Australia

The Australian law governing the recovery of purely economic loss shares some of the features of the English law on the subject. The following

---

85 *Ibid.*, 259–260, PER LORD GOFF.
86 *Mahesan s/o Thambiah* v. *Malaysia Government Officers' Co-Operative Housing Society Ltd* [1979] AC 374; *Island Records Ltd* v. *Tring International plc* [1996] 1 WLR 1256; *Tang Man Sit* v. *Capacious Investments Ltd* [1996] AC 514.

discussion is included here for the purpose of providing a framework within which to view the Australian cases concerning the victim's recovery for the carer's contribution. It is also necessary because, as cases such as *Veivers* v. *Connolly*[87] demonstrate, there may be scope in the Australian case law for the development of a direct claim by the carer against the tortfeasor allowing recovery of the carer's purely economic loss. Although the issue was not raised in *Kars* v. *Kars*, it seems arguable that in Australia the view that the carer has no direct claim must be qualified by the wider ambit of the rules in Australia governing the recovery of pure economic loss.

The cases fall into two groups. The first comprises those which are allied with the *Hedley Byrne* rule allowing recovery for negligent misstatements.[88] As in England, this category is not generally sensitive to the relationship between carer and victim and the existence of a duty of care owed to the carer is fortuitous. This discussion will not further explore the possibility of a duty of care in this category. The second group is made up of cases which allow recovery of purely economic loss as a result of negligent acts and omissions. This discussion will deal with these latter cases and consider whether they provide any avenue of redress for the carer.

Negligent acts or omissions

When compared to the English authorities, the unique feature of the Australian cases is that, without the need for the giving of information or advice, even as understood under an extended interpretation of *Hedley Byrne*, it is possible to claim damages for the negligent infliction of purely economic loss. Some cases purport to identify a ground of recovery independent of the principle set out in *Hedley Byrne & Co Ltd* v. *Heller & Partners Ltd*.[89] A

---

[87] *Veivers* v. *Connolly* (1994) Aust Torts Rep ¶81–309. See also *Foodlands Association Ltd* v. *Mosscrop* [1985] WAR 215 at 222 PER BURT CJ. Although *Foodlands* was not a case concerning services provided by a carer, it is relevant because it considers the existence of a duty of care owed by the tortfeasor to the husband of the victim. If successful, this claim would have allowed the husband to recover such damages as he may have sustained by reason of the tortfeasor's injury to the wife. Although recovery on the particular facts was denied, Burt CJ seems to suggest that in an appropriate case, a relationship of proximity might exist which would allow the husband to have recovered his own purely economic loss.

[88] *Esanda Finance Ltd* v. *Peat Marwick Hungerfords (Reg)* (1995–1997) 188 CLR 241; *Tepko Pty Ltd* v. *Water Board* [2001] 178 ALR 634. The earlier cases include: *Mutual Life & Citizens' Assurance Co Ltd* v. *Evatt* (1968) 122 CLR 556; *L Shaddock & Associates Ltd* v. *Parramatta City Council [No 1]* (1981) 150 CLR 225; *San Sebastian* v. *The Minister* (1986) 162 CLR 341.

[89] *Hedley Byrne & Co Ltd* v. *Heller & Partners Ltd* [1964] AC 465 and the Australian equivalent *Mutual Life & Citizens' Assurance Co Ltd* v. *Evatt* (1968) 122 CLR 556.

recent example of this type of case is *Hill (Trading as RF Hill & Associates)* v. *Van Erp*.[90] Mrs Hill was a solicitor who was instructed by the testator to prepare a new will leaving her house and its contents to her son and her friend Mrs Van Erp as tenants in common in equal shares. Mrs Hill procured Mr Van Erp to sign the will as one of the attesting witnesses. Unfortunately, s. 15(1) of the Succession Act 1981 (Qld) provided that if the spouse [Mr Van Erp] of an intended beneficiary [Mrs Van Erp] attested the signing of the will, the will was rendered null and void to the extent that it entitled the beneficiary to take property under it. Mrs Van Erp was thereby deprived of her inheritance and brought proceedings against the solicitor, Mrs Hill. The question for the court was whether Mrs Hill was liable in negligence for procuring Mr Van Erp to be an attesting witness whereby Mrs Van Erp failed to acquire the property which the testator intended to devise to her. A majority of the High Court of Australia applied the rule in *Caltex Oil* to find that Mrs Hill owed a duty of care to the intended beneficiary Mrs Van Erp:[91]

> And in *Caltex Oil (Australia) Pty Ltd* v. *The Dredge 'Willemstad'* this Court held that, although as a general rule damages are not recoverable for pure economic loss even when it is foreseeable, damages are recoverable where the defendant has the knowledge or means of knowledge that a particular class of person, not merely as a member of an unascertained class, will be likely to suffer economic loss as a consequence of his negligence. Again, the particular relationship between the parties was held to give rise to a duty of care. Of note is the statement of Stephen, J [(1984) 155 CLR 549 at 578–587] that there was a need for 'some control mechanism based upon notions of proximity between tortious act and resultant detriment.'

The application of the rule in *Caltex Oil* has more recently been applied by the High Court of Australia in *Perre* v. *Apand*,[92] in which Perre successfully recovered on account of pure economic loss. The claimant was a potato producer in South Australia, who wished to sell its crop on the Western

---

[90] *Hill (trading as RF Hill & Associates)* v. *Van Erp* (1995–1997) 188 CLR 159. The leading case is the decision of the High Court of Australia in *Caltex Oil (Australia) Pty Ltd* v. *The Dredge 'Willemstad'* (1976) 135 CLR 529. Discussed in R. Balkin and J. Davis, *Law of Torts* (2nd edn., Sydney, 1996), pp. 426–31; J. Fleming, *The Law of Torts* (9th edn., Sydney, 1998), pp. 199–200; Trindade and Cane, pp. 357–63.

[91] *Hill (trading as RF Hill & Associates)* v. *Van Erp* (1995–1997) 188 CLR 159 at 175 PER DAWSON J.

[92] *Perre* v. *Apand* (1999) 198 CLR 180.

Australian market, the advantage of doing so being the higher prices offered in Western Australia. A neighbouring farm had been supplied by Apand with potato seed affected by a disease called bacterial wilt. In order to prevent spread of the disease, the Western Australian authorities imposed a ban on importation of potatoes grown within a 20km radius of any affected farm. The Perre farm fell within this zone. Even though its crop was not actually affected by bacterial wilt, the claimant was not permitted to sell its crop in Western Australia. The claimant's economic loss did not flow from damage to person or property, but was nonetheless successfully recovered from the seed supplier, Apand, as pure economic loss. In allowing recovery, the majority of the High Court of Australia relied on the following factors as justifying the imposition of liability:[93]

> The losses suffered by the Perres were a reasonably foreseeable consequence of Apand's conduct in supplying the diseased seed; the Perres were a member of a class whose members, whether numerous or not, were ascertainable by Apand; the Perres' business was vulnerably exposed to Apand's conduct because the Perres were not in a position to protect themselves against the effects of Apand's negligence apart from insurance (which is not a relevant factor); imposing the duty on Apand does not expose it to indeterminate liability although its liability may be large; imposing the duty does not unreasonably interfere with Apand's commercial freedom because it was already under a duty to [the neighbouring farm] to take reasonable care; and Apand knew of the risk to potato growers and the consequences of that risk occurring.

Recovery by the carer

An example of a case in which *Caltex Oil* reasoning is invoked is *Veivers* v. *Connolly*.[94] The carer was a pregnant woman who had been concerned about the risk of rubella to her unborn child. The defendant was her

---

[93] *Ibid.*, 204 PER MCHUGH J. Similar reasons were advanced at 194–195 PER GLEESON CJ, 255–261 PER GUMMOW J, 303–308 PER HAYNE J and 326–329 PER CALLINAN J. Gaudron J at 201–202 allowed recovery on the ground that the act had caused a '... loss of impairment of legal rights possessed, enjoyed or exercised by another, whether as an individual or as a member of a class, and that that latter person is in no position to protect his or her own interests, there is a relationship such that the law should impose a duty of care on the former to take reasonable steps to avoid a foreseeable risk of economic loss resulting from the loss or impairment of those rights'. Kirby J at 275 and 292 held that some of the Perre interests should succeed in their claim on the basis that the three-stage test of reasonable foreseeability, proximity and that it was fair, just and reasonable to impose a duty of care had been satisfied.

[94] *Veivers* v. *Connolly* (1994) Aust Torts Rep ¶81–309.

general practitioner who was found to have been 'negligent in failing to carry out a proper regime of blood testing for the purpose of determining the first claimant's [the carer's] rubella status'.[95] As a result of the doctor's negligence, the victim Kylie was born suffering the effects of the rubella virus. She was 'gravely handicapped, born with congenital rubella embryopathy. She is profoundly deaf, almost blind, extremely retarded intellectually, and with other major physical difficulties and sensory deficiencies'.[96] At the time of trial the victim was eighteen years old. The carer sued the tortfeasor for an amount to compensate for, among other matters, the care and treatment provided in the past to the victim. The judgment of the court is clear that, although this claim could have been brought by the victim, in the case under discussion it was in fact the carer's claim.[97]

The carer succeeded. After referring to cases which assert the unavailability of the carer's direct claim,[98] the judge held that a direct duty of care was owed to the carer. Relying on the suggestion in *Caltex Oil* that in exceptional cases a sufficient degree of proximity will be established, the judge confirmed that the carer's losses were foreseeable and therefore recoverable:[99]

> She [the carer] presented herself to him as a responsible person extremely concerned to avoid that particular risk, and she plainly relied on him to exclude the risk. The defendant should have appreciated that it was quite likely that such a responsible person, should she produce a child suffering from rubella embryopathy through inter-uterine infection, would not abandon the child, despite her earlier anxiety to have a termination, and would undertake normal maternal responsibility for her upbringing, and that would necessarily involve substantial additional cost and personal loss. To my mind that is enough to characterise this as one of the 'exceptional cases' to which Gibbs, J. referred in *Caltex Oil*, apt to create 'sufficient degree of proximity to which Stephen J referred in *Griffiths* v. *Kerkemeyer*; and the heads of loss claimed here were, in general, foreseeable losses within the meaning of *Sutherland Shire Council*.

---

[95] *Ibid.*, 61,797 PER DE JERSEY J.   [96] N. 94 above at 61,795–61,796 PER DE JERSEY J.
[97] N. 94 above at 61,799 PER DE JERSEY J.
[98] *Donnelly* v. *Joyce* [1974] QB 454; *Griffiths* v. *Kerkemeyer* (1977) 139 CLR 161; *Van Gervan* v. *Fenton* (1992) 175 CLR 327 cited in *Veivers* v. *Connolly* (1994) Aust Torts Rep ¶81–309 at 61,799 PER DE JERSEY J.
[99] N. 94 above at 61,800, PER DE JERSEY J.

Veivers v. *Connolly* is therefore an example of a direct duty of care owed to the carer in respect of purely economic loss. The loss to the carer was reasonably foreseeable and the carer was a member of an ascertainable class. However, it must be acknowledged that there are few examples containing similar reasoning, and it is unlikely to be the model for future judicial action.

Canada

A leading commentator on the Canadian law concerning recovery for economic loss has noted that, until recently, the Canadian law on this subject largely mirrored that identified in the English courts.[100] However, recent decisions of the Supreme Court of Canada, such as *Canadian National Railway Co* v. *Norsk Pacific Steamship Co*,[101] have provided a unique line of authority. The law in Canada separates the cases into those which allow recovery for negligent misstatement on the basis of a *Hedley Byrne* type rule[102] and those which do not. It is this latter category of case which has developed a unique identity in the Canadian jurisprudence. This discussion will: (1) set out the decision of the Supreme Court of Canada in *Norsk*; and (2) briefly consider whether this provides any hope for recovery by the carer.

Canadian National Railway Co v. Norsk Pacific Steamship Co

The facts of *Canadian National Railway Co* v. *Norsk Pacific Steamship Co* are as follows. A railway bridge, ultimately owned by The Queen in Right of Canada, was damaged when struck by a barge owned and operated by Norsk. The accident caused extensive damage to the bridge, and it was closed for several weeks for repair. Norsk admitted negligence in causing physical

---

[100] B. Feldthusen, 'The Recovery of Pure Economic Loss in Canada: Proximity, Justice, Rationality and Chaos' in E. Bankas (ed.), *Civil Liability for Pure Economic Loss* (London, 1996), p. 131. However, it should be noted that despite both jurisdictions' (initial) hostility to recovery for pure economic loss, Canadian courts have retained the two-stage test for liability under which it is first asked whether there is proximity between the parties so as to establish a prima facie duty of care and then to ask whether any policy considerations operate to negative this conclusion. *Anns* v. *Merton London Borough Council* [1978] AC 278; *Kamloops (City)* v. *Nielsen* (1984) 10 DLR (4th) 641.

[101] *Canadian National Railway Co* v. *Norsk Pacific Steamship Co* (1992) 91 DLR (4th) 289.

[102] *Haig* v. *Bamford* [1977] 1 SCR 466.

damage to the bridge. As a result of the bridge being closed, Canadian National Railway (CNR) was required to detour rail traffic to an alternative bridge. CNR brought an action in tort against Norsk, claiming for the actual costs incurred by reason of the bridge closure. The claim was therefore on account of purely economic loss. The loss experienced by CNR was not dependent on damage to any property owned by CNR.

The Supreme Court of Canada rejected the principle underlying the English cases that economic loss is not, except in certain limited cases, recoverable. Rather, the majority allowed CNR's claim.[103] All judges accepted in principle that pure economic loss was recoverable. However, the court was divided in its reasoning. McLachlin J (L'Heureux-Dubé and Cory JJ concurring) proposed an approach which she identified with the dictum of Lord Wilberforce in Anns v. Merton London Borough Council.[104] On this view, pure economic loss is prima facie recoverable where, 'in addition to negligence and foreseeable loss, there is sufficient proximity between the negligent act and the loss'.[105] However, proximity alone will not guarantee recovery. In addition, the court must consider 'the purposes served by permitting recovery as well as whether there are any residual policy considerations which call for a limitation on liability. This permits courts to reject liability for pure economic loss where indicated by policy reasons not taken into account in the proximity analysis.'[106]

The alternative basis for recovery was that set out in the decision of La Forest J (Sopinka and Iacobucci JJ concurring). Although he ultimately denied recovery by CNR, La Forest did not depart from the fundamental point that pure economic loss is recoverable in some cases.[107] Rather than setting out a general template for recovery, he catalogued five different categories of economic loss cases, distinguishable by their unique facts and policy concerns. These were:[108]

---

[103] N. 101 above at 375–379 PER MCLACHLIN J with whom L'Heureux-Dubé and Cory JJ at 357 concurred. La Forest J at 353–357, with whom Sopinka J at 357 and Iacobucci J at 391 concurred, did not find for CNR. The balance was cast in favour of CNR by the judgment of Stevenson J at 390–391. Stevenson J allowed recovery by CNR on the basis that economic loss to CNR was foreseeable, and that liability was in no way indeterminate or uncertain. The loss to CNR was actually foreseen by Norsk. Stevenson J's approach has since been rejected in D'Amato v. Badger [1996] 8 WWR 390 at 401 PER MAJOR J who delivered the judgment of the Supreme Court of Canada.

[104] Anns v. Merton London Borough Council [1978] AC 728.

[105] N. 101 above at 369 PER MCLACHLIN J.   [106] N. 101 above at 371 PER MCLACHLIN J.

[107] N. 101 above at 299 PER LA FOREST J.   [108] N. 101 above at 299 PER LA FOREST J.

1. The Independent Liability of Statutory Public Authorities;
2. Negligent Misrepresentation;
3. Negligent Performance of a Service;
4. Negligent Supply of Shoddy Goods or Structures;
5. Relational Economic Loss.

The facts of CNR fell into the fifth category, relational economic loss. Relational economic loss has been defined as 'a loss which does not arise directly from an injury to the plaintiff or damage to the plaintiff's property, but rather from an interference with the plaintiff's relationship with a third party who has been directly injured, or whose property has been directly damaged by the defendant'.[109] La Forest J did not need to consider loss arising out of personal injury,[110] and did not therefore discuss the policy factors relevant to recovery by the claimant, such as a carer, in such a case. On the particular facts of *Norsk*, he confirmed that the claim fell into the narrow category of contractual relational economic loss, and that in general the law excludes such claims. On the facts of *Norsk*, there were no policy reasons to compel departure from that rule.[111]

After initial uncertainty,[112] these two approaches have now been rationalised. In *Martel Building Ltd* v. *Canada*[113] Iacobucci and Major JJ, delivering the judgment of the Supreme Court of Canada, referred to the categories identified by La Forest J, noting that recovery for contractual relational economic loss is presumptively excluded, subject to recovery for specified categorical exceptions.[114] Contractual relational economic loss was defined

---

[109] R. Bernstein, *Economic Loss* (London, 1993), p. 131.

[110] N. 101 above at 300 PER LA FOREST J.

[111] N. 101 above at 353–357 PER LA FOREST J.

[112] *D'Amato* v. *Badger* [1996] 8 WWR 390 at 400 PER MAJOR J who stated on behalf of the Supreme Court of Canada: 'While the tests of La Forest and McLachlin JJ in *Norsk* are different, they will usually achieve the same result. This is because in the identified categories outlined by La Forest J permitting pure economic recovery, McLachlin J's tests of proximity and foreseeability will also be met. For the reasons which follow, this is not one in which the plaintiff would succeed on one test, but not the other. A choice between the two will have to await the appropriate case.'

[113] *Martel Building Ltd* v. *Canada* (2000) 193 DLR (4th) 1. Previous cases have included: *Winnipeg Condominium Corp No 36* v. *Bird Construction Co* (1995) 121 DLR (4th) 193; *D'Amato* v. *Badger* [1996] 8 WWR 390; *Bow Valley Husky (Bermuda) Ltd* v. *St John Shipbuilding Ltd* (1997) 153 DLR (4th) 385 noted I. Duncan Wallace, 'Contractual Relational Loss in Canada' (1998) 114 *Law Quarterly Review* 370; *Hercules Managements Ltd* v. *Ernst & Young* (1997) 146 DLR (4th) 577. See generally B. Feldthusen, 'Liability for Pure Economic Loss: Yes, But Why?' (1999) 28 *University of Western Australia Law Review* 84.

[114] This point having earlier been conceded in *Bow Valley Husky (Bermuda) Ltd* v. *St John Shipbuilding Ltd* (1997) 153 DLR (4th) 385 at 406 PER MCLACHLIN J. In *Martel Building Ltd* v. *Canada*

to mean '... an economic loss suffered via a plaintiff's contractual relationship with a third party to whom the defendant is already liable for property damage'.[115] However, the categories in which recovery for purely economic loss are not closed[116] and it seems likely that the court would continue to evaluate the availability of a novel claim for pure economic loss on a case-by-case basis, weighing the unique policy considerations in each case.[117] In deciding the existence of a duty of care in these cases, the flexible *Anns* two-stage analysis identified by McLachlin J will be applied.

Recovery by the carer

McLachlin J's approach provides the most appropriate route for a claim by the carer. Assuming that foreseeability is established, her approach pivots on the finding that there is proximity between the carer and the tortfeasor, and that there are no policy considerations calling for a limitation on liability. McLachlin J defines 'proximity' in the following way:[118]

> Proximity is the controlling concept which avoids the spectre of unlimited liability. Proximity may be established by a variety of factors, depending on the nature of the case. To date, sufficient proximity has been found in the case of negligent misstatements where there is undertaking and correlative reliance (*Hedley Byrne*); where there is a duty to warn (*Rivtow*), and where a statute imposes a responsibility on a municipality towards the owners and occupiers of the land (*Kamploops*). But the categories are not closed. As more cases are decided, we can expect further definition on what factors give rise to liability for pure economic loss in particular categories of cases. In determining whether liability should be extended to a new situation, courts will have regard to the factors traditionally relevant to proximity such as the relationship between the parties, physical propinquity, assumed or imposed obligations and close casual connection. And they will insist on sufficient special factors to avoid the imposition of indeterminate and unreasonable liability.

(2000) 193 DLR (4th) 1 the following examples were identified at 14–15 PER IACOBUCCI and MAJOR JJ as falling within the exception to the rule against recovery for contractual relational economic loss: (1) where the claimant has a possessory or proprietary interest in the damaged property; (2) general average cases; and (3) where the relationship between the claimant and the property owner constitutes a joint venture.

[115] *Martel Building Ltd* v. *Canada* (2000) 193 DLR (4th)1 at 13 PER IACOBUCCI AND MAJOR JJ.

[116] *Ibid.*, 15 PER IACOBUCCI and MAJOR JJ.

[117] N. 115 above at 13 PER IACOBUCCI and MAJOR JJ.

[118] N. 101 above at 369–370 PER MCLACHLIN J. This formulation was adopted in *Martel Building Ltd* v. *Canada*, n. 115 above at 16 PER IACOBUCCI and MAJOR JJ.

Although difficult, it is possible to demonstrate the carer's proximity to the wrongdoer. In the same way that a rescuer is regarded as sufficiently connected to the tortfeasor, so might a carer be proximate. Liability will not be indeterminate because, as has been shown in chapter 2, there are various methods available to quantify the carer's loss. Irrespective of whether the measure is income forgone by the carer, or the market value of the carer's services, it is possible with some degree of precision to calculate the carer's claim. However, it seems that a court would be unlikely to extend the ambit of recovery for pure economic loss and allow a duty of care in favour of the carer.

Other requirements for the carer's claim

Even if the carer establishes a duty of care owed by the tortfeasor, the carer must also address the other elements of a claim in negligence: breach of duty, causation, remoteness of damage and defences. Particular difficulty may be presented by the requirement of causation to the extent that the carer's intervention may largely have been a matter of choice. The carer's financial losses may not have been an inevitable consequence of the tort-feasor's negligence.[119]

A related obstacle is the argument that the carer has voluntarily accepted the risk of harm when making the decision to intervene and help the victim. Particularly in a claim by the carer for her future care of the victim, it is difficult to see how the carer could escape this defence. At some point it might be expected that the carer's conduct will reflect her freedom of choice, rather than merely the emergency created by the tortfeasor's negligence.

As was foreshadowed at the start of this chapter, these further elements will not be canvassed in this book. The real difficulty for the carer is to demonstrate that the relevant duty of care exists. The purpose of this section is merely to acknowledge that, even supposing the courts could be persuaded to recognise a duty of care, the carer would still have to satisfy the other components of a claim.

Conclusion

The purpose of this chapter has been briefly to examine whether the carer holds a direct claim against the tortfeasor in negligence. Although there are

---

[119] *Allied Maples Group Ltd* v. *Simmons & Simmons* [1995] 4 All ER 907; *Barnett* v. *Chelsea and Kensington Hospital Management Committee* [1969] 1 QB 428; *Hotson* v. *East Berkshire Health Authority* [1987] 2 All ER 909.

examples of cases in which the carer has sued directly, these do not accord with the mainstream authority on this point. The assertion in *Hunt* v. *Severs* that the carer has no claim of her own appears to be correct. While there is scope for the development of a duty of care owed to the carer, such change does not seem likely via the development of a common law claim, nor does such change seem likely to be achieved via the enactment of legislation.[120]

The cases recognising the carer's direct claim are nonetheless of some relevance. Even if these are not a strong foundation for the carer's direct claim in tort, they are at least evidence of the law's desire to provide some redress for the carer. The solution which has more commonly been adopted is to impose a mechanism pursuant to which the carer obtains access to the fund of damages recovered. However, as will be discussed in chapter 6, the desire to provide a remedy for the carer cannot of itself explain the imposition of a mechanism in favour of the carer.

---

[120] The Law Commission has rejected the statutory enactment of a direct claim against the wrong-doer for private providers of gratuitous care. UK Law Commission, *Damages for Personal Injury: Medical, Nursing and Other Expenses; Collateral Benefits* (Law Com No 262, 1999), para. 3.53.

PART II

6

Direct claims: the problem remains unsolved

It is surprising that even a carer, who is entitled to share in the damages obtained by the victim, is assumed to have no claim of his own, against either wrongdoer or victim. This assumption is made both in those cases which recognise the carer's right to participate and those which do not. For example, the reasoning in *Hunt* v. *Severs* starts from the proposition that the carer has no claim against the wrongdoer in tort.[1] The carer's possible claim against the victim in unjust enrichment was raised in counsel's submissions but was not discussed by the House.[2] The same assumption is made in *Kars* v. *Kars*[3] in which the High Court of Australia, in line with its own previous authority,[4] confirmed that the carer has no right to share in the fund.[5] It is implicit in *Kars* that only the victim is entitled to sue the wrongdoer. The carer's possible direct claim was not referred to by the High Court, even though the market value of the carer's assistance was relevant when calculating the victim's damages.[6] Given the assumption in all jurisdictions[7] that the carer has no claim against wrongdoer or victim, why then should the carer be permitted in some jurisdictions to participate in the damages recovered? It is prima facie impossible to explain how anyone with no claim at all of her own can be given an interest in damages won by the victim.

---

[1] *Hunt* v. *Severs* [1994] 2 AC 350 at 358 PER LORD BRIDGE with whom the rest of the House agreed.

[2] *Ibid.*, at 354–355.

[3] *Kars* v. *Kars* (1996) 187 CLR 354.

[4] *Griffiths* v. *Kerkemeyer* (1977) 139 CLR 161; *Van Gervan* v. *Fenton* (1992) 175 CLR 327, now confirmed by *Grincelis* v. *House* (2000) 201 CLR 321.

[5] N. 3 above at 372 and 380 PER TOOHEY, MCHUGH, GUMMOW AND KIRBY JJ. *Grincelis* v. *House* (2000) 201 CLR 321 at 334 PER KIRBY J.

[6] *Van Gervan* v. *Fenton* (1992) 175 CLR 327 at 334–336 PER MASON CJ, TOOHEY AND MCHUGH JJ; *Grincelis* v. *House* (2000) 201 CLR 321 at 327 PER GLEESON CJ, GAUDRON, MCHUGH, GUMMOW AND HAYNE JJ.

[7] As recorded in chapter 5, there are examples in Canada where the carer has been allowed his own claim. However, these cases do not represent the mainstream position; see n. 8 below.

It might be thought that the carer's right to participate would be marginally less surprising if the carer possessed some rights of her own. The previous chapters of this book investigate the assumption that the carer has no claim against either the tortfeasor or the carer, and shows that this assumption is not always correct. On at least some facts, the carer does have a claim against the victim in contract or unjust enrichment. However, as chapters 3 and 4 show, the availability and success of such an action by the carer is by no means certain. Likewise, there are arguments which may be adopted by the carer to justify the existence of a claim against the tortfeasor in negligence on the basis of the carer's economic loss. However, chapter 5 demonstrates that there is little authority to support the existence of any claim by the carer in tort.

Even if these obstacles are overcome, and we are able to identify the basis of a direct claim for the carer, this direct claim cannot satisfactorily explain the carer's entitlement to participate in the damages obtained by the victim. Prima facie, the existence of the carer's direct claim of itself leads only to the conclusion that the carer could have pursued her claim. This conclusion is most obvious in relation to a claim by the carer against the wrong-doer in tort. While a direct claim against the wrongdoer is consistent with those rare decisions which allow the carer to sue the tortfeasor,[8] such a claim does not inform an analysis of the carer's participation in a fund of damages held by the victim, who is a third party to any suit brought by the carer against the wrongdoer. The carer's possible claim against the victim in un-just enrichment is of greater utility, as it at least has the advantage of being enforceable against the person holding the fund of damages. However, this chapter shows that the carer's direct claims, without more, are incapable of explaining those cases which recognise the carer's right to participate in the victim's damages.

Our difficulty of explanation arises from two particular characteristics of the cases in this study. The first characteristic is that, in those cases which recognise the carer's right to participate in the victim's damages, this right is only visible once the victim has successfully sued the tortfeasor. A direct

---

[8] For example: *Stevens et al* v. *Kachman* (1978) 10 AR 192; *Lapensée* v. *Ottawa Day Nursery Inc* (1986) 25 CCLT 129; *Howe* v. *Campbell* (1974) 7 NBR (2d) 144; *Roberts* v. *Bailey* (1975) 10 NBR (2d) 212; *Clark* v. *Warrington* (1958) 26 WWR 673 (the carer's claim failed); *Price* v. *Gebert* (1952–53) 7 WWR 426 (the carer's claim failed); *Thomas et al* v. *City of Winnipeg* (1937) 45 Man R 422 (the carer's claim failed); *Riordon* v. *Palmer* (1989) 226 APR 326; *Stewart et al* v. *Mayer* (1990) 243 APR 298; *Lang* v. *Ballash* (1989) 72 Alta LR (2d) 306; *Macdonald (Guardian ad litem of)* v. *Neufield* (1993) 85 BCLR (2d) 129; *Ostapowich* v. *Benoit* (1982) 14 Sask R 233.

right of action cannot explain an apparently contingent entitlement. The second perplexing aspect of these cases is that the carer seems not to be able to compel the victim to sue the wrongdoer. Given that the purpose of this portion of the victim's damages award is in some cases to compensate the carer, it is surely surprising that the carer has no way of enforcing this indirect right to compensation. Yet, in the cases which recognise the carer's entitlement to participate, this right to participate is not matched by a correlative right allowing the carer to force the victim to sue the wrongdoer. Each of these difficulties will be dealt with in turn.

The carer's right to participate is apparently contingent

Research has not revealed any case in which the court recognises the carer's right to participate on the basis of a pre-existing right of the carer to claim an amount from the victim. The carer's entitlement is not said to be in satisfaction of an antecedent debt owed by the victim to the carer. A superficial reading of the cases therefore seems to show that it is not until the victim has successfully sued the wrongdoer that the position of the carer is recognised. A portion of the damages awarded to the victim is at this point identified by the court to be for the benefit of the carer.

Further complexity is added by those cases in which the court does recognise the existence of a prior claim by the carer against the victim, and in which the carer's right to participate is doubted.[9] Chapter 3 deals with the possible claim by the carer against the victim on the basis of the victim's contractual or non-contractual promise to pay for benefits conferred. In the course of that discussion, reference is made to the now discredited rule, which links the availability of the victim's claim against the wrongdoer to the existence of an obligation on the victim to pay the carer.[10] Even though these cases are no longer relevant to a discussion of the availability of the victim's claim in tort, they are nonetheless helpful for this analysis. They are evidence that an obligation binding the victim to pay the carer will in some cases arise prior to the award of damages, and yet fail to correlate to the imposition of a mechanism in favour of the carer.

---

[9] *Blundell* v. *Musgrave* (1956) 96 CLR 73; *Gaydon* v. *Public Transport Commission* [1976] 2 NSWLR 44; *Nicholls* v. *Jack* [1963] Qd R 1; *Johns* v. *Prunell* [1960] VR 208.

[10] The following cases, among others, confirm that the victim's claim against the tortfeasor arises independently of an obligation to pay the carer: *Cunningham* v. *Harrison* [1973] 1 QB 942; *Housecroft* v. *Burnett* [1986] 1 All ER 332; *Hunt* v. *Severs* [1994] 2 AC 350; *Kars* v. *Kars* (1996) 187 CLR 354.

An example is *Blundell* v. *Musgrave*.[11] The victim was a naval rating, who was run over by a negligent motorist, and sustained injuries requiring hospital treatment. After a brief stay in a civilian hospital, the victim was taken to Flinders Naval Hospital, where he was treated by the Navy Department. Initially at least, no charge was imposed by the Navy Department for this care. The relevant statutory regime provided that '[t]he Naval Board may at their discretion disallow free medical attention or make a charge for such attendance in circumstances where they consider the cost should not be borne by the department'.[12] It was eventually decided that the cost of the victim's care would be charged against his pay account, although the Naval Board directed that the deduction would not be made until such time as he recovered the amount of the medical expenses from a third party. The victim commenced proceedings against the tortfeasor claiming, *inter alia*, the cost of his medical treatment and care. The case came to court in order to decide whether the victim could properly recover this amount.

At the time that *Blundell* v. *Musgrave* was decided, the availability of the victim's claim for the value of his care and treatment depended on whether or not he had incurred an obligation to pay the Navy. Put simply, the rule was that if the victim was not obligated to pay the service provider, the victim could not claim this amount from the wrongdoer. The facts of *Blundell* v. *Musgrave* caused difficulty because the effect of the Navy Department's decision was that the victim was not obliged to pay until he recovered damages from the tortfeasor. At the time of his suit, therefore, it was open to the tortfeasor to argue that no obligation to pay the Navy Department had yet arisen, and therefore this amount could not be claimed by way of damages. In the end, a majority of the High Court of Australia held that, notwithstanding the Naval Board's direction that the amount would not be collected until the victim had recovered damages from the wrongdoer, the victim was under a legal obligation to pay for his treatment and therefore the charge was recoverable as damages.[13]

Of utility to this analysis is the statement of principle made by Chief Justice Dixon. Although he disagreed with the majority in their application of the relevant rule to the facts, the following formulation is consistent with

---

[11]   *Blundell* v. *Musgrave* (1956) 96 CLR 73.
[12]   *Ibid.*, 78 PER DIXON CJ citing the Naval Financial Regulations made pursuant to the Naval Defence Act 1910–1952.
[13]   N. 11 above at 88 PER MCTIERNAN, WILLIAMS, WEBB AND TAYLOR JJ.

the majority's judgment and has been cited with approval in subsequent decisions:[14]

> It may be safely stated as a general proposition of law that, before a plaintiff can recover in an action of negligence for personal injuries an item of damage consisting of expenses which he has not yet paid, it must appear that it is an expenditure which he must meet so that at the time the action is brought, though he has not paid it, he is in truth worse off by that amount. Generally speaking the question whether he must meet the expense is to be decided as a matter depending on his legal liability to pay it. Indeed, it seems to have been taken for granted by Lord *Ellenborough* CJ in *Dixon* v. *Bell* [(1816) 1 Stark 287 at p. 289 171 ER 475, at p. 476] that legal liability was the only criterion… It may be that his Lordship went too far and that, where the situation of the plaintiff is such that as a matter of moral and social obligation he is bound to bear an expense which he could only escape at the expense of his reputation for honest dealing that is enough.

Chief Justice Dixon's formulation is helpful because it acknowledges that, even without a contract, the victim nonetheless may be obliged to pay the service provider or carer prior to the award of damages as a matter of moral or social obligation. Technically speaking, this statement is relevant only for the purpose of the now discredited rule that such an obligation is required as a precondition of the victim's tortious claim against the wrongdoer. However, in the context of this discussion it is evidence that in some cases at least, courts have regarded the victim as bound to pay the carer prior to any receipt of damages. Importantly, no mechanism was imposed allowing the carer access to the damages won by the victim. Notwithstanding the victim's prior obligation to pay the carer, Fullagar J expressly denied the carer's right to participate in the fund:[15]

> In an action for damages for personal injuries the court is concerned only with the interests of the plaintiff. It is in no way concerned with the interests of his creditors – still less with the interests of someone who may be thought to have a moral claim on him.

---

[14] N. 11 above at 79 PER DIXON CJ. Cited in: *Gaydon* v. *Public Transport Commission* [1976] 2 NSWLR 44 at 55 PER GLASS JA and 52 PER HUTLEY JA; *Nicholls* v. *Jack* [1963] Qd R 1 at 10–11 PER GIBBS J with whom the rest of the court agreed; *Johns* v. *Prunell* [1960] VR 208 at 210 PER SHOLL J.

[15] N. 11 above at 94 PER FULLAGAR J. His views are consistent with those of Dixon CJ.

Blundell v. *Musgrave* further adds to the mystery surrounding those cases in which the carer obtains access to the victim's fund. Even if, contrary to the assumption underlying the decision of the House in *Hunt* v. *Severs*, it is correct that the carer holds a direct claim against the victim or the tortfeasor, it is impossible to infer a right to share in the victim's damages from this direct right to claim. The existence of the carer's direct right to claim seems to point only to the conclusion that the carer could have enforced her own cause of action against the victim or the tortfeasor.

Direct claim against the tortfeasor

When the carer has a direct claim against the tortfeasor, it can suggest only that this cause of action could have been pursued. It cannot explain why the carer is entitled to share in the damages recovered by the victim. There is no suggestion in the cases that the victim sues as a representative of the carer[16] or that the carer is entitled to be joined as a claimant in the victim's suit.[17] Although a direct claim for the carer provides an avenue of redress, it does not contribute to an understanding of the carer's right to share in the fruits of litigation obtained by another.

Direct claim against the victim

Likewise, the existence of the carer's claims against the victim seem to indicate only that the carer could have pursued them directly. Earlier chapters of this book identified possible claims for the carer in contract (chapter 3) and unjust enrichment (chapter 4). Each will be briefly considered in turn.

Claim in contract

It is difficult to test the relevance of a contract to pay the carer because the cases in this study in which the victim was contractually obliged to pay the carer do not in general contain evidence of the carer's right to share in the fund. It is uncontroversial to argue that, the other requirements for a claim

---

[16] This would have to be argued by analogy with the position of a trustee who is the party of record in respect of a suit brought in respect of the trust property. The trustee's suit may be brought without joining to the proceedings any of the persons beneficially interested in the trust estate. S. Williams and F. Guthrie-Smith, *Daniell's Chancery Practice* (8th edn., London, 1985), p. 147.

[17] A person may be joined as a party to an action in respect of a joint interest against the defendant wrongdoer.

being made out, a victim who fails to perform his contractual obligation to pay is vulnerable to a claim by the carer for breach of contract. Such a claim by the carer does not, however, appear to explain why the carer should be granted access to the victim's damages.

In chapter 3 it was argued that there might be a correlation in the cases between those in which the victim was in breach of his contract, and those in which the carer was entitled to share in the fund. In this way, the absence in the contract cases of a mechanism granting the carer access to the fund might be explained by the fact that in none of these cases had the victim failed to perform his payment obligation. This argument is also consistent with the following explanation of *Cunningham* v. *Harrison*. In that case the victim and carer had entered into a contract for care. The complete facts are given in chapter 3. For the purposes of this discussion, all that must be observed is that, although not strictly required by the facts, Lord Denning MR held that the victim would have recovered damages subject to a trust in favour of the victim, but did not explain the basis of this trust. Chapter 3 records that the trust proposed in *Cunningham* v. *Harrison* is consistent with the general pattern if we take the view that the facts disclose a repudiatory breach of the contract by the victim so that the carer's contract was discharged. In this way, the existence of a breach of contract correlates with the imposition of a mechanism in favour of the carer.

However, even if the analysis in chapter 3 is correct, it cannot on its own explain the carer's right to share in the fund. The logical outcome of the conclusion that the victim Mr Cunningham had repudiated his contract is simply that Mrs Cunningham would have had the right to sue him for breach of contract or, as will be discussed below, assuming the contract was discharged, in unjust enrichment. The existence of the carer's contractual claim has no necessary connection to the carer's right to share in the victim's damages.

Claim in unjust enrichment

Chapter 4 investigates whether on certain facts the carer might hold a claim against the victim in unjust enrichment. The possible grounds of claim which are identified included those which qualify the carer's intention to benefit the victim (failure of basis and absence of basis) and a policy motivated claim based on necessity. None of these unjust factors commands clear support on the facts of the victim and carer cases.

The point of this chapter is to establish that, even if one of these grounds of claim is made out, the claim which it supports cannot explain the carer's right to share in the fund. The carer's claim in unjust enrichment entitles the carer only to bring this very claim against the victim. A further difficulty exists even if it is conceded that some connection exists between the carer's claim and her right to share in the fund. A claim in unjust enrichment which is generated by one of the above unjust factors arises at the moment of the victim's receipt of the relevant enrichment. For example, in a claim for the value of the services provided by the carer, the obligation to reverse an unjust enrichment arises when the services are provided. However, those cases which recognise the carer's right to share in the fund do so without reference to a pre-existing obligation on the victim to pay the carer. The carer's interest is visible only later in time, when the victim succeeds in his suit against the wrongdoer.

No right to compel the victim to sue

The prevailing orthodoxy is that the carer cannot compel the victim to sue the wrongdoer. The House of Lords has confirmed that the purpose of an award to the victim in these cases is, in part, to compensate the carer.[18] It is therefore astonishing that the carer is left bereft of any method to ensure that this indirect right to compensation is enforced. Without a right to compel the victim to procure these damages, the right of the carer to participate is surely rather hollow. It is not difficult to imagine the frustration of a carer who is left dependent on the vagaries of the victim in deciding whether or not to pursue a claim for compensation. Even worse, the victim may be incapacitated to the extent that a litigation guardian is appointed. In this situation, the carer would then have to persuade another person, with whom the carer may have no relationship and who may be unaware of the precise circumstances of the carer's intervention, to sue on account of the value of the carer's contribution. As the law currently stands, the carer has no right to compel the victim to sue the tortfeasor. It seems that the

---

[18] *Hunt* v. *Severs* [1994] 2 AC 350 at 363 PER LORD BRIDGE. Even in those cases where the stated objective of the court is to address the needs of the victim, the relevant amount is calculated by reference to the value of the carer's assistance. *Kars* v. *Kars* (1996) 187 CLR 354 at 380–382 PER TOOHEY, MCHUGH, GUMMOW AND KIRBY JJ; *Van Gervan* v. *Fenton* (1992) 175 CLR 327 at 334–336 PER MASON CJ, TOOHEY AND MCHUGH JJ.

vulnerable position of the carer has not yet been brought to the attention of the judiciary.

The identification of a direct right to sue the victim or the tortfeasor does not remove this difficulty. While the carer's right directly to sue either the victim or the tortfeasor may to some extent alleviate the need to rely on the indirect claim via the victim, this does not, of itself, create a method by which the carer could force the victim to sue. It may well be that, in the absence of a right to compel the victim in this way, more prominence will have to be given to the carer's direct rights of claim. Otherwise, the carer will be left without either certain recourse to the damages obtained by the victim or to his direct claim.

Conclusion

This chapter completes the ground clearing exercise commenced in chapter 1. Despite any advantages which the identification of a direct claim may offer in understanding these cases, our analysis is left with the unassailable fact that any direct claim held by the carer against either the tortfeasor or the victim does not explain the apparently contingent nature of the carer's right to participate in any damages recovered. A right to sue either the victim or the tortfeasor is just that. It is not obviously a right to share in the proceeds of any litigation brought by the victim against the wrongdoer. Following from this, it is equally clear that the identification of a direct claim does not assist in finding a method pursuant to which the carer might force the victim to sue in order to obtain the damages necessary to meet this contingent right to participate.

Although we have seen that on appropriate grounds there may be a direct claim available to the carer, we are no nearer explaining what the cases seem to reveal, namely a contingent right to share in the damages if they are recovered at the uncompellable initiative of the victim. This conclusion has powerful implications for the solutions suggested by this book. In answering why it is that the carer is entitled to participate in the fruits of the litigation held by the victim, it is also necessary that the characteristics of the cases discussed above are accommodated.

Chapters 7 and 8 of this book will advance a solution to this problem based on an analogy with the law of insurance subrogation. This solution is compatible both with the absence of a direct right in the carer to sue the tortfeasor and also with the notion that the carer's right to participate in the victim's damages is a contingent right. In addition, this model accommodates the existence of the carer's claim against the victim in unjust enrichment. More controversially, the subrogation solution in the end rejects the notion that the victim's suit is brought on his own uncompellable initiative. As will be seen, even if we are able to explain the contingent nature of the carer's right to participate in the victim's damages, this still leaves one conceptual mystery which relates to the seemingly uncompellable nature of the victim's right to sue the wrongdoer.

The subrogation solution suggests that, in addition to the right of the carer to participate in the victim's damages, the carer should also be entitled to force the victim to sue the tortfeasor. Without the right to compel the victim in this way, the carer is left to the vagaries of the victim in deciding whether or not to seek an award whose purpose is, in part, to compensate the carer. Although there is as yet no case law to substantiate this proposition, logic and justice necessitate that the carer must be able to compel the victim to sue. A right to share in the proceeds of litigation over which one has no control is indeed impossible to explain. However, a right to share in the proceeds of litigation which one is entitled to control is indeed not only explicable but also essential.

Insurance subrogation analogy

By recognising the carer's right to participate in the victim's damages, the House of Lords in *Hunt* v. *Severs*[1] has revealed three anomalies. The first is the apparently inexplicable nature of the carer's contingent right to participate in the victim's damages. The second is that the logical consequence of that right is that, when the tortfeasor is also the carer, the fund available to provide for the victim is much reduced.[2] The third is that the carer is left without any means of forcing suit against the wrongdoer. Rather, the law appears to adopt the bizarre configuration in which the carer's position is recognised, in that she is entitled to share in the victim's damages, but is not protected because the carer is unable to ensure that these damages actually are recovered.

The result in *Hunt* v. *Severs* occurred because the House of Lords held that the victim could not recover from the tortfeasor a sum which the tortfeasor, in her capacity as carer, would be entitled to have back. This book shows that the first and third anomalies are an illusion. The second anomaly, itself inescapable except by legislation,[3] is more easily tolerated than is the logical consequence of the High Court of Australia's approach in *Kars* v. *Kars*.[4] Consistent with its previous authority, the court denied

---

[1] *Hunt* v. *Severs* [1994] 2 AC 350.

[2] The dual identity of the intervener as both carer and tortfeasor cannot be dismissed as an aberrant coincidence. It is in the nature of things that a partner or spouse is likely to be the driver of a car in which the victim is injured.

[3] The Law Commission has recommended the statutory abolition of this anomaly. '... [W]e therefore recommend that there should be legislation reversing the decision in *Hunt* v. *Severs* and laying down that the defendant's liability to pay damages to the claimant for nursing or other care should be unaffected by any liability of the claimant, on receipt of those damages, to pay them or a proportion of them back to the defendant as the person who has gratuitously provided (or will provide) such care.' UK Law Commission, *Damages for Personal Injury: Medical, Nursing and Other Expenses; Collateral Benefits* (Law Com No 262, 1999), para. 3.76.

[4] *Kars* v. *Kars* (1996) 187 CLR 354; *Grincelis* v. *House* (2000) 201 CLR 321 at 333–334 PER KIRBY J and at 339 PER CALLINAN J.

that any carer has a right to share in the fund. The effect of this decision is to throw all carers back on the whim of the victim, subject only to any direct claim which may be held by the carer on some facts.

The first and third anomalies are exploded once we realise that there is at least one other example in the law in which a stranger to litigation obtains access to the damages obtained by a party to that litigation. The relevant example is the indemnity insurer which is entitled to exercise its rights of subrogation. As will be discussed in this chapter, it is possible to draw an analogy between the case of the indemnity insurer and the insured on the one hand, and the carer and the victim on the other. The purpose of doing so is to show that the rules allowing the carer access to the victim's damages are not arbitrary and incapable of explanation.[5] Rather, the carer's right to participate in the victim's damages resembles the right enjoyed by an indemnity insurer. In this way it will be argued that the carer's access to the fund is founded in principle. If the analysis in this chapter is correct, the rights of the insurer form a template for the law's future development. It will be argued that the carer should enjoy a right similar to the indemnity insurer's ability to compel litigation against the wrongdoer.

This chapter will proceed in two sections. The first section compares the position of the insurer with that of the carer and concludes that these are structurally similar. The discussion will set out the relevant rights of an indemnity insurer and determine the extent to which the same or similar rights are available to the carer. The second section deals with the juridical basis of these rights. The rights of the insurer are said to be an aspect of the law of subrogation.[6] The question to be answered in the second section is the extent to which a like principle may be in operation in the case of the victim and carer.

---

[5] The concern that the law in this area is characterised by 'exceptional' (at 368) principles which produce 'anomalies and absurdities' (at 382) and 'peculiar' (at 371) results in part led a majority of the High Court of Australia to reject the *Hunt* v. *Severs* trust. *Kars* v. *Kars* (1996) 187 CLR 354 PER TOOHEY, MCHUGH, GUMMOW AND KIRBY JJ. These criticisms have been repeated by Kirby J: 'Having, in *Griffiths* v. *Kerkemeyer*, embraced the principle that an injured plaintiff is entitled to recover damages for his or her needs met by the provision of gratuitous services by family or friends, this Court was set upon a path that has repeatedly demonstrated the "anomalies", "artificiality" and even "absurdities" of the "novel legal doctrine" which it adopted in substitution for its own earlier stated opinion.' *Grincelis* v. *House* (2000) 201 CLR 321 at 332 PER KIRBY J.

[6] The rules of subrogation also operate in other well-defined relationships which will not be discussed in this book. A more complete account of these is given in R. Meagher, W. Gummow and J. Lehane, *Equity: Doctrines and Remedies* (3rd edn., Sydney, 1992), chapter 9; Mitchell, part IV.

Analogy between the carer and the indemnity insurer

An analogy may be drawn between the carer and the indemnity insurer.[7] The characteristics which we observed in the victim and carer cases are also present in the insurance cases. This section describes the features and patterns of the cases common to both. The more difficult task of ascribing the juridical basis of these rights will not be tackled until the second section.

In drawing this analogy it is helpful to adopt the nomenclature employed by Mitchell in his work on the law of subrogation.[8] He observes that, in the case of simple subrogation,[9] the cases fall into a consistent factual pattern which allows us to assign a standard label to each participant in the simple subrogation model. This standardised label reflects each party's rights and obligations to the other participants in the model. This chapter shows that the same pattern is manifest in the cases concerning victims and carers, and therefore that the same nomenclature may be adopted.

Mitchell's model describes the relationship between three parties: PL, RH and S. The wrongdoer is called PL because she is primarily liable to one of the other parties in the picture. This primary liability will arise because she has acted wrongfully, for example by committing a tort, in relation to that other party. She is primarily liable to make good the loss. The person who has suffered this loss is the person who holds rights against PL. This person is therefore the Right Holder, designated in the model as RH. The third party is designated S because, as will be seen, it is she who will seek to rely on principles of subrogation. S will seek to be substituted or subrogated to the position of RH against PL.

S makes a payment to RH, the effect of which is to restore RH's position. The effect of this payment is only, as a matter of fact, to put RH into the position which she would have occupied had PL fulfilled his payment

---

[7] S. Degeling, 'Carers and Victims: The Law's Dilemma' (1997) 11 *Trust Law International* 30; S. Degeling, '*Kars* v. *Kars* – Balancing the Interests of Victims and Carers' (1997) 71 *Australian Law Journal* 882.

[8] Mitchell, chapter 1.

[9] Subrogation as it operates in the insurance context is the classic example of this type of subrogation. As will be seen, this simple subrogation operates to 'transfer subsisting rights of action from one party to another. This label is chosen to distinguish this first from a second, more complicated type of subrogation. This second type works to revive extinguished rights of action and then transfer them from one party to another.' Mitchell, p. 5. 'Simple' and 'Reviving' thus work to describe the contrast between transferring rights which have never been extinguished and transferring rights which, in order to be transferred, must be brought back to life. See also Birks and Mitchell, pp. 606–9.

obligation to RH. Importantly, the payment is neutral in its legal effect. PL's obligation to pay RH is not discharged. Without the intervention of subrogation, S cannot recover the value of her payment from PL. PL is still liable to RH, but is potentially benefited to the extent that RH, having been paid by S, is factually relieved of the need to pursue PL. Any cause of action that RH may hold against PL is not extinguished. It is therefore also possible that RH might, in addition to having received the payment from S, pursue her remedies against PL. In these circumstances, S may choose to be substituted or subrogated to RH's rights against PL.

The purpose of comparing the position of the carer and the indemnity insurer is better to understand the carer's right to share in the fund. Chapter 6 records that, even if the carer holds a direct right of claim, this cannot without more explain those cases which recognise the carer's right to share in the victim's damages. Chapter 6 attributes this difficulty of explanation to two particular characteristics of the victim and carer cases. The first characteristic is that, in those cases which recognise the carer's right to participate, this right becomes visible only once the victim has successfully sued the wrongdoer. The second characteristic relates to whether the carer is able to compel the victim to sue the wrongdoer. In examining the insurance cases, it becomes apparent that these peculiar features are also evident in the case of the indemnity insurer. Unofficiously, an insurer (S) pays an insured (RH) in respect of RH's loss. RH is factually relieved of the need to sue the tortfeasor (PL). PL's obligation to RH is, however, not discharged. Although apparently lacking direct rights against either RH or PL, S is nonetheless given rights in anything that RH recovers in reduction of her loss.[10] Finally, the insurer (S), although seemingly having no direct rights against RH or PL, is allowed by equity to compel RH to sue PL in its own name.

The analysis in this chapter draws on Mitchell's model in order to compare the rights available to the carer and the indemnity insurer. The purpose of so doing is to provide a foundation for the discussion of the legal basis of these rights which appears in the second section. The discussion will document the way in which both categories contain the following key aspects of Mitchell's model: (1) S intervenes unofficiously; (2) the obligations of PL are not discharged; (3) S participates in RH's recoveries; and (4) S can compel RH to sue.

---

[10] Although S may have no contractual rights against RH, RH may have been unjustly enriched at the expense of S.

S intervenes unofficiously

In order to take advantage of the remedy of subrogation, S must not be an officious intervener.[11] A claimant making a voluntary payment is not ordinarily entitled to recover that payment.[12] This requirement is satisfied in both the insurance example and also the victim and carer cases.

The insurer

Intervention pursuant to a contractual obligation, such as a contract of indemnity insurance, will not usually be regarded as officious, and S is thus entitled to be subrogated to RH's rights against PL.[13] However, even when S is not contractually obligated to intervene, there are other circumstances in which it is possible to conclude that S's intervention is non-officious. There is some evidence that when S intervenes without a contractual obligation to do so, but operates under a mistake or necessity, S is entitled to be subrogated to RH's rights against PL.[14] This discussion will deal separately with interventions made pursuant to: (1) contract; (2) mistake; and (3) necessity.

Contract   It is trite to say that an indemnity insurer which pays an insured pursuant to a contract of indemnity insurance between the insured and the

---

[11] Mason and Carter, p. 213; Goff and Jones, pp. 127–30; Mitchell, pp. 162–7.

[12] *King* v. *Victoria Insurance Company* [1896] AC 260 at 254–255 PER LORD HOBHOUSE who delivered the judgment of the Privy Council; *Esso Petroleum Co Ltd* v. *Hall Russell & Co Ltd* [1989] AC 643 at 662–663 PER LORD GOFF; *Orakpo* v. *Manson Investments Ltd* [1978] AC 95 at 106 PER LORD DIPLOCK. See also *Owen* v. *Tate* [1976] 1 QB 402 at 406–412 PER SCARMAN LJ and 412–413 PER STEPHENSON LJ; *Falcke* v. *Scottish Imperial Insurance Company* (1886) 34 Ch D 234 at 241 PER COTTON LJ, 248–249 PER BOWEN LJ and 252 PER FRY LJ; *In re Cleadon Trust Limited* [1939] 1 Ch 286 at 315 PER SCOTT LJ and 321–322 PER CLAUSON LJ; *Macclesfield Corporation* v. *Great Central Railway* [1911] 2 KB 528 at 536 PER VAUGHAN WILLIAMS LJ, 539 PER FARWELL LJ and 540–541 PER KENNEDY LJ.

[13] The contract of indemnity must be between S and RH. *Esso Petroleum Co Ltd* v. *Hall Russell & Co Ltd* [1989] AC 643 may be an example of a very strict application of this rule. Goff and Jones argue that S was denied subrogation because his obligation to indemnify RH arose not out of a contract with RH, but out of a contract between S and a third party. Goff and Jones, p. 128.

[14] For example: *King* v. *Victoria Insurance Company Limited* [1896] AC 250; *Canwest Geophysical Ltd et al* v. *Brown et al* [1972] 3 WWR 23 (mistake); *Nahhas* v. *Pier House (Cheyne Walk) Management Ltd* (1984) 270 EG 328 (necessity). Even if these case are not categorised as being cases of mistake or necessity, but are regarded properly as examples in which subrogation is allowed in support of a different policy objective, they are nonetheless examples of cases in which, despite the absence of a contractual obligation on S to intervene, S is subrogated to RH's rights against PL. To this extent, these cases demonstrate that interventions outside of contract are in some cases non-officious, thus entitling S to be subrogated to RH's rights against PL.

insurer is not a volunteer. The insurer is entitled to be subrogated. Although dealing specifically with a payment made by a guarantor, Scarman LJ in *Owen* v. *Tate* provides some guidance:[15]

> The broad analysis of a guarantor situation suffices, and it is this: if, as in this case, there is *no antecedent request, no consideration or consensual basis* for the assumption of the obligation of a guarantor [S], he who assumes that obligation is a volunteer.

Mistake   An insurer which pays the insured, mistakenly believing that it is contractually obligated to do so, is entitled to rely on the remedy of subrogation. The requirements are that a valid contract exists between the insurer and the insured and that, although not required by the contract, the insurer mistakenly indemnifies the insured.

King v. *Victoria Insurance Company Limited* provides an illustration.[16] The Bank of Australasia ('Bank') had taken out insurance on a cargo of wool due to be shipped from Townsville to London. The insurer was Victoria Insurance Company Limited ('Victoria Insurance'). While the cargo was in Townsville awaiting shipment, a storm arose and the ship on which the wool was being stored was damaged by small punts, owned by the Government of Queensland, which had broken free of their anchorage. The Bank sued the Government of Queensland for loss. In addition, the Bank made an honest and reasonable[17] claim on its insurance policy, and Victoria Insurance honestly and reasonably acceded to this claim, paying *l* 920 in respect of the Bank's loss.[18] In fact, the loss was not within the terms of

---

15   *Owen* v. *Tate* [1976] 1 QB 402 at 408 PER SCARMAN LJ (emphasis added). The converse is also true. Although the insurer was in part denied relief because it had not indemnified the insured for loss, *John Edwards and Co* v. *Motor Insurance Ltd* [1922] 2 KB 249 at 259 PER MCCARDIE J is an example in which the insurer's payment pursuant to a void contract was not recoverable. The insurance contract was a ppi policy which was held at 255 to be void 'on much the same footing as a wager on a horse-race'.

16   *King* v. *Victoria Insurance Company Limited* [1896] AC 250; *John Edwards and Co* v. *Motor Insurance Co Ltd* [1922] 2 KB 249. Although these were strictly speaking claims to recover funds paid by way of contribution, see also *GRE Insurance Ltd* v. *QBE Insurance Ltd* [1985] VR 83 at 95–96 PER MURRAY J and 101–103 PER MCGARVIE J; *Austin* v. *Zurich General Accident and Liability Insurance Co Ltd* [1944] 2 All ER 243 at 246 PER TUCKER J. Another subrogation case is *Leduc* v. *British Canadian Insurance Co* [1924] 1 DLR 196 at 197 PER GUERIN J. Although not argued as such, *Leduc* might be viewed as a case in which the insurer paid according to a mistaken liability to do so, not being aware of the true facts of the case, and was nonetheless entitled to rights of subrogation.

17   *King* v. *Victoria Insurance Company Limited* [1896] AC 250 at 255 PER LORD HOBHOUSE who delivered the judgment of the Privy Council.

18   *Ibid.*, 255 PER LORD HOBHOUSE.

the insurance policy and Victoria Insurance was not contractually obliged to indemnify the Bank. Victoria Insurance had also taken a formal assignment from the Bank of all of '. . . their rights and causes of action against the government, the bank stipulating that the assignment should not authorise the use of their name in legal proceedings'.[19] Victoria Insurance then commenced proceedings against the Government of Queensland, claiming damages in respect of the loss suffered by the Bank owing to the Government's negligence. In effect, Victoria Insurance stood in the shoes of the Bank in its claim against the Government of Queensland. Victoria Insurance succeeded.

The Government of Queensland appealed, arguing that the loss was not within the terms of the policy of insurance. On this basis, it was argued that the character of Victoria Insurance's payment was not an indemnity given by Victoria Insurance pursuant to the contract. Rather, it was said, the payment was in the nature of a voluntary payment made to the Bank by a stranger. The Government argued that Victoria Insurance was not entitled to rely on the rights of the Bank in bringing a suit. It was also argued that, even if Victoria Insurance was entitled to the benefit of the Bank's rights, it was not permitted pursuant to the rules of subrogation to pursue these in its own name. Rather, it was argued, the suit must be brought in the name of the insured, the Bank.

Lord Hobhouse confirmed that there was no contractual requirement on Victoria Insurance to indemnify the Bank. However, this was not fatal to Victoria Insurance's claim against the Government of Queensland. Leaving aside for one moment the question of in whose name the action ought to have been brought, Lord Hobhouse made clear that if the action had been brought by the Bank after having been indemnified by Victoria Insurance, then Victoria Insurance would nonetheless have been entitled to participate in the damages recovered. The fact that Victoria Insurance had not been contractually obliged to indemnify the Bank was not relevant to whether Victoria Insurance was entitled to the benefit of the Bank's rights:[20]

> Their Lordships have no doubt that if, after receiving payment from the plaintiffs, the bank had got damages from the government, a Court of Equity would have treated them as trustees for the plaintiffs to the extent of the payment, and that if it had been necessary to use the name of the bank a Court of Equity would have compelled the bank to permit it on the usual terms.

[19] N. 17 above at 253 PER LORD HOBHOUSE.
[20] N. 17 above at 255–256 PER LORD HOBHOUSE.

Lord Hobhouse also upheld the purported assignment by the Bank to Victoria Insurance of its rights against the Government. On this basis, it overcame the Government's objection that Victoria Insurance was not able to sue in its own name, while acknowledging that without the assignment, the action should have been brought in the name of the Bank.[21]

The above explanation of *King* is given only to illustrate the proposition that when an insurer pays the insured, mistakenly believing that it is contractually obligated to do so, the remedy of subrogation may be available to the insurer. However, it must be admitted that other interpretations of *King* are possible. Mitchell notes that the case may also be explained on policy grounds.[22] He suggests that '... courts wish as a matter of general policy to encourage insurers to pay their insureds notwithstanding that they are not strictly bound to do so under the terms of the insurance policy'.[23]

Necessity   The insurer may be in a position where the principle of necessity applies to the decision to indemnify the insured. The law may decide that certain interventions will not be condemned as officious on the policy ground that necessitous interventions should not be discouraged. Even though the insurer is not contractually obliged to intervene, the indemnity insurer will nonetheless be entitled to rights of subrogation. *Nahhas* v. *Pier House (Cheyne Walk) Management Ltd*[24] provides some support for this position. Mrs Nahhas was the lessor of a flat managed by Pier House. As a result of Pier House's negligence, jewellery worth £23,250 was stolen from her flat. Mrs Nahhas had insured the jewellery kept on the premises, but had unfortunately understated its value. Her insurer refused liability on the policy, but made an ex gratia payment of £3,000 which was insufficient to cover her loss.

---

[21]   N. 17 above at 256 PER LORD HOBHOUSE.

[22]   Mitchell, p. 106. Clarke also suggests that the decision can be supported on policy grounds, arguing that the result in *King* is in the public interest against unnecessary litigation. In addition, he refers to the submission, unsuccessfully made by the Government of Queensland, that Victoria Insurance was not entitled to rely on the rights of the Bank in bringing a suit. Clarke defends the decision on the basis that it is not open to a third party (Government of Queensland) to raise a defence which is based on a contract to which he is not a party (contract of insurance), is not raised by either party to the contract (Victoria Insurance and the Bank) and is not intended by them to be for the benefit of the third party. M. Clarke, *The Law of Insurance Contracts* (3rd edn., London, 1997), p. 856. Goff and Jones, pp. 139–40, n. 68.

[23]   Mitchell, p. 106.

[24]   *Nahhas* v. *Pier House (Cheyne Walk) Management Ltd* (1984) 270 EG 328.

Her insurance had been arranged through a firm of insurance brokers, Reed Stenhouse, who also acted for her father. 'For reasons of benevolence, mixed with the commercial desirability of cementing and maintaining the business relations with her father, which was worth some £50,000 to them in commissions, they [Reed Stenhouse] agreed with her father to pay her out for the jewellery provided that the family co-operated with them in pursuing the action, whether against the underwriters on the insurance policy or against the present defendants [Pier House]'.[25] Therefore, a second contract of indemnity was entered into, pursuant to which Reed Stenhouse agreed to indemnify Mrs Nahhas for her loss. In return, an action was to be brought against Pier House in her name, and she was contractually obligated to account to Reed Stenhouse for any proceeds of this litigation. The defendant disputed Mrs Nahhas' right to claim, arguing that owing to the payment made by Reed Stenhouse, she had suffered no loss. Mr Denis Henry QC, sitting as a deputy judge of the Queen's Bench division, disagreed and allowed her claim.

Strictly speaking, *Nahhas* v. *Pier House (Cheyne Walk) Management Ltd* concerned a contract, the terms of which expressly stipulated the insurer's rights of subrogation. However, Mr Denis Henry QC went further and, independently of the contract, justified the insurer's rights. His reasons for doing so were first, that Reed Stenhouse was motivated or compelled by a genuinely benevolent desire to help Mrs Nahhas and secondly, that necessitous interveners, such as Reed Stenhouse, should not be discouraged. Importantly, he drew a parallel between the position of the insurer and that of the carer. This parallel is a bridge between the insurance cases and those concerning victims and carers. The following statement suggests that the rights enjoyed by the indemnity insurer are conceptually the same as those available to the carer:[26]

> For my part, it seems to me that the right policy is that wrongdoers [PL] should pay and that third parties [S] motivated by a genuine benevolent and/or commercial regard for the plaintiff [RH], arising as it does from a pre-existing relationship, should not be discouraged from helping victims at a time when they need that help most . . . I am happy to find that this appears to be in line with, or at any rate not inconsistent with, authority: see *Donnelly* v. *Joyce* [1974] QB 454; *Cunningham* v. *Harrison* [1973] QB 942; and *Dennis* v. *The London Passenger Transport Board* [1948] 1 All ER 779.

---

[25] *Ibid.*, 334 PER MR DENIS HENRY QC (NOW DENIS HENRY LJ).
[26] N. 24 above at 334 PER MR DENIS HENRY QC.

The decision in *Nahhas* is supported by those cases which show that, in a non-insurance and therefore non-contractual context, an intervener acting in circumstances of necessity will also negate a charge of officiousness. It is possible to observe this pattern in the funeral cases,[27] cases concerning the extension of the doctrine of agency of necessity,[28] and various other categories.[29] By way of example, *The 'Zuhal K' and 'Selin'* concerned a ship (*The Selin*) which had been arrested at Rotterdam harbour on the basis that the cargo was damaged. The cargo owners would not release the ship until security was provided by or on behalf of the ship owners. A third party intervened and issued in favour of the cargo owner a guarantee securing the obligations of the ship owner. At the time that this guarantee was made available, there was no legal obligation binding the third party to do so. The ship owner was unaware that the guarantee was provided by a third party. The third party recovered from the ship owner the payments made pursuant to the guarantee. The basis for the third party's successful claim was that the payments were made in circumstances of necessity:[30]

> If that question is asked, there can be no doubt that it was reasonably necessary in the interests of the ship owners that the guarantee should be given. Pursuant to that guarantee, payment had to be made. To my mind, it is clearly just and reasonable that a right of reimbursement should arise.

The victim and carer cases

The carer's intervention is also unofficious. Chapter 4 sets out the elements of the carer's claim against the victim in unjust enrichment. One of the possible unjust factors identified is that the carer intervenes in an emergency sufficient to invoke the principle of necessity. In respect of the minority of cases, in which a policy-based argument founded on necessity might succeed, it is therefore open to the carer to argue that her intervention was

---

[27] *Jenkins* v. *Tucker* (1788) 1 Hy Bl 90; *Rogers* v. *Price* (1829) 3 Y&J 28; *Ambrose* v. *Kerrison* (1851) 10 CB 776.

[28] *Great Northern Railway* v. *Swaffield* (1874) LR 9 Ex 132.

[29] For example: medical care provided to a pauper *Tomlinson* v. *Bentall* (1826) 5 B & C 738; the necessitous payment of another's debt *Owen* v. *Tate* [1976] 1 QB 402; a guarantee given to secure the release of the defendant's ship *The 'Zuhal K' and 'Selin'* [1987] 1 Lloyd's Rep 151; necessitous services rendered by a liquidator *In re Berkeley Applegate (Investment Consultants) Ltd* [1989] Ch 32.

[30] *The 'Zuhal K' and 'Selin'* [1987] 1 Lloyd's Rep 151 at 156 PER SHEEN J.

non-officious. However, the analysis in chapter 4 concludes that in general, necessity cannot be sustained in the victim and carer cases.[31] Although the carer's intervention is clearly necessary, the necessity analysis does not sit well with those cases in which the victim, although badly injured, is able to communicate meaningfully with the victim. In addition, it seems unlikely that the state of emergency generating the necessity for the carer's intervention will operate over the extended period of time in which the carer may provide services to the victim.

In most cases, therefore, the carer will have to rely on a different argument to negate the charge of officiousness. The carer is entitled to argue that her intervention is non-officious because, as a matter of policy, the law should not operate to discourage such necessary interventions made out of love and affection. The carer in most cases is a friend or relative of the victim and usually has no professional qualifications or training. However, it is clear that the carer in fact benefits the victim and that this benefit is conferred out of love and affection. The necessitous quality of the carer's intervention, as opposed to the length of time over which it occurs or the ability of the victim to communicate her wishes, is not disputed. The defects causing the failure of the application of necessity as an unjust factor do not derogate from this conclusion.

The obligations of PL are not discharged

The carer (S) and the insurer (S) both make good the loss of the claimant (RH). The carer (S) does so by providing necessary services and assistance to the victim of a tort (RH). Even after having received this assistance, the victim's (RH's) right of action against the tortfeasor (PL) is not extinguished. The victim (RH) still holds a right to claim damages from the tortfeasor (PL) referable, in part, to the value of services provided and expenses paid by the carer (S).

The same pattern exists in the insurance cases. The insurer (S) makes good the loss of the insured (RH) by paying, as it may be contractually bound to do, on the policy of indemnity insurance. Even though the loss of the insured has thereby been made good, the insured (RH) retains any right of action it may have against the tortfeasor (PL). The corollary of this argument is that the money paid to the insured (PL) pursuant to the insurance contract

---

[31] Chapter 4, pp. 91–100.

is disregarded by the court when quantifying the damages recoverable by the insured (RH) in any action against the tortfeasor (PL).

An early example of this reasoning, which is one of the foundations of the modern law of insurance, is *Bradburn* v. *The Great Western Railway Company*.[32] Bradburn was a passenger on a train operated by the Great Western Railway Company and was injured owing to the latter's negligence. He had taken out insurance with Accidental Insurance Company, which paid *l* 31 to Bradburn on account of his injuries. Bradburn sued the Great Western Railway Company for damages and obtained judgment for *l* 217. The Great Western Railway Company appealed against this decision, arguing that the insurance payment had reduced Bradburn's loss by *l* 31 and therefore that this sum should be deducted from his award. The court rejected this analysis, holding that the money received by Bradburn by way of indemnity had no bearing on his '... suing upon his common law right for injuries caused to him by the defendants' negligence'.[33] Pigott B stated:[34]

> The plaintiff is entitled to recover the damages caused to him by the negligence of the defendants, and there is no reason or justice in setting off what the plaintiff has entitled himself to under a contract with third persons, by which he has bargained for the payment of a sum of money in the event of an accident happening to him. He does not receive that sum of money because of the accident, but because he has made a contract providing for the contingency; an accident must occur to entitle him to it, but it is not the accident, but his contract, which is the cause of his receiving it.

Despite these similarities, there is one important difference between the insurance cases and the victim and carer cases. This difference is relevant to chapter 9, the task of which is to account for the fact that in some cases the carer's access to the fund is proprietary in nature, and is described in more detail in that chapter. Although in both categories S's intervention leaves PL's obligations to RH undischarged, the effect of this intervention on the value of RH's claim against PL is different. In the case of the carer, not only does intervention by the carer (S) fail to release the tortfeasor (PL) from liability, but actually operates to increase the value of the victim's (RH's)

---

[32] *Bradburn* v. *The Great Western Railway Company* (1874) LR 10 Ex 1. Other examples are: *Central Insurance Co Ltd* v. *Seacalf Shipping Corporation (The Alios)* [1983] 2 Lloyd's LR 25 at 33 PER OLIVER LJ; *Hobbs* v. *Marlowe* [1978] AC 16 at 37 PER LORD DIPLOCK.

[33] *Bradburn* v. *The Great Western Railway Company* (1874) LR 10 Ex 1 at 3 PER BRAMWELL B AND PIGGOTT B. Amphlett B concurred.

[34] *Ibid.*, 3 PER PIGGOTT B.

claim against the tortfeasor (PL). This can be illustrated by reference to *Hunt v. Severs*.[35]

It will be recalled that Miss Hunt was negligently injured when travelling as a pillion passenger on a motorcycle driven by her fiancé Mr Severs. As a result of the accident, Miss Hunt required a great deal of care and assistance, much of which was provided by Mr Severs. She claimed damages, among other matters, on account of his care of her to the date of trial and estimated future care to be provided by him. The facts were complicated by Mr Severs' dual identity as carer and tortfeasor. Mr Severs, expressing the interest of his insurer, argued on appeal to the House of Lords that he should not have to pay damages in respect of his care of Miss Hunt because in providing those services gratuitously, he would in a non-monetary form be meeting his own obligations as tortfeasor. In effect Mr Severs argued that his intervention as carer operated to discharge his obligations as wrongdoer.

The House of Lords did not agree. Although the quantum of damages was reduced by the value of his past and estimated future care of Miss Hunt, this was not on the basis that the liability of the tortfeasor had been discharged. Rather, it was because the House of Lords held that the carer was entitled to share in the fund of damages. If Mr Severs had been required to pay the undiscounted amount in damages, he would in effect be paying money into a fund of which, in his capacity as carer, he was beneficiary. It was therefore to avoid the anomalous consequence of a tortfeasor paying damages to himself that the quantum of Miss Hunt's award was reduced.

Despite the reduction in the victim's award, the underlying principle which was applied by the House of Lords is the rule that '...an injured plaintiff may recover the reasonable value of gratuitous services rendered to him by way of voluntary care by a member of his family'.[36] The law therefore explicitly responds to the services provided by the carer in allowing the victim to claim a corresponding amount by way of damages. The application of this rule means that if no past care is provided, then no damages can be claimed by the victim in a suit against the wrongdoer.[37] However, if the carer intervenes to assist by providing services to the victim which are of the requisite quality, the victim is entitled to claim the reasonable value of these services from the wrongdoer. There is thus a direct relationship

---

[35] *Hunt* v. *Severs* [1994] 2 AC 350.   [36] *Ibid.*, 363 PER LORD BRIDGE.

[37] The same argument applies in relation to the future care of the victim. Discussed in chapter 9, pp. 255–7.

between the carer's services to the victim and the heads of damage available to the victim. The carer contributes to the value of the victim's claim against the wrongdoer. In effect, the carer's intervention enlarges the chose in action held by the victim which is generated by the tortfeasor's negligence.[38]

The claim by an insured (RH) against the wrongdoer (PL) is different. Even though an indemnity provided by the insurer (S) does not discharge PL's liability to RH, the value of RH's claim against PL is not altered. The size of the insured's claim is limited to her own loss. The court does not, in addition, look to the amount paid out by the insurer by way of indemnity. As a practical matter, it is of course likely that the insured's loss will exactly correlate, and in some cases may exceed, the value of the insurer's indemnity. To an extent, leaving aside the situation where the insured is not fully covered for loss, one will be a mirror image of the other. However, the two are not directly linked. If the victim receives no care, then no claim can be made in respect of the value of this care. In the insurance example, if the insured is not indemnified, this does not derogate from the quantum of her suit against the wrongdoer. This difference is not important for the purpose of this chapter. It is documented here merely for the sake of convenience, but will become relevant in chapter 9.

S has a contingent right to share in RH's damages

Chapter 6 records that in those cases in which the court recognises the right of the carer (S) to participate in the damages awarded to the victim (RH), this right is apparently contingent on the victim (RH) having successfully brought a claim against the tortfeasor (PL). As was discussed in chapter 6, research has revealed no case in which the carer (S) is allowed to share in the damages on the basis of an antecedent right to be paid.

An example is *Thornton* v. *Board of School Trustees of School District No 57 (Prince George)*[39] in which Gary Thornton was made paraplegic due to an accident which occurred through the negligence of his school gymnastics

---

[38] It is not intended to suggest here that the carer is acting in a dishonest way. Not all services provided by the carer are recoverable. The law strictly limits recovery by insisting that the care be of an extraordinary quality, beyond what would normally be the care given by one person to another in the day-to-day life of their relationship.

[39] *Thornton* v. *Board of School Trustees of School District No 57 (Prince George)* (1978) 83 DLR (3d) 480 upholding the relevant part of the decision of the British Columbia Court of Appeal reported at *Thornton* v. *Board of School Trustees of School District No 57 (Prince George)* (1976) 73 DLR (3d) 35.

instructor. Gary was cared for at home for a time after the accident by his mother and step father, Mr and Mrs Tanner. The British Columbia Court of Appeal, *inter alia*, allowed Gary to sue for the value of the care provided by Mr and Mrs Tanner. Damages were awarded to Gary in trust for his carers, thus allowing them to participate in the damages obtained by him. Taggart JA stated:[40]

> I ... am of the opinion that while Mr and Mrs Tanner have no claim against the appellants the respondent Gary Thornton may claim as an item of special expense an appropriate amount to compensate those who have rendered services to him of a nursing character. That result should obtain irrespective of whether there exists between the respondent Gary Thornton and those rendering the services a contract pursuant to which he agrees to reimburse them ... [referring to the sum of $7,500 awarded on this basis] That amount should be paid to Gary Thornton but held by him on trust to be paid over to Mrs Tanner.

The same characteristic is present in the insurance cases. Leaving to one side the form that this access takes, it is clear that on the insured (RH) receiving damages or another payment in diminution of the loss made good by the insurer (S), the insurer (S) is entitled to the benefit of the appropriate portion of those damages.[41] The leading case is *Lord Napier and Ettrick* v. *Hunter*.[42]

The claimants were 987 Lloyds Names who had been members of the Outhwaite Syndicate of Lloyds of London ('Names'). In 1989 the Names commenced proceedings against R.H.M. Outhwaite Underwriting Agencies Ltd ('Outhwaite') claiming that Outhwaite had been negligent in performing underwriting services for the Names. The Names alleged that policies in respect of asbestos claims had been written on their behalf without adequate

---

[40] *Thornton* v. *Board of School Trustees of School District No. 57 (Prince George)* (1976) 73 DLR (3d) 35 at 55 PER TAGGART JA with whom the rest of the court agreed.

[41] Earlier cases such as *Randal* v. *Cockran* (1748) 1 Ves Sen 98 and *Blaaupot* v. *Da Costa* (1758) 1 Eden 130 impose a trust. However, the House of Lords has confirmed that the insurer is the beneficiary not of a trust but an equitable lien. *Lord Napier and Ettrick* v. *Hunter* [1993] AC 713 at 741–742 and 744–745 PER LORD GOFF, 737–738 PER LORD TEMPLEMAN and 752 PER LORD BROWNE-WILKINSON.

[42] *Lord Napier and Ettrick* v. *Hunter* [1993] AC 713. Discussed in Mitchell, pp. 82–6; C. Mitchell, 'Subrogation and Insurance Law: Proprietary Claims and Excess Clauses' [1993] *Lloyd's Maritime and Commercial Law Quarterly* 192. *Lord Napier and Ettrick* v. *Hunter* was cited with approval in *Banque Financière de la Cité* v. *Parc (Battersea) Ltd* [1999] 1 AC 221 at 231–232 PER LORD HOFFMANN with whom Lord Griffiths agreed.

reinsurance, thus leaving the Names in a vulnerable position should they be called on to pay in respect of these policies. In the event, the Names were required to pay on these policies and consequently suffered underwriting losses, precipitating their suit against Outhwaite.

Some of the Names were able to ameliorate their position by virtue of the fact that they had taken out Stop Loss indemnity insurance with other syndicates at Lloyds ('Stop Loss Insurers'). The terms of the Stop Loss policies provided, *inter alia*, that the Stop Loss Insurers would indemnify the insured Names in respect of underwriting losses. Therefore, prior to the proceedings against Outhwaite, some of the Names had received insurance payments from the Stop Loss Insurers in reduction of their underwriting losses.

Outhwaite negotiated a settlement of the Names' suit and £116 million in settlement monies was paid to Richards Butler, a firm of solicitors acting for the Names. Disputation then arose as to whom the settlement monies held by Richards Butler should be distributed. The Corporation of Lloyds asserted that the settlement monies could not be distributed because they were subject to the terms of Lloyd's Premium Trust Deeds which had been entered into by each Name. This claim by the Corporation of Lloyds was rejected by Saville J, and no appeal was lodged in relation to this part of his decision.[43]

In the course of the proceedings to determine the Corporation of Lloyds' claim to the settlement monies, the Stop Loss Insurers claimed an equitable proprietary interest in the settlement monies, and were added as parties to the proceedings. Saville J held against the Stop Loss Insurers who then took the matter to the Court of Appeal,[44] and ultimately the House of Lords, the decision under consideration here. Two issues arose for determination by the House:[45]

> (1) whether the stop loss insurers had an equitable proprietary interest in any of the settlement moneys and/or whether any of the settlement moneys were impressed with a trust in favour of the stop loss insurers; (2) whether, in any

---

[43] *Baron Napier and Ettrick* v. *RF Kershaw* unreported Saville J 14 May 1992. See now *Society of Lloyd's* v. *Robinson* in which the House of Lords held that, after subsequent amendments to the Lloyd's Premium Trust Deed in 1995, damages recovered for negligent underwriting are subject to the trust. *Society of Lloyd's* v. *Robinson* [1999] 1 WLR 756 at 763 PER LORD STEYN with whom the rest of the House agreed.

[44] *Baron Napier and Ettrick* v. *RF Kershaw* [1993] 1 Lloyd's Rep 10.

[45] *Lord Napier and Ettrick* v. *Hunter* [1993] AC 713 at 716.

event, in determining the amount that the stop loss insurers were entitled to claim in respect of the settlement moneys, the stop loss insurers were entitled to be reimbursed any indemnity paid by them to an assured before that assured was fully indemnified by applying his share of the settlement moneys to a loss occurring below the excess in that assured's policy.

Lord Napier and Ettrick v. *Hunter* is dealt with again below. For the present discussion, all that must be observed is that in respect of the first question posed above, all members of the House agreed that the Stop Loss Insurers were entitled to recoup their indemnity from the settlement monies paid to the Names, and held that this right to recover was proprietary in nature, being an equitable lien. Lord Templeman stated:[46]

> The principles which dictated the decisions of our ancestors and inspired their references to the equitable obligations of an assured person towards an insurer entitled to subrogation are discernible and immutable. They establish that such an insurer has an enforceable equitable interest in the damages payable by the wrongdoer. The assured person is guilty of unconscionable conduct if he does not provide for the insurer to be recouped out of the damages awarded against the wrongdoer. Equity will not allow the assured person to insist on his legal rights to all the damages awarded against the wrongdoer and will restrain the assured person from receiving or dealing with those damages so far as they are required to recoup the insurer under the doctrine of subrogation.

The same pattern therefore exists in the insurance example and the victim and carer cases. In both models, RH (insured/victim) may suffer a loss attributable to the wrongdoing of PL (tortfeasor). S (insurer/carer) may indemnify RH and make good this loss. If RH recovers money referable to the loss already made good by S, S is entitled to share in the fund. The form of S's access to the fund varies. As *Thornton* v. *Board of School Trustees of School District No 57 (Prince George)*[47] demonstrates, the carer in some cases is the beneficiary of a trust and in others is merely entitled to rely on

---

[46] *Ibid.*, 738 PER LORD TEMPLEMAN. Consistent formulations of principle are to be found at 744–745 PER LORD GOFF, 746–747 PER LORD JAUNCEY, and 752 PER LORD BROWNE-WILKINSON. Lord Slynn agreed with the speech of Lord Templeman.

[47] *Thornton* v. *Board of School Trustees of School District No 57 (Prince George)* (1978) 83 DLR (3d) 480 upholding the relevant part of the decision of the British Columbia Court of Appeal reported at *Thornton* v. *Board of School Trustees of School District No 57 (Prince George)* (1976) 73 DLR (3d) 35.

a direction to pay.[48] In the insurance example, *Lord Napier and Ettrick* v. *Hunter* imposes an equitable lien. Chapter 9 returns to the question why in some cases the carer's access is proprietary and in others is not. At this point, all that we seek to show is that in both models, S participates in the fruits of the litigation brought by RH against PL.

S can compel RH to sue PL

The insurer (S) may compel the insured (RH) to enforce its rights against the wrongdoer (PL). The suit must be brought in the name of the insured since the right of action against the wrongdoer belongs to the insured.[49] In order to bring litigation, the insured must therefore consent to the insurer using the insured's name as the claimant of record.[50] If the insured does not consent, the insurer must go to a court of equity to compel the insured to lend her name to the proceedings. The award of subrogation is an equitable remedy and is thus discretionary. The court may refuse to compel the insured to lend her name if the terms are not just and equitable.[51]

As the law currently stands, the carer (S) cannot force the victim (RH) to sue the wrongdoer (PL). However, the possibility that the carer might hold such a right has never been tested by a court, and the contrary position produces a result which is an anathema to both logic and justice. The result of the prevailing orthodoxy is that the carer is left to the whim of the victim, who alone has the capacity to decide whether to recover damages whose purpose in part is to compensate the carer. It is therefore remarkable that the carer is left without a method of ensuring that the tortfeasor does not indirectly obtain the benefit of the carer's intervention. Without a right to force a claim against the tortfeasor, the carer cannot make certain that the tortfeasor will pay damages referable to the services provided and expenses paid by the carer. As will be argued later in this chapter, if the subrogation analogy that we are here seeking to draw is correct, then the law may in the

---

[48] For example: *Hunt* v. *Severs* [1994] 2 AC 350 proposed a trust of the damages. *Coderre* v. *Ethier* (1978) 85 DLR (3d) 621 imposed a direction to pay the carer.

[49] *Esso Petroleum Co Ltd* v. *Hall Russell & Co Ltd* [1989] 1 AC 643.

[50] As a matter of practicality, many contracts of indemnity insurance contain terms pursuant to which the insured gives this consent. In addition, the insurer may insist on an assignment of the rights of action against PL, even though an assignment is not necessary for the award of subrogation.

[51] *Yorkshire Insurance Co Ltd* v. *Nisbet Shipping Co Ltd* [1962] 2 QB 330; *Esso Petroleum Ltd* v. *Hall Russell & Co Ltd* [1989] 1 AC 643.

future recognise the carer's vulnerability and accord to the carer the same rights as the insurer.

Conclusion

The insurance example and the victim and carer cases contain the same pattern. Each fits the model described by Mitchell in the following way: PL (wrongdoer) causes loss to RH (insured/victim) and is thereby obligated to compensate RH. S (insurer/carer) intervenes and makes good part of this loss. S may compel RH to sue PL. If RH recovers damages in a suit against PL, S is entitled to participate in the fruits of this litigation.

The recognition of the subrogation analogy can thus be seen to have two potential benefits, which together transform the unsatisfactory condition of the present law. First, it takes us one step forward in explaining the carer's right to participate in the victim's damages. Secondly, this explanation brings with it what seemed impossible, a means of releasing the carer from the victim's power to decide whether or not to sue. In short, it becomes apparent that the carer's right to participate must include a right to compel suit.

Juridical foundation of the subrogand's rights

The first section has recorded the characteristics which are identified by Mitchell and are present in both the insurance cases and also the victim and carer cases. The two categories display the same pattern. The existence of this uniform pattern raises the possibility that the juridical basis of the insurer's rights might also provide a foundation for the carer's rights. In this section it will be argued that, to the extent that we are able coherently to explain the source of the insurer's rights, a similar principle operates in the case of the victim and carer. The task of the remainder of this chapter is twofold. First, it argues that the carer should, in common with the indemnity insurer, hold the right to force suit against the tortfeasor. Secondly, it paves the way for the argument that the carer's right to participate in the victim's damages is given to reverse the unjust enrichment which would otherwise remain. Chapter 4 has already explored this possibility but failed, according to the existing unjust factors, satisfactorily to identify the reason for restitution. As will be shown in chapter 8, the unjust factor is the policy against accumulation. This chapter, therefore, begins to explain the juridical basis of the carer's right to participate in the fund.

The taxonomy adopted in this book views the recognition of a right, or its correlative remedy, as the law's response to one of a generic list of events.[52] For example, the list of events to which the law responds includes at a minimum consent, unjust enrichment and wrongdoing. In this model, the rights held by the indemnity insurer must be attributable to the happening of one of these events to which the law responds. The first section demonstrated that the pattern of rights and obligations held by RH, S and PL are the same in both the insurance example and also the victim and carer cases. This section will argue that these rights are generated by the same event.

A few qualifications must be made at the outset. The first is that this book is about explaining the carer's right to share in the victim's damages. In the course of doing so, the analysis draws on our understanding of the rights available to an indemnity insurer. The point must be made, however, that it is not the work of this book to conduct a detailed examination of the insurance cases. While the discussion will hopefully add to our understanding of the rights given to the indemnity insurer, the work of other scholars addresses these in detail.[53] The second point is one of labelling. Lord Hoffmann has warned, '. . . the subject of subrogation is bedevilled by problems of terminology and classification which are calculated to cause confusion'.[54] Scholars use the term 'subrogation' differently. Taken literally, it means 'substitution'. It is in this sense that Mitchell uses it, limiting its scope to the right of S to control litigation brought by RH against PL.

---

[52] P. Birks, 'Equity in the Modern Law: An Exercise in Taxonomy' (1996) 26 *University of Western Australia Law Review* 1; P. Birks, 'Definition and Division: A Meditation on *Institutes* 3.13' in P. Birks (ed.), *The Classification of Obligations* (Oxford, 1997) 1; P. Birks, 'The Law of Restitution at the End of an Epoch' (1999) 28 *University of Western Australia Law Review* 13; P. Birks, 'Unjust Enrichment and Wrongful Enrichment' (2001) 79 *Texas Law Review* 1767. Other systems of classification have been proposed but will not be considered. For example: P. Cane, *The Anatomy of Tort Law* (Oxford, 1997), chapter 6; J. Davies, 'Restitution and Equitable Wrongs: An Australian Analogue' in F. Rose (ed.), *Consensus Ad Idem. Essays on Contract in Honour of Guenter Treitel* (London, 1996), pp. 158–78; R. Grantham and C. Rickett, 'On the Subsidiarity of Unjust Enrichment' (2001) 117 *Law Quarterly Review* 273; J. Stapleton, 'A New "Seascape" for Obligations: Reclassification on the Basis of Measure of Damages' in P. Birks (ed.), *The Classification of Obligations* (Oxford, 1997) 193.

[53] Mitchell; R. Derham, *Subrogation in Insurance Law* (Sydney, 1985).

[54] *Banque Financière de la Cité* v. *Parc (Battersea) Ltd* [1999] 1 AC 221 at 231 PER LORD HOFFMANN.

Although he agrees that the right of S to share in the damages obtained by RH is a right available to the insurer, he denies that this is a right properly described as subrogation.[55] Other scholars and judges use the term 'subrogation' more loosely, intending it to refer to the bundle of rights held by S, including both the right to control litigation and the right to share in the fund.[56] For the purposes of this chapter, the distinctions drawn in relation to the use of the term subrogation are not material. It is the substance of the rights enjoyed by S which are the subject of our analogy.

These qualifications having been given, this section will determine the extent to which the same event gives rise to the right to participate in the fund. The discussion will revolve around the two rights said to be available to the insurer after having indemnified the insured.[57] As set out above, these are that the insurer is able to compel the insured to bring proceedings against the wrongdoer and the insurer is entitled to the benefit of a equitable lien over the fund containing damages recovered by the insured in diminution of loss.[58]

Right to control litigation

The first right available to the indemnity insurer is the right to control litigation against the wrongdoer. The cause of action against the wrongdoer belongs to the insured. Such litigation must therefore be brought in the name of the insured. If the insured refuses to lend her name to such a suit, the insurer may go to a court of equity for orders compelling the insured to co-operate.[59] The task of this discussion is to show how the right to force litigation against the wrongdoer may be understood as being given in response to the insured's unjust enrichment. This section will:

---

[55] Mitchell, pp. 68–74. The same view is taken by Tettenborn, p. 56.

[56] For example: Burrows, p. 78; *Lord Napier and Ettrick* v. *Hunter* [1993] AC 713 at 732 and 738 PER LORD TEMPLEMAN.

[57] J. Birds, *Modern Insurance Law* (London, 1993), pp. 272ff; R. Derham, *Subrogation in Insurance Law* (Sydney, 1985), chapter 1; E.R. Hardy Ivamy, *General Principles of Insurance Law* (London, 1993), pp. 497–8; N. Leigh-Jones et al (eds.), *MacGillivray & Parkington on Insurance Law* (9th edn., London, 1997), chapter 22.

[58] A concise statement is given in *Lonrho Exports Ltd* v. *Export Credits Guarantee Department* [1996] 4 All ER 673 at 690 PER LIGHTMAN J. The insurer may also claim as money had and received the value of money paid to the insured on account of a loss in respect of which the insured has already received money from a third party. The insurer's personal claim will not be considered here.

[59] *Morris* v. *Ford Motor Co Ltd* [1973] 1 QB 792 at 800 PER LORD DENNING MR.

(1) outline the view that the insurer's right to control litigation is generated by unjust enrichment; (2) consider the consequence of this analysis for our understanding of the carer's rights; and (3) apply this analysis to the victim and carer cases.

Unjust enrichment analysis

Recent judicial statements confirm that the insurer's subrogation rights are given to reverse unjust enrichment.[60] *Banque Financière de la Cité* v. *Parc (Battersea) Ltd*[61] concerned the claim of Banque Financière to be subrogated to the security interest held against the property of Parc by a first registered charge holder. The decision is properly located not with the rights of sub-rogation held by an indemnity insurer, so-called 'simple subrogation', but in the category reviving subrogation.[62] Lord Hoffmann's speech, however, confirms that both species of subrogation are given to reverse an unjust enrichment. After referring to *Orakpo* v. *Manson Investments Ltd* [1978] AC 95 and *Lord Napier and Ettrick* v. *Hunter* [1993] AC 713, he said:[63]

> Furthermore, your Lordships drew attention to the fact that it is customary for the assured, on payment of the loss, to provide the insurer with a letter of subrogation, being no more nor less than an express assignment of his rights of recovery against any third party. Subrogation in this sense is a contractual arrangement for the transfer of rights against third parties. But the term is also used to describe an equitable remedy to reverse or prevent unjust enrichment which is not based upon any agreement or common intention of the party enriched and the party deprived. The fact that contractual subrogation and subrogation to prevent unjust enrichment both involve transfers of rights or something resembling transfers of rights should not be allowed to obscure the fact that one is dealing with radically different institutions. One is part of the law of contract and the other part of the law of restitution.

Mitchell argues that, properly described, only the right of the insurer to be substituted to the insured's claims against the wrongdoer falls within the

---

[60] The speech of Lord Diplock in *Orakpo* v. *Manson Investments Ltd* [1978] AC 95 at 104 acknowledges that subrogation is a remedy given to reverse unjust enrichment. However, at the time that case was decided, the House did not have the benefit of the widespread recognition of unjust enrichment which has occurred in the modern law.

[61] *Banque Financière de la Cité* v. *Parc (Battersea) Ltd* [1999] 1 AC 221 noted C. Mitchell, 'Subro-gation, Unjust Enrichment and Remedial Flexibility' [1998] *Restitution Law Review* 144.

[62] Mitchell, pp. 9–11.

[63] N. 61 above at 231–232 PER LORD HOFFMANN with whom Lord Griffiths and Lord Clyde agreed.

category subrogation.[64] It will be recalled that in his model PL (wrongdoer) causes loss to RH (insured/victim) and is thereby obligated to compensate RH. S (insurer/carer) intervenes and makes good part of this loss. S may compel RH to sue PL. If RH recovers damages in a suit against PL, S is entitled to participate in the fruits of this litigation. This discussion is concerned only with S's ability to be substituted to RH's claim against PL. In Mitchell's model, S is given the right to be substituted to RH's claim against PL in order to prevent the unjust enrichment of RH which would otherwise occur. The function of subrogation in his model is prophylactic.[65] The model thus contemplates that subrogation is given prospectively to reverse RH's enrichment. Put simply, by forcing RH to sue PL, two objectives are achieved. First, RH is divested of the right to sue PL and secondly, PL is forced to meet her liability to RH instead of having her obligations de facto discharged by the intervention of S. 'In order to prevent the insured from thus recovering more than a full indemnity for the insured loss, and secondarily in order to prevent the burden of paying for the insured loss from falling on the insurer rather than on the third party, the insurer is entitled in these circumstances to be simply subrogated to the insured's right of action.'[66]

Despite the obvious utility of the above analysis, certain difficulties exist. The first relates to failure of the analysis specifically to identify RH's enrichment. Mitchell states that '[t]he primary function of awarding S simple subrogation to RH's rights is to prevent RH from thus unjustly benefiting from S's payment'.[67] The problem with this statement is that, of itself, the right to force RH to sue PL does not remove this enrichment. On the contrary, it exacerbates it. Without more, the right of S to force suit against PL is merely a right to force RH to realise the value of her own enrichment. The proceeds of RH's suit against PL belong beneficially to the insured.[68] Merely by forcing RH to sue does not give S redress.

---

[64] Mitchell, pp. 74–80. Mitchell's work was cited with approval in *Banque Financière de la Cité* v. *Parc (Battersea) Ltd* [1999] 1 AC 221 at 228 PER LORD STEYN. However, Mitchell's views are not without criticism. M. Quinn, 'Review Essay. Subrogation, Restitution and Indemnity' (1996) 74 *Texas Law Review* 1361.

[65] Mitchell, p. 10. Mitchell restates this view in 'Subrogation, Unjust Enrichment and Remedial Flexibility' [1998] *Restitution Law Review* 144 at 145 and in Birks and Mitchell, p. 608 speaking of subrogation as a remedy to reverse potential enrichment.

[66] Mitchell, p. 74.   [67] Mitchell, p. 9.

[68] *Lonrho Exports Ltd* v. *Export Credits Guarantee Department* [1996] 4 All ER 673 at 690 PER LIGHTMAN J.

Mitchell's model might be enhanced if it is realised, as will be suggested in chapter 8, that the enrichment of RH is triggered by S's payment but reflected in the fact that RH continues to hold a right to sue PL. Mitchell is correct in his analysis that by forcing RH to sue PL, the rights of subrogation given to S ensure that RH is divested of the enrichment represented by RH's right to claim, but only when the enrichment is in that form. It is at this point that the other right of the insurer, the right to share in the fund, is essential. In this way, the two rights available to the indemnity insurer may be seen as two remedies designed to reverse the unjust enrichment of the insured. Lightman J in *Lonrho Exports Ltd* v. *Export Credit Guarantee Department* states the position:[69]

> The significant facts in such a situation are that: (a) the cause of action or right to recover belongs beneficially and (unless assigned) at law to the insured; (b) the insurer is entitled through the medium of the insured to enforce the cause of action to secure his recoupment; (c) while the House of Lords in *Lord Napier and Ettrick* v. *Hunter* left open whether the insurer has an equitable charge on the cause of action, he has an equitable lien on the recoveries. In short the insurer enforces a cause of action belonging beneficially to the insured for the joint benefit of the insured and the insurer and in the fruit of that endeavour the insurer has only a limited interest.

The other advantage of recognising that RH's enrichment is reflected in RH's ability to sue PL, notwithstanding a payment by S, is that Mitchell's model ceases to be one concerned with a prophylactic remedy. Burrows has criticised Mitchell's model on the basis that S's right to force RH to sue PL '... is not concerned to reverse an enrichment already received by the insured but rather prevents the possibility of the insured becoming enriched by recovery from D. On an extreme view that puts the first subrogation right outside the law of restitution. At the very least, it belongs outside the mainstream of restitution.'[70] If we take the view that RH's enrichment is already constituted when RH holds both the value of S's intervention, and also a right to claim against PL, this objection is removed. As will be shown in chapter 8, it is possible to view the damages recovered by RH as simply the substitute of the chose in action held against PL, which was itself enriching.[71]

---

[69] *Ibid.*
[70] Burrows, p. 81. See also R. Williams, 'Preventing Unjust Enrichment' [2000] *Restitution Law Review* 492.
[71] This argument is explored in greater depth in chapter 9, pp. 251ff.

The second difficulty with Mitchell's simple subrogation analysis is that it fails adequately to identify the unjust factor pursuant to which RH's enrichment is rendered unjust, and by which S is given the remedy of subrogation. Although he acknowledges the role of the policy against accumulation,[72] Mitchell advances two unjust factors said to explain the insurer's right, legal compulsion and necessity.

Dealing first with legal compulsion, he notes that it might be argued that an insurer's entitlement to be simply subrogated arises because it has made a payment under legal compulsion. With respect, this argument cannot be sustained. Leaving aside whether or not legal compulsion is properly recognised as an unjust factor in the law of restitution, the insurer is not legally compelled to intervene. Rather, the insurer pays the insured as it is contractually obligated to do according to a contract of indemnity insurance. Of itself, this cannot yield a right to claim in unjust enrichment. The second argument is that the insurer intervenes to benefit RH in necessitous circumstances thus entitling it to a claim against RH in unjust enrichment. Mitchell[73] himself expresses doubts similar to those noted in chapter 4 concerning the difficulties associated with recognising a right to restitution based on the policy ground of necessity. While there may be cases in which the insurer does intervene in circumstances of necessity, not all insurers will be entitled to this type of claim.

It may be easier simply to recognise that the right of the insurer to force litigation against the wrongdoer is based on the same policy objective which underpins the insurer's right to share in the fund. Mitchell refers extensively to the principle of indemnity, pursuant to which an insured whose loss is covered by an indemnity policy must never be more than fully compensated for his loss.[74] If RH's enrichment is seen to arise at the time that RH holds both the value of S's contribution and also the right to sue PL, it makes sense that the reason that RH is divested of this right is the law's concern that RH should not be doubly indemnified, or accumulate, in respect of the same loss.

Victim and carer cases

The first section of this chapter demonstrated that there are strong structural similarities between the indemnity insurer and the carer. In both cases, the claimant on the record is the party who is beneficially and legally the owner

---

[72] Described as the policy against overindemnity. Mitchell, p. 67.
[73] Mitchell, p. 101.   [74] Mitchell, chapter 6.

of the cause of action. Subrogation does not operate to effect an assignment of the insured's right of action to the insurer. The right remains that of the insured. Similarly, the carer has no cause of action against the wrongdoer. Rather, the cause of action is that of the victim.

This book argues that the carer's rights mirror those of the insured to the extent that the carer should also be able to compel the victim to lend her name to proceedings brought against the wrongdoer. The possibility that the carer might hold such a right has never been tested by a court, and the contrary position produces a result which is contrary to both justice and logic. If the subrogation analogy thus far revealed is correct, what we are seeing is the tip of an iceberg. Without the right to compel the victim in this way, the carer is left to the vagaries of the victim in deciding whether or not to seek an award. The unjust enrichment of both the carer and also the tortfeasor will thus remain. This conclusion follows from the powerful arguments put by Mitchell. In the absence of such a right for the carer, the tortfeasor will indirectly obtain the benefit of the carer's contribution because she will not be forced to pay damages calculated by reference to the carer's intervention. The victim will be unjustly enriched because she will continue to hold both the value of the care given and also the right to claim the value of this care from the tortfeasor.

It might erroneously be thought that conferring such rights on the carer raises the possibility of gold digging carers, who provide services and assistance to the victim not out of love and affection, but motivated by a desire to earn income. This risk must not be overstated. The situation currently prevailing is that the victim is entitled to sue the tortfeasor in respect of the carer's contribution and, in England and Canada, the victim is obligated to share these damages with the carer. The carer's existing entitlements are not, in a legal sense, a function of the altruism of the carer. Rather, the court looks to the fact that the carer has contributed necessary services in a situation of crisis. The novel right suggested for the carer, the right to compel suit by the victim against the wrongdoer, is simply the corollary of the carer's existing right to share in the fund. Returning to the insurance subrogation analogy, it must be remembered that an award of subrogation is an equitable remedy and is thus discretionary. The parallel right enjoyed by the insurer is therefore given only in the discretion of the court and the carer's right should likewise be exercised only if it is just and equitable to do so.

It is therefore essential that the carer be given a right equivalent to that of the insurer to force litigation. This book rejects the view that the victim's suit is brought against the tortfeasor on her own uncompellable initiative. Although there is as yet no case law to substantiate this proposition, logic and justice dictate that the carer must hold such a right. Without it, not only is the carer's position left vulnerable to the whim of the victim in deciding whether or not to sue, but the carer's right to share in the fund, which is established in the cases, becomes very difficult to explain.

The right to participate in the fruits of litigation

We are here concerned with the existence of a right pursuant to which the insurer is entitled to participate in the damages obtained by the insured, and the apparently similar right of the carer to share in the damages won by the victim. What must be established is whether the rights enjoyed by the carer and insurer are generated by the same event. In order to do so it is necessary to identify the juridical basis of the insurer's rights. Leaving aside those cases in which the parties agree as a matter of contract that the insurer will have the right to participate, it is arguable that the right of the insurer to participate in the fund is generated by the event labelled 'unjust enrichment'. The discussion in this section will show how an unjust enrichment analysis is capable of explaining the insurer's right to the fund and suggest that the same framework applies in the victim and carer cases.

Unjust enrichment analysis

Burrows argues that the insurer's right to participate is given to reverse the enrichment of the insured which would otherwise arise if the insured were permitted to retain both the payment by the insurer and the damages paid by the wrongdoer.[75] The two difficulties he identifies are first, that the enrichment does not easily meet the 'at the expense of' requirement of such a claim and secondly, that it is not certain what is the unjust factor or reason for restitution.[76] These will be dealt with in reverse order.

---

[75] Burrows, pp. 79–81; Mitchell, pp. 82–6; Tettenborn, p. 56. See also S. Degeling, 'A New Reason for Restitution: The Policy Against Accumulation' (2002) 22 *Oxford Journal of Legal Studies* 435.

[76] Burrows, p. 80.

Turning first to the reason for restitution. It is possible to construct arguments based on mistake[77] and failure of basis.[78] For example, it might be argued that the insurer intervenes mistakenly believing it is obligated to do so, or unaware that the insured's loss has already been made good.[79] Equally, it might be argued that the insurer agrees to indemnify the insured on the basis only that the insured is suffering a loss. If, before the insurer's payment, the insured has received a loss-ameliorating payment from the wrongdoer, the basis of the insured's payment may be seen to have failed. The difficulty with these unjust factors is that they will never consistently explain the juridical basis of the insurer's rights. While it is true that on some facts they will be of utility, these unjust factors do not systematically explain the insurer's entitlement to share in the fund.

Burrows and Mitchell[80] both concede that a better way of understanding the insurer's right to participate may be located in the policy rationale invoked by the courts when explaining the insurer's rights. The right of an insurer to recover amounts paid by way of indemnity is '... founded upon the general policy laid down by the courts that an insured whose loss is covered by an indemnity policy must never be more than fully indemnified for his loss'.[81] To allow the insured to retain both the funds paid by way of indemnity and any damages awarded runs the risk that the insured will be doubly indemnified or accumulate in respect of the same loss. Another way of saying this is to recognise that on recovering compensatory damages from the tortfeasor, the loss of the insured has been made good. In this way, the insured is no longer suffering a loss. Therefore, the insurer is no longer obliged to indemnify the insured and should be entitled to claw back any funds paid by way of indemnity. The policy rationale underpinning the insurer's right to participate will be explored more fully in chapter 8. As will be shown, the insurer's entitlements are an example of an unjust factor

---

[77] Mitchell, chapter 9; Burrows, p. 80.   [78] Mitchell, chapters 10 and 11; Burrows, p. 80.

[79] *King* v. *Victoria Insurance Company Limited* [1896] AC 250.

[80] Burrows, p. 80 and Mitchell, p. 67.

[81] Mitchell, p. 67. *Darrell* v. *Tibbitts* (1880) 5 QBD 560 at 562 PER BRETT LJ; *Castellain* v. *Preston* (1883) 11 QBD 380 at 386 PER BRETT LJ; *Re Miller, Gibb & Co Ltd* [1957] 2 All ER 266 at 271–272 PER WYNN-PARRY J; *England* v. *Guardian Insurance Ltd* [2000] Lloyd's Rep IR 404 at 409–410 PER JUDGE THORNTON QC; *Arab Bank plc* v. *John D Wood Ltd* [2000] 1 WLR 857 at 875 PER MANCE LJ; *Caledonia North Sea Ltd* v. *Norton (No 2) Ltd* (*in Liquidation*) [2002] 1 All ER (Comm) 321 at 328–329 PER LORD BINGHAM.

called the policy against accumulation. A convenient statement of the policy is that given by Brett LJ in *Castellain* v. *Preston*:[82]

> The very foundation, in my opinion, of every rule which has been applied to insurance law is this, namely, that the contract of insurance contained in a marine or fire policy is a contract of indemnity, and of indemnity only, and that this contract means that the assured, in case of a loss against which the policy has been made, shall be fully indemnified, but shall never be more than fully indemnified.

The second difficulty is the 'at the expense of' element. This is demonstrated by *Lord Napier and Ettrick* v. *Hunter*. The Names (RH) commenced proceedings against Outhwaite (PL) in respect of the latter's negligence. This litigation was settled and settlement monies were paid by Outhwaite and held by a third party on behalf of the Names. The House of Lords granted the Stop Loss Insurers (S) an equitable lien over the fund of settlement monies. The problem is to do with the identity of the specific enrichment in relation to which restitution is given. The general law of unjust enrichment says that the defendant (RH/Names) is enriched at the expense of the claimant (S/Stop Loss Insurer) and is thus liable to make restitution. The fund over which the lien in favour of the Stop Loss Insurer attached was the fund of settlement moneys held on behalf of the Names. The problem was that directionally, this money came not from the claimant in the unjust enrichment claim (S/Stop Loss Insurer), but from the tortfeasor (PL/Outhwaite). Strictly speaking, the only enrichment which passed from the Stop Loss Insurer was its payment pursuant to the contract of indemnity. Burrows attempts to resolve this conflict by pointing out that the insurance subrogation example is an exception to the '...normal privity rule in that the benefit is being rendered by someone other than the plaintiff'.[83]

However, as discussed in chapter 8, it is possible to avoid the difficulties posed by the 'at the expense of' element via recognition of the policy against accumulation as an unjust factor. At this point, all that must be noticed is that the existing unjust factors are not satisfactorily able to account for the insurer's right to share in the fund. They command little consistent support on the facts of the indemnity insurance cases, and lead to

---

[82] *Castellain* v. *Preston* (1883) 11 QBD 380 at 386 PER BRETT LJ.
[83] Burrows, p. 80.

difficulties in satisfying the 'at the expense of' element of the unjust enrichment analysis.

Victim and carer cases

The consequence of the above analysis for the victim and carer cases is to reveal the existence of a policy motivated ground of restitutionary claim. Chapter 8 will show that the carer's right to participate is likewise given to reverse the unjust enrichment of the victim which would otherwise remain, and that this right is supported by the policy against accumulation.

Conclusion

The purpose of this section has been to briefly show that the two rights available to the insurer are given to reverse unjust enrichment. In Mitchell's model PL (wrongdoer) causes loss to RH (insured/victim) and is thereby obligated to compensate RH. S (insurer/carer) intervenes and makes good part of this loss. S may compel RH to sue PL. If RH recovers damages in a suit against PL, S is entitled to participate in the fruits of this litigation.

S is given two rights: the right to force RH to sue PL and the right to share in the fund of damages recovered by RH. RH's enrichment is triggered when S intervenes and lies in RH's ability to hold both the value of S's contribution and also the right to sue PL. By forcing RH to sue PL, S divests RH of the enrichment in this form. The damages won by RH's suit are a substitute of her right to sue and it is this enrichment which is reversed by S's right to share in the fund.

Conclusion

The task of this chapter has been to document the analogy which exists between the indemnity insurer and the insured on the one hand, and the carer and victim on the other. In doing so two objectives have been achieved. First, we have argued for the recognition of the carer's right to force litigation against the wrongdoer. Secondly, we have revealed the basis on which the carer's right to share in the fund will convincingly be explained.

The first section observes that, leaving aside the nature of the insurer's rights, the same pattern exists in both categories. Each conforms to the pattern identified by Mitchell. This book argues that the right of the carer to participate, apparently arbitrary and unprincipled, is not isolated but is an example of an existing category. The following pattern exists both in the insurance cases and those concerning victims and carers: (1) S (insurer/carer) intervenes unofficiously; (2) the obligations of PL (wrongdoer) are not discharged; (3) S participates in RH's (insured/victim) recoveries; and (4) S can compel RH to sue.

The second section sets out the components of the view which sees the insurer's rights as being generated by the event labelled 'unjust enrichment'. The reason for restitution is the policy objective of preventing the overindemnification of the insured. Chapter 8 will show that this policy motivation underpins the novel unjust factor called the 'policy against accumulation'. This unjust factor is present in the victim and carer cases, and also the insurance cases, thus explaining S's entitlement to share in the fund and completing the subrogation analogy.

So far as the law now stands, the subrogation analogy is strictly sustainable only in respect of the insurer's right to recoup the value of any indemnity paid. It does not yet exist in relation to the right of the insurer to force the insured to bring litigation against the wrongdoer. However, it is the great merit of this explanation of the carer's participation that it promises to eliminate the bizarre configuration in which the carer is on the one hand entitled to participate in the damages, but on the other hand is unable to ensure that these damages are recovered by forcing suit against the wrongdoer. We have seen that one part of the carer's right to be subrogated is the right to participate in the victim's damages. We may yet see the other part, namely the carer's right to use the victim's name in litigation against the tortfeasor.

The categories of subrogation are not closed, and there is evidence that an insurance subrogation analysis continues to be considered and applied in novel situations.[84] The reader may not agree that the rules regulating the carer's access to the victim's damages are a hitherto unrecognised example of the rights accorded to an indemnity insurer. However, this does not preclude the argument that the rights are very similar. To this extent, we are able to explain the carer's right to participate in the damages obtained by the victim. In this sense at least, the concern expressed by the majority

---

[84] *In re TH Knitwear (Wholesale) Ltd* [1988] 1 Ch 275 (whether VAT Commissioners could rely on a subrogated claim against the liquidator of an insolvent company). See also the general statements of principle in *Orakpo* v. *Manson Investments Ltd* [1978] AC 95 at 104 PER LORD DIPLOCK.

Justices of the High Court of Australia in *Kars* v. *Kars*,[85] that the law in this area is persistently characterised by absurdities and anomalies, is unfounded. In recognising the analogy between the position of the carer and the indemnity insurer, the right of the carer to participate in the victim's damages is placed on a principled foundation.

---

[85] *Kars* v. *Kars* (1996) 187 CLR 354 at 382 PER TOOHEY, MCHUGH, GUMMOW AND KIRBY JJ.

The policy against accumulation

This chapter is concerned with the novel policy motivated unjust factor called the policy against accumulation. The unjust enrichment framework adopted in this book separates the unjust factors into two categories.[1] The first category establishes injustice on the ground that the claimant's intention to benefit the defendant is in some way deficient or qualified. The second comprises the so-called policy motivated unjust factors, according to which the law recognises particular grounds of claim in order to promote policy objectives. The policy against accumulation falls into the latter category, and is relevant where a claimant receives a benefit, or has the right to recover a debt or damages from another party, and receives, or has the right to receive, in respect of the *same debt or damage* from a third party. The claimant may not be permitted to receive value from both parties. If she does, she must reverse one transfer, thereby preventing her accumulation in respect of the same debt or damage.[2] The claimant's obligation to return value is given to reverse the unjust enrichment which would otherwise remain.

The question to be answered by this book is to explain the juridical basis of the carer's right to share in the fund of damages recovered by the victim. The insurance subrogation analogy set out in chapter 7 shows us that the indemnity insurer's right to share in the insured's damages also requires explanation. It seems tolerably clear that both are rights raised to reverse unjust enrichment. The difficulty has been to identify the relevant unjust factor. This chapter argues that both are explicable by the policy against accumulation. In doing so, the subrogation analogy commenced in chapter 7 is completed. By recognising that the insurance cases, and also the victim and carer cases, conform to Mitchell's model, various difficulties

---

[1] Birks and Mitchell, pp. 543–4 and n. 89 on p. 548.

[2] This chapter is a further development of ideas earlier expressed in S. Degeling, 'The Policy Against Accumulation as an Unjust Factor' in E. Schrage, *Unjust Enrichment and the Law of Contract* (The Hague, 2001), pp. 167–92.

are exposed. The first is that as the law currently stands, the carer has no means of forcing the victim to seek redress from the wrongdoer. Chapter 7 shows that this is an anomaly, and argues for the recognition of a right for the carer similar to the insurer's ability to compel suit against the wrongdoer. The second difficulty is to explain the juridical basis of the right to share in the fund. This chapter places on a principled foundation the carer's and the insurer's right to share in the fund. Both are raised to reverse unjust enrichment on the basis of the policy against accumulation.

It must be conceded that the policy against accumulation is a novel ground of claim which has received little attention by scholars and judges.[3] This chapter therefore proceeds in four parts. The first is an outline of the unjust factor. The second briefly identifies the evidence which may be marshalled to support the existence of this new unjust factor. The third applies the policy against accumulation to the carer and also the indemnity insurer, demonstrating how it best explains their respective rights to share in the fund. Finally, the fourth part considers the broader ramifications of the unjust factor, examining other cases in which it might also apply.

Outline of the policy against accumulation

The policy against accumulation applies where a claimant (RH) receives a benefit, or has the right to recover a debt or damages from another party (PL), and receives or has the right to receive, in respect of the *same debt or damage* from a third party (S). The claimant will not usually be entitled to retain the value transferred by both PL and S. In conformity with the policy, the claimant will not be permitted to accumulate in respect of this debt or damage and must reverse one transfer. In order to apply the policy, an anterior question must first be answered. It is necessary to know whether it is the value transferred to RH by PL or S which must be returned. This is a question to be answered on the facts of each category of case, taking into account the unique policy considerations. For example, on the facts of the

---

[3] There has been some work done to establish its existence. S. Degeling, 'The Policy Against Accumulation as an Unjust Factor' in E. Schrage, *Unjust Enrichment and the Law of Contract* (The Hague, 2001), pp. 167–92; S. Degeling, 'A New Reason for Restitution: The Policy Against Accumulation' (2002) 22 *Oxford Journal of Legal Studies* 435; S. Degeling, 'Carers' Claims: Unjust Enrichment and Tort' [2000] *Restitution Law Review* 172 at 186–8. As was outlined in chapter 7, Burrows suggests the policy against overcompensation as an unjust factor in connection with the indemnity insurer's right to claw back the value of its indemnity. Burrows, p. 80. See also A. Burrows, 'Improving Contract and Tort' in *Understanding the Law of Obligations: Essays on Contract, Tort and Restitution* (Oxford, 1998), p. 188.

victim and carer cases, we know it is the value transferred from the carer which must be returned.

In common with the established unjust factors, an unjust enrichment claim founded on the policy against accumulation must also satisfy the other elements of a claim. Chapter 4 documents how these are met on the facts of the victim and carer cases. The discussion in this chapter completes the unjust enrichment analysis, the element of injustice being met by application of the policy against accumulation. The next section of this chapter sets out the evidence supporting the existence of the unjust factor. When reading this evidence it is vital to note that the analysis operates at two levels. At the macro level, it is necessary to recognise the existence of a general theme or policy against accumulations in our private law. More relevant is that working at the micro level, in which the policy is operating as an unjust factor. It is important to keep in mind this distinction because it is not always the case that the policy operates to found a claim in unjust enrichment.

Evidence to support the existence of the policy against accumulation

As has been said, the policy against accumulation is relevant between three parties: the claimant (RH) who receives a benefit, or has the right to recover a debt or damages from another party (PL), and receives, or has the right to receive, in respect of the *same debt or damage* from a third party (S). The evidence presented below is an outline of that available in support of the policy, noting in particular cases where it appears in addition to operate as an unjust factor. Broadly speaking, there are three categories of case: (1) only PL is required to transfer value to RH; (2) both PL and S are required to transfer value to RH; and (3) the rare case in which RH is permitted to accumulate.

Only PL is obligated to transfer value to RH

The following are examples in which only PL is required to transfer value to RH, for example via payment of money or the performance of services. Although S is not obligated to do so, S transfers value to RH. The policy against accumulation dictates that RH may not retain the value given by both PL and S. RH must therefore return value; in the cases below it is that given by S.

Payment of debts

Let us assume the case where a creditor (RH) is owed money by a debtor (PL). The third party (S) is not obligated to meet this debt but pays RH anyway. If PL also pays, RH will not be permitted to retain both payments. RH cannot accumulate in respect of the same debt. Irrespective of whether PL's debt is thereby discharged, the pattern of the cases is consistent with the policy against accumulation.

PL's debt is not discharged   The general rule is that unless previously authorised or ratified by the debtor (PL), the payment made by the third party (S) will not discharge the debt to the creditor (RH). There is some evidence that if S pays in circumstances of necessity, or under legal compulsion, the debt automatically will be discharged.[4] Thus if S mistakenly pays RH in respect of PL's debt, and we assume RH does not subsequently adopt the payment, PL's debt will not be discharged. Since the debt remains, RH is still entitled to look to PL for payment. The potential therefore exists for R to accumulate value in respect of the same debt.

On such facts it is likely that RH's accumulation will be prevented by the mistake pursuant to which S paid. It is uncontroversial that S may establish an unjust enrichment claim against RH, seeking return of the value transferred by mistake. Subject to the usual question of enrichment and the availability of defences, S will succeed against RH if the mistake caused the payment.[5] In this way, RH's vulnerability to an unjust enrichment claim based on the mistake works to reverse any accumulation. The presence of the policy against accumulation in such cases is not so obvious since other unjust factors, such as mistake, can do the work. However, it is important to notice that the result is consistent with the policy against accumulation. RH is not entitled to be paid twice in respect of the same debt.

---

[4] *Owen* v. *Tate* [1976] 1 QB 402 at 409–410 PER LORD SCARMAN; *The 'Zuhal K' and the 'Selin'* [1987] 1 Lloyd's Rep 151 at 156 PER SHEEN J; *Exall* v. *Partridge* (1799) 8 TR 308 at 311 PER BLANC J; *Moule* v. *Garrett* (1872) LR 7 Exch 101 at 104 PER COCKBURN J. For discussion of the principles governing the discharge of debts see P. Birks and J. Beatson, 'Unrequested Payment of Another's Debt' (1976) *Law Quarterly Review* 188; Burrows, pp. 222–30; Mitchell, pp. 19–26; Goff and Jones, pp. 16–17 and 204–8; Virgo, pp. 225–30.

[5] *Barclays Bank Ltd* v. *WJ Simms Son and Cooke (Southern) Ltd* [1980] QB 677; *Kleinwort Benson Ltd* v. *Lincoln City Council* [1998] 3 WLR 1095; *David Securities Pty Ltd* v. *Commonwealth Bank of Australia* (1992) 175 CLR 353.

PL's debt is discharged It is of course possible to concede that the third party (S) might have paid in circumstances of necessity, or under the force of legal compulsion. As has been said, in such cases, irrespective of whether the debtor (PL) adopts the payment, it may be argued that the debt automatically is discharged. Since the debt is discharged, the creditor (RH) is not entitled to pursue PL for payment. RH is not permitted to accumulate. Once again, the role of the policy against accumulation is not as prominent as in other examples. This is because the work is done by other unjust factors and the rules concerning the discharge of debts. However, the result is consistent with the policy against accumulation.

Tort victims and carers

A victim of tort (RH) is permitted to claim from the tortfeasor (PL) damages in order to compensate for loss.[6] In all jurisdictions under investigation in this book, as part of this damages claim, RH is entitled to recover on account of necessitous assistance provided by the carer (S).[7] PL's liability to RH is not affected by this intervention. There is therefore a risk that, by virtue of the fact that RH holds a right to sue PL which is not reduced by the value of S's intervention, RH will accumulate in respect of the same loss. In those cases which permit the carer access to the victim's damages, chapter 4 briefly records that there is some evidence that the courts have invoked the policy against accumulation to justify the right to participate.[8] The evidence in the victim and carer category is particularly important as it recognises not only the existence of the policy, but provides evidence of its operation as an unjust factor.

Our starting point is *Hunt* v. *Severs*.[9] Miss Hunt (RH) was injured through the negligence of her fiancé Mr Severs (PL) when travelling as a pillion passenger on a motorcycle driven by him. She suffered terrible injuries, including extreme paraplegia. Much of her care was provided by Mr Severs (S). Miss Hunt claimed damages on account of his care of her up until the date of trial and his estimated future care to be provided to her. The facts were complicated by Mr Severs' dual identity as carer and tortfeasor.

---

[6] *British Transport Commission* v. *Gourley* [1956] AC 185.

[7] *Hunt* v. *Severs* [1994] 2 AC 350; *Griffiths* v. *Kerkemeyer* (1977) 139 CLR 161; *Kars* v. *Kars* (1996) 187 CLR 354; *Grincelis* v. *House* (2000) 201 CLR 321; *Thornton* v. *Board of School Trustees of School District No 57 (Prince George)* (1978) 83 DLR (3d) 480.

[8] Chapter 4, p. 86.   [9] *Hunt* v. *Severs* [1994] 2 AC 350.

On the basis that he would, in his capacity as carer, be entitled via a trust to share in Miss Hunt's damages, the House of Lords reduced Miss Hunt's award by the value of Mr Severs' past and estimated future care. Importantly, this reduction was not on the basis that his liability as tortfeasor had been discharged. Rather, it was because the House of Lords held that as carer, he was entitled to participate via a trust in the fund of damages. The reasoning of the House was that, if Mr Severs had been required to pay an undiscounted sum by way of damages, he would in effect be paying money into a fund of which, in his capacity as carer, he was beneficiary. It was therefore to avoid the anomalous consequence of the tortfeasor paying himself that the amount of Miss Hunt's damages award was reduced. On the facts of *Hunt* v. *Severs* therefore, Miss Hunt (RH) did not in fact accumulate, because she was not entitled to recover from Mr Severs (or more accurately his insurer) (PL) the value of necessary services provided by him (S). However, this was only to avoid the bizarre configuration which would otherwise result. Of relevance to this chapter is the configuration in the normal case, where the victim holds damages in trust for the carer.

Their Lordships' decision to impose a trust in such cases was in part based on the desire of the House to harmonise the relevant laws of England and Scotland. Lord Bridge referred to those provisions of Part II of the Administration of Justice Act 1982 which apply to Scotland.[10] S. 8(1) imposes on the person responsible for the victim's loss an obligation to pay damages to the victim in part comprising such sum as represents reasonable remuneration for the necessary services provided by a relative, and any reasonable expenses incurred in connection with these services. S. 8(2) imposes on the victim a statutory obligation to account to the carer for any such damages recovered. The report of the Scottish Law Commission pursuant to which s. 8(2) was enacted justified the victim's obligation to account on the basis of the risk that the victim would otherwise be compensated for a loss which, as a matter of practicality, he had not suffered. In effect, the desire of the legislature was to prevent the victim accumulating in respect of loss. Para. 22 of the report states:[11]

---

[10] *Ibid.*, 362 PER LORD BRIDGE.
[11] Scottish Law Commission, *Damages For Personal Injuries, Report on (1) Admissibility of Claims For Services (2) Admissible Deductions* (Report No 51, 1978), para. 22. Cited in *Hunt* v. *Severs* [1994] 2 AC 350 at 362 PER LORD BRIDGE.

In cases where services have been rendered gratuitously to an injured person, it is artificial to regard that person as having suffered a net loss in the events which happened. The loss is in fact sustained by the person rendering the services, a point vividly illustrated in cases where he has lost earnings in the course of rendering those services. We suggest, therefore, that it is wrong in principle, in cases where services have been rendered gratuitously by another to an injured person, to regard the latter as having in fact suffered a loss.

In result, the position in Scotland is that the victim (RH) may claim against the wrongdoer (PL) for the value of the carer's (S's) intervention. In recognition of the risk that this will allow the victim to accumulate in respect of loss, the victim is obligated to account to the carer for any such damages won in the suit.[12] The other solutions to this problem, such as reducing the victim's damages claim by the value of the assistance or alternatively allowing the carer a direct claim, were not adopted. In permitting the carer access to the fund the House purported merely to harmonise the relevant laws of England and Scotland. Closer analysis reveals that this reason in the end reduces to an argument supporting the carer's access on the basis that it removes any accumulation by the victim which would otherwise remain.

Such arguments had earlier been presented in *Donnelly* v. *Joyce*,[13] even though not a case in which a mechanism was imposed in favour of the carer. The infant victim Christopher Donnelly (RH) was negligently injured in a road accident. He required hospitalisation and after his release from hospital, his mother Mrs Donnelly (S) gave up her job in order to care for her son. The victim commenced proceedings against the tortfeasor (PL) claiming damages calculated by reference to the value of his mother's forgone wages for the period in which he was in her care. The case came to the Court of Appeal in order to decide whether the victim could properly recover the value of his mother's care.

The tortfeasor argued that the availability of the victim's claim depended on whether or not the victim had a legal obligation to pay the carer. In the absence of a contractual obligation to pay his mother, the tortfeasor argued that the victim could not claim in respect of her care. The Court of Appeal rejected this submission, holding that the victim was entitled to claim for the

---

[12] Administration of Justice Act 1982 s. 8(2): 'The relative shall have no direct right of action in delict against the responsible person in respect of the services or expenses referred to in this section, but the injured person shall be under an obligation to account to the relative for any damages recovered from the responsible person under this section.'

[13] *Donnelly* v. *Joyce* [1974] 1 QB 454.

cost of meeting the needs generated by the tortfeasor's negligence.[14] The victim thus recovered an amount on account of the carer's services. The Court of Appeal made clear that the right of the victim to claim against the wrongdoer was not a function of the victim's obligation to pay the carer. The Court did not dispute that such an obligation might arise, but questioned whether it was relevant for the claim against the tortfeasor. In particular, the Court acknowledged that a moral obligation to pay the carer may bind the conscience of the victim. Such an obligation arises when the victim accumulates in respect of the same loss:[15]

> Suppose the provider [S], being a charitable person, the Good Samaritan of St. Luke's Gospel, for example, has advanced money to provide nursing treatment for an injured neighbour [RH] who had suffered injuries by the crime or negligence of another [PL]. It might well be thought, by the Good Samaritan and other right-minded people, that there was no moral obligation on the injured man to repay unless and until he recovered compensation from the wrongdoer. But it might well be thought, also, by right-minded people that, if and when he recovered compensation, there *would* be such a moral obligation to at least offer repayment.

Consistent arguments are to be found in *In the Matter of GDM and the Protected Estates Act 1983 (NSW)*.[16] This was a case before the Protective Division of the Supreme Court of New South Wales. GDM (RH) had suffered severe brain damage at the age of two months when he was thrown from a car owned by his father and driven by his mother (PL). He sued his parents in negligence and his claim was compromised, a verdict of $2.5 million being entered by the consent of the parties. An order was made under the Protected Estates Act 1983 (NSW) pursuant to which the Protective Commissioner was appointed as the manager of GDM's estate. This claim, brought when GDM was eight years old, concerned his parents' entitlement to be paid out of the fund administered on his behalf. In particular, they claimed payment for their past and estimated future care of GDM. The Protective Commissioner sought the guidance of the court as to whether he should pay the parents (S).

Powell J ordered that an amount should be paid out of GDM's estate on account of past care and expenses, and that a continuing carer's allowance

---

[14] *Ibid.*, 462 PER MEGAW LJ who read the judgment of the Court of Appeal.
[15] N. 13 above at 463, PER MEGAW LJ.
[16] *In the Matter of GDM and the Protected Estates Act 1983 (NSW)* (1992) Aust Torts Rep ¶81–190.

be awarded for future care.[17] Of interest is the reasoning adopted by the court in reaching this decision. It must be remembered that the accepted position in Australia is that the damages belong beneficially to the victim. There is no legal obligation binding the victim to share the damages with the carer.[18] However, for example when considering the carer's entitlement to share in the fund of damages managed on behalf of an incapable victim, the courts have acknowledged a moral obligation binding the victim to pay the carer.[19] In *GDM*, the court went one step further and identified the basis for this moral obligation. The victim is obligated to pay the carer to avoid accumulating in respect of his loss:[20]

> ... it is not the fact that services have been gratuitously provided, [by the carer] but the fact that an *amount representing the value of those services has been included in the plaintiff's verdict*, which gives rise to a moral – but not legal, or equitable – obligation to the provider of the services...

Finally, reference must be made to *Feng* v. *Graham*, in which the damages recovered by the victim were impressed with a trust in favour of the carer. The victim was Mrs Feng (RH) who was struck by the tortfeasor's vehicle and suffered a leg injury. As a result, she was unable to perform her usual household chores, and from March 1984 until the end of April 1985 these were performed by her husband Mr Feng (S). Mrs Feng sued the tortfeasor (RH) claiming the value of the household chores performed by Mr Feng. The trial judge allowed her claim and awarded $5,000 in damages '... in trust for any person or even a relative who assisted in the homemaking'.[21] The tortfeasor appealed against this part of the trial judge's decision, questioning only the value of compensation awarded

---

[17] *Ibid.*, 61,692.

[18] *Griffiths* v. *Kerkemeyer* (1977) (139) CLR 161; *Kars* v. *Kars* (1996) 187 CLR 354; *Grincelis* v. *House* (2000) 201 CLR 321.

[19] The cases involve the protective jurisdiction of the court and a claim by the carer for payment out of the fund of damages administered on behalf of a severely incapacitated victim. Examples include: *Re B* [2000] NSWSC 44; *Beasley* v. *Marshall (No 4)* (1986) 42 SASR 407; *Re DJR and the Mental Health Act 1958* [1983] 1 NSWLR 557; *Re ES and the Mental Health Act 1958* [1994] 3 NSWLR 341; *In the Matter of GDM and the Protected Estates Act 1983 (NSW)* (1992) Aust Torts Rep ¶81–190; *Goode* v. *Thompson and Anor* (2001) Aust Torts Reports ¶81–617; *Jones* v. *Moylan [No 2]* (2000) 23 WAR 65; *Re N* (2001) 33 MVR 237; *W* v. *Q* (1992) 1 Tas R 301.

[20] *In the Matter of GDM and the Protected Estates Act 1983 (NSW)* (1992) Aust Torts Rep ¶81–190 at 61,686–61,687 PER POWELL J, emphasis added.

[21] *Feng* v. *Graham* (1988) 25 BCLR (2d) 116 at 125 PER WALLACE JA quoting the decision of the trial judge.

on account of the carer's contribution. The imposition of a trust was not challenged. The British Columbia Court of Appeal upheld the trial judge's award and made the following observations about the use of a trust in favour of the carer. After referring to the *dicta* of Lord Denning MR in *Cunningham* v. *Harrison* that the victim should hold the damages in trust for the carer, Wallace JA observed that such a trust reverses accumulation by the victim:[22]

> This direction creates a problem. If the spouse does not have a legal right to compensation – having agreed to perform the services gratuitously – it is difficult to perceive how she could enforce the trust. Unless this desirable objective is obtained, the court may well be compensating the victim for a loss which he has not suffered and thus unjustly enriching him at the expense of a good samaritan.

Both PL and S are obligated to transfer value to RH

There are also examples in which RH is entitled against both PL and S. In general RH is not permitted actually to seek value from both. If RH does end up being paid twice, she is not permitted to retain both transfers.

Passing on a tax burden

In certain cases a party obligated to pay tax (RH) passes the cost of this tax onto third parties (S), but is nonetheless entitled to sue the revenue (PL) in unjust enrichment. An example is the Australian case of *Commissioner of State Revenue (Victoria)* v. *Royal Insurance Ltd*[23] which concerned the payment of stamp duty. The Stamps Act 1958 (Vict) imposed on Royal Insurance (RH) the obligation to pay stamp duty on certain policies of insurance. It was Royal's practice to pass the cost of the stamp duty onto its policy holders (S). Royal discovered that the Stamps Act had been amended and that it had mistakenly overpaid the Revenue (PL). Royal therefore sued the Revenue in unjust enrichment, seeking to recover the overpayments. The Revenue resisted the claim, arguing that the payments had not been at the expense of Royal Insurance because it had passed the burden of the duty onto its policy holders. This argument failed and Royal succeeded,

---

[22] *Ibid.*, 126 PER WALLACE JA who delivered the judgment of the British Columbia Court of Appeal.

[23] *Commissioner of State Revenue (Victoria)* v. *Royal Insurance Ltd* (1994) 182 CLR 51.

notwithstanding that it had recouped from policy holders the cost of the stamp duty.[24]

Of relevance to this chapter is the brief reference in the case to the risk that, in being permitted to sue the Revenue in respect of a duty it had passed onto the policy holders, Royal would be 'overcompensated'[25] or accumulate recoveries in respect of the same debt. The narrow purpose of Mason CJ's remarks were to confirm that in Australia the 'at the expense of' element of an unjust enrichment claim does not require a corresponding impoverishment of the claimant. All that is required is that the payment came, as a matter of direction, from Royal Insurance to the Revenue. Therefore, the fact that the burden of the stamp duty had ultimately been borne by the policy holders, and Royal had suffered no corresponding impoverishment, did not derogate from Royal's entitlement to claim against the Revenue in unjust enrichment. However, Mason CJ also dealt with the risk that, in pursuing such a claim, Royal Insurance would accumulate recoveries. He stated that, subject to the evidential difficulties inherent in identifying the relevant policy holders, Royal Insurance should be obligated to return value to them:[26]

> Even if it had been established that Royal [RH] charged the tax as a separate item to its policy holders so that it was a constructive trustee of the moneys representing the separate charge when it made payments to the Commissioner [PL], it would have been entitled to recover from the Commissioner, provided that it satisfied the court that it will account to its policy holders [S].

Similar issues arose in *Roxborough* v. *Rothmans of Pall Mall Australia Limited*.[27] Tobacco wholesalers and retailers in New South Wales were obligated to pay a periodic licence fee to the New South Wales government. The fee was calculated by reference to the relevant tobacco sales for the previous period, and it was the usual practice for the cost of the licence to be passed on to consumers in the form of higher tobacco prices. In the transaction in question, a retailer had purchased for re-sale tobacco from Rothmans, a wholesaler. The price paid reflected two distinct components. The first was the cost of the tobacco. The second was an amount referable to the licence fee. The retailer each period therefore paid the price of the tobacco plus an amount to put Rothmans in funds to pay the licence fee. The problem

---

[24] *Ibid.*, 75 PER MASON CJ.   [25] N. 23 above at 75 PER MASON CJ.

[26] N. 23 above at 78 PER MASON CJ. See also Brennan J at 90, with whom Toohey J and McHugh J agreed.

[27] *Roxborough* v. *Rothmans of Pall Mall Australia Limited* [2001] HCA 68.

was that the High Court of Australia in *Ha* v. *State of New South Wales* had declared the New South Wales legislation to be unconstitutional.[28] The retailer in *Roxborough* therefore sought restitution of the amount it had paid to Rothmans on account of the licence fee. The claim succeeded.

The facts of *Roxborough* display the pattern attracting the operation of the policy against accumulation. The retailer (RH) had paid to Rothmans (PL) an amount on account of the licence fee which it would recoup from consumers (S). Due to constitutional invalidity, the retailer was entitled to recover the payment from Rothmans. As stated by Gleeson CJ, Gaudron and Hayne JJ there was thus a risk that RH would accumulate in respect of the transfers of value from PL and S:[29]

> In all probability, whoever succeeds in these proceedings will have made a windfall gain. In the absence of some legislative intervention, the appellants [RH], if they succeed, are unlikely to be obliged to pass on the fruits of the success to the smokers [S] who bore the financial burden of the invalid tax.

After referring with approval to the passages from *Royal Insurance* cited above, Gleeson CJ, Gaudron and Hayne JJ determined that, notwithstanding that the retailer had passed the cost of the licence fee onto consumers, it could satisfy the 'at the expense of' element of the unjust enrichment claim, and succeed in its suit against Rothmans for money had and received.[30] On the surface it therefore seems that the retailer (RH) was permitted to accumulate recoveries. However, the court did not exclude or rule out the possible claim by tobacco consumers, and there is no doubt that such a claim would reverse RH's accumulation.

In a powerful dissenting judgment Kirby J refused the retailer's claim, in part because to allow it would entrench RH's accumulation. Rather than allowing the claim, Kirby J held that the value should remain in the hands of Rothmans, pending legislative intervention to disgorge this value to the consumers of tobacco products.[31] In reaching this conclusion, Kirby J was

---

28 *Ha* v. *State of New South Wales* (1997) 189 CLR 465 dealing with the Business Franchise Licences (Tobacco) Act 1987. The court declared that the licence fee imposed by this Act was in reality a duty of excise within s. 90 of the Constitution. On the basis that the power to impose excise is reserved exclusively for the Commonwealth, the Act was held invalid as being beyond the competence of any State Parliament.

29 N. 27 above at para. 5. The risk of the windfall to the retailers is also referred to at para. 114 PER KIRBY J.

30 N. 27 above at paras. 29 and 30.   31 N. 27 above at para. 174 PER KIRBY J.

influenced by the possibility that to allow the retailer to recover risked RH's accumulation in respect of the same debt or damage:[32]

> ... in my view, Australian law (as in the law of the United States, Canada and the European Union) is free to, and does, take into account the fact (if it be established) that the plaintiff taxpayer [RH], seeking recovery, *has already passed on the tax in question to third party consumers [S] and has not done, or will not do, anything to reimburse those consumers* but instead seeks only to make a private gain for itself. In a given case, it may mean that the taxpayer has, in fact, suffered no loss and is entitled to no legal recovery.

On the current state of the law this category of case is evidence only for the existence of the law's general policy against accumulation. As yet, the role of the policy as an unjust factor in this configuration has not been realised. We will return to *Roxborough* later in this chapter. The discussion will demonstrate the future role of the policy against accumulation as an unjust factor in support of the claim by S against RH.

Indemnity insurance

Chapter 7 records the role of the policy against indemnity, pursuant to which an insured may not recover from the insurer amounts in excess of actual loss. As stated by Brett LJ in *Castellain* v. *Preston*:[33]

> The very foundation, in my opinion, of every rule which has been applied to insurance law is this, namely, that the contract of insurance contained in a marine or fire policy is a contract of indemnity, and of indemnity only, and that this contract means that the assured, in case of a loss against which the policy has been made, shall be fully indemnified, but shall never be more than fully indemnified.

The policy against accumulation is reflected in the situation where the insured (RH) is entitled to be indemnified by an insurer (S) under a policy of insurance, and also to recover in respect of the same loss from another indemnity insurer or a wrongdoer (PL). In each of these cases, RH is not

---

[32] N. 27 above at para. 143 PER KIRBY J, emphasis added.

[33] *Castellain* v. *Preston* (1883) 11 QBD 380 at 386 PER BRETT LJ. See also *Darrell* v. *Tibbitts* (1880) 5 QBD 560 at 562 PER BRETT LJ; *Re Miller, Gibb & Co Ltd* [1957] 2 All ER 266 at 271–272 PER WYNN-PARRY J; *England* v. *Guardian Insurance Ltd* [2000] Lloyd's Rep IR 404 at 409–410 PER JUDGE THORNTON QC; *Arab Bank plc* v. *John D Wood Ltd* [2000] 1 WLR 857 at 875 PER MANCE LJ; *Caledonia North Sea Ltd* v. *Norton (No 2) Ltd (in liquidation)* [2002] 1 All ER (Comm) 321 at 328–329 PER LORD BINGHAM.

permitted to retain the value transferred by both S and PL. Rather, one payment must be reversed.

Payment by another indemnity insurer   It is possible that the insured (RH) may take out more than one policy of insurance, so that RH is entitled to look to more than one insurer (PL) and (S) to indemnify for loss. The principle of indemnity, described above, applies to this configuration so that RH '... shall be fully indemnified, but shall never be more than fully indemnified' for loss.[34] RH is entitled to call on either PL or S to cover her loss but cannot recover twice. This means that if PL indemnifies for RH's whole loss, RH is not entitled then to seek any further payment from S.[35] RH is not permitted to accumulate. The position between the two insurers PL and S is governed by the law of contribution, each insurer being obligated to bear a rateable proportion of RH's loss.[36] Analysis between the position of the insurers inter se is not relevant for the purpose of this chapter. Rather, what must be observed is that RH is not permitted to accumulate.

Payment by the wrongdoer   We have in chapter 7 seen that the insured (RH) may be entitled, in addition to a claim against the indemnity insurer (S), to claim compensatory damages from the wrongdoer (PL). RH is not permitted to accumulate in respect of the same damage, and is thus not permitted to retain the value transferred by both S and PL. Rather, as between the wrongdoer and the insurer, the law allocates RH's loss so that it is factually to be borne by PL. It is therefore the transfer from S which must be reversed, and to whom RH must return value. There are two examples of this pattern, differentiated by the timing of the respective transfers.[37]

---

[34]   *Castellain* v. *Preston* (1883) 11 QBD 380 at 386 PER BRETT LJ.

[35]   *Godin* v. *London Assurance Company* (1758) 1 Burr 489; *Newby* v. *Reid* (1763) 1 Wm Bl 416.

[36]   *Caledonia North Sea Ltd* v. *Norton (No 2) Ltd (in liquidation)* [2002] 1 All ER (Comm) 321 at 329 PER LORD BINGHAM. *Legal and General Assurance Society Ltd* v. *Drake Insurance Ltd* [1992] QB 887 at 898 PER NOURSE LJ and 892–893 PER LLOYD LJ. See also *North British and Mercantile Insurance Company* v. *London, Liverpool and Globe Insurance Company* (1876) 5 Ch D 569; *Eagle Star Insurance Co Ltd* v. *Provincial Insurance plc* [1993] 1 All ER 1. It has been suggested that contribution between indemnity insurers should be governed by The Civil Liability (Contribution) Act 1978. *Firme C-Trade SA* v. *Newcastle P&I Association* [1991] 2 AC 1 at 35–36 PER LORD GOFF; *Astopolos Konstantine Ventouris* v. *Trevor Rex Mountain (The Italia Express No 2)* [1992] 2 Lloyd's Rep 281 at 285 PER HIRST J. See C. Mitchell, 'The Civil Liability (Contribution) Act 1978' [1997] *Restitution Law Review* 27 at 29 (especially n. 23); Goff and Jones, p. 397.

[37]   The significance attached to the timing of payments has been the subject of criticism. Mitchell makes the point that if the difference between the case where the insurer is entitled to a proprietary remedy (via an equitable lien) and that where the insurer is entitled only to a personal

These cases are not only evidence of the law's policy against accumulation. In addition, it is arguable that they are evidence of the policy in its role as an unjust factor.

The situation explored in chapter 7 is where the insurer (S) pays the insured (RH) prior to the latter's receipt from the wrongdoer (PL) damages or any correlative amount in settlement. As shown by *Lord Napier and Ettrick* v. *Hunter*,[38] this configuration triggers a proprietary response, and the insurer is entitled to an equitable lien over the fund to the extent of the value of any indemnity provided. As Lord Templeman stated:[39]

> The principles which dictated the decisions of our ancestors and inspired their references to the equitable obligations of an assured person towards an insurer entitled to subrogation are discernible and immutable. They establish that such an insurer has an enforceable equitable interest in the damages payable by the wrongdoer. The assured person is guilty of unconscionable conduct if he does not provide for the insurer to be recouped out of the damages awarded against the wrongdoer. Equity will not allow the assured person to insist on his legal rights to all the damages awarded against the wrongdoer and will restrain the assured person from receiving or dealing with those damages so far as they are required to recoup the insurer under the doctrine of subrogation.

In this configuration, the insured (RH) is therefore not permitted to accumulate in respect of the same damage. Having received damages from the wrongdoer (PL), and funds paid by way of indemnity from the insurer (S), RH must reverse one transfer. In conformity with the policy against accumulation RH, via the equitable lien, returns the value provided by S. As was discussed in chapter 7, the juridical basis of the insurer's right to participate in the fund of damages recovered by the insured is controversial.[40] As will be shown later in this chapter, the insurer's entitlement is given to reverse unjust enrichment based on the policy against accumulation. The

---

remedy (via an action for money had and received) is simply the order in which the payments were received by RH, this creates '... an anomaly for which there is no justification'. Mitchell, p. 84. These criticisms have received judicial support in *England* v. *Guardian Insurance Ltd* [2000] Lloyd's Rep IR 404 at 415 PER JUDGE THORNTON QC. Chapter 9 explains why in some cases the third party's right to share in the fund is proprietary, although ultimately concluding that the insurer's right to claw back value should only ever be reflected in a personal claim.

[38] *Lord Napier and Ettrick* v. *Hunter* [1993] AC 713.

[39] *Ibid.*, 738 PER LORD TEMPLEMAN. Consistent formulations of principle are to be found at 744–745 PER LORD GOFF, 746–747 PER LORD JAUNCEY and 752 PER LORD BROWNE-WILKINSON. Lord Slynn agreed with the speech of Lord Templeman.

[40] Chapter 7, pp. 177–90.

Lord Napier and Ettrick v. *Hunter* configuration is therefore evidence not only of the existence of the policy against accumulation, but also of its operation as an unjust factor.

The alternative pattern is raised when the insured (RH) receives from the wrongdoer (PL) damages or settlement monies prior to any insurance payments from the insurer (S). The insurer thus pays in respect of a loss already made good. In this configuration, a personal response is triggered. The insurer is entitled to claim as money had and received the value paid to the insured in respect of the loss already made good. S is likely to found this unjust enrichment on mistake, claiming that its intention to benefit RH was affected by a mistake. Alternatively, S may say that its intention was qualified and that the basis of the transfer has failed.[41] Even though other unjust factors are likely to operate in this configuration, this example is still important, because the result is consistent with the law's policy against accumulation. In conformity with the principle that RH '... shall be fully indemnified, but shall never be more than fully indemnified...'[42] for loss, RH is not permitted to accumulate in respect of the same debt or damage.

More than one tortfeasor

A claimant (RH) may have suffered loss in respect of which an action in tort may be commenced against two tortfeasors, (S) and (PL). The policy against accumulation is reflected in the fact that RH is not permitted to recover in respect of the same damage from both S and PL. To the extent, for example, that PL compensates all of RH's loss, RH is not permitted to recover any more from S. RH may only in addition pursue S to recover damage insufficiently compensated by PL.[43]

This principle is shown by *Jameson* v. *Central Electricity Generating Board*.[44] David Jameson had died of malignant mesothelioma in respect of which his former employer (Babcock), and the owner–occupier of the power station where he worked (Central Electricity Generating Board), were jointly and severally liable. Prior to his death, Jameson settled an action against his former employer Babcock, accepting as full and final settlement

---

[41] Burrows, pp. 81–2; Mitchell, pp. 80–2.

[42] *Castellain* v. *Preston* (1883) 11 QBD 380 at 386 PER BRETT LJ.

[43] As between PL and S, so long as the payment is in respect of the same damage, PL may sue S for contribution under the Civil Liability (Contribution) Act 1978.

[44] *Jameson* v. *Central Electricity Generating Board* [1999] 3 WLR 141.

THE POLICY AGAINST ACCUMULATION

a sum which was in reality only two-thirds the value of his claim.[45] On Jameson's death this money was inherited by his widow, who also sought damages for loss of dependency. Jameson's executors brought a separate action against the Central Electricity Generating Board under the Fatal Accidents Act 1976. The widow's entitlement to claim depended on whether, before his death, Jameson would have been able to sue Central Electricity, even though he had settled his claim against Babcock.[46] The House of Lords held that Jameson would not have been entitled to maintain the second action, and therefore that his widow was likewise prevented from suing.[47] As Lord Hope makes clear, Jameson (or his widow) (RH) was not permitted to recover in respect of the same damage from both Babcock (PL) and Central Electricity (S). The case is evidence of the law's policy against accumulation:[48]

> The basic rule is that *a plaintiff cannot recover more by way of damages than the amount of his loss.* The object of an award of damages is to place the injured party as nearly as possible in the same financial position as he or she would been in but for the accident. The liability which is in issue in this case is that of concurrent tortfeasors, because the acts of negligence and breach of statutory duty which are alleged against Babcock and... [Central Electricity]... respectively are not the same. *So the plaintiff has a separate cause of action against each of them for the same loss.* But the existence of damage is an essential part of the cause of action in any claim for damages. It would seem to follow, as a matter of principle, that *once the plaintiff's claim has been satisfied by any one of several tortfeasors, his action for damages is extinguished against all of them.*

The exceptional position in which accumulation is permitted

It must be conceded that there are rare cases in which the law's policy against accumulation is relaxed, and RH is permitted to accumulate. However, closer examination reveals that these are cases where by consent the

---

[45] *Ibid.,* 144 PER LORD HOPE.
[46] Fatal Accidents Act 1976 s. 1(1). N. 44 above at 149 PER LORD HOPE.
[47] N. 44 above at 156 PER LORD HOPE with whom at 156 Lord Browne-Wilkinson and at 147 Lord Clyde agreed. Lord Clyde at 163 also denied the widow her claim. Lord Lloyd at 145–146 allowed the claim, holding that Jameson's acceptance of an amount from Babcock which was in fact less than the value of his claim did not bar proceedings against the Central Electricity.
[48] N. 44 above at 150 PER LORD HOPE, emphasis added.

parties have departed from the policy. In other words, the party who would otherwise have been entitled to recover value transferred has accepted the risk that RH will accumulate.

Contingency insurance

A contingency insurer does not indemnify for loss. Rather, the obligation is to pay the insured on the happening of a specified event, such as accident or death. The amount paid to the insured will not necessarily reflect loss, but will be the amount specified in the contract.[49] It is possible that the insured (RH) will have taken out a contingency policy with more than one insurer, (S) and (PL) each specifying payment on the happening of the same event. Subject to the terms of the insurance contracts, the usual position is that RH will be entitled to retain value transferred by S and PL. Unlike the case of indemnity insurance, where RH is not permitted to accumulate, in the case of contingency insurance '. . . it will clearly have been contemplated by all the parties that the insured should have the right to accumulate recoveries in respect of the same insured loss'.[50] S and PL thus accept the risk that RH will accumulate.

Gifts

This book documents many examples where a victim of tort (RH) receives services from the carer (S), in addition to holding a right to claim damages from the tortfeasor (PL). In some cases, it seems a reasonable conclusion that the carer intended this intervention to be a transfer of value in addition to any damages paid by the tortfeasor. In benefiting the victim, the carer accepts the possibility that the victim will in addition recover damages from the tortfeasor. Arguably, S accepts the risk that RH will thereby accumulate in respect of the same damage.

This configuration is illustrated by *Kars* v. *Kars*.[51] It will be remembered that Mrs Kars (RH) was injured through the negligence of her husband (PL), when the car in which she travelled as passenger was involved in a motor vehicle accident. As a result of the accident, Mrs Kars required a great deal of day-to-day care, and this was provided by her tortfeasor

---

[49] M. Clarke, *The Law of Insurance Contracts* (3rd edn., London, 1997), pp. 81–2.
[50] C. Mitchell, 'Claims in Unjustified Enrichment to Recover Money Paid Pursuant to a Common Liability' (2001) 5 *Edinburgh Law Review* 1 at 26.
[51] *Kars* v. *Kars* (1996) 187 CLR 354.

husband Mr Kars (S). Mrs Kars sued the tortfeasor for damages on account of her loss, including an amount calculated by reference to the care to be provided by him. A majority of the High Court of Australia allowed her claim, ordering that Mr Kars could not, in effect, discharge his obligations as tortfeasor in kind. Rather, his insurer was obligated to pay damages to Mrs Kars undiscounted by the value of his care.[52]

Of relevance to this chapter is the analysis of Dawson J. Although in result the learned judge agreed with the decision of the other members of the court, and ordered that Mr Kars' liability was not reduced by his contributions as carer,[53] he justified the outcome by reference to the character of the carer's contribution as a gift:[54]

> The provision of gratuitous services to an injured plaintiff by a friend or relative is, to my mind, clearly to be characterised as an act of benevolence where there is no intention that it should result in the reduction of damages recoverable by the injured person... [referring to *National Insurance Co of New Zealand Ltd* v. *Espagne* (1961) 105 CLR 569 at 599–600 PER WINDEYER J] where personal injury is productive of private benevolence (and also some other forms of bounty), it is the intent of the donor which is crucial in deciding whether the benefit should be enjoyed in addition to and not in diminution of any claim for damages. If that is the purpose of the benevolence then the law will give effect to it.

In this model, the intentions of the carer (S) in providing benefits to the victim (RH) are given effect, such that S is permitted to accumulate. On the facts of *Kars* v. *Kars*, the victim recovered from the tortfeasor (PL) damages undiscounted by the value of the care provided by Mr Kars (S). No obligation was imposed on the victim to return value to either PL or S. In Dawson J's model, RH was permitted to accumulate because S had accepted the risk of this occurring.

Application of the policy against accumulation as an unjust factor

The discussion thus far has given the evidence in support of the existence of a general policy against accumulation running through various categories of case, noting where relevant those categories in which it also operates as an unjust factor. The policy governs the position of the claimant (RH)

[52] *Ibid.*, 382–383 PER TOOHEY, MCHUGH, GUMMOW AND KIRBY JJ.
[53] N. 51 above at 364 PER DAWSON J.   [54] N. 51 above at 362–363 PER DAWSON J.

who receives a benefit, or has the right to recover damages from another party (S) and receives, or has the right to receive, in respect of the *same debt or damage* from a third party (PL). If RH has in fact received value from both S and PL, RH must reverse one transfer. In conformity with the policy, RH is not permitted to accumulate. In certain cases, the policy against accumulation operates as an unjust factor pursuant to which RH's obligation to return value is given to reverse the unjust enrichment which would otherwise remain.

The evidence indicates two categories of case in which the policy presently operates as an unjust factor, that of the carer and victim and the indemnity insurer and insured. The task of this section is to complete the analysis commenced in chapters 4 and 7. In each of these cases, the third party (S) is entitled to participate in the damages recovered by the claimant (RH). This right is given to remedy RH's enrichment at the expense of S. As will be seen, there are arguably two moments in time when RH accumulates. The first is when RH actually recovers in her claim against PL. The second is when RH's cause of action accrues. These will both be considered when applying the policy against accumulation to (1) the victim and carer cases and (2) the indemnity insurance cases.

The victim and carer cases

Hunt v. *Severs*[55] is an example of this configuration. The tortfeasor Mr Severs (PL) caused loss to Miss Hunt (RH) thereby incurring an obligation to compensate her. In his capacity as carer (S), he intervened and in part made good this loss, although his liability as PL was *not* thereby discharged. Miss Hunt sued Mr Severs, including an amount calculated by reference to the services provided by him. On the particular facts of *Hunt* v. *Severs*, in which PL and S were the same person, the House did not require that RH hold these damages on trust for S. This was only to avoid the bizarre configuration which would have resulted had the trust been imposed. It was pointless to require the tortfeasor to pay damages to the victim as these would immediately be carried back to the tortfeasor in his capacity as carer.[56] In the standard configuration, RH is obligated to share the fruits of this litigation with S.[57]

---

[55] *Hunt* v. *Severs* [1994] 2 AC 350.   [56] *Ibid.*, 363 PER LORD BRIDGE.
[57] N. 55 above at 366 PER LORD BRIDGE.

Chapter 4 commences the unjust enrichment analysis, and shows how the enrichment and 'at the expense of' elements of an unjust enrichment claim may be satisfied. The victim is enriched by receipt from the carer of loss ameliorating benefits, and these satisfy at least one of the tests of enrichment which have been proposed.[58] Of greatest utility is the test of incontrovertible enrichment. The carer, in providing necessary services and meeting the carer's expenses, anticipates the victim's inevitable expenditure. Had the carer not intervened, the victim would have been forced to obtain care from another provider and to herself pay related expenses.

Williams argues that Miss Hunt was not enriched, and that the carer's right to share in the fund is not given to reverse unjust enrichment. His basis for doing so hinges on the proprietary aspect of that case, that a trust of the victim's damages would ordinarily be imposed. He states that Miss Hunt was not enriched '... by any damages awarded in respect of benefits received, for he or she never takes beneficial title to those damages. The trust cannot therefore be said to reverse any such enrichment.'[59] Williams' approach fundamentally misunderstands the position and is misleading for two interlinked reasons. First, it fails correctly to identify the relevant benefit and secondly, it ignores those cases in which the carer's right to share is personal.

Turning first to the relevant benefit, it is clear that the value carried by the trust back to the carer reflects the benefits, such as nursing or other care and assistance provided by the carer. The value is that which was originally transferred by the carer to the victim, in respect of which the victim has an undiminished right to recover from the tortfeasor. As was emphasised by Lord Bridge in *Hunt* v. *Severs*, the whole point of the carer's entitlement is to '... enable the voluntary carer to receive proper recompense for his or her services...'[60] Consistently with this position, the courts attribute a value to the carer's contribution and it is this value which is returned in those cases recognising the carer's entitlement.[61] The other defect to Williams' analysis is that he ignores those cases in which the carer's right to share

---

[58] Chapter 4, pp. 53–65.
[59] R. Williams, 'Preventing Unjust Enrichment' [2000] *Restitution Law Review* 492 at 509.
[60] N. 55 above at 363 PER LORD BRIDGE.
[61] N. 55 above at 363 PER LORD BRIDGE. The methods by which the courts value the carer's contribution are dealt with in chapter 4.

in the fund is only ever personal in nature.[62] Although it is true that the response identified by the House of Lords in *Hunt* v. *Severs* is proprietary, there are other instances where this is not so. These cases demonstrate that the remedial response is not always in specie. They are evidence that it is not the value inherent in the damages paid by the tortfeasor which must be passed back to the carer. Rather, it is the value of the benefits provided by carer to victim. It is important to separate our investigation of the carer's right to share in the fund *at all* from the form that this right takes. As shown by the cases in which the carer's right is personal, the value carried back to the carer is that which was originally transferred to the victim by the carer. The proprietary nature of the carer's entitlement will be considered in chapter 9.

The 'at the expense of' element is uncontroversial, although requires particular care when applying the policy against accumulation as unjust factor. The policy states that, in respect of the same debt or damage, RH is not permitted to accumulate. To the extent that RH holds value transferred by both S and PL, RH is unjustly enriched and must reverse one transfer. In applying the policy, it is therefore necessary to determine whether it is the value given by RH or S which is vulnerable. The choice between S and RH is a policy decision which must be made prior to an unjust enrichment claim against RH. On the facts of the victim and carer cases, it is clear that the courts have decided it is the value given by the carer (S) which must be returned. In order to satisfy the 'at the expense of' element of an unjust enrichment claim, the court must therefore simply ask whether the value in question did travel, as a matter of direction, from S to RH.[63]

Despite the fact that it is relatively easy to demonstrate the victim's enrichment at the carer's expense, earlier chapters highlight two barriers to the success of an unjust enrichment analysis. Briefly to recapitulate, these are that: (1) the elements of the established unjust factors are not established; and (2) the carer's entitlement is not visible at the moment of the

---

[62] *Coderre* v. *Ethier* (1978) 85 DLR (3d) 621 at 632 PER LERNER J; *Turnbull* v. *Hsieh* (1990) 269 APR 33 at 42 PER HOYT JA who delivered the judgment of the Court; *Rawson* v. *Kasman* (1956) 3 DLR (2d) 376 at 381 PER SCHROEDER JA with whom Hogg and MacKay JJA agreed.

[63] As discussed in chapter 4, it might controversially be suggested that RH needs, in addition, to show a corresponding impoverishment. The position prevailing in Australia and England is that this is not required, it being sufficient that the value travelled directionally from S to RH. However, even if this view was incorrect and rather, as required in Canada, RH must show detriment, it remains the case that the carer does in general suffer loss by devoting himself to the victim.

victim's receipt of benefits conferred. Rather, it is not until the victim has successfully sued the wrongdoer that the carer's entitlement to share in the victim's damages is recognised. A direct claim in unjust enrichment apparently cannot explain a contingent entitlement. The discussion which follows demonstrates that, when viewed as an unjust enrichment claim rendered unjust via the policy against accumulation, these barriers are removed.

The elements of the unjust factor are not established

Chapter 4 considers the unjust enrichment claim of the carer pursuant to two categories of unjust factor, cases where the claimant's intention to transfer wealth is qualified, and a policy motivated claim based on necessity. Turning first to qualified transfer, the discussion notes that the unjust factors possibly relevant to the victim and carer cases are failure of basis and absence of basis.

In relation to failure of basis, chapter 4 concludes that none of the cases in this study disclose a claim for the carer in unjust enrichment founded on this unjust factor.[64] Quite simply, the facts of the cases do not support the application of this unjust factor. In few cases do the victim and carer actually agree a basis for the carer's intervention. Those rare cases in which the victim has promised to pay the carer do not in general disclose any failure of basis sufficient to generate a claim. In none of these examples has the court imposed a mechanism, as at the date of judgment, enforcing the carer's right to be paid. This is because as at the date of trial, the victim is not in breach of any payment obligation. Neither does absence of basis command clear support. For one thing the existence of the unjust factor is not sufficiently settled. In addition, as demonstrated above, properly understood it is difficult to see how the basis of the carer's intervention could fail. Assuming, as suggested by the evidence, the carer intervenes out of love and affection, the basis of the carer's assistance is not likely to fail.

Necessity fares little better. Chapter 4 concludes that the facts of the victim and carer cases do not systematically reveal the elements of this unjust factor. It is difficult to see how the emergency or state of crisis which may have existed immediately following the victim's accident will continue far into the future. It is simply not possible to have a permanent state of emergency. The requirement that the intervener must be unable to obtain rational instructions also poses difficulty. Even if it is possible initially to meet this

[64] Chapter 4, pp. 74–6 and 78–9.

element, it is likely that over time the victim's ability to communicate with the carer would improve.

At this point, it is trite to point out that the facts of the victim and carer cases do meet the elements of the policy against accumulation. As has been shown, the relationship between them is that the victim (RH) is injured through the negligence of the tortfeasor (PL). The carer (S) intervenes and provides necessary services to RH, although the effect of such services is not to discharge PL's obligation to compensate RH. RH is entitled to claim damages from PL, including an amount calculated by reference to the con-tribution of S. Unless forced to return value to the carer, RH will accumulate in respect of the same damage. A mechanism is therefore imposed pursuant to which RH returns value to S.[65]

The carer's entitlement is not visible at the moment of the victim's receipt

Even if one of the unjust factors identified in chapter 4 is established, a further difficulty remains. A claim in unjust enrichment generated by any one of these unjust factors arises at the moment of the plaintiff's receipt of the relevant enrichment. However, the carer's right to share in the fund only becomes visible when the victim has successfully sued the wrongdoer. An initial reading of the cases reveals no entitlement at the moment of the victim's receipt from the carer. Rather, the victim's entitlement seems to be contingent on the success of the victim's claim against the wrongdoer. Chapter 6 demonstrates that even if one of these grounds of claim in unjust enrichment had been made out, this claim cannot explain the carer's right to share in the fund. The existence of such a ground of claim for the carer seems only to entitle the carer to bring this very claim against the victim. Without more it cannot explain a contingent entitlement.

The policy against accumulation removes both of these difficulties, pro-viding a credible explanation for the carer's right to share in the fund. Importantly, it is consistent with the carer's apparently contingent right to participate in the victim's damages. It is possible to identify an accumulation

---

65 This may either be via a proprietary mechanism such as the trust identified in *Hunt* v. *Severs* or a personal obligation such as was recognised in *Coderre* v. *Ethier* (1978) 85 DLR (3d) 621 at 632 PER LERNER J; *Turnbull* v. *Hsieh* (1990) 269 APR 33 at 42 PER HOYT JA who delivered the judgment of the Court; *Rawson* v. *Kasman* (1956) 3 DLR (2d) 376 at 381 PER SCHROEDER JA with whom Hogg and MacKay JJA agreed. The form of S's entitlement, whether personal or proprietary, is covered in chapter 9.

by the victim at two distinct moments in the story. The first is when the victim actually recovers damages from the wrongdoer. The second is prior in time when the victim's cause of action accrues. Both versions of the policy are capable of explaining the carer's right to share in the fund. As outlined earlier in this chapter, when applying the policy it is necessary already to know whether it is the value given by S or PL which is vulnerable. The answer to this question is a function of the policy considerations raised by the particular category of case. *Hunt* v. *Severs* shows that in the victim and carer example, it is the value transferred by the carer which must be returned.

At the time the victim wins damages   The victim (RH) accumulates when RH actually recovers damages from the wrongdoer (PL). The event triggering the right of the carer (S) to share in the fund is not merely the victim's receipt from the carer of enriching services and other benefits. It is the victim's receipt of damages from the tortfeasor, when the victim has already benefited in kind through the carer's intervention. The carer's right to participate in the damages does not arise until the victim has been successful in her suit against the wrongdoer, because it is at this moment that the victim accumulates in respect of the same damage.

This model is also capable of accommodating the fact that the court may award damages on account of future care to be provided by the carer to the victim. For example, in *Hunt* v. *Severs* the claim was also on account of future care to be provided by Mr Hunt. Although this aspect of the trust has been criticised,[66] it seems clear that it was intended to cover damages

---

[66] Chapter 9 will deal with the proprietary, rather than personal, nature of the carer's right to share in the fund. The trust of damages on account of future care has been the subject of academic criticism. P. Matthews and M. Lunney, 'A Tortfeasor's Lot is not a Happy One?' (1995) *Modern Law Review* 395; L. Hoyano, 'The Dutiful Tortfeasor in the House of Lords' (1995) 3 *Tort Law Review* 63; A. Reed, 'A Commentary on *Hunt* v. *Severs*' (1995) 15 *Oxford Journal of Legal Studies* 133. The UK Law Commission has recommended that there should be no legal duty on the victim to pay over damages recovered on account of future gratuitous care. Rather, the victim should be entitled to dispose of these funds as he or she considers appropriate. The Law Commission adopted this position in recognition of the fact that many victims will voluntarily use their damages to pay their carers or that families may enter into contracts (however informal) for care. Without challenging these arguments, this discussion simply notes that the removal of the obligation to pay over damages on account of future care risks unjustly enriching the victim by accumulation. UK Law Commission, *Damages for Personal Injury: Medical, Nursing and other Expenses; Collateral Benefits* (Law Com No 262, 1999), paras. 3.59 and 3.62. See S. Degeling, 'Carers' Claims: Unjust Enrichment and Tort' [2000] *Restitution Law Review* 172 at 187.

on account of future care. Leaving aside the proprietary aspects of that decision, which will be dealt with in chapter 9, it is enough to observe that the court envisaged the case where the carer (S) would be entitled to share in the fund on account of future care.

At first sight, this configuration appears not to conform with the policy against accumulation. However, it is possible to show that the victim (RH) also accumulates in respect of damages recovered for future care. On the day of judgment, the court awards damages to RH in respect of future care to be provided. On the basis of RH's physical incapacity, the court is sufficiently certain that future care will, without doubt, be necessary. Thus, although care has yet actually to be provided, the court awards damages on account of future care. As at the day of judgment therefore, RH accumulates because she holds the fund of damages calculated by reference to the value of future necessary care, and the court is certain that this care will in the future be provided. A very narrow application of the policy against accumulation says that RH does not accumulate until that moment, later in the story, when necessary services are actually given. On this narrow application, RH accumulates on actual receipt of S's services. RH holds both the value of S's intervention and the fund of damages calculated in part by reference to the value of it.

However, careful analysis allows us to identify RH's accumulation at the point when damages are awarded. The touchstone of RH's entitlement to claim from PL is that such care will, in the future, continue to be necessary. When awarding damages on account of future care, the court is therefore satisfied that, as a matter of factual certainty, such care will actually be provided. In other words, the court is certain that S, or a commercial provider, will provide services to RH. In doing so, the law commits us to a model of damages liability which relies on this element of certainty. It is therefore not possible for us to second guess the court. We must assume, as does the court, that RH will in the future receive necessary care and assistance from S. RH accumulates at the moment damages are awarded because, being factually certain that such care will be provided, RH at the date of judgment holds the damages calculated by reference to the value of this care.

At the time the victim's cause of action accrues   The victim (RH) accumulates at the moment her cause of action accrues. RH is entitled to sue the wrongdoer (PL) for damages, including an amount calculated by reference to the value of the carer's (S's) assistance. At the moment her claim accrues, RH holds both the value transferred by S and the ability to claim a correlative amount from PL. RH thus accumulates in respect of the same damage.

This model is consistent with the general view in the law of unjust enrichment that the claimant's right arises at the moment of receipt of the relevant enrichment. If it is argued that the victim accumulates prior to the exercise of her claim against the wrongdoer, then it is at this moment that the carer's right to participate arises. RH has received a benefit from S, in respect of which she has the right to recover damages from PL. The difficulty with this analysis is of course that the carer's right to share is visible only when the court imposes a mechanism, at the date of judgment, granting the carer access to the victim's damages. In order for this version of the policy to be sustainable, it is therefore necessary to argue that although RH accumulates earlier in time, it is not visible until RH succeeds in the claim.

The operation of this model can be more clearly illustrated if we return to the insurance subrogation analogy established in chapter 7. The leading case is the decision of the House in *Lord Napier and Ettrick* v. *Hunter*.[67] The Names (RH) commenced proceedings against Outhwaite (PL) in respect of the latter's negligence. This litigation was settled and settlement monies were paid by Outhwaite and held by a third party on behalf of the Names. The House of Lords granted the Stop Loss Insurers (S) an equitable lien over the fund of settlement monies. Although not finally deciding the issue,[68] all members of the House in *Lord Napier and Ettrick* v. *Hunter* identified the possibility that the insurer's interest, expressed via the equitable lien, may have attached not only to the fund but also to a prior asset held by the insured, the chose in action exercisable against the tortfeasor Outhwaite. Lord Goff stated:[69]

> There is one particular problem to which I wish to refer, although, as I understand it, it does not fall to be decided in the present case. Does the equitable proprietary interest of the insurer attach only to a fund consisting of sums

---

[67] *Lord Napier and Ettrick* v. *Hunter* [1993] AC 713.

[68] It must be conceded that their Lordships expressed no concluded view about this possibility. The point was not directly addressed in argument and their Lordships were careful to emphasise that further consideration would be required in order to give a firmer opinion. *Ibid.*, 740 PER LORD TEMPLEMAN who acknowledged that 'reconsideration in the light of further research' would be required. Lord Goff at p. 745 expressly reserved his opinion as did Lord Browne-Wilkinson at p. 752 who preferred to 'express no concluded view'.

[69] N. 67 above at 745 PER LORD GOFF. Refer also to 740 PER LORD TEMPLEMAN and 752–753 PER LORD BROWNE-WILKINSON. Lord Slynn agreed with Lord Templeman and Lord Jauncey agreed with Lord Templeman, Lord Goff and Lord Browne-Wilkinson.

which come into the hands of the assured in reduction of the loss paid by
the insurer? Or does it attach also to a right of action vested in the assured
which, if enforced, would yield such a fund? The point is not altogether easy.
I can see no reason in principle why such an interest should not be capable
of attaching to property in the nature of a chose in action.

Lord Goff's tentative solution is also capable of operation in the victim and
carer cases. Leaving to one side the proprietary aspects, his analysis shows
that the victim's accumulation arises earlier in time, when the carer provides
enriching services. The victim's chose in action against the tortfeasor arises
by operation of law. At this moment, the victim holds both the value of
the carer's contribution, and a right to sue the tortfeasor in respect of this
assistance. The victim thus accumulates in respect of the same damage. The
accumulation does not become visible until the victim recovers damages
because, as will be explored in more detail in chapter 9, it is possible to view
the victim's damages as being the substitute of this chose in action.

   This model of the policy against accumulation is also capable of explaining the carer's entitlement on account of damages awarded for future care.
Once again, it is necessary to rely on the court's certainty that care will in
the future be provided. RH's accumulation arises at the moment she is by
operation of law entitled to claim from PL. At this moment, RH holds the
ability to sue PL for the value of future care in circumstances where the
court is certain that this care will be provided. To the extent that the law
will allow her claim on account of future assistance, RH accumulates in
respect of the same damage.

The indemnity insurance cases

The insurance subrogation analogy commenced in chapter 7 reveals two
rights for the indemnity insurer, the right to control litigation against the
wrongdoer and the right to participate, via an equitable lien, in the fund
of damages recovered by the insured in diminution of loss.[70] Chapter 7
records that, following the work of Mitchell, the right to control litigation is
properly understood as a right raised to reverse unjust enrichment. Leaving
aside those cases in which the insurer participates by virtue of a contractual
right to do so, it also seems clear that the right of the insurer to share in

---

[70] *Lonrho Exports Ltd* v. *Export Credits Guarantee Department* [1996] 4 All ER 673 at 690 PER
LIGHTMAN J.

the insured's damages is given to reverse unjust enrichment. Of difficulty is to satisfy the 'at the expense of' element, and satisfactorily to identify an unjust factor. The policy against accumulation eliminates these barriers to demonstrate that the insurer's entitlement is to reverse the insured's enrichment which would otherwise remain.

Turning first to 'at the expense of'. In applying the policy it is necessary to determine whether it is the value given by S or PL which is vulnerable. This is a policy choice to be made prior to an unjust enrichment claim against RH. On the facts of the indemnity insurance cases, it is clear that it is the value given by the insurer (S) which must be returned. In order to satisfy the 'at the expense of' element of the unjust enrichment claim, the court is simply confirming that, as a matter of direction, the value travelled from S to RH. In other words, that the value in respect of which RH accumulates came from S. As in the victim and carer example, it is possible to identify the insured's accumulation at two distinct periods in time.

At the time the insured wins damages

The insured (RH) accumulates when she exercises her claim and recovers damages or settlement monies from the wrongdoer (PL). RH is not obligated to return value to the insurer (S) unless and until RH wins in her claim against PL. The event triggering the insurer's entitlement is not merely the insured's receipt of money under the policy of insurance. It is the insured's receipt of damages from the wrongdoer, when she has already been indemnified by the insurer. On receipt of the damages or settlement monies the insured accumulates in respect of the same damage.

At the time the insured's cause of action accrues

By operation of law, the insured (RH) is entitled to claim against the wrongdoer (PL) for loss. Under the policy of insurance, the insured also receives from the insurer (S) an amount on account of loss. The insured thus accumulates at the moment of receipt from the insurer, because it is at this moment that RH receives, or has the right to receive, from both PL and S in respect of the same damage.

As with the victim and carer cases, the problem is that the insurer's entitlement is visible only when the court imposes a mechanism, at the date of judgment, granting the insurer a right to share in the fund. It is therefore necessary to show that, although RH's accumulation is not visible until RH succeeds in its suit against PL, the accumulation actually arose earlier in time, at the point when S indemnified RH. This construction is supported by the decision of the House in *Lord Napier and Ettrick* v. *Hunter*. As has been noted, all members of the House conceded the possibility, without finally deciding the issue, that the insurer's entitlement, expressed via an equitable lien, may have attached not only to the fund but also a prior asset, the chose in action held by the insured against the wrongdoer.[71]

Relying on the argument that the insured's damages are the substitute of the chose in action, we can see that although only visible when damages were recovered, the insurer's accumulation arose earlier in time. By operation of law the insured holds a chose in action exercisable against the tortfeasor. At the time of the insurer's intervention, therefore, the position of the insured has to an extent already been ameliorated. This explanation is illustrated by the following extract from Lord Goff's speech in *Esso Petroleum Co Ltd* v. *Hall Russell & Co Ltd*:[72]

> There can of course be no direct claim by Esso [S] against Hall Russell [PL] in restitution, if only because Esso has not by its payment discharged the liability of Hall Russell; if anybody has been enriched, it is the Crofters [RH], to the extent that they have been indemnified by Esso and yet continue to have vested in them rights of action against Hall Russell in respect of the loss or damage which was the subject matter of Esso's payment to them.

Leaving to one side the form of the insurer's right to participate, it is thus possible to see how the enrichment is received by the insured (RH) at the expense of the insurer (S). Restitution is given to prevent the insured from accumulating in respect of the same debt or damage. The accumulation does not arise at the moment when the insured recovers damages from the wrongdoer (PL), but commences when the insurer indemnifies the insured. RH has, by operation of law, been given a right to seek redress from PL. RH accumulates since she holds a right to sue PL undiminished by the value transferred, or expected to be transferred, by S.

---

[71] *Lord Napier and Ettrick* v. *Hunter* [1993] AC 713 at 745 PER LORD GOFF, 740 PER LORD TEMPLEMAN and 752–753 PER LORD BROWNE-WILKINSON. Lord Slynn agreed with Lord Templeman and Lord Jauncey agreed with Lord Templeman, Lord Goff and Lord Browne-Wilkinson. Lord Templeman acknowledged that reconsideration in the light of further research would be required. Lord Goff expressly reserved his opinion as did Lord Browne-Wilkinson who preferred to express no concluded view. This aspect of *Lord Napier* is discussed above on pp. 217–18.

[72] *Esso Petroleum Co Ltd* v. *Hall Russell & Co* [1989] 1 AC 643 at 663 PER LORD GOFF. The statement was made in the context of a discussion of the insurer's right to compel litigation.

Conclusion

The above discussion shows that the policy against accumulation best explains the rights of both the carer and the indemnity insurer to share in the fund of damages recovered. It must of course be conceded that other unjust factors on particular facts may also go some way to explaining the right to participate. The advantage of the policy against accumulation is that it systematically solves the problem. It goes to the heart of the relationship between the three parties in the equation and demonstrates, at a structural level, why RH's enrichment is unjust. Importantly, it is consistent with the pattern in the cases whereby S's entitlement to share is contingent on the success of RH's suit. We are not able to see S's right to participate until RH has recovered against PL. This is because it is not until then, or prior in time when RH's claim against PL accrues, that RH accumulates in respect of the same debt or damage.

As has been said, in order to apply the policy against accumulation as an unjust factor, it is necessary already to have decided whether it is the value transferred by S or PL which must be returned. This is a policy question to be answered prior to the claim against RH. At least in the cases of the carer and insurer, it is their value which must be returned. Two models of the policy have been identified. In the first RH accumulates when RH recovers in his suit against PL, her loss already having been ameliorated via the transfer of value from S. In the second, RH accumulates prior in time when RH's right to sue PL accrues. For the purpose of explaining RH's entitlement to share in the fund of damages, it is not necessary to commit to either version of the policy. Both are capable of explaining the contingent entitlement.

At this point in the discussion, the analysis commenced in chapter 7 is complete. The use throughout of the labels adopted by Mitchell is in part for ease of exposition. However, it also highlights the fact that the subrogation analogy is now fully accomplished. By recognising the symmetrical pattern of the victim and carer cases, and the insurance cases, various anomalies are highlighted. This chapter examines the apparently inexplicable nature of the carer's and also the insurer's entitlement to share in the fund. Via the policy against accumulation, it is possible to place on a principled foundation the right of both the carer and the indemnity insurer to share in the fund of damages recovered. The right is given to reverse the unjust enrichment by accumulation which would otherwise remain. The second element of the puzzle revealed by the subrogation analogy is that, as the law currently stands, the carer is given no means of forcing suit against the wrongdoer. Chapter 7 shows that this latter difficulty is an anomaly, and strongly argues that the carer should enjoy a right similar to the indemnity insurer's ability to compel litigation against the wrongdoer.

The future role of the policy against accumulation

The law discloses a novel policy motivated unjust factor called the policy against accumulation. As has been said, this applies whenever the claimant (RH) receives a benefit, or has the right to recover damages from another party (PL) and receives, or has the right to receive, in respect of the *same debt or damage*, from a third party (S). RH is not in general permitted to accumulate. If RH has in fact received value from both PL and S, she must reverse one transfer. Two observations may be made about the future role of the policy against accumulation.

The first is that additional work is required to determine the extent that the policy applies more generally. In any given fact situation, it is necessary to determine whether the relationship under investigation is one to which the policy applies, in other words whether in the configuration in question RH is permitted to accumulate. The policy against accumulation is an unjust factor capable of broad application. However, as shown by examples such as the case of the contingency insurer, it is not always that the policy will be relevant. On rare facts it is possible that the parties may take the risk of accumulation. Precise analysis requires that we reveal the relationships to which the policy applies.[73]

The second observation follows from the first. In applying the policy, it is not sufficient simply to know that the configuration under investigation is one to which the policy applies. If we conclude that the relationship between the parties is such that RH is not permitted to accumulate in respect of the same debt or damage, we must also know whether it is the transfer of value from S or PL that must be reversed. The answer to this question is a function of the attendant policy considerations. In the cases under investigation in this book, the overwhelming evidence is that it is the value given by the carer

---

[73] Mitchell has conducted such an analysis in the context of some banking cases. C. Mitchell, 'Distributing the Burden of Alternate and Co-Extensive Liabilities: Some Banking Cases Considered' in F. Rose (ed.), *Restitution and Banking Law* (Oxford, 1999) 27, pp. 31–2. See also Birks and Mitchell, p. 579; C. Mitchell, 'Claims in Unjustified Enrichment to Recover Money Paid Pursuant to a Common Liability' (2001) 5 *Edinburgh Law Review* 1 at 25–7.

and indemnity insurer (S) which must be reversed. Careful consideration of the relative position of S and PL is therefore required in order to satisfy the 'at the expense of' element of the unjust enrichment claim.

These general caveats having been given, there are two configurations which appear to invite the future application of the policy against accumulation. These are those revealed in *Dimond* v. *Lovell*[74] and *Roxborough* v. *Rothmans of Pall Mall Australia Limited*.[75]

Dimond v. Lovell

Mrs Dimond's car was negligently damaged by Mr Lovell (PL) in a traffic accident. Mrs Dimond (RH) temporarily hired a replacement car from 1st Automotive (S), the total hiring charge being £346.63. In common with industry practice, the contract of hire contemplated that 1st Automotive would pursue Mrs Dimond's claim against Mr Lovell at its own expense, and satisfy her obligation to pay the hiring charge out of any damages awarded. Any such claim would have been brought in the name of Mrs Dimond and judgment entered in her name.

The issue for the court was whether Mrs Dimond could recover this amount from Mr Lovell in her damages claim against him. The difficulty was caused by the fact that the contract of hire was by statute rendered unenforceable.[76] Mrs Dimond therefore had no contractual obligation to pay for the car hire. 1st Automotive tried to establish an obligation on Mrs Dimond, arising in unjust enrichment, to make restitution of the benefits conferred on her. The purpose of doing so was to establish her obligation to pay for the hire, thus laying the foundation for her damages claim against Mr Lovell for this amount.

Mrs Dimond was clearly enriched at the expense of 1st Automotive because she had the use of the replacement car for eight days without paying. However, 1st Automotive's unjust enrichment claim failed because the policy rendering the contract unenforceable also operated to bar an unjust enrichment claim:[77]

---

[74] *Dimond* v. *Lovell* [2002] 1 AC 384(HL).

[75] *Roxborough* v. *Rothmans of Pall Mall Australia Limited* [2001] HCA 68.

[76] The contract was a regulated agreement within the terms of the Consumer Credit Act 1974. The statute required that the contract state the amount of credit, represented by the hiring charge, on the face of the document. Because this amount was not stated, the contract was improperly executed and rendered unenforceable. N. 74 above at 397 PER LORD HOFFMANN.

[77] N. 74 above at 398 PER LORD HOFFMANN with whom the other Law Lords agreed.

The real difficulty, as it seems to me, is that to treat Mrs Dimond as having been unjustly enriched would be inconsistent with the purposes of section 65(1) [of the Consumer Credit Act]. Parliament intended that if a consumer credit agreement was improperly executed, then subject to the enforcement powers of the court, the debtor should not have to pay. This meant that Parliament contemplated that he might be enriched and I do not see how it is open to the court to say that this consequence is unjust and should be reversed by a remedy at common law...

The role of the policy against accumulation is revealed if we vary slightly the facts, and assume that the policy of the Consumer Credit Act 1974 did not preclude a claim by 1st Automotive against Mrs Dimond. In other words, let us assume that 1st Automotive was entitled to sue Mrs Dimond in unjust enrichment for the value of benefits conferred. To succeed, 1st Automotive would obviously have been required to establish an unjust factor. One possibility is that 1st Automotive's intention to benefit Mrs Dimond was vitiated by a mistake. Although difficult to sustain, 1st Automotive might have argued that it hired the car to Mrs Dimond, mistakenly believing the contract was enforceable against her. The evidence that it was through 1st Automotive's own policies that the hiring charge was not inserted on the face of the agreement may in the end suggest that 1st Automotive was not mistaken.[78] However, let us assume that the mistake argument succeeded and Mrs Dimond was found to have been unjustly enriched at the expense of 1st Automotive. It is at this point that the configuration invites the application of the policy against accumulation. We have assumed that Mrs Dimond received the benefit of the replacement car hired by 1st Automotive, and that Mrs Dimond was in addition entitled to claim from Mr Lovell damages undiminished by the value of the car hire. As the analysis below demonstrates, Mrs Dimond was thereby unjustly enriched by accumulation.

Turning first to the question of enrichment, Mrs Dimond was clearly enriched since she had obtained the use of a replacement car. This was a benefit she had bargained for and promised to pay for once her damages claim against Mr Lovell succeeded. As has been said, when applying the policy against accumulation it is necessary already, as a matter of policy,

---

[78] *Dimond* v. *Lovell* [2000] 1QB 216 at 233 PER SIR RICHARD SCOTT VC who pointed out that 1st Automotive could have inserted an '... estimate of the [hiring charge] or amount of credit with an indication of the assumptions on which the estimate was made'. 1st Automotive might on such evidence be characterised a risk taker rather than a party affected by mistake.

to know whether it is the value given by S or PL which is vulnerable to return. On the facts of *Dimond* v. *Lovell*, it is clearly the transfer from 1st Automotive (S) which is vulnerable. In satisfying the 'at the expense of' element, it is a relatively simple matter to demonstrate that, as a matter of direction, the enrichment passed from S to RH.

Of interest is the unjust factor. On the revised facts of *Dimond* v. *Lovell*, we have assumed that the policy which rendered the contract of hire unenforceable did not preclude a claim in unjust enrichment by 1st Automotive against Mrs Dimond. The purpose of doing so was to establish a liability on Mrs Dimond (RH), for example founded in mistake, to make restitution to 1st Automotive (S) for benefits conferred. Pursuant to this restitutionary obligation, Mrs Dimond would then have been entitled to claim a correlative amount by way of damages from the wrongdoer (PL). The facts thus resemble those attracting the policy against accumulation. RH is entitled to claim from PL damages in respect of a loss ameliorated by benefits provided by S. RH holds in respect of the same damage value transferred by both S and PL.

Of course, on the revised version of *Dimond* v. *Lovell*, RH's accumulation would have been reversed by the obligation, founded on mistake, to make restitution to S. However, the point is to realise that the policy against accumulation would also have been available. Had Mrs Dimond's receipt from both S and PL not been reversed by the unjust enrichment claim founded on S's mistake, the policy against accumulation would have satisfied the question of injustice. By the policy against accumulation, RH's enrichment would have been reversed, and she would have been forced to return value to S. *Dimond* v. *Lovell* thus illustrates a configuration which potentially attracts the policy against accumulation as an unjust factor. The consequence of a system of tort liability which does not deduct from RH's damages claim against PL the value of S's loss ameliorating contribution entrenches injustice. It creates a structural anomaly by which, owing to the interrelationship between RH's ability to receive value from both S and PL, RH will accumulate in respect of the same damage. Recognition of the policy against accumulation as an unjust factor addresses this issue.

Roxborough *v.* Rothmans of Pall Mall Australia Limited

The facts of this case were given above on pp. 201–2. Briefly stated, the New South Wales government imposed a licence fee on tobacco wholesalers and retailers. The retailer in question purchased for resale tobacco from

Rothmans. The price paid included two distinct components. The first was the price of the tobacco, the second an amount referable to the licence fee. It was industry practice to pass the cost of this licence fee onto consumers in the form of higher retail prices for tobacco products. An intervening High Court decision[79] declared unconstitutional the New South Wales fee. The retailer therefore commenced proceedings against Rothmans to recover amounts paid on account of this licence fee.[80] The claim succeeded.

Of relevance to this discussion is the observation that the configuration in *Rothmans* is a category of case raising the application of the policy against accumulation. The retailer (RH) recovered an amount from Rothmans (PL) in respect of which it also received from tobacco consumers (S). The effect of the court's decision was therefore to permit RH to accumulate in respect of the same debt or damage. There is clear evidence that the justices of the High Court of Australia were uneasy about the risk of RH's accumulation. Although ultimately allowing the retailer's claim, the majority was content to let the windfall lie in the hands of the retailer.[81] In relation to the risk of accumulation, Gleeson CJ, Gaudron and Hayne JJ stated:[82]

> In all probability, whoever succeeds in these proceedings will have made a windfall gain. In the absence of some legislative intervention, the appellants [RH], if they succeed, are unlikely to be obliged to pass on the fruits of their success to the smokers [S] who bore the financial burden of the invalid tax.

Kirby J also identified the windfall to RH:[83]

> The attempt of the retailers to recover a share of the wholesaler's windfall was not a selfless one, ventured on behalf of their customers. Neither before the proceedings reached this Court, nor in answer to repeated questions asked of their counsel, did the retailers indicate the slightest interest in recovering the whole, or any part, of the windfall for the benefit of the consumers. They wanted the windfall for themselves ... Must part of the windfall to the wholesaler, who is undeserving, be passed to the retailers, equally undeserving, without any provision, sought or offered, to recompense the consumers, who are deserving because they ultimately paid amounts towards the unrecovered licence fees?

---

[79] *Ha* v. *New South Wales* (1997) 189 CLR 465.
[80] *Roxborough* v. *Rothmans of Pall Mall Australia Limited* [2001] HCA 68.
[81] *Ibid.*, paras. 30 and 31.   [82] N. 80 above at para. 5.   [83] N. 80 above at paras. 114 and 115.

In contrast to the majority position, Kirby J ultimately denied the retailer's claim, pending legislation which might be enacted to strip tobacco wholesalers of their gain and return this value to tobacco consumers.[84] The difficulties of analysis faced by the court might have been avoided had the policy against accumulation been realised in its role as an unjust factor. As shown by the following paragraphs, the policy against accumulation would have reversed the retailer's enrichment which was by the result in *Roxborough* allowed to remain.

Prior to any unjust enrichment claim against RH, it is necessary to determine whether the relationship in question is one to which the policy against accumulation applies. Further, we must ask whether it is the value transferred by S or PL which must be returned. The above extract from the judgment of Kirby J demonstrates that, in connection with the factual transfer of liability to pay the licence fee, the relationship between S, PL and RH attracts the policy against accumulation. Neither the tobacco consumers (S), nor Rothmans (PL), accepted the risk that the retailer (RH) would accumulate. Kirby J also confirms that it is the value from S which must be returned, since in his view both Rothmans and the retailer are equally undeserving.[85] It is therefore relatively easy to satisfy the 'at the expense of' element of the claim. RH is enriched at the expense of S since it is this value which must be returned. There is no doubt that, as a matter of direction, the payment travelled from consumers (S) to the retailer (RH).

The question of enrichment is similarly uncontroversial. The retailer (RH) received from tobacco consumers (S) value on account of the licence fee. S paid money to RH. It is relatively easy to demonstrate this payment is enriching because money is always enriching, it is the very measure of value. As stated by Robert Goff J '... [m]oney has the peculiar character of a universal medium of exchange. By its receipt, the recipient is inevitably benefited...'[86]

Finally, we come to the relevant unjust factor. It must be remembered that the unjust factor under investigation is that underlying S's potential claim against RH. The question of RH's accumulation arises only because RH is permitted to recover from PL value on account of an unconstitutional licence fee. The unjust factor surrounding this separate claim is not the focus of this discussion. Rather, we must assume that the retailer (RH) recovers

---

[84] N. 80 above at paras. 174 and 175.   [85] N. 80 above at para. 115.
[86] *BP Exploration Co (Libya)* v. *Hunt (No 2)* [1979] 1 WLR 783 at 789 PER ROBERT GOFF J.

against Rothmans (PL), having already been paid this amount by purchasers of tobacco products (S). It will be difficult for S to establish injustice on the basis of another unjust factor. In relation to the terms of sale, it is likely that S's intention to transfer value was qualified only to the extent that RH agreed to supply the product. It is highly unlikely that specific reference was made to that proportion of the price paid which was in fact referable to the licence fee. Similarly, in most cases it is not likely that S could rely on a mistake to recover that part of the price paid on account of the licence fee. Even if a mistake could be established, it is unlikely that such a mistake could render deficient S's intention to transfer value. It will be hard to prove, in relation to the tobacco consumer, that it was the mistake which caused S's transfer of value to RH.

The policy against accumulation is thus uniquely able to supply the foundation for S's unjust enrichment claim against RH. RH accumulates because it has, in respect of the same debt or damage, received value from both S and PL. In order to reverse this accumulation, RH must therefore return to S amounts paid on account of the licence fee. It must be conceded that on the particular facts of *Roxborough* this would present evidential and practical difficulties because the class of claimants, tobacco consumers who had paid the higher tobacco price, was very large. However, through the mechanisms of class or representative actions the law has in the past overcome these obstacles. Even if on the facts of *Roxborough* such difficulties prove insoluble, the unassailable fact remains that in a configuration where S is represented by not such a large number of claimants, the policy against accumulation should operate as an unjust factor. In this way, the concerns of the High Court of Australia in *Roxborough* that to allow RH's claim would create a windfall are overcome. It is true that *without* the policy against accumulation the result in the case is to entrench RH's ability to accumulate at the expense of S. It is therefore vital to recognise the role of the policy as an unjust factor.

Conclusion

The task of this chapter has been to outline the novel policy motivated unjust factor called the policy against accumulation. The policy applies where the claimant (RH) receives a benefit, or has the right to recover a debt or damages from another party (PL), and receives, or has the right to receive, in respect of the same debt or damage, from a third party (S). It is possible to identify RH's accumulation at two moments in the story. The first is when RH actually recovers from both S and PL. The second is earlier in time when RH is entitled to receive from S and PL. In those categories of case where it applies as an unjust factor, the policy against accumulation dictates that RH must return value to reverse her enrichment which would otherwise remain. In the cases in this study, RH has returned the value transferred by S.

Both versions of the policy are capable of explaining RH's obligation to share her damages with S. However, there is an important limit to this analysis, relevant to the second version of the policy by which RH accumulates when her cause of action accrues. Taken literally, this might mean that RH would be obligated to return value at this moment, even before having exercised a claim against PL. This is a very strong application of the policy, which might be considered draconian in effect. However, it must be realised that the impact of the policy against accumulation will in some configurations be tempered by the fact that, in addition to the ability to share in RH's damages, S holds the ability to force RH to sue PL.

The primary examples under investigation in this book are the carer and victim and the indemnity insurer and insured. It is uncontroversial that the indemnity insurer (S) is entitled to be substituted to the insured's (RH's) claim against the wrongdoer (PL).[87] This book has argued for recognition of a parallel right for the carer. At least in these configurations, in which S may force litigation against RH, it might be thought acceptable that RH's accumulation is assessed when her claim accrues. In other cases, the better view may well be that RH accumulates only when she actually recovers from PL.

Leaving aside the above qualification, this book demonstrates that two categories in which the policy unequivocally applies are that of the carer and victim, and the indemnity insurer and insured. The carer and the indemnity insurer are both entitled to participate in the fund of damages recovered. This chapter shows that these rights of participation are given to reverse RH's enrichment which would otherwise remain. Not all carers are entitled to share in the victim's damages. In Australia, the prevailing orthodoxy is that damages belong beneficially to the victim, and there is no legal obligation on the victim to pay the carer. This is manifestly unjust.

---

[87] Chapter 7, pp. 176–7 and 179–83.

In those cases where the victim's damages are under the control of another party, by reason of the victim's incapacity, there is evidence that the carer will succeed in a claim to be paid out of the victim's estate.[88] However, not all carers obtain such protection, and most rather fall to the vagaries of the victim who may or may not decide to return value to the carer. As described by Callinan J:[89]

> Experience recalls to mind the incredulous expressions of delight of plaintiffs, and of disbelieving dismay of defendants, on being told that damages for gratuitous care and services at common law are available, and that there is no legal obligation in this country for them to be paid to the gratuitous carer and provider of services.

One of the reasons that the Australian courts have entrenched the victim's ability to accumulate is for want of a basis on which rationally to distribute the victim's damages, and to reverse the value transferred by the carer. Recognition of the policy against accumulation provides a foundation on which to rest the carer's entitlement. The law in Australia requires urgent attention to remedy the situation currently prevailing where the victim is unjustly enriched by accumulation.

The policy against accumulation is an unjust factor capable of application beyond the configurations disclosed by the carer and victim and the indemnity insurer and insured. The anomaly in the Australian treatment of carers occurred in part because the role of the policy against accumulation was not properly understood. We are in danger of repeating this error. As shown by the above discussion of *Roxborough*, there are other configurations in which RH's ability to accumulate is being entrenched. The broader significance of this book is therefore to reveal the existence of this unjust factor.

---

[88] N. 19 above.
[89] *Grincelis* v. *House* (2000) 201 CLR 321 at 339 PER CALLINAN J.

PART III

9

The proprietary claim

This chapter explains why the carer's access to the fund is proprietary in nature, being expressed through the mechanism of a trust. Although on the particular facts a trust was not actually imposed, the House of Lords in *Hunt* v. *Severs* held that in the case where carer and tortfeasor are not the same person, the victim will hold in trust for the carer that portion of the damages award calculated by reference to the value of the carer's intervention.[1] As has been discussed, their Lordships failed to identify the juridical basis of the trust. It is important to separate the fact of the carer's entitlement to participate in the fund from the form of the right to do so. This book has shown that the right to participate is raised to reverse the enrichment which would otherwise remain, the unjust factor being the policy against accumulation. However, even with this analysis, it is still necessary to account for the fact that the carer's entitlement is proprietary.

This chapter contends that the policy against accumulation itself triggers the proprietary nature of the carer's entitlement. The particular feature of the cases justifying a proprietary, rather than a personal award, is that the carer's intervention directly enlarges the victim's patrimony. The model of damages liability adopted by the court makes the value of the victim's claim, in part, a function of the value of the services provided by the carer. Put simply, the more services a carer provides or is reckoned in the future to provide, the more valuable will be the victim's chose in action against the wrongdoer. The carer's intervention thus creates new value in the hands of the victim.

The suggestion of a trust for the carer has been controversial. In Australia, judicial suspicion of the trust has contributed to the position whereby in that jurisdiction the victim always accumulates. In *Kars* v. *Kars*[2] the High Court

---

[1] *Hunt* v. *Severs* [1994] 2 AC 350 at 363 PER LORD BRIDGE.
[2] *Kars* v. *Kars* (1996) 187 CLR 354.

of Australia considered the imposition of a trust in favour of the carer. Regarding such a trust as 'peculiar',[3] the majority of the court rejected the argument that the *Hunt* v. *Severs* trust should be incorporated into Australian law. One of the reasons for doing so was that such a device would result in a diminution in the fund available to the victim in the case where the tortfeasor and carer are the same person.[4] In result, the court denied the right of all carers, whether personal or proprietary, to share in the fund. Any damages awarded belong beneficially to the victim and '... contractual or other legal liability apart, whether the plaintiff actually reimburses the provider is entirely a matter between the injured plaintiff and the provider'.[5] The outcome of this position is that the victim who recovers damages calculated by reference to the carer's contribution always accumulates in respect of the same damage. Although it is possible such victims will by voluntary payment return value to the carer, this is not the model mandated by law. As argued in chapter 8, the entrenchment of this position was in part caused by the failure to recognise the policy against accumulation as an unjust factor. This was compounded by a failure properly to understand the carer's trust. This has led to the anomalous position graphically described by Callinan J:[6]

> ... there is implicit in their reasoning [referring to the suggestion in *Donnelly* v. *Joyce* that the victim would be subject to a moral obligation to pay the carer] ... an optimism about human nature unhappily rather infrequently encountered in practice. Experience calls to mind the incredulous expressions of delight of plaintiffs, and of disbelieving dismay of defendants, on being told that damages for gratuitous care and services at common law are available, and that there is no legal obligation in this country for them to be paid to the gratuitous carer and provider of services.

Leaving aside the juridical basis of the carer's entitlement, the trust has been criticised as being unworkable. Serious problems with the administration of such a trust remain unresolved.[7] The first is that which relates to an

---

[3] *Ibid.*, 371 PER TOOHEY, MCHUGH, GUMMOW AND KIRBY JJ.

[4] N. 2 above at 380 PER TOOHEY, MCHUGH, GUMMOW AND KIRBY JJ.

[5] N. 2 above at 372 PER TOOHEY, MCHUGH, GUMMOW AND KIRBY JJ.

[6] *Grincelis* v. *House* (2000) 201 CLR 321 at 339 PER CALLINAN J.

[7] These are documented in P. Matthews and M. Lunney, 'A Tortfeasor's Lot is not a Happy One?' (1995) *Modern Law Review* 395 at 402–4; L. Hoyano, 'The Dutiful Tortfeasor in the House of Lords' (1995) 3 *Tort Law Review* 63 at 73; A. Reed, 'A Commentary on *Hunt* v. *Severs*' (1995) 15 *Oxford Journal of Legal Studies* 133 at 139.

award of damages in respect of future services to be given by the carer to the claimant. There are examples of cases in which the victim recovers the value of future care and a trust for the carer is recognised.[8] An obvious problem in these cases is that it is not certain whether the carer will continue to be the person responsible for the victim's care. As explained by Callinan J:[9]

> There are other matters which perhaps have not always attracted the attention that they deserve in the assessment of damages for gratuitous care, either past or prospective. Some relationships are more fragile and less enduring than others. Care provided gratuitously, for a time, may cease to be available or may simply cease because of fatigue or exhaustion.

Depending on the way in which the trust is described, it is possible that the only beneficiary is the precise carer who was in view at the time of the award. If this person dies, a narrow construction says that this carer is the only beneficiary of the trust and that the funds cannot be held to meet the cost of intervention by a second or subsequent carers.

The second problem with the administration of the carer's trust derives not from the award in respect of future care, but is a function of the degree of incapacity suffered by the victim who is now a trustee. The general rule is that, if a person is capable of holding or disposing of legal or equitable property, then that person also possesses the capacity to be a trustee.[10] An extreme example is the victim in *Pickering* v. *Deakin*, who suffered injuries to the left temporal lobe of his brain and was left with a profound loss of intellectual ability. Lambert JA described his condition as follows:[11]

> Steven has major defects in speech and language functioning and his judgment is impaired. He does not have a realistic understanding of his deficiencies and he does not understand or even appreciate his incapacity.

The trial judge in that case awarded a proportion of the damages to the claimant Steven to be held in trust for his carer wife.[12] Cases such as this

---

[8] *Hunt* v. *Severs* [1994] 2 AC 350; *Taylor* v. *Bristol Omnibus Co* [1975] 1 WLR 1054; *Lunnon* v. *Reagh* (1978) 25 NSR (2d) 196.

[9] N. 6 above at 343 PER CALLINAN J.

[10] An obvious exception to this is the minor who cannot be a trustee. Section 20 of the Law of Property Act 1925.

[11] *Pickering* v. *Deakin* [1985] 1 WWR 289 at 292 PER LAMBERT JA.

[12] *Ibid.*, 293 PER LAMBERT JA quoting from the decision of the trial judge reported at [1983] BCWLD 1953. The trial judge's decision in respect of past care was not affected by the appeal.

obviously call for the appointment of a receiver or like person to administer the affairs of the victim, including the administration of any trusts of damages.[13] It must be questioned whether the victim has the capacity to be a trustee on facts such as these.

The need to explain the proprietary nature of the third party's access to the fund is compounded by the observation that the indemnity insurer's right to participate is also proprietary. Earlier chapters have described the insurer's parallel right to share in the fund. Chapter 8 shows that the right to participate is given to reverse the insured's enrichment by accumulation which would otherwise remain. In *Lord Napier and Ettrick* v. *Hunter*[14] the House of Lords confirmed that, where the insured recovers damages having first been indemnified by the insurer, the form of the insurer's entitlement is expressed via an equitable lien over the fund of damages or settlement monies.[15] The proprietary nature of the insurer's entitlement has been subject to criticism. Particularly puzzling is the fact that it is the timing of the insurer's payments which appears to trigger this result. In the case where the insured first recovers damages from the wrongdoer, and is then indemnified by the insurer, the insured is vulnerable only to a personal claim for money had and received. However, as shown by *Lord Napier*, in the configuration where the insured is paid first by the insurer, the response is proprietary.[16]

The purpose of this chapter is therefore to explain why the third party's entitlement to share in the fund is proprietary. It thus provides a way of explaining both the carer's trust and also the lien in favour of the indemnity

---

13 For example: *Cassell* v. *Hammersmith and Fulham Health Authority* [1992] 1 PIQR Q1 and *Fairhurst* v. *St-Helens and Knowsley Health Authority* [1995] 4 PIQR Q1 in which the administration of the victim's award was placed in the hands of the Court of Protection. In neither of those cases was a trust of the damages awarded. However, any doubt as to the capacity of the trustee would have been avoided. See also *Re DJR and the Mental Health Act* [1983] 1 NSWLR 557 and *W* v. *Q* (1992) 1 Tas R 301. In both of these cases the mental deficit suffered by the victim required that a commissioner or public trustee be appointed to stand in the shoes of the victim, including the power to pay the carer.

14 *Lord Napier and Ettrick* v. *Hunter* [1993] AC 713.

15 *Ibid.,* 738–739 PER LORD TEMPLEMAN, 744–745 PER LORD GOFF, 748 PER LORD JAUNCEY who agreed with Lord Goff and Lord Browne-Wilkinson, 752 PER LORD BROWNE-WILKINSON and 753 PER LORD SLYNN who agreed with Lord Templeman.

16 The significance attached to the timing of payments has been the subject of criticism. Mitchell makes the point that, if the difference between the case where the insurer is entitled to a proprietary remedy (via an equitable lien), and that where the insurer is entitled only to a personal remedy (via an action for money had and received), is simply the order in which the payments were received by RH, this creates '. . . an anomaly for which there is no justification'. Mitchell, p. 84. These criticisms have received judicial support in *England* v. *Guardian Insurance Ltd* [2000] Lloyd's Rep IR 404 at 415 PER JUDGE THORNTON QC.

insurer. The difficulties of administration of the carer's trust can be solved only via legislative reform, and as noted below, statutory abolition of the carer's trust has been recommended.[17] However, better to understand the existing law requires an explanation of the proprietary nature of the carer's entitlement and this is the question addressed by this chapter.

This discussion does not argue prescriptively in favour of a proprietary entitlement for either the carer or the insurer. The Law Commission has recommended statutory reform which would fundamentally alter the nature of the carer's entitlements. In particular, the Law Commission has proposed abolition of the carer's trust, and suggested that the victim should be subject only to a personal obligation to pay over damages in respect of past care.[18] The discussion likewise notes that the proprietary quality of the insurer's entitlement has been criticised, and might instead be recognised only by a personal claim. These possible future developments are relevant but do not derogate from the central purpose of this chapter. The discussion seeks only to show how the existing entitlements may be placed on a principled foundation.

Four important qualifications must be made at the outset. The first is to recognise that the subject of proprietary claims is itself an area of prolific study and debate. Our understanding of the law in this area has been the concern of many leading scholars and judges. This chapter purports to do no more than determine the extent to which a proprietary claim for the carer and the insurer (S) may be explained by reference to existing theories of proprietary restitution. The purpose of this chapter is not to examine the ambit of proprietary restitutionary claims in general, but rather to understand better S's proprietary right to participate in the fund of damages held by the claimant (RH).

The second qualification is one of labelling. This analysis assumes that the proprietary language employed by the court is intended in substance to refer to proprietary rights. The argument excludes the possibility that the proprietary language is intended to refer only to a personal obligation to account.[19] While the litmus test is whether S's right to

---

[17] UK Law Commission, *Damages for Personal Injury: Medical, Nursing and Other Expenses; Collateral Benefits* (Law Com No 262, 1999), para 3.62.

[18] *Ibid.*, Discussed in S. Degeling, 'Carers' Claims: Unjust Enrichment and Tort' [2000] *Restitution Law Review* 172.

[19] Sir P. Millett, 'Restitution and Constructive Trusts' in W. Cornish et al (eds.), *Restitution Past, Present & Future* (Oxford, 1998) 199 p. 200; A. Oakley, *Constructive Trusts* (3rd edn., London, 1997) pp. 188–90.

participate survives the bankruptcy, death or divorce of RH, there is no evidence in the cases supporting the contrary assumption. The analysis therefore excludes the possibility that the language adopted by the court is intended to refer to anything other than a proprietary right enforceable against RH.

More difficult problems of understanding arise from the use of the labels constructive and resulting trusts. Classification of the carer's trust as constructive or resulting will not be attempted. While the analysis ultimately provides an explanation for the fact that the carer's entitlement is expressed via a trust, and the insurer's via an equitable lien, this book rejects the use of the labels constructive and resulting. These descriptors do not make any attempt at all to identify the events by which these non-express trusts arise. At least one judge appears to classify the trust as a constructive trust[20] and another says it is a 'notional trust',[21] but in the final analysis these categories do nothing to illuminate the juridical basis for the trust and the reason why the law's response in such a case is proprietary rather than personal.

There have been recent academic and judicial efforts to understand the true nature of trusts raised to reverse unjust enrichment. Lord Browne-Wilkinson suggested in *Westdeutsche Landesbank Girozentrale* v. *Islington London Borough Council*[22] that the role of the constructive trust should not be limited to the province of wrongs. Rather, he proposed that the development of proprietary restitution should be via the recognition of the remedial constructive trust.[23] Lord Browne-Wilkinson's model has not been followed, and the Court of Appeal has since unequivocally rejected recognition in English law of the remedial constructive trust.[24]

Chambers has controversially suggested that the primary vehicle for proprietary restitution of unjust enrichment is the resulting trust. He argues

---

[20] *Burdis* v. *Livesey* [2001] 1 WLR 1751 at 1762 PER GRAY J. This was in fact a claim to recover the value of car repairs from the tortfeasor who had negligently damaged the claimant's car.

[21] '... Alberto has received and will need to receive from the various friends and relatives. Those sums of course on the *Hunt* v. *Severs* principles are held in a *notional trust* for those who have provided them.' *Bordin* v. *St Mary's NHS Trust* unreported Queen's Bench Division 26 January 2000 PER CRANE J.

[22] *Westdeutsche Landesbank Girozentrale* v. *Islington London Borough Council* [1996] AC 669 (HL).

[23] *Ibid.*, 716 PER LORD BROWNE-WILKINSON.

[24] *Re Polly Peck (No 2)* [1998] 3 All ER 813 at 831 PER NOURSE LJ. This contrasts starkly with the position in Canada where the remedial constructive trust is alive and well. *Soulos* v. *Korkontzilas* (1997) 146 DLR (4th) 214.

that all resulting trusts arise in response to unjust enrichment.[25] On this view, a resulting trust arises whenever property is transferred into the hands of a recipient, in circumstances where the provider of the property did not intend to benefit the recipient.[26] The absence of intention to benefit the recipient may arise either because the transferor was unaware or ignorant of this shift of wealth, her intention was vitiated, or the basis of the transfer had failed prior to the recipient obtaining unfettered ownership of the enrichment. In this model, other unjust factors are not capable of raising a proprietary response. In such other categories of unjust enrichment, although there is a right to restitution, the claimant is affected by '... neither impairment of judgment or qualification...' and it is difficult to see why a resulting trust should arise.[27] Writing extra judicially, Lord Millett has expressed some sympathy with Chambers' model.[28] Although in *Twinsectra Limited* v. *Yardley*[29] Lord Millett disagreed with Chambers' explanation of the *Quistclose* trust,[30] his Lordship does not appear to disagree with Chambers' central thesis about the true basis of the resulting trust.[31]

A discussion of the correct analysis of resulting and constructive trusts is therefore only just beginning. However, what we really want to know is not the true nature of resulting and constructive trusts, but rather whether non-express trusts ever arise from wrongs or breaches or duty and whether

---

[25] R. Chambers, *Resulting Trusts* (Oxford, 1997). A similar view had earlier been expressed by P. Birks, 'Restitution and Resulting Trusts' in S. Goldstein (ed.), *Equity and Contemporary Legal Developments* (Jerusalem, 1992), 335.

[26] Chambers, p. 21.   [27] *Ibid.*, p. 229.

[28] Sir P. Millett, 'Restitution and Constructive Trusts' in W. Cornish et al (eds.), *Restitution Past, Present & Future* (Oxford, 1998), pp. 201–2, 209–10 and 215.

[29] *Twinsectra Limited* v. *Yardley* [2002] 2 AC 164.

[30] *Ibid.*, 190–193 PER LORD MILLETT. Lord Millett at 190–191 endorsed the criticisms made by L. Ho and P. St J. Smart, 'Re-interpreting the *Quistclose* Trust: A Critique of Chambers' Analysis' (2001) 21 *Oxford Journal of Legal Studies* 267.

[31] N. 29 above at 190. In *Air Jamaica Ltd* v. *Charlton* [1999] 1 WLR 1399 at 1413 Lord Millett, giving the advice of the Privy Council, appeared to lend some support to Chambers' analysis. A pension scheme set up for the employees of Air Jamaica Ltd was effectively discontinued. In an action to determine the destination of an actuarial surplus which had built up in the pension fund, the Privy Council held that the surplus should be paid to members and Air Jamaica in equal shares, via the mechanism of resulting trust. The return of value to the employees and the company reflected their respective contributions. One factor influencing Lord Millett in reaching this position was that '[o]ne of the benefits [the employees] had bargained for was that the trustees should be obliged to pay them additional benefits in the event of the scheme's discontinuance'. The trust of the surplus which would otherwise have arisen was void ab initio. Therefore, in the language of Chambers, since the basis of the transfer had failed ab initio, the recipient fund had never obtained unrestricted use of the money, thus justifying the recognition of a resulting trust in favour of employees.

they ever arise from unjust enrichment. This chapter regards the carer's entitlement as being given to reverse unjust enrichment. The focus of this inquiry is to determine whether this right to restitution yields a proprietary response. In other words, we ask whether the carer's trust is an unjust enrichment trust.

The third qualification is that the evidence presented in the victim and carer cases is inconsistent. Even after the decision of the House of Lords in *Hunt* v. *Severs*, which purports to establish that the victim normally holds the relevant portion of damages in trust for the carer,[32] the cases remain unsettled. For example, in *Jolley* v. *London Borough of Sutton*[33] the victim sued the London Borough of Sutton in respect of personal injuries sustained in the grounds of a block of council flats owned by the defendant. The victim recovered an '... allowance for the care and attention afforded by his family beyond the normal call of duty and beyond natural love and affection'. Despite noting that the purpose of such an award was to allow recompense to the person who rendered the services, and citing as authority the decision of the House in *Hunt* v. *Severs*, the trial judge failed to impose a trust of the damages. He did not specifically refuse a trust, but rather remained silent as to whether the carer had any right to participate in the damages awarded. Leaving aside the fact that in *Jolley* the mere existence of the carer's right to participate was apparently ignored, it is also an example of a case in which the court failed to conform to the trust mechanism suggested by the House of Lords. The only reason that a trust was not imposed in *Hunt* v. *Severs* was Mr Severs' dual identity as carer and tortfeasor. The carer in *Jolley* was not implicated in the wrongdoing.

The Canadian cases are also unstable. *Thornton* v. *Board of School Trustees of School District No 57 (Prince George)* is authority for the recognition of a trust of the damages in favour of the carer.[34] Notwithstanding the endorsement of this trust by the Supreme Court of Canada, there are examples

---

[32] *Hunt* v. *Severs* [1994] 2 AC 350 at 363 PER LORD BRIDGE with whom the rest of the House agreed.

[33] *Jolley* v. *London Borough of Sutton* [1998] Lloyd's Rep 433. Another example is *Simpson* v. *Portsmouth & South East Hampshire Health Authority* unreported Queen's Bench Division 16 July 1997, Mantell J.

[34] *Thornton* v. *Board of School Trustees of School District No 57 (Prince George)* (1976) 73 DLR (3d) 35 at 55 PER TAGGART JA with whom Branca and Carrothers JJA agreed on this issue. The decision of the British Columbia Court of Appeal was upheld by the Supreme Court of Canada reported at (1978) 83 DLR (3d) 480 at 491 PER DICKSON J who delivered the judgment of the court.

in which the victim has recovered damages from the wrongdoer calculated by reference to the value of the carer's contribution, but in respect of which no trust is recognised.[35] Despite the pattern of instability, this chapter nevertheless attempts to make some sense of the possibilities, and nudges the wandering cases towards something resembling order. Earlier chapters present a model of the victim and carer cases which requires that the carer obtain access to the victim's damages in order to reverse the unjust enrichment of the victim which would otherwise remain. While noting that there are exceptions, this analysis is based on a core configuration which is typified in England by the trust proposed in *Hunt* v. *Severs*, and in Canada by that proposed in *Thornton* v. *Board of School Trustees of School District No 57 (Prince George)*. This chapter attempts to provide a rationalisation only for the observation that in some cases the carer's right to share is proprietary. It does not purport to explain the form of the carer's right in every example to share in the fund.

The fourth impediment is that although there is some evidence of various policy considerations weighing on the minds of the judges, the courts rarely explicitly identify why a particular policy factor is relevant. Judicial analysis often fails to separate out whether a policy consideration is relevant to any or all of: (1) the availability and success of this head of damage in the victim's claim; (2) the reason justifying the carer's participation in the victim's award; and (3) the form of this participation. Courts do not specify whether the policy objective is being used to discriminate between those cases in which the carer is entitled to a proprietary right in the victim's award or merely a personal right exercisable against the victim. Even in those cases where the carer's right to participate is proprietary, judicial analysis does not explain why one form of proprietary remedy, such as a trust, is imposed in preference to another such as a lien. So far as the evidence allows, this chapter is concerned only with the reasons given in support of a particular form of mechanism.

This chapter proceeds in three sections. The first section very briefly documents the species of device by which the carer obtains access to the victim's damages. As has been said, the major feature of the victim and carer cases is that there are prominent examples in which the carer is the

---

[35] For example the following cases in which no mechanism was imposed: *Millett* v. *McDonald's Restaurants of Canada Limited* (1984) 29 Man R (2d) 83; *Newell* v. *Hawthornthwaite* (1988) 26 BCLR (2d) 105; *Redden* v. *Hector* (1980) 42 NSR (2d) 96; *Yepremian et al* v. *Scarborough General Hospital et al* (1980) 110 DLR (3d) 513.

beneficiary of a trust of the damages. However, there are exceptions. In some examples, the carer's access to the fund is not proprietary in nature. The question of precisely when a claim in unjust enrichment will be met by a proprietary remedy has yet satisfactorily to be resolved. For the purpose of better understanding the nature of the proprietary response, the next section will record briefly the relevant accounts of the law's proprietary response to unjust enrichment. The third section returns to the two versions of the unjust factor called the policy against accumulation. It will be recalled that there are two points in time when the claimant's (RH's) accumulation may be identified. In the first, RH accumulates when RH actually recovers damages from the wrongdoer (PL). In the second, RH accumulates at the moment her cause of action accrues. RH accumulates because she holds both the value transferred by the third party (S) and the right to sue PL for a correlative amount. The third section applies these models in order to determine whether either discloses a proprietary claim for S. As will be demonstrated, when applied both to the carer and the indemnity insurer, the policy against accumulation is capable of generating a proprietary response to reverse RH's unjust enrichment.

Mechanisms implementing the carer's right to participate

The purpose of this section is briefly to document the means by which the carer obtains access to the victim's damages. The cases exhibit a spectrum of responses implementing the carer's right to participate. These responses, progressing from weakest to strongest, are as follows. First, there are cases of judicial silence about the entitlement of the carer.[36] There is no obvious correlation between the cases in which the court is silent and the existence of any particular consideration, whether factual or policy based. It must also be admitted that the contents of a judgment will in part be a product of the arguments put to the court by counsel. Especially when we cannot be sure whether the carer actually requested access to the fund, it would be unwise to place undue emphasis on judicial silence.

[36] *A* v. *National Blood Authority* [2001] 3 All ER 289; *Joy* v. *Newell* unreported Queen's Bench Division 27 February 1998, Campbell J; *Jolley* v. *London Borough of Sutton* [1998] 1 Lloyd's Law Rep 433, appealed on other grounds to the Court of Appeal [1998] 1 WLR 1546 (CA) and the House of Lords [2000] 1 WLR 1082 (HL); *Parry* v. *North West Surrey Health Authority* unreported Queen's Bench Division 29 November 1999, Penry-Davey J; *Stacey* v. *National Leisure Catering Ltd* [2001] EWCA Civ 355; *Simpson* v. *Portsmouth & South East Hampshire Health Authority* unreported Queen's Bench Division 16 July 1997, Mantell J.

The silence cases are best regarded as neutral as to the existence and form of the carer's right to participate. The only exceptions to this position are perhaps those cases in which the victim has promised to pay the carer. It is hardly surprising that the court is silent, because there appears to be no case in which the victim is, at the date of judgment, in breach of an obligation to pay the carer. The victim and carer may agree that the carer will intervene in return for payment, if and when the victim is put in funds by an award of damages from the wrongdoer. It is impossible to be more specific about the terms of these agreements because such matters fall to be decided by the parties. The crucial point is that the reports of these cases seem to indicate that, at the date of judgment, the victim is not in breach of an obligation to pay the carer.[37] In this situation it is hardly surprising that the court remains silent. Without a breach of an obligation, it is difficult to see how the existence of a promise to pay could have any relevance to the imposition of a mechanism granting the carer access to the victim's damages. Unless the promise has been repudiated, there is no need for judicial intervention.

The second category is those cases which recognise a moral obligation on the victim to pay the carer.[38] Unfortunately, there is no factor which

---

[37] For example: *Gibeault* v. *Schultz* (1978) 11 AR 584; *Redden* v. *Hector* (1980) 42 NSR (2d) 96; *Johnson* v. *Shelest* (1988) 22 BCLR (2d) 230; *Haggar* v. *de Placido* [1972] 2 All ER 1029. The only exception may be *Cunningham* v. *Harrison* [1973] 1 QB 942. This case is consistent with the other evidence if it is regarded as a case in which the victim repudiated his obligations to pay the carer. There are oblique references in the judgments of the members of the Court of Appeal to Mr Cunningham's unfavourable disposition. Lord Denning MR at 952 describes him as 'a very autocratic and talkative man who would not fit well with others in a home for the disabled'. Lawton LJ at 956 notes the trial judge's observation that he had a 'personality which may not be congenial to many'. Doubtless also the court was influenced by the plight of Mrs Cunningham who felt compelled to take her own life prior to trial.

[38] For example: *Altmann* v. *Dunning* [1995] 2 VR 1 at 25 PER HEDIGANN J who states '[i]t is clearly now accepted that there is no legal or equitable obligation on the victim to reward or account to the person who voluntarily provided the service, although it may be appropriate that that should be done'. *Marsland* v. *Andjelic* [No 2] (1993) 32 NSWLR 649 at 653 PER KIRBY AND MEAGHER JJA who speak of the need for the victim to 'be enabled to reimburse' the carer. *Van Gervan* v. *Fenton* (1992) 175 CLR 327 at 335 PER MASON CJ, TOOHEY AND MCHUGH JJ who were concerned that the victim should have the ability to pay the carer. *Gow* v. *Motor Vehicle Insurance Trust* [1967] WAR 55 at 58 PER NEGUS J although the moral obligation in this case might also have been a matter going to the victim's right to claim from the wrongdoer. The following cases concern an application to determine whether the carer should be paid out of a fund of damages administered on behalf of an incapacitated victim. In each, the court acknowledges a moral obligation binding the victim to pay the carer: *Re B* [2000] NSWSC 44 at para. 11 PER YOUNG J; *Beasley* v. *Marshall (No 4)* (1986) 42 SASR 407 at 410 PER KING CJ; *Re DJR and the Mental Health Act 1958* [1983] 1 NSWLR 557 at 561 and 564–565 PER POWELL J; *Re ES and the Mental Health Act 1958* [1984] 3 NSWLR 341 at 343 PER POWELL J; *Goode*

consistently triggers this response. The existence of the moral obligation by which the carer participates in the victim's damages is often merely asserted by the court. There is no reason or policy justification consistently invoked to justify its existence.[39] In the third category, the court imposes a condition on the victim's award, so that the victim is obligated to pay the carer. The victim and carer cases contain evidence of two methods by which the victim's conditional recovery is implemented. Those cases in which the court directs the victim to pay the carer[40] and other cases in which the victim recovers on the basis of his undertaking to the court that the appropriate portion of damages will be paid to the carer.[41]

v. *Thompson and Anor* (2001) Aust Torts Rep ¶81–617 at 67,179 PER AMBROSE J (also the victim's damages claim); *In the Matter of GDM and the Protected Estates Act 1983 (NSW)* (1992) Aust Torts Rep ¶81–190 at 61,686–61,687; *Jones* v. *Moylan [No 2]* (2000) 23 WAR 65 at 89–90 PER MCKECHNIE J; *Re N* (2001) 33 MVR 237 at 238 PER YOUNG J; *W* v. *Q* (1992) 1 Tas R 301 at 304–305 PER CRAWFORD J. See also *Kobs* v. *Merchants Hotel* et al (1990) 62 Man R (2d) 210 at 215 PER SMITH J approved (1990) 70 Man R (2d) 178; *Valois* v. *Long* (1984) 56 NBR (2d) 191 at 205 PER DAIGLE J; *Donnelly* v. *Joyce* [1974] 1 QB 454 at 463 PER MEGAW LJ who delivered the judgment of the Court of Appeal; *Roach* v. *Yates* [1938] 1 KB 256 at 263 PER GREER LJ who stated that the victim 'would naturally feel that he ought to compensate' the carer.

[39] An important exception to this statement is *In the Matter of GDM and the Protected Estates Act 1983 (NSW)* (1992) Aust Torts Rep ¶81–190 at 61,686–61,687 PER POWELL J. As discussed in chapter 8, Powell J identified the risk of accumulation as the basis of the victim's moral obligation to pay the carer: '. . . it is not the fact that services have been provided, but the fact that an amount representing the value of those services have been included in the plaintiff's verdict, which gives rise to a moral – but not a legal, or equitable – obligation to the provider of the services'.

[40] *Coderre* v. *Ethier* (1978) 85 DLR (3d) 621 at 632 PER LERNER J; *Turnbull* v. *Hsieh* (1990) 269 APR 33 at 42 PER HOYT JA who delivered the judgment of the court; *Rawson* v. *Kasman* (1956) 3 DLR (2d) 376 at 381 PER SCHROEDER JA with whom Hogg and MacKay JJA agreed.

[41] *Schneider* v. *Eisovitch* [1960] 2 QB 430 at 440 PER PAULL J; *Hasson* v. *Hamel* (1977) 78 DLR (3d) 573 at 578 PER ZALEV CO CT J. It is difficult to separate out whether the court requires this undertaking as a matter merely going to the existence of the victim's right to sue, or in addition as a matter going to the carer's right to participate in the fund. The two questions are frequently collapsed into the same inquiry. In *Wattson* v. *Port of London Authority* [1969] 1 Lloyd's Rep 95 at 102 Justice Megaw relaxed the requirement that the victim must undertake to pay the carer. In *Wilson* v. *McLeay* (1961) 106 CLR 523 at 526–527 PER TAYLOR J the victim stated in evidence that she was prepared to give an undertaking but the court did not consider this relevant. The court justified her claim against the wrongdoer on the basis that the presence of the carers at her bedside was necessary and therefore that an amount should be recoverable on account of the comfort and assistance given by them. On this view, the undertaking is relevant only as an ingredient of the victim's right to claim. Its role as a mechanism for the benefit of the carer is not taken into account.

The final category comprises those cases which impose a trust of the damages in favour of the carer. There are cases in which a trust is asserted without explanation,[42] those in which the court attempts some justification[43] and cases in which the court recognises that it has both proprietary and non-proprietary mechanisms available to allow the carer to participate in the victim's damages.[44]

There is little evidence in the cases of why, in some examples, a trust is recognised, and in others, a non-proprietary mechanism is imposed. Judicial analysis gives little, if any, explanation for the diversity of remedial devices implementing the carer's right to share. In addition, even in those cases where justifications are given by the court, it is difficult to determine whether the existence of the reason is matter relevant to the form of the carer's participation rather than a matter germane only to the prior question of whether the carer holds a right to do so. Judicial analysis fails to discriminate between these two core issues. The impoverished analysis offered by the cases therefore reveals little about why in some examples the carer's right to share is proprietary. The application of an unjust enrichment framework explains the form of the carer's right to participate and it is to this discussion that we now turn.

[42] For example: *Bissky* v. *Trottier* (1984) 54 BCLR 288; *Bordin* v. *St Mary's NHS Trust* unreported Queen's Bench Division 26 January 2000 PER CRANE J; *Brown et al* v. *University of Alberta Hospital et al* (1997) 145 DLR (4th) 63; *Gerow* v. *Reid* (1989) 225 APR 34; *Grover* v. *Lowther* (1982) 52 NSR (2d) 22; *Kirby* v. *British Columbia (Attorney General)* British Columbia Supreme Court 15 July 1997 PER BAUMAN J; *Lankenau* v. *Dutton* (1989) 56 DLR (4th) 364; *Lusignan (Litigation Guardian of)* v. *Concordia Hospital* [1997] 6 WWR 185, supplementary reasons at [1999] 1 WWR 733; *Lunnon* v. *Reagh* (1978) 25 NSR (2d) 196; *Matheson* v. *Bartlett* (1993) 335 APR 373; *Mitchell* v. *U-Haul Co of Canada Ltd* (1986) 73 AR 91; *Scarff* v. *Wilson* (1987) 39 CCLT 20; *Thornton* v. *Board of School Trustees of School District No 57 (Prince George)* (1978) 83 DLR (3d) 480; *Mackinlay* v. *MacEachern* (1983) 123 APR 175; *Pickering* v. *Deakin* [1985] 1 WWR 289.

[43] For example: *Cunningham* v. *Harrison* [1973] 1 QB 942; *Hunt* v. *Severs* [1994] 2 AC 350; *Taylor* v. *Bristol Omnibus Co* [1975] 1 WLR 1054; *Thomson* v. *MacLean* (1983) 57 NSR (2d) 436; *Feng* v. *Graham* (1988) 25 BCLR (2d) 116; *Crane* v. *Worwood* (1992) 65 BCLR (2d) 16. In *Oliver (Guardian ad Litem of)* v. *Ellison* British Columbia Court of Appeal 18 May 2001 at para. 122 PER SOUTHIN J the judge noted '[t]hese "in trust" awards which owe their origin to Lord Denning in *Cunningham* v. *Harrison* . . . are difficult to justify in legal theory . . . the court does not say the victim holds those amounts "in trust" for his creditors and I am unable to see the difference between the position of the family member who renders services and any other person who has a claim against the victim'.

[44] For example: *Housecroft* v. *Burnett* [1986] 1 All ER 332; *Griffiths* v. *Kerkemeyer* (1977) 139 CLR 161; *Kars* v. *Kars* (1996) 187 CLR 354; *Hall* v. *Miller* (1989) 41 BCLR (2d) 46; *McLeod* v. *Palardy* (1980) 4 Man R (2d) 218; *Turnbull* v. *Hsieh* (1990) 108 NBR (2d) 33; *Curator of Estates* v. *Fernandez* [1976] 16 ALR 445.

Unjust enrichment generated proprietary rights

Both the carer and the indemnity insurer (S) are entitled to share in the fund of damages won by the claimant (RH) in RH's suit against the wrong-doer (PL). As has been said, in explaining the proprietary nature of S's right to share in the fund, it is not helpful, in the case of the carer's trust, to attempt to understand the trust by assigning one of the hitherto accepted labels such as 'resulting trusts' or 'constructive trust'. These labels have been much misused, and do not tell us the answer to the relevant question. Previous chapters have demonstrated that S's entitlement to the fund is given to reverse RH's enrichment by accumulation. We want to know whether, in response to RH's unjust enrichment at the expense of S, the law will grant S a proprietary remedy. The question of precisely when a claim in unjust enrichment will be met by a proprietary remedy has yet satisfactorily to be resolved. For the purpose of better understanding the nature of S's entitlement, the discussion will record briefly the relevant accounts of the law's proprietary response to unjust enrichment.

The dominant model is that which links the availability of a proprietary response to the particular unjust factors, and the correlative impact on the transfer of value from claimant to defendant. As stated by Smith, '... not every case in which unjust enrichment is established will support the creation of proprietary rights. One could say that the more defective was the transfer from the plaintiff to the defendant, the stronger is the argument for a proprietary remedy.'[45] Following this approach, it is possible to survey the accepted unjust factors, documenting those in which proprietary restitution seems to be available.[46]

The strongest case for the award of proprietary restitution is that where the claimant either had no intention to benefit the recipient, or her intention to do so was impaired, for example by mistake. In these cases, the transfer of value may be declared voidable, conferring on the claimant the power to re-vest title in herself.[47] The claimant's entitlement to do so is an example of

---

[45] Smith, p. 296.

[46] *Ibid.*, p. 298; Birks and Mitchell, pp. 598–601; W. Swadling, 'Property and Unjust Enrichment' in J. W. Harris (ed.), *Property Problems: From Genes to Pension Funds* (London, 1997), pp. 133–8; Sir P. Millett, 'Restitution and Constructive Trusts' in W. Cornish et al (eds.), *Restitution Past, Present & Future* (Oxford, 1998), pp. 215–16; R. Goode, 'Proprietary Restitutionary Claims' in W. Cornish et al (eds.), *Restitution Past, Present & Future* (Oxford, 1998), pp. 75–7.

[47] At law this is expressed via the remedy of rescission: *Car & Universal Finance* v. *Caldwell* [1965] 1 QB 525. In equity, the exercise of the power leads to a trust in favour of the transferor: *Lonrho*

proprietary restitution of unjust enrichment.[48] Cases of qualified intent are different. In these cases the claimant does have an intention, albeit qualified, to benefit the recipient and the courts should therefore be careful about transforming the status of this claim from personal to proprietary. It has been suggested that there will only ever be a personal claim if, before the basis of the transfer fails, the recipient obtains unrestricted use of the property transferred.[49] We have already shown that the carer's entitlement to share in the fund is not generated by one of these unjust factors.[50] This model of proprietary restitution therefore has very little to offer in explaining the carer's proprietary entitlement.

Another school of thought links the availability of a proprietary remedy to the question of whether the claimant has taken a risk on the solvency of the defendant.[51] It is only when the claimant has not taken the risk of the defendant's solvency that the claimant will be entitled to a proprietary remedy. This model recognises the powerful impact that a proprietary remedy will have against an insolvent defendant. The claimant is protected because, by virtue of the proprietary response, the asset claimed does not form part of the estate of the insolvent, but is instead protected for the benefit of the claimant. Burrows is one exponent of this approach. In his analysis, in those

plc v. *Fayed* [1992] 1 WLR 1 at 11–12 PER MILLETT J. An alternative view is that which says, in relation to equity's response, that on completion of the transfer the recipient immediately holds in trust for the transferor. As stated by Chambers at p. 184, '... it turns out to be well established that a person who is entitled to recover property through the exercise of [the right of rectification or rescission] has an equitable interest in the property. That right arises at the outset...' See generally Chambers, pp. 171–84.

[48] Care must be taken to separate those cases in which, as a result of such deficient or absent intention, the transfer is declared void. In these cases, it is true that a proprietary remedy is given. However, the remedy is not given to reverse unjust enrichment. Rather, the cases are best understood as preserving the claimant's pre-existing title which was not transferred to the recipient.

[49] Chambers, p. 148. *Neste Oy* v. *Lloyd's Bank* [1983] 2 Lloyd's Rep 658; *Re Goldcorp Exchange Ltd* [1995] 1 AC 74. Lord Millett has rejected this explanation in relation to money paid for a particular purpose pursuant to a structure commonly associated with the decision in *Barclays Bank Ltd* v. *Quistclose Investments* [1970] AC 567. *Twinsectra Limited* v. *Yardley* [2002] 2 AC 164 at 190–193 PER LORD MILLETT.

[50] To the extent that the trust proposed in *Cunningham* v. *Harrison* [1973] QB 942 is explicable as a response to the victim's repudiation of his obligation to pay his carer wife, the trust may be consistent with this model of trusts raised to reverse unjust enrichment.

[51] A. Burrows, 'Proprietary Restitution: Unmasking Unjust Enrichment' (2001) 117 *Law Quarterly Review* 412; D. Paciocco, 'The Remedial Constructive Trust: A Principled Basis for Priorities Over Creditors' (1989) *Canadian Bar Review* 315; C. Rotherham, 'Tracing and Justice in Bankruptcy' in F. Rose (ed.), *Restitution and Insolvency* (London, 2000). Such arguments are critiqued by Chambers, pp. 235–6.

cases where the enrichment is rendered unjust by the claimant's vitiated or absent intention to benefit the recipient, it is normally possible to conclude that no risk of insolvency was taken by the claimant. In such cases, proprietary restitution is justified, because the claimant is in an analogous position to a secured creditor of the defendant's estate. Neither took the risk of the defendant's insolvency. Similarly, a claimant who is entitled to recover on a failure of basis will not ordinarily be entitled to proprietary relief.[52] It is difficult to apply this analysis to the facts of the victim and carer cases because, as noted above, the unjust factor disclosed by those cases is not the carer's vitiated or qualified intention but rather a policy motivated unjust factor. Burrows does not specifically address the availability of proprietary restitution based on the policy motivated unjust factors. However, applying his key principle, we should ask whether the carer is '... or is analogous to a secured creditor who has not taken the risk of the defendant's insolvency'. Even though the carer's intention to benefit the victim is not vitiated or otherwise defective, it remains the case that there is little evidence that the carer in such cases takes a risk on the victim's solvency. This conclusion would tend to support the carer's proprietary entitlement.

The final explanation for proprietary relief to be canvassed is that recognised by Lord Browne-Wilkinson in *Westdeutsche Landesbank Girozentrale* v. *Islington Borough Council*.[53] We know that one of the characteristics of property held in trust is that legal title is vested in the trustee and equitable title is vested in the beneficiary. Lord Browne-Wilkinson emphasised that, until the happening of a significant event which triggers the recognition of equitable title, it is not correct to regard the holder of legal title as also holding the equitable title to an asset:[54]

> [a] person solely entitled to the full beneficial ownership of money or property, both at law and in equity, does not enjoy an equitable interest in that property. The legal title carries with it all rights. Unless and until there is a separation of the legal and equitable estates, there is no separate equitable title.

The factor which will trigger equity in this way, says Lord Browne-Wilkinson, is that the conscience of the holder of legal title has been

---

[52] A. Burrows, 'Proprietary Restitution: Unmasking Unjust Enrichment' (2001) 117 *Law Quarterly Review* 412 at 426–7.
[53] *Westdeutsche Landesbank Girozentrale* v. *Islington Borough Council* [1996] AC 669 (HL).
[54] *Ibid.*, 706 PER LORD BROWNE-WILKINSON.

affected. 'Unless and until the trustee is aware of the factors which give rise to the supposed trust, there is nothing which can affect his conscience.'[55] The effect of this model is to transform the recipient into a trustee for the transferor. This is shown by his Lordship's application of the rule to the facts of *Chase Manhattan Bank NA* v. *Israel British Bank (London) Ltd*.[56] Chase Manhattan mistakenly transferred US$2 million to the recipient. Crucially, the defendant bank knew of the mistake within two days of receipt of the funds. Goulding J held that the claimant was entitled to proprietary restitution, declaring the defendant a trustee of the money.[57] Although Lord Browne-Wilkinson disagreed with Goulding J's reasoning, his Lordship justified the finding of trust by reference to the knowledge affecting the conscience of the recipient:[58]

> ... [T]he mere receipt of the moneys, in ignorance of the mistake, gives rise to no trust, the retention of the moneys after the recipient bank learned of the mistake may well have given rise to a constructive trust.

Lord Browne-Wilkinson's model therefore suggests that knowledge of the claimant's restitutionary entitlements, while the enrichment is still in the hands of the recipient, justifies elevating what would otherwise be only a personal claim. His Lordship's analysis has been criticised,[59] but seems to have some currency.[60] Birks and Mitchell[61] locate it within a broader spectrum of cases such as *Neste Oy* v. *Lloyd's Bank*[62] which transform the right to restitution on the basis of the knowledge by the recipient of the

---

[55] N. 53 above at 706 PER LORD BROWNE-WILKINSON. This requirement has been the subject of much debate as it is not clear exactly whether his Lordship intended the outcome which has been set out in this discussion. Nevertheless, it is a prevailing interpretation of his remarks. L. Smith, 'Constructive Fiduciaries?' in P. Birks (ed.), *Privacy and Loyalty* (Oxford, 1997) 249, pp. 265–7; W. Swadling, 'The Law of Property' in P. Birks and F. Rose (eds.), *Lessons of the Swaps Litigation* (Oxford, 2000) 242, pp. 257–64; Birks and Mitchell, pp. 596–7.

[56] *Chase Manhattan Bank NA* v. *Israel British Bank (London) Ltd* [1981] Ch 105.

[57] *Ibid.*, 119 PER GOULDING J.

[58] N. 53 above at 714–715 PER LORD BROWNE-WILKINSON.

[59] W. Swadling, 'The Law of Property' in P. Birks and F. Rose (eds.), *Lessons of the Swaps Litigation* (Oxford, 2000) 242, pp. 257–72; W. Swadling, 'Property and Unjust Enrichment' in J.W. Harris (ed.), *Property Problems: From Genes to Pension Funds* (London, 1997), p. 141; W. Swadling, 'Property and Conscience' (1998) *Trust Law International* 228, pp. 231–6; Sir P. Millett, 'Restitution and Constructive Trusts' in W. Cornish et al (eds.), *Restitution Past, Present & Future* (Oxford, 1998), pp. 212–13.

[60] *Bank of America* v. *Arnell* [1999] Lloyd's Rep Banking 399.

[61] Birks and Mitchell, pp. 595–7.

[62] *Neste Oy* v. *Lloyd's Bank* [1983] 2 Lloyd's Rep 658.

claimant's entitlement. The addition made by Lord Browne-Wilkinson is that knowledge is tested, not merely at the moment of receipt, but at any moment while the enrichment is traceably in the hands of the recipient.[63] It is difficult to apply Lord Browne-Wilkinson's analysis to the victim and carer cases. To generate a proprietary claim for the carer what must be shown is that, at the moment of receipt from the carer, the victim knows that the carer is entitled to restitution. In those cases where the victim and carer have agreed the carer would be paid, it is possible to conceive that the victim might have some knowledge of the carer's entitlement. However, leaving aside these rare examples, Lord Browne-Wilkinson's model does not fit the pattern of the victim and carer cases. It cannot explain the carer's proprietary entitlement.

The carer's entitlement is to prevent RH's accumulation, and as such falls into the category of policy motivated unjust factors. The policies calling for restitution occasionally mandate a proprietary response. For example, the successful maritime salvor is in part allowed a quantum meruit award for his assistance. This award is secured by a maritime lien over the property salved.[64] It has been argued that the reason for the salvor's right to recover is to encourage necessitous interventions such as rescue of property at sea.[65] The extension of this argument is that, not only does the policy of encouraging necessitous interventions support the mere existence of the claim for the salvor, but also the existence of a proprietary remedy. Rose states that the '... salvor's security rights derive partly from the proprietary basis of the jurisdiction of the admiralty courts and are currently justifiable by the mobility of vessels and the practical difficulties of enforcing claims where international considerations are involved'.[66] Whatever the basis of the salvor's lien, the reasons are highly specific to the facts of salvage cases. It is difficult to detect the principles dictating a proprietary remedy across all the policy motivated unjust factors. There is no systematic reason for this response. What must therefore be asked is whether a particular policy

---

[63] N. 53 above at 715 PER LORD BROWNE-WILKINSON.

[64] D. Steel and F. Rose (eds.), *Kennedy's Law of Salvage* (5th edn., London, 1995), pp. 1–2; F. Rose, 'Restitution for the Rescuer' (1989) 9 *Oxford Journal of Legal Studies* 167.

[65] Birks, pp. 304–8; Burrows and McKendrick, p. 725.

[66] F. Rose, 'Restitution for the Rescuer' (1989) 9 *Oxford Journal of Legal Studies* 167 at 199. Similar arguments are advanced by Swadling, who points to evidence that the lien is given in recognition of the fact that there is neither time nor facility to enquire into the creditworthiness of the owner of the goods to be saved. W. Swadling, 'Property and Unjust Enrichment' in J.W. Harris (ed.), *Property Problems: From Genes to Pension Funds* (London, 1997), p. 138.

motivated unjust factor triggers a proprietary entitlement. The next section of this chapter therefore considers the possible proprietary consequences of the policy against accumulation.

The policy against accumulation

The policy against accumulation applies whenever a claimant (RH) receives a benefit, or has the right to recover a debt or damages from another party (PL), and receives, or has the right to receive, in respect of the same debt or damage from a third party (S). RH is not permitted to accumulate and must reverse one transfer. On the facts of the cases in this study, we have shown that a victim of tort (RH) accumulates when RH recovers damages from the tortfeasor (PL) including an amount calculated by reference to the assistance provided and to be provided by the carer (S). Similarly, the insured (RH) accumulates when RH, in addition to recovering damages or settlement monies from the tortfeasor (PL), is indemnified in respect of the same loss by an insurer (S). In each case, RH must reverse the transfer of value made at the expense of S in order to remedy RH's unjust enrichment. Chapter 8 records that it is possible to identify RH's accumulation at two distinct moments in time. The first is when RH actually recovers damages from PL. The second is when RH's cause of action accrues. As will be shown below, both models are consistent with the proprietary nature of the carer's and the indemnity insurer's entitlements.

The policy against accumulation triggers a remedy reversing RH's unjust enrichment. It is necessary to determine why this response is proprietary. The answer lies in the effect of S's intervention on RH's claim against PL. There is a direct correlation between the value given by S, and RH's claim against PL. In the case of the carer's contribution, it is clear that the valuation of RH's claim against PL is in part a direct function of the services provided by the carer. These services created new value in the hands of RH by increasing the worth of RH's claim against the wrongdoer. It is this contribution to value which justifies the carer's proprietary award. Similarly, in the case of the indemnity insurer, the insurer contributes to RH's general financial position, thus supporting RH's ability to sue PL.

Before moving to a detailed application of the policy against accumulation, it is therefore necessary to notice that what is being proposed is that the unjust factor itself justifies the proprietary response. There are examples in which a proprietary remedy has been granted for reasons which are unique to the particular category of case. The discussion above refers to the case of the successful maritime salvor who is in part allowed a quantum meruit award for assistance. This award is secured by a maritime lien over the property salved. Whatever the true basis of the salvor's proprietary award, it is clear that the reason is unique to the particular circumstances of this type of case. The policy motivated unjust factor justifying recovery, probably necessity, generates a proprietary response when applied to maritime salvors.

Similar observations may be made about cases in which the commission of a wrong generates a proprietary response. A controversial example is *AG for Hong Kong* v. *Reid*.[67] The defendant Reid was the Acting Director of Public Prosecutions employed by the Government of Hong Kong. In the course of his duties he had accepted bribes in breach of his fiduciary obligations to his employer. Reid used these bribes to purchase real estate in New Zealand. The Government of Hong Kong sued in the New Zealand courts, claiming a proprietary interest in this real estate. Invoking the equitable maxim that equity regards as done that which ought to be done, the Privy Council held that Reid was a trustee of both the bribes and also the real estate:[68]

> ...a fiduciary must not be allowed to benefit from his own breach of duty, that the fiduciary should account for the bribe as soon as he receives it and that equity regards as done that which ought to be done. From these principles it would appear to follow that the bribe and the property from time to time representing the bribe are held on a constructive trust for the person injured.

The facts of *AG for Hong Kong* v. *Reid* are not on all fours with the victim and carer cases. The case was about the commission of a wrong and the claim was both to the wrongfully taken bribe and also its substitute assets. However, the case is helpful for this analysis because it may be interpreted as an example of a limited category in which the unique circumstances

---

[67] *AG for Hong Kong* v. *Reid* [1994] 1 AC 324. Noted P. Birks, 'Property in the Profits of Wrongdoing' (1994) 24 *University of Western Australia Law Review* 8 at 14; S. Gardner, 'Two Maxims of Equity' [1995] *Cambridge Law Journal* 60 at 63.

[68] *AG for Hong Kong* v. *Reid* [1994] 1 AC 324 at 336 PER LORD TEMPLEMAN who delivered the advice of the Privy Council.

themselves generate proprietary rights.[69] The case is evidence that the wrong defined as a breach of fiduciary duty is capable of generating proprietary rights. More narrowly, we might point to the fact that the defaulting fiduciary was a corrupt government official whose conduct flew in the face of his professional obligations as a public prosecutor. On this narrower view, the novel facts raised judicial concerns about the existence of corruption which engendered a proprietary response.

It must be conceded that this explanation for the incidence of proprietary interests raises legitimate concerns about the proliferation of proprietary remedies. The danger of this type of argument is that the circumstances in which a trust is available are reduced to a list of examples in which historically such a remedy has been granted. This category-by-category approach has the tendency to mask the common event to which the trust in each case might be responding. However, it has to be said that the explanations of proprietary restitution set out above do little to carry forward our understanding of the proprietary response to accumulation. There may be room for the recognition of a uniquely generated proprietary right. This discussion therefore assumes that the policy against accumulation may itself be capable of generating a proprietary response. The paragraphs which follow examine the proprietary nature of both the carer's and the insurer's entitlements. In conformity with the two moments in the story when RH accumulates, the discussion will consider separately the position (1) when RH wins damages from PL; and (2) when RH's cause of action accrues.

At the time RH wins damages

In this model the claimant (RH) accumulates when RH actually recovers damages from the wrongdoer (PL). The event triggering the entitlement of the third party (S) to share in the fund is not merely RH's receipt from S of enriching benefits. It is RH's award of damages from PL when RH has already benefited through S's intervention. Having received from both PL and S, RH accumulates in respect of the same damage. S is entitled to share in the fund of damages recovered.

---

[69] This suggestion is rejected by Birks who cautions that the case is not '... authority for raising a novel property in response to an evaluation of the merits of a particular claim'. P. Birks, 'Establishing a Proprietary Base' [1995] *Restitution Law Review* 83 at 85. R. Goode, 'Proprietary Restitutionary Claims' in W. Cornish et al (eds.), *Restitution Past, Present & Future* (Oxford, 1998) 63, pp. 69–74.

The key to understanding why S's right is proprietary lies in the effect of S's intervention on RH's claim against PL. The carer (S) and the insurer (S) both make good the loss of the claimant (RH). The carer does so by providing to RH necessary services and assistance. The insurer does so by paying an amount of money to indemnify RH for loss. In neither case does S's intervention discharge the wrongdoer's (PL's) liability to RH. However, this is not to say that the effect of S's intervention on RH's claim is neutral. Rather, as shown below, it produces dramatic results.

Victim and carer

The core example of this configuration is *Hunt* v. *Severs*.[70] Katherine Hunt was negligently injured when travelling as a pillion passenger on a motor-cycle driven by Mr Severs. She suffered terrible injuries, including extreme paraplegia and other complications. As a result of the accident, Katherine required a great deal of care and assistance, much of which was provided by Mr Severs. She claimed damages on account of her husband's care of her to the date of trial and an amount in respect of the estimated future care to be provided by him. The case was complicated by the fact that the carer and the tortfeasor were the same person. Mr Severs, expressing the interest of his insurer, argued on appeal to the House of Lords that he should not have to pay damages in respect of his care of his wife because in providing those services gratuitously, he would in a non-monetary form be meeting his own obligations as tortfeasor. His argument was that as carer he discharged his obligations as wrongdoer.

The House of Lords did not agree. Although the quantum of damages was reduced by the value of his past and estimated future care of his wife, this was not on the basis that the liability of the tortfeasor had been discharged. Rather, it was because the House of Lords held that the carer was entitled to share in the fund of damages. If Mr Severs had been required to pay the undiscounted amount in damages, he would in effect be paying money into a fund of which, in his capacity as carer, he was beneficiary. It was therefore to avoid the anomalous consequence of a tortfeasor paying damages to himself that the quantum of Katherine Hunt's award was reduced.

Despite the reduction in the victim's award, the underlying principle which was applied by the House is the rule that '... an injured plaintiff may recover the reasonable value of gratuitous services rendered to him by way

---

[70] *Hunt* v. *Severs* [1994] 2 AC 350.

of voluntary care by a member of his family'.[71] The law therefore explicitly responds to the services provided by the carer by allowing the victim to claim a corresponding amount in damages. The application of this rule means that, if no past care is provided, then no damages can be claimed. On the other hand, if the carer intervenes to assist by providing services which are of the requisite quality, then the victim will be entitled to claim the reasonable value of these services. There is thus a direct relationship between the relevant services having been provided and the heads of damage available to the victim. The carer thus not only contributes services and assistance, but in doing so also enlarges the value of the victim's claim against the wrongdoer.

The same analysis is possible in relation to an award for the future care of the victim. Chapter 8 explains that the victim (RH) accumulates in respect of damages for future care. On the day of judgment, the court awards to RH damages in respect of future care to be provided. The court is satisfied, as a matter of factual certainty, that care will in the future actually be provided by the carer (S). As at the day of judgment, RH accumulates because RH holds the fund of damages calculated by reference to the value of future care and the court is satisfied that this care in the future will be provided.

The fact that the care has not yet actually been provided does not derogate from this analysis. The key is this element of certainty. In adopting a model of damages liability which relies on this element of certainty to justify awards on account of future care, the law has committed us to this conclusion about the future. It is not possible to go behind the court's reasoning and deny RH's accumulation. We are certain, because the court is certain, that RH will in the future receive necessary services and assistance from S. RH therefore accumulates when damages are awarded because the court is convinced that future care will be necessary, and RH holds damages calculated by reference to the value of this care. S's entitlement to share in damages awarded by reference to future care is given to reverse RH's accumulation.

Once again, the proprietary nature of S's entitlement is justified by the fact that the value given by S operates to increase the worth of RH's chose in action against PL. This is shown by *Taylor* v. *Bristol Omnibus Co.*[72] The infant Paul Taylor sued the tortfeasor by his father and next friend. Paul was crippled after a car in which he was a passenger was negligently hit by a

---

[71] *Ibid.*, 363, PER LORD BRIDGE.
[72] *Taylor* v. *Bristol Omnibus Co* [1975] 1 WLR 1054.

coach owned by the defendants. As a result, Paul required constant care and supervision. He was looked after by his parents and grandparents. In relation to his future care needs, Lord Denning MR noted that compensation was available for the services rendered by Paul's parents and imposed a trust:[73]

> Taking values at the date of trial, the cost of a house, help and compensation for the parents' services can be put together at £20 a week ... I would add that, although this sum is only recoverable by Paul, it is really for the costs incurred and services rendered by the parents. If a trust is created, as I think it should be, this fact should be borne in mind in administering the trust.

The trigger for the award of damages is therefore defined by a matter external to the victim. It is to the value of the carer's contribution that specific reference is made. Of course, the quantum of damages assessed depends on an estimation of the future care needs and life expectancy of the victim. In addition, the court will obviously also make an assessment of the likelihood that the carer will be the person providing the necessary services. Thus, despite the fact that the services have not yet been provided by the carer and in this sense the carer has as yet done nothing to enlarge the victim's claim, the same analysis applies. The court is sufficiently certain that the services will be provided, otherwise damages would not be awarded. The external influence of the carer on the quantum of the victim's claim is still present. The same argument may be made in relation to the victim's debts which are paid by the carer. The carer may pay certain of the victim's debts incurred as a result of the tortfeasor's negligence. In doing so, the carer contributes to the value of the victim's claim against the wrongdoer. The carer's contribution thus affects the value of the victim's chose in action.

The proprietary nature of the carer's entitlement is therefore justified by the fact that the carer's contribution operates to enlarge the victim's claim. This is true both in respect of awards on account of the victim's expenses and also on account of past and future care. This analysis is not to suggest that the provision of services is conscious action by the carer taken to increase the size of the victim's award. Rather, it is the fact that a component of the victim's damages is calculated by reference to the contribution of the carer. While there is obviously a factual connection between the contribution of the carer and the incapacity suffered by the victim, itself recognised by the requirement that the carer's services be necessary, the law computes the

---

[73] *Ibid.*, 1059 PER LORD DENNING MR.

victim's claim in part by reference to the value of the carer's intervention. It is this connection which justifies a proprietary response to unjust enrichment.

Insured and indemnity insurer

Lord Napier and Ettrick v. *Hunter*[74] is authority for the proposition that the insurer is entitled to the benefit of an equitable lien securing the insured's obligation to return value. The facts of this case are given in chapter 7 but may be briefly summarised as follows. The Names (RH) commenced proceedings against Outhwaite (PL) in respect of the latter's negligence. This litigation was settled and settlement monies were paid by Outhwaite and held by a third party on behalf of the Names. The House of Lords granted the Stop Loss Insurers (S) an equitable lien, reflecting the value of the indemnity, over the fund of settlement monies.

A lien is an interest by way of security only. It is a proprietary interest created over the property of the defendant in order to secure the performance of a particular obligation. The lien is defeasible on performance of that obligation and does not, in contrast to the trust, carve out in favour of the holder separate ownership of the asset over which the lien is attached.[75] In the insurance example, RH is obligated to return to S value for which S has indemnified RH and RH has recovered in a claim against the wrongdoer PL. RH's obligation to do so is secured via an equitable lien over the fund of damages recovered.

The response to RH's accumulation is thus proprietary. The paragraphs which follow show how the proprietary nature of S's entitlement may be explained. However, it must be conceded that the insurer's lien has been heavily criticised, and that the better view is that in this configuration the policy against accumulation does not trigger a proprietary remedy. To the extent that we are able to explain the insurer's proprietary entitlement, it does not rest on any contribution by the insured to the value of RH's claim. Rather, it flows from the effect of S's intervention on the general financial position of RH.

As indicated above, S's contribution does not alter the value of RH's claim against PL. In common with the victim and carer cases, S's contribution

---

[74] *Lord Napier and Ettrick* v. *Hunter* [1993] AC 713 at 738–739 PER LORD TEMPLEMAN, 745–746 PER LORD GOFF and 752 PER LORD BROWNE-WILKINSON.

[75] R. Chambers, 'Tracing, Trusts and Liens' (1997) 11 *Trust Law International* 86; S. Worthington, *Proprietary Interests in Commercial Transactions* (Oxford, 1996), chapters 7–9.

does not discharge PL's liability to RH. However, unlike the victim and carer cases, the worth of RH's claim is limited to RH's own loss. The court does not, in addition, look to the value transferred by S by way of indemnity. As a practical matter it is of course possible that RH's loss will correlate exactly to the value of S's indemnity. To an extent, leaving aside the situation where RH is not fully covered for loss, one will be a mirror image of the other. However, the two are not directly linked. The value of RH's claim against PL is not a function of the value transferred from S. If S provides no indemnity, this will not derogate from the quantum of RH's suit against PL.

The argument that the insurer's entitlement is proprietary rests on the observation that the insurer's contribution enhances the insured's general financial position, and thus improves RH's ability to bring litigation against the wrongdoer. In this connection, it is helpful to refer to the general proposition that, the claimant who contributes to the improvement or maintenance of an asset, will be entitled to the benefit of an equitable lien.[76] RH's ability to sue PL is an asset in the hands of RH. To the extent that S's intervention contributes to RH's ability to realise the value of that asset, and bring litigation against PL, S assists in the maintenance of this asset. In this way, it is arguable that S's intervention justifies recognition of an equitable lien.

The application of these rules has been controversial and produces results which have been criticised. In particular, it is often artificial to draw a distinction between the acquisition of an asset and its maintenance. Contributions to the payment of a mortgage are often treated as the maintenance or improvement of the mortgaged asset. However, it has been observed that, particularly when the mortgage secures repayment of the purchase price, it would be more accurate to regard the mortgage payments as going to the acquisition of the asset, arguably therefore justifying recognition of a trust.[77] In addition, doubt has been cast on the status of the rule confining the improver's remedy to a lien by the House of Lords' decision in *Foskett* v. *McKeown*.[78]

The claimants in *Foskett* were the beneficiaries of a trust. In breach of trust, the trustee used trust money to pay various premiums under a life

---

[76] *Foskett* v. *McKeown* [1998] Ch 265 (CA). Noted P. Birks and W. Swadling, 'Restitution' in [1997] *All ER Annual Review* 385, pp. 402–5; R. Chambers, 'Tracing, Trusts and Liens' 110 *Trust Law International* 86; C. Mitchell, 'Tracing Trust Funds into Life Insurance Proceeds' [1997] *Lloyd's Maritime and Commercial Law Quarterly* 465; L. Smith, 'Tracing into Life Assurance Proceeds' (1997) 113 *Law Quarterly Review* 552.

[77] Smith, pp. 146–52, 353–6.   [78] *Foskett* v. *McKeown* [2001] 1 AC 102 (HL).

insurance policy. This policy was held for the benefit of the trustee's children. The trustee died and the insurer paid on the policy. Disputation then arose as to the entitlement to these funds, and the claimants argued for a proportionate share of the proceeds of the policy. The House of Lords rejected an argument which had been successful in the Court of Appeal, which was that by analogy to the case where trust money was used to maintain or improve the property of a third party, the claimants' money was used to maintain the insurance policy, an asset owned by the children. Arguing by analogy, the claimants argued that the use of their funds to maintain the policy gave them an equitable lien over the proceeds. This analogy was rejected. Thus, having on the facts rejected the analogy of improvements, it is not clear whether restriction confining the improver to a lien will survive.[79]

It must be admitted that the case for a proprietary remedy for the insurer is weak. Birks has attempted to ring fence the decision in *Lord Napier* to allow a proprietary remedy, suggesting that the case '... may be the rare exception, not a model for judicial action'.[80] Mitchell is also critical of the Stop Loss Insurer's proprietary claim. While not disputing that the insurers '... owed a duty to account to their insurers for sums received from third party sources to the extent that these more than fully indemnified them for their insured losses, they were wrong to hold that the insurers should therefore have been given a corresponding proprietary claim in respect of these sums'.[81] Surprisingly, a contrary position is taken by Sir Peter Millett. Far from cutting back the proprietary remedy, he aligns the case with *AG for Hong Kong* v. *Reid* and argues that the Stop Loss Insurer should have been the beneficiary of a constructive trust.[82] Yet it must not be overlooked that Reid was a wrongdoer acting in breach of fiduciary duty. An analogy is not easily drawn between a wrong and a merely subtractive unjust enrichment.

Given that the insurer, unlike the carer, does not contribute to the value of RH's claim against PL, the better conclusion is that the insurer should be entitled only to a personal claim. This discussion has dealt only with the nature of S's entitlement to share in the fund. It does not derogate from the earlier conclusion, which is that without an obligation to return value, RH accumulates in respect of the same debt or damage. The insurer is entitled

---

[79] *Ibid.*, 137 PER LORD MILLETT.
[80] P. Birks, 'Overview: Tracing, Claiming and Defences' in P. Birks (ed.), *Laundering and Tracing* (Oxford, 1995) 289, p. 314.
[81] Mitchell, p. 83.
[82] Sir P. Millett,'Restitution and Constructive Trusts' in W. Cornish et al (eds.), *Restitution Past, Present & Future* (Oxford, 1998) 199, p. 206.

to participate in the fund of damages recovered by RH to reverse the latter's unjust enrichment which would otherwise remain. However, when applied to the particular case of the indemnity insurer, the better view is that the policy against accumulation does not engender a proprietary response. This is because, unlike the carer's intervention, the insurer does not enlarge RH's patrimony.

At the time RH's cause of action accrues

In this model the claimant (RH) accumulates at the moment RH's cause of action accrues. RH receives, or is entitled to receive, value from the carer or the insurer (S). By operation of law, RH is given the right to sue the wrongdoer (PL) for loss. RH accumulates when RH's cause of action accrues, because she holds the right to sue PL for an amount undiminished by the value transferred from S. RH therefore accumulates in respect of the same debt or damage.

As discussed in chapter 8, the difficulty with this model is that even though RH accumulates when her claim against PL arises, we know that S's trust or lien is imposed over the damages won by RH in her suit against PL. Our analysis must accommodate the fact that the value by which RH accumulates at the moment RH's cause of action against PL accrues is not immediately returned to S. Rather, the enrichment is reversed via a trust or lien later in time, when RH wins in her suit against the wrongdoer.

This difficulty is removed if it is recognised that the damages won by RH in her suit against PL are the substitute of RH's chose in action. In this way it may be argued that S's proprietary interest in RH's damages was actually capable of recognition prior to the day of judgment. The position is more clearly illustrated if we return to the decision of the House in *Lord Napier and Ettrick* v. *Hunter*.[83] Although not finally deciding the issue, all members of the House identified the possibility that the insurer's interest, expressed via the equitable lien, may have attached not only to the fund but also to a prior asset held by the insured, the chose in action exercisable against the tortfeasor Outhwaite. Lord Goff stated:[84]

---

[83] *Lord Napier and Ettrick* v. *Hunter* [1993] AC 713.
[84] *Ibid.*, 745, PER LORD GOFF. Refer also to 740, PER LORD TEMPLEMAN; 752, PER LORD BROWNE-WILKINSON; 753. Lord Slynn agreed with Lord Templeman and Lord Jauncey agreed with Lord Templeman, Lord Goff and Lord Browne-Wilkinson.

There is one particular problem to which I wish to refer, although, as I understand it, it does not fall to be decided in the present case. Does the equitable proprietary interest of the insurer attach only to a fund consisting of sums which come into the hands of the assured in reduction of the loss paid by the insurer? Or does it attach also to a right of action vested in the assured which, if enforced, would yield such a fund? The point is not altogether easy. I can see no reason in principle why such an interest should not be capable of attaching to property in the nature of a chose in action.

It must be conceded that their Lordships expressed no concluded view about this possibility. The point was not directly addressed in argument and their Lordships were careful to emphasise that further consideration would be required to give a firmer opinion.[85] The point of this discussion is simply to explore the possibility that, to the extent that S's interest may have attached not only to the fund but also to the chose in action exercisable against PL, the model identified in *Lord Napier* assists in understanding S's right to participate in RH's damages.

What is needed is a method of connecting S's rights at the time RH's cause of action accrues, to the fund of damages yielded by exercise of that cause of action. The law of tracing allows us to do this. By connecting the damages as the substitute of RH's claim against PL, we are able to account for the fact that S's entitlement is not visible until RH's claim has actually succeeded. To the extent that S had a proprietary interest in RH's chose in action against PL, S is later able to assert a proprietary interest in the substitute of that asset, the damages recovered by RH in pursuing this claim. This argument proceeds in three stages. First, to show that S has a proprietary base such that it is possible to justify the recognition of a proprietary interest in the substitute asset. Secondly, to connect via the process of tracing RH's claim against PL and the damages awarded in satisfaction of this claim. Finally, to show that S's entitlement does not offend the rules against maintenance and champerty.

Proprietary base

In connecting S's entitlement at the moment RH's cause of action accrues to S's entitlement when damages are actually recovered, it is necessary to

---

[85] N. 83 above at 740 PER LORD TEMPLEMAN who acknowledged that 'reconsideration in the light of further research' would be required. Lord Goff at p. 745 expressly reserved his opinion as did Lord Browne-Wilkinson at p. 752 who preferred to 'express no concluded view'.

demonstrate that S has an undestroyed proprietary base.[86] Put simply, this argument says that if S has a proprietary interest in RH's chose in action against PL then, to the extent that the damages recovered by RH are the traceable proceeds of this chose in action, the damages recovered may also be the subject of S's proprietary claim. S must therefore demonstrate that she holds a proprietary interest in RH's chose in action exercisable against PL.

Victim and carer   The discussion on pp. 253–7 explains why the carer's intervention triggers a proprietary response as at the date of judgment. The same arguments are applicable when accumulation is measured at the moment RH obtains the ability to sue PL. The carer's proprietary entitlement is justified, because the carer's contribution increases the value of the victim's patrimony. The law adopts a model of damages liability whereby the value of RH's claim against PL is in part a function of the value of the care and assistance provided by S. The more necessary care is provided by S, the greater the value of RH's claim against PL on account of this care. The same is true on account of awards for future care. Based on judicial certainty that care will in the future be necessary, RH accumulates at the moment she is by operation of law entitled to claim from PL on account of future care. At this moment, RH holds the ability to sue PL for the value of future care in circumstances where the court is certain that this care will be provided. RH has a proprietary base, because the policy against accumulation itself triggers a proprietary response.

These arguments are sufficient to justify a proprietary base for the carer. However, in case further support is necessary, it is worth noting another prominent example, in which services themselves create new value in the hands of the recipient, and are capable of constituting a proprietary base for a proprietary claim in respect of the new asset.[87] Cases concerning the division of family property after the breakdown of a relationship are evidence of the extent to which courts will go in this exercise. Typically in these cases the defendant has title to the family home in which the other party to the relationship, the claimant, seeks an interest. Leaving aside the

---

[86] P. Birks, 'Property and Unjust Enrichment: Categorical Truths' [1997] *New Zealand Law Review* 623 at 663, Smith, pp. 299–301 and pp. 361–9; Birks and Mitchell, pp. 594–5.
[87] Smith, pp. 239 and 367.

question of whether such cases are evidence of a restitutionary response,[88] it is clear that the value of services provided by the claimant is used as a foundation for the recognition by the court that, although legal title in the home is vested in the defendant, this title is subject to a trust in favour of the claimant service provider.[89] Some services, such as repairing or painting, result directly in an improvement to the physical condition of the asset. However, the family property cases tell us that this proposition is secure even where the services provide a more indirect contribution. For example, in *Peter* v. *Beblow*[90] the claimant's contribution comprised the housekeeping and home making services that she had provided on a gratuitous basis over the relevant period. This had saved the defendant large sums of money, allowing him to pay off his mortgage in what had become the family home. It was this saved expenditure, generated by the claimant's labours, which was reflected in the constructive trust imposed by the court over the house.

Indemnity insurer and insured   It is difficult to identify a proprietary base for the indemnity insurer. To the extent that the analysis on pp. 257–8 is correct, it might be thought that the justification for the insurer's lien at the time damages are awarded also justifies a proprietary interest in the insured's right of action against PL. In *Lord Napier and Ettrick* v. *Hunter*, the House of Lords cautiously proposed that the insurer's equitable proprietary interest might attach to the right of action held against PL.[91] Unfortunately, their Lordships did not explain why the initial proprietary interest might arise. The discussion on p. 258 suggests that the insurer's proprietary entitlement rests on the observation that the insurer's contribution enhances the insured's general financial position. By analogy with the rules by which a claimant who improves and maintains an asset is entitled to an equitable lien, we observed that the insurer's intervention improves RH's ability to bring litigation against the wrongdoer. Although difficult to explain, the current law is that the indemnity insurer is entitled to an equitable lien.

---

[88] The consensus of opinion is that these cases are not about the reversal of unjust enrichment but rather carry into effect the intentions or expectations of the parties. S. Gardner, 'Rethinking Family Property' (1993) 109 *Law Quarterly Review* 263; Chambers, pp. 228–9; Smith, p. 368; Elias, pp. 9–16.

[89] *Peter* v. *Beblow* [1993] 3 WWR 337.

[90] *Ibid.*, 351–353 PER MACLACHLIN J. La Forest, Sopinka and Iacobucci JJ concurred.

[91] N. 84 above and n. 85.

The above analysis suggests one way in which we may supply a proprietary base.

However, as has been said, the proprietary nature of the insurer's entitlement has proved difficult to explain. It therefore seems likely that the policy against accumulation is not capable of generating a proprietary response when applied to the indemnity insurer. This is because the insurer's intervention produces no new value in the hands of the insured. Unlike the case of the carer, the value of RH's claim against the wrongdoer is not thereby enhanced. The consequence of this conclusion for this model of the policy against accumulation is that in order to reverse RH's unjust enrichment, the insurer should be entitled only to a personal claim against the insured.

Tracing

By whichever route we arrive at the conclusion that a proprietary base is available to carer or indemnity insurer (S), our analysis must still account for the fact that S's right to participate in the claimant's (RH's) damages does not become visible until RH has recovered damages from the wrongdoer (PL). What is therefore needed is a method of connecting S's right in the chose in action to the fund of damages yielded by the enforcement of that chose in action. Tracing is an exercise which is neutral as to the existence of rights, allowing a claimant to demonstrate in a legally relevant way that the value she claims in an asset which exists at the beginning of a chain of events is the substitute of an asset which is identifiable at the end of that chain.[92]

It is possible to characterise the damages won by RH as the traceable substitute of S's right to bring litigation against PL. A helpful description of the model being proposed is that given in an American case in which a restaurant owner had been erroneously charged cabaret tax by the New York revenue authorities. Despite the fact that the restaurant owner had passed this tax onto his customers as a separate item on their bill, he sued the revenue for a refund of the taxes which had been erroneously collected. Learned Hand J contemplated that the claim against the revenue would be

---

[92] Smith, pp. 10–14. *Foskett* v. *McKeown* [2001] 1 AC 102 at 109 PER LORD BROWNE-WILKINSON, 113 PER LORD STEYN and 127–128 PER LORD MILLETT.

held by the restaurant owner in trust for his customers, for whom he would also hold the proceeds of the claim:[93]

> That claim [against the revenue] was certainly a substitute for the money whose payment had created it; in equity it was the same as though the plaintiff [restaurant owner] had used the money actually to purchase the claim; and, if a constructive trust attached to the money, the same trust attached to the claim ... If the plaintiff collects this claim, it will therefore hold it as trustee for its guests.

Although the conclusion is not absolutely certain, it does now seem that one positive contribution to have been made by Lord Browne-Wilkinson in *Westdeutsche* is that the requirement that a fiduciary relationship was necessary before a tracing exercise could begin has been removed. Although such a requirement was on certain facts rather easily met,[94] it now seems that the statement that we may trace through a thief warrants the conclusion that this requirement has been dropped.[95] Failing this, it would have been necessary to identify a fiduciary relationship somewhere in the facts.[96]

The damages recovered by RH can only be the substitute of the chose in action previously held by RH against PL. It is of course possible to construct more complicated facts in which, for example, RH sues more than one tortfeasor and recovers damages from each. This does not derogate from our analysis. All that it means is that more complex rules of identification will be applied. The underlying proposition that the enforcement of a chose in action yields a fund of damages is not disturbed.

Maintenance and champerty

The success of the analysis in this section is contingent on it being accepted that RH's right to sue PL is a form of property which is capable of being held in trust. If this argument fails, then it is not possible to argue that S's proprietary right to share in the fund has as its base S's right to claim a proprietary interest in the chose in action. One objection which might

---

[93] *123 East Fifty-Fifth Street Inc* v. *United States* (1946) 157 F Rep (2d) 68 at 71 PER LEARNED HAND J relied on in *Commissioner of State Revenue (Victoria)* v. *Royal Insurance Australia Limited* (1994) 182 CLR 51 at 77–79 PER MASON CJ.

[94] For example the fiduciary relationship identified in *Chase Manhattan Bank NA Ltd* v. *Israel-British Bank (London) Ltd* [1981] Ch 105.

[95] N. 53 above at 716 PER LORD BROWNE-WILKINSON.

[96] L. Smith, 'Constructive Fiduciaries?' in P. Birks (ed.), *Privacy and Loyalty* (Oxford, 1997) 249, p. 255; Smith, pp. 120–30.

be raised is the suggestion that a trust of RH's damages offends the rules against champerty.

There is authority which supports the proposition that a chose in action is an item of property which is capable of being held in trust. For example, the benefit of rights under a contract may be held for a third person who is not a party to the contract. In this situation the trustee will hold the rights under the contract subject to an equitable obligation in favour of the beneficiary third party.[97] Of difficulty is the suggestion that the particular quality of the chose in action in the victim and carer cases, and the insurance cases, renders impossible a proprietary interest in this chose in action. On the facts of the cases in this study the victim's right to sue the tortfeasor is a claim in tort. Similarly, many of the insurance cases concern damages recovered by the insured in tort.[98] It might be argued that a trust of, or other proprietary interest in, a chose in action concerning a claim in tort offends the rule against champerty. Although not explicitly decided on the basis of the rule against champerty, an example of this type of reasoning is *Bradstock Trustee Services Ltd* v. *Nabarro Nathanson (A Firm)*.[99] Judge Paul Baker QC had to decide, *inter alia*, whether a chose in action comprising a claim in negligence against the defendant Nabarro Nathanson was held as trust property. In contradistinction from the position had the claim against Nabarro Nathanson been in contract, the judge held that the claim in negligence was *not* capable of being held in trust:[100]

> More importantly, the cause of action I am concerned with here is an action in tort for negligence. It is true that an action for negligence against solicitors can be based on breach of contract, or breach of the duty of care in tort. The former confronts the applicants with insuperable difficulties under the Limitation Act 1980, as will appear later. Where the action sounds in tort there can be no question of the trustees constituting themselves as trustees of a chose in action right from the moment that they first consulted the solicitors. As I see it the claim cannot be regarded as part of the trust property, although doubtless any damages which may be recovered would be.

---

[97] *Beswick* v. *Beswick* [1968] AC 58; *Re Schebsman* [1944] Ch 83; *Vandepitte* v. *Preferred Accident Insurance Corp of New York* [1933] AC 70.

[98] *Esso Petroleum Co Ltd* v. *Hall Russell & Co Ltd* [1989] 1 AC 643; *King* v. *Victoria Insurance Company Limited* [1896] AC 250; *Lord Napier and Ettrick* v. *Hunter* [1993] AC 713.

[99] *Bradstock Trustee Services Ltd* v. *Nabarro Nathanson (A Firm)* [1995] 1 WLR 1405.

[100] *Ibid.*, 1411 PER JUDGE PAUL BAKER QC. The question of whether a claim in negligence could be held in trust was left open in *Wills* v. *Cook and Others*, an unreported decision of Slade J in the Chancery Division dated 2 April 1979. An account of the case is given in the *Law Society's Gazette* 11 July 1979, 706.

Maintenance is the practice of giving assistance or encouragement to one of the parties in litigation by a person who has neither an interest in the litigation nor any other motive recognised by the law as justifying her interference. Champerty is a species of maintenance, pursuant to which maintenance is given in return for a promise to give the maintainer a share in the proceeds of the action.[101] Although the tort and crime of maintenance have been statutorily abolished,[102] recent authority has noted that the abolition of this criminal and civil liability '... shall not affect any rule of [the law of England and Wales] as to the cases in which a contract is to be treated as contrary to public policy or otherwise illegal'.[103] It might be argued that S's proprietary claim to RH's chose in action runs contrary to the rule against champerty.

The relevant prohibition is that which relates to the assignment of a bare right of action. Although there are also rules regulating the assignment of the fruits of litigation, these do not relate to the model being considered here.[104] What is being suggested is that S has a proprietary interest in RH's right to bring litigation against PL, not merely a proprietary interest in the fruits of this litigation. The leading authority is the decision of the House in *Trendtex Trading Corporation* v. *Credit Suisse*, which deals with the prohibition on the assignment of a bare right of action.[105] Lord Roskill states the rule as follows:[106]

> I cannot agree that... 'The old saying that you cannot assign a "bare right to litigate" is gone.' I venture to think that that still remains a fundamental principle of our law. But it is today true to say that in English law an assignee who can show that he has a genuine commercial interest in the enforcement of the claim of another and to that extent takes an assignment of that claim to himself is entitled to enforce that assignment unless by the terms of that

---

[101] *Halsbury's Laws of England Volume Nine* (4th edn., 1974), p. 272 para. 400. Y. Tan, 'Champertous Contracts and Assignments' (1990) 106 *Law Quarterly Review* 656; A. Walters, 'A Modern Doctrine of Champerty?' (1996) 112 *Law Quarterly Review* 560; D. Capper, 'A Modern Doctrine of Champerty? – A Postscript' (1997) 113 *Law Quarterly Review* 49.

[102] Criminal Law Act 1967 s. 14.

[103] *Giles* v. *Thompson* [1994] 1 AC 142 at 153–154 PER LORD MUSTILL with whom the rest of the House agreed. *In re Oasis Merchandising Services Ltd* [1998] Ch 170.

[104] *Ibid.*

[105] *Trendtex Trading Corporation* v. *Credit Suisse* [1982] AC 679.

[106] *Ibid.*, 703 PER LORD ROSKILL. Lord Wilberforce at 694–695 referred to the need for the assignee to have 'a genuine and substantial interest in the success' of the litigation in the context of 'the agreement as a whole'. Lord Edmund-Davies, Lord Fraser and Lord Keith agreed with the reasons of Lord Roskill and Lord Wilberforce.

assignment he falls foul of our law of champerty, which, as has often been said, is a branch of our law of maintenance.

The assignment will therefore be upheld if it is of a property right or interest, and the cause of action being assigned is ancillary to that right or interest, or if the assignee has a genuine commercial interest in taking the assignment and enforcing it for her own benefit.[107] Strictly speaking, this formulation concerns the assignment of a claim for breach of contract. However, it arguably also applies to the assignment of a claim in tort.[108] There are certainly judicial statements which contemplate that a right to litigate in tort can be assigned. For example, in *Esso Petroleum Co Ltd* v. *Hall Russell & Co Ltd*, the question for the House of Lords was in part whether Esso could bring a claim in tort against Hall Russell in its own name or whether Esso had to sue in the name of the crofters to whom the claim in tort accrued. The House in the end decided that the subrogated claim had to be brought in the name of the crofters. However, Lord Goff contemplated that the crofters could have assigned their claim in tort to Esso.[109]

The question to be asked is whether the carer has a genuine commercial interest in the victim's right to bring litigation against the tortfeasor. The difficulty for the carer is that, leaving to one side those examples in which the victim and carer have entered into a contract for care, there is no pre-existing commercial relationship between the carer and victim. It might therefore be difficult to assess whether the carer has a genuine commercial interest in the victim's right to sue the wrongdoer. Some assistance is provided by the rules set out in *Giles* v. *Thompson*. Although on a narrow reading that case concerned an assignment of the fruits of litigation, Lord Mustill warned that the tests laid down in *Trendtex* '... were addressed to transactions of the kind then before the House; they are not to be understood as if they had statutory force; and I see no reason to impose the procedure thus evolved on situations which are entirely different'.[110] The more flexible approach in *Giles* v. *Thompson* condemns the transaction when '... there is wanton and officious intermeddling with the disputes of others in where the meddler has

---

[107] N. 105 above at 703 PER LORD ROSKILL.

[108] *Brownton Ltd* v. *Edwards Moore Inbucon Ltd* [1985] 3 All ER 499 at 509 PER LLOYD LJ whose formulation of the *Trendtex* rule applies to the assignment of a bare right to litigate in contract and tort. In the Court of Appeal phase of *Trendtex* [1980] 1 QB 629 Lord Denning MR and Oliver J were in favour of maintaining a rule against the assignability of personal tort claims.

[109] *Esso Petroleum Co Ltd* v. *Hall Russell & Co Ltd* [1989] 1 AC 643 at 663 PER LORD GOFF.

[110] N. 103 above at 163–164 PER LORD MUSTILL with whom the rest of the House agreed.

no interest whatever, and where the assistance he renders to one or the other party is without justification or excuse'.[111] The unjust enrichment analysis in chapter 4 makes clear that the carer is not an officious intermeddler. The carer's intervention is necessary, and arises in the context of the relationship of love and affection between the carer and victim. In such circumstances it would be hard to argue that the carer's intervention is without justification or excuse. A trust of the victim's claim against the wrongdoer is not affected. Similarly, the indemnity insurer has a genuine commercial interest in the insured's right to sue the wrongdoer.

Conclusion

Both the carer and the indemnity insurer (S) are entitled to share in the fund of damages recovered by the claimant (RH) in a suit against the wrongdoer (PL). As suggested by *Hunt* v. *Severs*, the carer's entitlement appears to be via a trust. Similarly, we know after *Lord Napier* that the indemnity insurer is entitled to an equitable lien secured over the fund of damages recovered. It is vital to keep in mind the distinction between two separate issues. The first is the juridical basis of S's right to participate in RH's damages. The second is the form of that right to participate, whether personal or proprietary. We have already shown that S's right to participate *at all* is given to reverse unjust enrichment on the basis of the policy against accumulation. This chapter has been concerned with the second issue, to explain the nature of S's right to participate. The purpose of this chapter has therefore been to shed some light on how the proprietary nature of S's entitlement might be explained.

The key to understanding why S's right is proprietary lies in the effect of S's intervention on RH's claim against PL. The carer (S) and the insurer (S) both make good the loss of the claimant (RH). The carer does so by providing to RH necessary services and assistance. The insurer does so by paying to RH an amount of money to indemnify for loss. In neither case does S's intervention discharge the wrongdoer's (PL's) liability to RH. However, this is not to say that the effect of S's intervention on RH's claim is neutral. In the case of the carer, the value of RH's claim against the wrongdoer is

---

[111] N. 103 above at 164 PER LORD MUSTILL, relied on in *Grovewood Holdings plc* v. *James Capel & Co Ltd* [1995] 2 WLR 70 at 74 PER LIGHTMAN J. See *Dimond* v. *Lovell* [2002] 4 AC 384 (HL).

a direct function of the services and assistance provided by the carer. S's contribution enlarges RH's patrimony. It enhances the worth of an asset in the hands of RH, the claim against PL. It is for this reason that a proprietary response is triggered by RH's enrichment by accumulation.

The indemnity insurer's proprietary entitlement is harder to explain. Unlike the carer, the insurer's payment does not increase the value of RH's claim against PL. As the law currently stands, the insurer is entitled to the benefit of an equitable lien over the fund of damages recovered. One explanation for this proprietary entitlement might be that, although the insurer does not add value to RH's asset, the insurer's contribution does nonetheless maintain and support that asset. The insurer contributes to RH's general financial position and thus RH's ability to sue PL. However, it must be conceded that the insurer's lien has been criticised and the better view may well be that the insurer's entitlement should only ever be personal. On this view, the insurer is entitled to share in the fund of damages won by RH in order to reverse the latter's unjust enrichment on the policy against accumulation. The claim should only ever be personal, because the insurer does not increase RH's patrimony. As applied to the indemnity insurer, the policy against accumulation does not trigger a proprietary remedy.

10

Conclusion

This book explains why a stranger to litigation is entitled to share in the fruits of that litigation. The central example around which discussion revolves is the carer, who is entitled to share in the fund of damages won by the victim in her suit against the wrongdoer. The same pattern is evident in the indemnity insurance cases, in which the indemnity insurer is entitled to participate in the fund of damages won by the insured in diminution of loss.

In exploring this central issue three features of the cases have been revealed. The first is that the pattern of the cases seems to reveal the carer's entitlement as a contingent entitlement. There are no cases in which a mechanism implementing the carer's right to share is imposed in recognition of a prior obligation on the victim to pay the carer. Superficially at least, it appears that the carer's right therefore springs to life only when the victim has succeeded in her damages claim against the wrongdoer.

Secondly, the difficulty is aggravated by the assumption that the carer has no direct rights of claim. A contingent entitlement is already difficult to explain. A contingent entitlement vested in someone with no rights exercisable against either the person paying damages or the person holding the fund is doubly anomalous. In advancing an explanation of the carer's entitlements it has therefore been necessary separately to consider the possible claims available in contract, tort and unjust enrichment. This book has shown that even if the carer does hold a claim in contract or tort, this claim cannot explain a contingent entitlement to participate in the damages recovered by the victim. Rather, it seems only to entitle the carer to bring that very claim against the victim or tortfeasor. The claim against the victim is more helpful, but, according to the known unjust factors, cannot explain the carer's right to share.

Thirdly, it seems, as the law now stands, that the carer has no right to force the victim to claim against the wrongdoer. The possibility that the carer might hold such a right has never been tested by a court. The negative now commonly assumed produces a result which is contrary to both logic and justice. Without the right to compel the victim in this way, the carer is left to the whim of the victim in deciding whether or not to seek an award. In the absence of such a right for the carer, the tortfeasor may indirectly obtain the benefit of the carer's intervention. If the victim chooses not to sue, the tortfeasor will not be forced to pay damages calculated by reference to the carer's intervention.

As has been said, the primary relationship under investigation has been that of carer and victim. However, the phenomenon under investigation in these cases is also present in the case of the indemnity insurer and insured. The technique of this book has therefore been to observe that a structural analogy exists between the position of the carer and the indemnity insurer. Both intervene to make good the loss of the claimant and both are entitled to share in the fund of damages recovered. Chapter 7 demonstrates that the victim and carer cases contain the key elements of the model of insurance subrogation identified by Mitchell. In both categories, S (insurer/carer) intervenes unofficiously for the benefit of RH (insured/victim). The obligations of PL (wrongdoer) to RH are not discharged and S participates in RH's recoveries. S (insurer) can compel RH to sue and, in the case of the carer, this book argues that the carer ought to be able to do so.

The analogy with the position of the indemnity insurer reveals not only that the two categories reveal the same characteristics, but suggests that the rights of the insurer and carer might be generated by the same event. The analogy provides the foundation for a better understanding of the rights available to the carer and the indemnity insurer (S). This book addresses three aspects of S's entitlement: (1) the juridical basis of the right to participate in the fund; (2) the right to force litigation against the wrongdoer; and (3) the nature of the right to participate.

The right to participate in the fund

S is entitled to participate in the fund of damages recovered by RH in order to reverse RH's unjust enrichment. Chapter 8 demonstrates the existence of a novel policy motivated unjust factor called the policy against accumulation. The policy against accumulation applies whenever a claimant (RH) receives a benefit, or has the right to recover damages from the wrongdoer (PL) and receives, or has the right to receive, in respect of the same debt or damage from another party (S). The policy against accumulation dictates that RH is not usually entitled to receive from both PL and S. To the extent that RH does receive value from both, RH may have to reverse one transfer in order to reverse her own enrichment by accumulation. In the configurations investigated in this book, RH returns value to the carer and the indemnity insurer in order to reverse her enrichment which would otherwise remain.

There are two models of the policy against accumulation. The first is that which measures RH's accumulation at the moment she actually recovers damages from PL, in addition to having been benefited in kind by S. The second considers RH's position earlier in the story, when her entitlement to claim damages from PL actually accrued. For the purpose only of explaining S's entitlement to share in the fund, both versions satisfactorily account for S's right to participate. The right of S to force litigation against the wrongdoer is discussed in the next paragraph. This book argues that the right to participate works in tandem with the right to force litigation against the wrongdoer. To the extent that both rights are available to S, it seems rational to argue that RH accumulates at the moment her cause of action accrues. However, it is possible that the rights will be free standing, and that RH will accumulate without the correlative right to force litigation against the wrongdoer. To this extent, the more cautious model of accumulation, in which RH accumulates when she actually recovers from PL, will in most cases be applicable.

Whichever model of the policy gains dominance, it remains the case that the application of the policy is not limited to the configurations disclosed by the carer and victim and the indemnity insurer and insured. Rather, it applies whenever we are satisfied that the facts under investigation attract the policy against accumulation. As discussed in chapter 8, it is possible to identify categories where the parties have by consent accepted the risk of accumulation and excluded the operation of the policy. It will be a case-by-case process to determine the categories to which the novel unjust factor applies, probably having most utility in categories which do not disclose one of the existing unjust factors. As shown by cases such as *Roxborough*, we are in grave danger of repeating the errors of the past, and entrenching RH's ability to accumulate. This book has shown that the position in Australia, where the victim is not obligated to share damages with the carer, is anomalous and should be reversed. The law discloses a novel policy motivated unjust factor called the policy against accumulation and this should be applied in appropriate categories. In the case of the carer and victim, recognition of this unjust factor solves the mystery of the carer's contingent entitlement.

The right to control litigation

The analogy between the carer and victim, and the insurer and insured, assists in removing another disturbing aspect of the cases, that the carer apparently has no right to force litigation against the wrongdoer. Chapter 7 argues that the rights of the indemnity insurer form a template for the law's future development, and that the carer should enjoy a right parallel to that of the insurer to force litigation. This book in the end rejects the view that the victim's suit is brought by the victim against the tortfeasor at her own uncompellable initiative. Although there is no case law to substantiate this proposition, logic and justice dictate that the carer must hold such a right. Without it, the carers left vulnerable to the whim of the victim in deciding whether or not to sue.

The nature of the right to participate

The central observation of this book is that the carer's entitlement, and also the insurer's entitlement, to share in the fund is generated by the law of unjust enrichment, resting on the novel unjust factor called the policy against accumulation. Of difficulty is that there is evidence that in both categories this right is implemented via a proprietary mechanism to share. *Lord Napier and Ettrick* v. *Hunter* tells us that the insurer is entitled to the benefit of an equitable lien and there are other cases conforming to the carer's trust proposed in *Hunt* v. *Severs*.

It is a matter of debate as to when a right to restitution will be expressed as a proprietary, rather than a personal, right. Chapter 9 has shown that, within the confines of current debate, it is very difficult to explain why a proprietary response is given to RH's unjust enrichment. Chapter 9 controversially argues that it is the policy against accumulation itself which generates the proprietary nature of S's entitlement. The key to understanding this phenomenon is to determine the effect of S's intervention on the value of RH's claim. In the case of the victim and carer, it is possible to justify recognition of a trust because the carer's intervention increases the victim's patrimony. The consequence of the model of tort liability currently prevailing is that the value of the victim's claim against the wrongdoer is in part a direct function of the services and assistance the carer provides and is reckoned in the future to provide. The more necessary assistance given by the carer, the more value can be claimed from the wrongdoer. Arguably, it is this contribution which justifies a proprietary response for the carer.

The indemnity insurer is different. Although it is possible to construct an argument drawing an analogy with the rights of other parties who are entitled to a lien, on the foundation of their contribution to the maintenance of an asset, these arguments are not wholly convincing. The insurer's entitlement is given to reverse the insured's enrichment by accumulation which would otherwise remain. Unlike the carer, however, the insurer does not increase the worth of the insured's chose in action against the wrongdoer. Since the insurer's intervention does not create new value in the hands of the insured, the insurer should be entitled only to a personal claim.

BIBLIOGRAPHY

Aitken, L., 'Negotiorum Gestio and the Common Law: A Jurisdictional Approach' (1988) 11 *Sydney Law Review* 566

Balkin, R. and Davis, J., *Law of Torts* (2nd edn., Sydney, 1996)

Beatson, J., 'Benefit, Reliance and the Structure of Unjust Enrichment' (1987) 40 *Current Legal Problems* 71

Beatson, J., *The Use and Abuse of Unjust Enrichment* (Oxford, 1991)

Bernstein, R., *Economic Loss* (London, 1993)

Birds, J., *Modern Insurance Law* (London, 1993)

Birks, P., 'Negotiorum Gestio and the Common Law' (1971) 24 *Current Legal Problems* 110

Birks, P., 'Restitutionary Damages for Breach of Contract: Snepp and the Fusion of Law and Equity' [1987] *Lloyd's Maritime and Commercial Law Quarterly* 421

Birks, P., *An Introduction to the Law of Restitution* (rev. edn., Oxford, 1989)

Birks, P., 'In Defence of Free Acceptance' in A. Burrows (ed.), *Essays on the Law of Restitution* (Oxford, 1991) 105

Birks, P., 'Restitution and Resulting Trusts' in S. Goldstein (ed.), *Equity and Contemporary Legal Developments* (Jerusalem, 1992) 335

Birks, P., 'No Consideration: Restitution after Void Contracts' (1993) 23 *University of Western Australia Law Review* 195

Birks, P., 'Property in the Profits of Wrongdoing' (1994) 24 *University of Western Australia Law Review* 8

Birks, P., 'Establishing a Proprietary Base' [1995] *Restitution Law Review* 83

Birks, P., 'Overview: Tracing, Claiming and Defences' in P. Birks (ed.), *Laundering and Tracing* (Oxford, 1995) 289

Birks, P., 'Equity in the Modern World: An Exercise in Taxonomy' (1996) 26 *University of Western Australia Law Review* 1

Birks, P., 'Change of Position and Surviving Enrichment' in W. Swadling (ed.), *The Limits of Restitutionary Claims* (London, 1997) 36

Birks, P., 'Definition and Division: A Meditation on *Institutes* 3.13' in P. Birks (ed.), *The Classification of Obligations* (Oxford, 1997) 1

Birks, P., 'Property and Unjust Enrichment: Categorical Truths' [1997] *New Zealand Law Review* 623

Birks, P., 'Equity, Conscience and Unjust Enrichment' (1999) 23 *Melbourne University Law Review* 1

Birks, P., 'The Law of Restitution at the End of an Epoch' (1999) 28 *University of Western Australia Law Review* 13

Birks, P., 'At the Expense of the Claimant: Direct and Indirect Enrichment in English Law' (2000) *Oxford U Comparative Law Forum* 1 at ouclf.iuscomp.org

Birks, P., 'Private Law' in P. Birks and F. Rose (eds.), *Lessons of the Swaps Litigation* (Oxford, 2000) 1

Birks, P., 'Rights, Wrongs and Remedies' (2000) *Oxford Journal of Legal Studies* 1

Birks, P., 'Unjust Enrichment and Wrongful Enrichment' (2001) 79 *Texas Law Review* 767

Birks, P. and Beatson, J., 'Unrequested Payment of Another's Debt' (1976) *Law Quarterly Review* 188

Birks, P. and Chambers, R., *The Restitution Research Resource* (2nd edn., Oxford, 1997)

Birks, P. and Mitchell, C., 'Unjust Enrichment' in P. Birks (ed.), *English Private Law, Volume* II (Oxford, 2000), chapter 15.

Birks, P. and Swadling, W., 'Restitution' in [1997] *All ER Annual Review* 385

Burrows, A., 'Free Acceptance and the Law of Restitution' (1988) *Law Quarterly Review* 576

Burrows, A., *The Law of Restitution* (London, 1993)

Burrows, A., 'Swaps and the Friction Between Common Law and Equity' [1995] *Restitution Law Review* 15

Burrows, A., 'Improving Contract and Tort' in *Understanding the Law of Obligations: Essays on Contract, Tort and Restitution* (Oxford, 1998) 164

Burrows, A., 'Proprietary Restitution: Unmasking Unjust Enrichment' (2001) 117 *Law Quarterly Review* 412

Burrows, A. and McKendrick, E., *Cases and Materials on the Law of Restitution* (Oxford, 1997)

Byrne, D., 'Benefits-for Services Rendered' in M. McInnes (ed.), *Restitution: Developments in Unjust Enrichment* (North Ryde, 1996) 87

Cane, P., *The Anatomy of Tort Law* (Oxford, 1997), chapter 6

Capper, D., 'A Modern Doctrine of Champerty? – A Postscript' (1997) 113 *Law Quarterly Review* 49

Chambers, R., 'Change of Position on the Faith of the Receipt' [1996] *Restitution Law Review* 100

Chambers, R., *Resulting Trusts* (Oxford, 1997)

Chambers, R., 'Tracing, Trusts and Liens' (1997) 11 *Trust Law International* 86

Clarke, M., *The Law of Insurance Contracts* (3rd edn., London, 1997)

Cooper-Stephenson, K., *Personal Injury Damages in Canada* (2nd edn., Scarborough, 1996)

Davies, J., 'Restitution and Equitable Wrongs: An Australian Analogue' in F. Rose (ed.), *Consensus Ad Idem: Essays on Contract in Honour of Guenter Treiter* (London, 1996)

Davies, J., 'Tort' in P. Birks (ed.), *English Private Law, Volume II* (Oxford, 2000), chapter 14.

Dawson, J., 'Rewards for the Rescue of Human Life?' in *The Good Samaritan and the Law* (New York, 1966)

Degeling, S., 'Carers and Victims: The Law's Dilemma' (1997) 11 *Trust Law International* 30

Degeling, S., '*Kars* v. *Kars* – Balancing the Interests of Victims and Carers' (1997) 71 *Australian Law Journal* 882

Degeling, S., 'Carers' Claims: Unjust Enrichment and Tort' [2000] *Restitution Law Review* 172

Degeling, S., 'The Policy Against Accumulation as an Unjust Factor' in E. Schrage (ed.), *Unjust Enrichment and the Law of Contract* (The Hague, 2001)

Degeling, S., 'A New Reason for Restitution: The Policy Against Accumulation' (2002) 22 *Oxford Journal of Legal Studies* 435

Derham, R., *Subrogation in Insurance Law* (Sydney, 1985)

Dugdale, A. (et al) (eds.), *Clerk and Lindsell on Torts* (18th edn., London, 2000)

Duncan Wallace, I., 'Contractual Relational Loss in Canada' (1998) 114 *Law Quarterly Review* 370

Edelman, J., 'Profits and Breach of Contract' (2001) *Lloyd's Maritime and Commercial Law Quarterly* 9

Edelman, J., 'Restitutionary Damages and Disgorgement Damages for Breach of Contract' [2000] *Restitution Law Review* 129

Elias, G., *Explaining Constructive Trusts* (Oxford, 1990)

Feldthusen, B., 'Liability for Pure Economic Loss: Yes, But Why?' (1999) 28 *University of Western Australia Law Review* 84

Feldthusen, B., 'The Recovery of Pure Economic Loss in Canada: Proximity, Justice, Rationality and Chaos' in E. Banakas (ed.), *Civil Liability for Pure Economic Loss* (London, 1996) 131

Fleming, J., *The Law of Torts* (9th edn., Sydney, 1998)

Fox, D., 'Restitutionary Damages to Deter Breaches of Contract' (2001) *Cambridge Law Journal* 33

Friedmann, D., 'Restitution of Profits Gained by Party in Breach of Contract' (1988) 104 *Law Quarterly Review* 383

Friedmann, D., 'Valid, Voidable, Qualified, and Non-existing Obligations: An Alternative Perspective on the Law of Restitution' in A. Burrows (ed.), *Essays on the Law of Restitution* (Oxford, 1991) 247

Fung, E. and Ho, L., 'Change of Position and Estoppel' (2001) 117 *Law Quarterly Review* 14

Fung, E. and Ho, L., 'Establishing Estoppel After the Recognition of Change of Position' [2001] *Restitution Law Review* 52

Gardner, S., 'Rethinking Family Property' (1993) 109 *Law Quarterly Review* 263

Gardner, S., 'Two Maxims of Equity' [1995] *Cambridge Law Journal* 60

Garner, M., 'Benefits for Services Rendered: Commentary' in M. McInnes (ed.), *Restitution: Developments in Unjust Enrichment* (Sydney, 1996) 109

Garner, M., 'The Role of Subjective Benefit in the Law of Unjust Enrichment' (1990) 10 *Oxford Journal of Legal Studies* 42

Goff, R. and Jones, G., *The Law of Restitution* (5th edn., London, 1998)

Goode, R., 'Proprietary Restitutionary Claims' in W. Cornish et al (eds.), *Restitution Past, Present & Future* (Oxford, 1998) 63

Grantham, R. and Rickett, C., 'On the Subsidiarity of Unjust Enrichment' (2001) 117 *Law Quarterly Review* 273

Hardy Ivamy, E.R., *General Principles of Insurance Law* (London, 1993)

Ho, L. and Smart, P. St J., 'Re-interpreting the *Quistclose* Trust: A Critique of Chambers' Analysis' (2001) 21 *Oxford Journal of Legal Studies* 267

Hoyano, L., 'The Dutiful Tortfeasor in the House of Lords' (1995) 3 *Tort Law Review* 63

Jackman, I., 'Restitution for Wrongs' (1989) 48 *Cambridge Law Journal* 302

Jewell, M., 'The Boundaries of Change of Position – A Comparative Study' [2000] *Restitution Law Review* 1

Jones, G., 'The Recovery of Benefits Gained From Breach of Contract' (1983) 99 *Law Quarterly Review* 442

Jones, G., *Restitution in Public and Private Law* (London, 1991)

Key, P., 'Change of Position' (1995) 58 *Modern Law Review* 505

Klippert, G.B., *Unjust Enrichment* (Toronto, 1983)

Krebs, T., 'In Defence of Unjust Factors' (2000) *Oxford U Comparative Law Forum* 3 at ouclf.iuscomp.org

Leigh-Jones, N. et al (eds.), *MacGillivray & Parkington on Insurance Law* (9th edn., London, 1997)

Luntz, H., *Assessment of Damages for Personal Injury and Death* (3rd edn., Sydney, 1990)

Luntz, H., 'Voluntary Services Provided by the Defendant: A Postscript' (1994) 2 *Torts Law Journal* 184

Luntz, H., 'Damages for Voluntary Services Provided by the Tortfeasor' (1997) 113 *Law Quarterly Review* 201

Maddaugh, P. and McCamus, J., *The Law of Restitution* (Aurora, 1990)

Mason, J. and Carter, J., *Restitution Law in Australia* (Sydney, 1995)

Matthews, P. and Lunney, M., 'A Tortfeasor's Lot is not a Happy One?' (1995) *Modern Law Review* 395

McCamus, J.D., 'Necessitous Intervention: The Altruistic Intermeddler and the Law of Restitution' (1979) 11 *Ottawa Law Review* 297

McGregor, H., *McGregor on Damages* (16th edn., London, 1997)

McInnes, M., ' "At The Plaintiff's Expense": Quantifying Restitutionary Relief' [1988] 57 *Cambridge Law Journal* 472

McInnes, M., 'Restitution and the Rescue of Life' (1994) 32 *Alberta Law Review* 37

McInnes, M., 'The Canadian Principle of Unjust Enrichment: Comparative Insights into the Law of Restitution' (1999) 37 *Alberta Law Review* 1

McKendrick, E., 'The Reason for Restitution' in P. Birks and F. Rose (eds.), *Lessons of the Swaps Litigation* (Oxford, 2000) 84

McKendrick, E., 'Work Done in Anticipation of a Contract which does not Materialise' in W. Cornish et al (eds.), *Restitution Past, Present & Future* (Oxford, 1998) 163

Meagher, R., Gummow, W. and Lehane, J., *Equity: Doctrines and Remedies* (3rd edn., Sydney, 1992)

Millett, Sir P., 'Restitution and Constructive Trusts' in W. Cornish et al (eds.), *Restitution Past, Present & Future* (Oxford, 1998) 199

Mitchell, C., 'Subrogation and Insurance Law: Proprietary Claims and Excess Clauses' [1993] *Lloyd's Maritime and Commercial Law Quarterly* 192

Mitchell, C., *The Law of Subrogation* (Oxford, 1994)

Mitchell, C., 'The Civil Liability (Contribution) Act 1978' [1997] *Restitution Law Review* 27

Mitchell, C., 'Tracing Trust Funds into Life Insurance Proceeds' [1997] *Lloyd's Maritime and Commercial Law Quarterly* 465

Mitchell, C., 'Subrogation, Unjust Enrichment and Remedial Flexibility' [1998] *Restitution Law Review* 144

Mitchell, C., 'Distributing the Burden of Alternate and Co-Extensive Liabilities: Some Banking Cases Considered' in F. Rose (ed.), *Restitution and Banking Law* (Oxford, 1999) 27

Mitchell, C., 'Claims in Unjustified Enrichment to Recover Money Paid Pursuant to a Common Liability' (2001) 5 *Edinburgh Law Review* 1

Muir, G., 'Unjust Sacrifice and the Officious Intervener' in P. Finn (ed.), *Essays on Restitution* (1990) 297

Mullany, N. and Handford, P., *Tort Liability for Psychiatric Damage: The Law of Nervous Shock* (North Ryde, 1993)

Napier, M. and Wheat, K., *Recovering Damages for Psychiatric Injury* (London, 1995)

Nolan, R., 'Change of Position' in P. Birks (ed.), *Laundering and Tracing* (Oxford, 1995) 135

Oakley, A., *Constructive Trusts* (3rd edn., London, 1997)

Paciocco, D., 'The Remedial Constructive Trust: A Principled Basis for Priorities Over Creditors' (1989) *Canadian Bar Review* 315

Quinn, M., 'Review Essay. Subrogation, Restitution and Indemnity' (1996) 74 *Texas Law Review* 1361

Reed, A., 'A Commentary on *Hunt* v. *Severs*' (1995) 15 *Oxford Journal of Legal Studies* 133

Rose, F., 'Restitution for the Rescuer' (1989) 9 *Oxford Journal of Legal Studies* 167

Rotherham, C., 'Tracing and Justice in Bankruptcy' in F. Rose (ed.), *Restitution and Insolvency* (London, 2000) 113

Scottish Law Commission, *Damages For Personal Injuries, Report on (1) Admissibility of Claims For Services (2) Admissible Deductions* (Report No 51, 1978)

Smith, L., 'The Province of the Law of Restitution' (1992) 71 *Canadian Bar Review* 672

Smith, L., 'Breach of Confidence – Constructive Trusts – Punitive Damages – Disgorgement of the Profits of Wrongdoing: *Ontex Resources Ltd v Metalore Resources Ltd*' (1994) 73 *Canadian Bar Review* 259

Smith, L., 'Disgorgement of the Profits of Breach of Contract: Property, Contract and Efficient Breach' (1994) 24 *Canadian Business Law Journal* 121

Smith, L., 'Constructive Fiduciaries?' in P. Birks (ed.), *Privacy and Loyalty* (Oxford, 1997) 249

Smith, L., *The Law of Tracing* (Oxford, 1997)

Smith, L., 'Tracing into Life Assurance Proceeds' (1997) 113 *Law Quarterly Review* 552

Stapleton, J., 'Duty of Care and Economic Loss: A Wider Agenda' (1991) 107 *Law Quarterly Review* 249

Stapleton, J., 'In Restraint of Tort' in P. Birks (ed.), *The Frontiers of Liability, Volume 2* (Oxford, 1994) 83

Stapleton, J., 'Duty of Care: Peripheral Parties and Alternative Opportunities for Deterrence' (1995) 111 *Law Quarterly Review* 301

Stapleton, J., 'Tort, Insurance and Ideology' (1995) 58 *Modern Law Review* 820

Stapleton, J., 'A New "Seascape" for Obligations: Reclassification on the Basis of Measure of Damages' in P. Birks (ed.), *The Classification of Obligations* (Oxford, 1997) 193

Stapleton, J., 'Duty of Care Factors: A Selection from the Judicial Menus' in P. Cane and J. Stapleton (eds.), *The Law of Obligations. Essays in Celebration of John Fleming* (Oxford, 1998) 59

Steel, D. and Rose, F. (eds.), *Kennedy's Law of Salvage* (5th edn., London, 1995)

Stoljar, S., 'Negotiorum Gestio' in *The International Encyclopaedia of Comparative Law* vol. X (London, 1984) 10

Stoljar, S., 'Unjust Enrichment and Unjust Sacrifice' (1987) 50 *Modern Law Review* 603

Stoljar, S., *The Law of Quasi Contract* (2nd edn., Sydney, 1989), chapter 7

Swadling, W., 'Property and Conscience' (1998) *Trust Law International* 228

Swadling, W., 'Property and Unjust Enrichment' in J. W. Harris (ed.), *Property Problems: From Genes to Pension Funds* (London, 1997) 130

Swadling, W., 'Restitution for No Consideration' [1994] *Restitution Law Review* 73

Swadling, W., 'The Law of Property' in P. Birks and F. Rose (eds.), *Lessons of the Swaps Litigation* (Oxford, 2000) 242

Tan, Y., 'Champertous Contracts and Assignments' (1990) 106 *Law Quarterly Review* 656

Tettenborn, A., *Law of Restitution in England and Ireland* (2nd edn., London, 1996)

Trindade, F. and Cane, P., *The Law of Torts in Australia* (2nd edn., Oxford, 1993)

UK Law Commission, *Mentally Incapacitated Adults and Decision-Making: An Overview* (Consultation Paper 119, 1991)

UK Law Commission, *Mental Incapacity. Item 9 of the Fourth Programme of Law Reform: Mentally Incapacitated Adults* (Law Com No 231, 1995)

UK Law Commission, *Damages for Personal Injury: Medical, Nursing and Other Expenses* (Consultation Paper No 144, 1996)

UK Law Commission, *Liability for Psychiatric Illness* (Law Com No 249, 1998)

UK Law Commission, *Damages for Personal Injury: Medical, Nursing and Other Expenses; Collateral Benefits* (Law Com No 262, 1999)

Virgo, G., *The Principles of the Law of Restitution* (Oxford, 1999)

Walters, A., 'A Modern Doctrine of Champerty?' (1996) 112 *Law Quarterly Review* 560

Williams, R., 'Preventing Unjust Enrichment' [2000] *Restitution Law Review* 492

Williams, S. and Guthrie-Smith, F., *Daniell's Chancery Practice* (8th edn., London, 1985)

Witting, C., 'Distinguishing Between Property Damage and Pure Economic Loss
in Negligence: A Personality Thesis' (2001) 21 *Legal Studies* 481

Witting, C., 'Justifying Liability to Third Parties for Negligent Misstatements' (2000)
20 *Oxford Journal of Legal Studies* 615

Worthington, S., *Proprietary Interests in Commercial Transactions* (Oxford, 1996)

INDEX

absence of basis *see* non-voluntary
    unjust factors
account of profits, 45–6, 237–8
accumulation, policy against
    contingency insurance, 208
    gifts, 208–9
    permitted, 207–9
    policy motivated unjust factor, 6–8,
      86, 110, 186–9, 191–3, 209–22,
      228–30, 251–65, 272–4
    debt payments, 194–5
    evidence, 193–209
    future role, 222–30
    indemnity insurance, 203–6,
      218–20, 257–60, 263–4
    meaning, 191–3
    proprietary restitution, 251–3,
      274–5; timing of accumulation,
      253–65
    several tortfeasors, 206–7
    taxes, 10, 200–3, 225–8
    timing, 213–18, 218–20, 253–65,
      273
    transfers by those primarily liable,
      193–200
    transfers by those primarily liable
      and third parties, 200–7
    victims and carers, 86, 195–200,
      210–18, 254–7, 262–3
actio per quod consortium et servitium
    amisit, 111
administration of funds, 25, 198–9,
    235–6
agency, of necessity, 89–90, 168
agreements with carers *see also*
    contracts for care, promises
    capacity to communicate, 53

capacity to consent, 49–53
    generally, 49–53
assignment, rights of action, 166, 182,
    184, 267–9
at the expense of, 72, 187–8, 212, 219,
    225, 227
Australia
    accumulation, 198–9, 200–3, 208–9,
      225–8, 229–30, 233–5, 273
    carer's right to funds, 3, 24–6, 85,
      198–9, 229–30, 233–5, 273
    direct claim for carer, 139–41
    pure economic loss, 136–41
    unjust enrichment, 25, 72
    victims and carers, 3, 22–6, 28

bad faith, 104, 105
bankruptcy, 218, 238
bargained-for benefit test, 58–9
bribes, 252–3, 259
burial cases, 90

Canada
    accumulation, 199–200, 241
    direct claim for carer, 1, 21, 149–50
    participation in funds, 3, 4, 20–1,
      240–1
    pure economic loss, 141–5
    right to force litigation, 3–4, 7
    trusts for carers, 3, 4, 22, 220–1,
      240–1
    unjust enrichment, 72
    victims and carers, 3, 19–22, 28
capacity
    communication, 53, 57, 59, 64
    consent: medical treatment, 50–1;
      victims, 49–53

incapacity *see* defences, unjust enrichment
  mental incapacity, 108
  minors, 107–8
care, past and future care, 14, 19, 23, 69, 95, 97, 215–16, 218, 233, 234–5, 255–6
carers
  access to damages *see* participation in funds
  accounting for carer's intervention: Australia, 24; Canada, 20–1; England, 15–17
  agreements with victims, 30–3
  analogy with indemnity insurers, 161–77, 188–9
  compensation for loss: approaches to damages, 17, 20–1; valuation of contribution, 66–7
  direct claims *see* direct claims
  dual identity as tortfeasors: Australia, 22–4, 25–6, 209, 234; England, 14–15, 18–19, 195–6, 210, 254
  duty of care to *see* duty of care
  economic loss, 111–15
  expenses, 49, 61–3, 71
  functions, 2
  moral obligations of, 4, 90, 169, 269
  opportunity cost, 65, 66, 68, 70
  participation in funds *see* participation in funds
  physical injuries to, 113
  proprietary entitlement *see* proprietary restitution
  reasonable remuneration, 65, 67, 68–9, 83–5
causation, 145
champerty, 265–9
choses in action, 218, 220, 254–7, 259–64, 264–9
civilian systems, 109
communication
  acceptance of benefits, 57, 64
  capacity, 53: and bargained-for benefit, 59; and instructions to carer, 95–7; and subjective test of enrichment, 64

consent
  capacity, victims, 49–53
  medical treatment, 50–1, 92–3
  tests of enrichment, 55–9
constructive trusts, 238–9, 246, 249
  bribes, 252, 259
  remedial constructive trusts, 238
contingency insurance, 208, 222
contingent rights to participate, 26–7, 78–9, 100, 151–6, 159, 172–6, 214–20, 271–4
contracts
  breach, assignment of actions, 268
  indemnity insurance, 4, 163–4
  unenforceable contracts, 223–4
  victims and carers *see* contracts for care
  void contracts, 76
contracts for care *see also* promises
  breach of contract: account of profit, 45–6; claims founded on, 44
  case law, 29–33
  direct claim for carers, 154–5
  no breach of contract, 42–4
  participation in funds, 5, 6, 20
  relevance, 33–42: for carer's participation, 38–44; for victim's claim, 33–8
  sham contracts, 34
  unconscionability, 30

damages
  breach of victims' contracts with carers, 46
  carers' access to *see* participation in funds
  heads of damages: carers' contribution, 13, 14–15, 19–20, 22–4; pecuniary and non-pecuniary losses, 15, 33–8; statutory modification, 19, 23, 159
  purpose, 15
death, 238
debts
  discharge by carers: accumulation, 194–5; free acceptance, 56–7; necessity, 60–1, 98–9; and valuation of, 71
  of victim: 48

defences, unjust enrichment, 101–8
  change of position, 101–6
  incapacity, 106–8
direct claims
  by carers against tortfeasors:
    Australia, 139–41; Canada, 1, 21;
    consequences, 154; generally, 47,
    111–46
  by carers against victims:
    contractual, 29–46, 154–5;
    generally, 154–6; unjust
    enrichment, 47–110, 155–6,
    210–18, 254–7, 262–3
divorce, 238
duty of care
  economic loss, 116–46: Australia,
    136–41; Canada, 141–5
  factual duty, 116
  fair, just and reasonable, 132–6
  foreseeability of harm, 127–8
  notional duty, 116, 119–24
  novel claim, 125–36
  proximity, 128–32, 142, 144–5
  psychiatric injuries, 125–7,
    130–2
  rescuers, 132–3
  victim and carer cases, 123–4,
    139–41, 144–5

economic loss, 111, 112–15, 116–36
  Australia, 136–41
  Canada, 141–5
  duty of care   see duty of care
  from injury to property, 115
  from physical injury to the person,
    112–14
  relational economic loss, 143:
    contractual, 143–4
  victim and carer cases, 123–4,
    139–41, 144–5
election, 136
emergency interventions
  unjust enrichment, 91–5, 213–14
England
  accumulation, 194–8, 203–8,
    210–20, 223–5, 254–65
  carer's right to funds, 4, 18–19,
    242–5
  direct claim for carer, 47

pure economic loss, 112–15
  right to force litigation, 3–4, 7
  unjust enrichment, 48, 72
  victims and carers, 13–19
enrichment, tests of, 53–4
  bargained-for benefit, 58–9
  consent based, 55–9
  free acceptance, 55–8
  incontrovertible enrichment,
    59–63
  necessity, 59–63
  objective, 54–5
  subjective, 63–5
  subjective devaluation   see
    subjective devaluation
equitable liens
  accumulation, 257–61, 263–4
  improvement of assets, 258–9
  insurers, 1, 8, 175, 182, 187, 205,
    217: criticism, 236
expenses, carers', 14, 19, 49, 61–3,
    71

failure of basis   see non-voluntary
    unjust factors
forcing litigation
  conceptual problem, 3–4, 7, 9–10,
    27, 156–7
  insurers, 7, 176–7, 179–83
  interveners, 9–10
  right, 3–4, 7, 151, 156–7, 159, 189,
    271–2, 274
  subrogation rights, 179: unjust
    enrichment, 180–3; victim and
    carer cases, 183–5, 271–2, 274
free acceptance, 55–8
funds   see administration of funds;
    participation in funds
funeral cases   see burial cases

gifts, 77–8, 208–9
guarantees, 168

hire contracts, 223–4

incapacity defence, 106–8
incontrovertible enrichment,
    59–63
insolvency, 238, 247–8

insurance
    contingency insurance, 208
    contracts, 4, 163–4
    influence on litigation, 14
    liens   see equitable liens
    policy against accumulation, 186–8,
        203–6, 208, 218–20, 257–60,
        263–4, 270, 272–4
    proprietary restitution, 236, 257–61,
        263–4
    subrogation   see subrogation
interest swap agreements, 76, 106

Law Commission
    abolition of carers' trusts, 237
    damages for personal injuries, 19
    direct claims by carers, 135
    future gratuitous care, 215, 237
    legal capacity to consent, 49, 50
    mental disorder or disability, 51
    reversing Hunt v. Severs, 19, 159
legal relationships
    carers also wrongdoers, 14–15, 18
    carers to victims, 135
    carers, victims and wrongdoers, 4–5
    insurers and insured, 4, 163–4
liens   see also equitable liens
    maritime salvage, 250
    nature, 252
litigation
    forcing   see forcing litigation
    influence of insurers, 14
    right, assignment, 166, 182, 184,
        267–9

maintenance and champerty, 265–9
maritime salvage, 98, 250, 252
medical treatment, consent, 50–1, 92–3
mental disability
    consent to treatment, 51–2
    definition, 51
    factual patterns, 49–53
    unjust enrichment, 108
minors
    consent to treatment, 52–3
    factual patterns, 49–53
    unjust enrichment, 107–8
mistake
    subrogation, 164–6

unjust enrichment, 73, 78, 186, 206,
    225–8, 246
Mitchell, C.
    model of subrogation, 6, 161–2,
        163–77, 177, 188–90, 221–2,
        272
    right to control litigation, 179–83
    right to participate in fund, 186–8,
        222
moral obligations
    carers to victims, 4, 90
    or gifts, 77–8, 208–9
    participation in funds, 85, 153,
        198–9, 243–4
    victims to carers, 37–8, 75–6, 85,
        153, 198–9, 243–4
    justification for carer's entitlement,
        81–3

necessity
    principle, 91–5: appropriate
        interveners, 97–8; emergency,
        91–5; impossible or impractical
        to obtain instructions, 95–7;
        requirements, 90–1
    subrogation, 166–8
    test of enrichment, 59–63
    unjust enrichment, 88–100, 183:
        discharge of victims' debts, 98–9,
        193–4
    utility as an unjust factor, 99–100,
        155–6, 213–14
negligence
    carers' claims, 111–15
    causation and remoteness, 145
    duty of care   see duty of care
    requirements, 115, 145
negotiorum gestio, 63, 108–10
non-voluntary unjust factors, 73–9
    absence of basis, 76–8, 193
    failure of basis, 74–6, 186, 193–4
    mistake   see mistake
    utility of unjust factors, 78–9, 155–6,
        186, 213–14

officiousness, 97–8, 163–9, 184
opportunity cost valuation of carer's
        contribution, 65, 66, 68
    value of method, 70

participation in funds
  Australia, 24–6
  Canada, 22, 78–9, 99–100
  conceptual problems, 26–7, 151–6,
    185–8, 213–14, 272–4
  contingent right, 26–7, 78–9, 100,
    151–6, 159, 172–6, 214–20, 271–4
  England, 18–19
  mechanisms, 242–8
  personal rights, 4, 8, 22, 24–6,
    175–6, 179, 204–6, 214, 236, 237,
    240–1, 243–4, 257, 259–60, 264,
    270, 274–5
  policy justifications, 79–87:
    accumulation by victims, 86;
    necessary intervention by carers,
    81–3; no direct claim by carers,
    86; right to reasonable
    remuneration, 83–5
  proprietary rights, 18, 22, 31,
    199–200, 205, 233–7, 240–1,
    242–6, 254–64, 269–70
  relevance of promises, 38–42, 43–4
  right of carers, 2–3, 5–7, 18–19, 22,
    24–6, 31, 150–6, 172–3, 188,
    195–200, 210–18, 233–7, 242–6,
    254–7, 262–3, 272–4: carers also
    tortfeasors, 18–19; carers not
    tortfeasors, 18
  right of insurer, 5–7, 8, 173–6, 185–8,
    203–6, 218–20, 257–60, 263–4
  right of other parties, 9–10, 201–3,
    223–8
policy motivated unjust factors
  accumulation   see accumulation
  generally, 73, 79
  necessity   see necessity
poor and parish, 90
promises to pay carer
  breach of promise, 29, 42–6
  case law, 29–33
  contractual promises, 29–32, 36–7
  failure of basis   see non-voluntary
    transfer of benefits
  non-contractual promises, 29, 32–3,
    37; informality, 33; moral
    obligations, 33, 37–8
  relevance, 33–46, 154–5

proprietary restitution
  generally, 7–8, 238–40, 242, 246–51,
    251–3
  indemnity insurance, 236, 257–62,
    263–5
  policy against accumulation, 7–8,
    242, 251–70, 274–5: insurers,
    257–60, 263–5, 270, 275; timing
    of accumulation, 253–65, 269–70,
    273
  proprietary base, 261–4
  victims and carers, 254–7, 262–3,
    269–70, 274–5
proximity, negligence, 128–32, 142,
  144–5
psychiatric injuries, 125–7, 130–2

Quistclose trusts, 239
  see also resulting trusts

relationships   *see* legal relationships
remuneration
  promises   *see* promises
  reasonable remuneration:
    justification for carer's
    participation, 83–5; valuation of
    services, 65, 67, 68–9
rescuers, 132–3
resulting trusts, 238–9, 246
Roman law, 109

salvage, 98, 250
Scotland
  reasonable remuneration, 84, 196
  Scots and English law, 121, 196
  statutory rights of carers, 196–7
  victims' duty of account to carers,
    18, 196–7
Scottish Law Commission, 196–7
services
  accounting for carers' services:
    Australia, 24; Canada, 20–1;
    England, 15–17
  nature, 48–9
  necessity, 59–61, 81–3
  quantification of damages, 46
  valuation, 65–71: arbitrary value,
    65, 70–1; comparison of

approaches, 69–71; compensation of carers, 66–7; methods, 65–6; needs of victims, 67–9; opportunity cost approach, 65, 66, 68, 70; reasonable remuneration, 65, 67, 68–9, 83–5
stamp duty, 200–1
structural paradoxes, 4–10, 26–7, 149–58, 272–5
subjective benefits, 63–5
subjective devaluation, 54–5, 56–63
subrogation
  categories, 180–1, 189
  equitable remedy, 176, 180, 184
  forcing litigation, 176–7, 179–83: victim and carer cases, 183–5
  insurance, 1, 6: analogy, 157, 160, 161–77
  juridical foundation, 177–88
  meaning, 9, 178–9
  Mitchell's model, 6, 161–2, 163–77, 177, 188–90, 221–2, 272: primary liability undischarged, 169–72; right to control litigation, 179–83; right to participate in fund, 186–8, 222; unofficious intervention, 163–9

taxes
  unconstitutional taxes, 9, 10, 200–3, 225–8, 230, 273
  unjust enrichment, 200–3, 225–8, 230, 273
  constructive trusts, 264
tobacco licensing, 10, 200–3, 225–8
tort
  assignment of claims, 166, 182, 184, 267–9
  maintenance and champerty, 265–9
  negligence see duty of care; negligence
  right to sue, 2, 6
tortfeasors
  dual identity as carers, 14–15, 18–19, 22–4, 25–6, 195–6, 209, 210, 234, 254: approaches to damages, 17, 18–19, 20–1

duty of care see duty of care
several tortfeasors, 206–7
tracing, 264–5
trustees, 235–6
trusts
  choses in action, 254–7, 259–64, 264–9
  terminology, 237–8, 246
trusts for carers, 2–3
  administrative problems, 233–7
  Australia, 3, 24–6
  Canada, 3, 20, 22, 172–3, 199–200
  champerty, 265–9
  England, 2–3, 18–19, 31–2, 195–8
  judicial controversy, 24–6, 215–16, 233–6, 245
  reasons, 5–8
  reversing unjust enrichment, 27–75, 251–65

unconscionability, 30
unconscious victims, 51–3, 95–8
unjust enrichment
  accumulation see accumulation, policy against
  at carers' expense see at the expense of
  Australia, 25, 72
  defences see defences, unjust enrichment
  direct claims by carers see direct claims
  elements, 48
  emergency interventions, 88–90, 91–5, 213–14
  enrichment see enrichment, tests of; factual patterns, 49–53
  proprietary remedies, 238–40, 246–51
  subrogation rights see subrogation
  taxes see taxes
  unjust factors, 6–7, 48, 72–100, 155–6, 183, 186–7: absence of basis: see non-voluntary unjust factors; categories, 73; failure of basis see non-voluntary unjust factors; legal compulsion, 183; mistake see mistake; necessity

unjust enrichment (*cont.*)
    see necessity; non-voluntary
    transfers   *see* non-voluntary
    unjust factors; policy motivated
    unjust factors   *see* policy
    motivated unjust factors
  valuation   *see* valuation of unjust
    enrichment
  void contracts, 76
unjust sacrifice, 91

valuation of unjust enrichment
  debts of victim, 71
  expenses of carer, 71
  generally, 65, 72
  services, 65–71: arbitrary value, 65,
    70–1; comparison of approaches,
    69–71; compensation of carers,
    66–7; needs of victim, 67–9;
    opportunity cost approach, 65, 66,
    68, 70; reasonable remuneration,
    65, 67, 68–9, 70

victims
  accumulation   *see* accumulation,
    policy against
  agreements with carers,
    30–3
  capacity as trustees, 235–6
  needs of victim: approaches to
    damages, 15–17, 21, 39;
    Australia, 24; Canada, 21;
    England, 15–17, 21; relevance of
    promises, 33–8; valuation of
    services, 67–9
  promises to pay for services
    see promises
  unjust enrichment   *see* unjust
    enrichment
void contracts, 76

wills, 120–1, 136–8
wrongful births, 121–3, 124–5
wrongs, restitution for, 45–6, 47, 238,
  252–3

2048308

Made in the USA